Date: 1/26/16

**The civil rights movement in
America :from Black Nationalism**

The Civil Rights
Movement in America

The Civil Rights Movement in America

From Black Nationalism to the Women's Political Council

Peter B. Levy, Editor

Movements of the American Mosaic

 GREENWOOD™

An Imprint of ABC-CLIO, LLC
Santa Barbara, California • Denver, Colorado

Copyright © 2015 by ABC-CLIO, LLC

Library of Congress Cataloging-in-Publication Data

The civil rights movement in America : from Black Nationalism to the Women's Political Council / Peter B. Levy, editor.
    pages cm. — (Movements of the American mosaic)
Includes bibliographical references and index.
ISBN 978–1–61069–761–3 (hard copy : alk. paper) — ISBN 978–1–61069–762–0 (ebook) 1. Civil rights movements—United States—History—Encyclopedias. 2. African Americans—Civil rights—History—Encyclopedias. 3. Civil rights workers—United States—Biography—Encyclopedias. 4. United States—Race relations—Encyclopedias. I. Levy, Peter B., editor.
E185.61.C6148   2015
323.1196′073—dc23   2014044237

ISBN: 978–1–61069–761–3
EISBN: 978–1–61069–762–0

19 18 17 16 15   1 2 3 4 5

This book is also available on the World Wide Web as an eBook.
Visit www.abc-clio.com for details.

Greenwood
An Imprint of ABC-CLIO, LLC

ABC-CLIO, LLC
130 Cremona Drive, P.O. Box 1911
Santa Barbara, California 93116-1911

This book is printed on acid-free paper ∞

Manufactured in the United States of America

Every reasonable effort has been made to trace the owners of copyrighted materials in this book, but in some instances this has proven impossible. The editor and publisher will be glad to receive information leading to more complete acknowledgments in subsequent printings of the book and in the meantime extend their apologies for any omissions.

Contents

Introduction

This book traces a heroic struggle for freedom in America, the modern civil rights movement. It takes as its major premise Martin Luther King Jr.'s pronouncement that the movement had a vast array of heroes, men and women, old and young, well known and unknown, and that the words and actions of these individuals counted. Or, as he put it in his "Letter From Birmingham Jail" (1963), one day the South would recognize its real heroes, like James Meredith, who "courageously and with a majestic sense of purpose" faced "jeering and hostile mobs," and like the "72-year-old woman" from Montgomery, Alabama, "who rose up with a sense of dignity and with her people decided not to ride the segregated buses, and responded to one who inquired about the tiredness with ungrammatical profundity. 'My feet is tired, but my soul is rested.' " This book also seeks to display the veracity of King's argument that the modern civil rights movement stood up for the "American dream and the most sacred values" of Western culture, that it sought to turn the ideal of the Declaration of Independence and Christian morality into a reality for all of America's citizens.

The majority of the over 120 entries are biographies of some of the most important men and women who comprised the movement. They were a remarkably varied group. They included Harvard PhDs like Ralph Bunche, who worked closely with Eleanor Roosevelt to craft the United Nations' Declaration of Human Rights; to Fannie Lou Hamer, a poor sharecropper from the Mississippi Delta who moved the nation with her gripping testimony on the terrorism she faced for trying to exercise her right to vote. Some, like Ella Baker, worked primarily behind the scenes as a mentor and/or sage; others, like James Meredith, largely marched alone. From James Lawson, who studied the principles of nonviolence in Gandhi's India, to H. Rap Brown, who once declared that violence was as American as cherry pie, they neither practiced nor preached the same tactics. But even if they were not always united in terms of their background, tactics, or personalities, collectively they shared a similar goal: to overcome racism and to achieve equality.

A sizable chunk of the entries in this book examine events like the March on Washington, where Martin Luther King Jr. delivered his famous "I Have a Dream" speech, and the Los Angeles (Watts) Riot of 1965, which made clear that race was a national problem, not just a southern problem. Just as many describe organizations, from the National Association for the Advancement of Colored People (NAACP), which had been fighting for equality since the early decades of the twentieth century; to the Student Nonviolent Coordinating Committee, which burst onto the public scene following the sit-ins of 1960. Some of the entries discuss key pieces of legislation, such as the Voting Rights Act of 1965, which enabled millions of blacks to vote for the first time; or court cases, such as *Loving v. Virginia*, which overturned age-old laws that barred people of different races from marrying one another. Since the movement did not operate in a vacuum, a number of the entries focus on some of the foes of the civil rights movement, such as George Wallace, who proclaimed his defense of segregation "forever" in his 1963 gubernatorial inaugural address; and the White Citizens' Council, which organized to resist racial reform.

This volume also includes a dozen key documents, ranging from the Supreme Court's decision in *Brown v. Board of Education*, which ruled segregated public education unconstitutional; to excerpts from the FBI's secret file on Malcolm X, which reminds us that the movement had friends as well as foes in the federal government. A number of these documents are laws that still have a profound impact upon how we live. The Civil Rights Act of 1964, for instance, provides the basis for protecting women from sexual harassment in the workplace and in schools. And several of the documents are addresses delivered by the presidents who were in office as the civil rights movement emerged as a major factor in American life. While reading these laws, court cases, and speeches, readers are encouraged to consider why successive presidents of the United States have publicly defended the rights of blacks, whereas for years American leaders had averted doing so.

In order to help readers understand the answer to this question, it is important to have at least some sense of the history of the black struggle for freedom. In almost every way that the status of African Americans can be measured, they were second-class citizens as the United States emerged from World War II. At roughly midcentury, blacks had half the average annual income and twice as high unemployment and poverty rates as whites. While U.S. scientific technology, consumer goods, colleges and universities, and suburban homes were the envy of the world, millions of African Americans continued to battle the age-old problems of inadequate health care, education, and housing. Even blacks who were not poor faced legal and extralegal barriers to full citizenship. In the South, blacks faced a rigid set of Jim Crow laws that limited where they could go to school, eat, recreate, and much more. Only a minority of blacks enjoyed the right to vote, and they were rarely allowed to exercise it in cases that could affect public policies. While blacks who migrated to the North or West, as blacks did in extraordinary numbers in the middle decades of the twentieth century, left behind Jim Crow laws and a society that openly espoused its belief in white supremacy, they found themselves living in segregated neighborhoods and limited by customs and codes in terms of employment and their public lives. Moreover, though African Americans in the North could vote, and on occasion elected black officials, only rarely did whites face the prospect of having African Americans set the laws and policies for majority-white communities. In sum, in the midst of the Cold War, as American leaders touted the freedom of the West versus the tyranny of the East, African Americans were not a free people. As President John F. Kennedy rhetorically observed in a nationally televised address in June 1963: "Who among us [meaning whites] would be content to have the color of his skin changed and stand in his [meaning blacks] place?"

The modern civil rights movement clearly sought a revolution in race relations in America. It sought to dramatically alter the answer to President Kennedy's question. While blacks differed over the best way to achieve equality and disagreed over the extent to which the American system would have to be changed in the process, as the 1960s dawned, they became increasingly confident that they could achieve their ultimate goal. They did so, in part, because the modern civil rights movement did not emerge out of thin air. Rather, it built on a long history of struggle and sacrifice. Put somewhat differently, like bars of steel, African Americans were tempered and hardened by their experiences. Black women, for instance, built up personal and collective reservoirs of strength upon which they could and did draw in the 1950s and 1960s. In the years before the modern civil rights movement, African Americans developed institutions that provided resources and an organizational foundation for the movement's rapid growth in the mid-1950s. The most important institution was the black church, which served as a training ground for charismatic leaders, enlisted a mass and decentralized leadership, accumulated a reservoir of fund-raising experiences, and preached a doctrine that at its core contradicted the ideology of white supremacy. Other important institutions that blacks established in the years before the modern civil rights movement included civil or human rights organizations, most notably the NAACP, black colleges and universities, and the black press. Blacks also joined labor unions, particularly those associated with the Congress of Industrial Organization (CIO), which in their own way aided the movement in the 1960s.

Broader historical or structural developments also accounted for and shaped the modern civil rights movement. With the Great Migration from the rural South to the North and West and urban South, millions of blacks gained a modicum of political power, the space to join and form interracial organizations, and greater access to the media than ever before. World War II and then the Cold War, coupled with the decolonization of much of the nonwhite world from Asia to Africa, inspired African Americans to fight for their own equality at home and prodded American leaders to support race reforms, lest they look hypocritical by proclaiming to stand as the defenders of freedom. Broad socioeconomic changes, from the rise of national chain stores and brands to the allure of Hollywood films and television shows, also undermined local folkways that reinforced white supremacy.

Yet, if structural changes and long-term developments set the state for the emergence of the modern civil rights movement, ultimately, it depended on the actions of individuals to make the most of these favorable conditions. Thousands of men and women, like Rosa Parks, Robert Moses, and even Muhammad Ali, had to make the personal decision to risk their well-being to fight for the rights of others. Civil rights leaders like Martin Luther King Jr. had to ignore the counsel of others who told him that conditions, though improved, were not ripe enough for demonstrations in the streets. Indeed, one of the central legacies of the modern civil rights movement is that it reminded people of their own power to make history. They learned—and showed—that freedom does not grow like a leaf on a tree, but that it is the product of struggle. And even though the movement fell short of the ultimate goal of freedom for all, it left thousands of individuals with a newfound sense of their own power, a lesson that should not be forgotten.

A

Abernathy, Ralph David

Ralph David Abernathy (1926–1990) was a leading civil rights activist. He was born on March 21, 1926, in Lindon, Alabama. After serving in the U.S. Army in World War II, he became an ordained Baptist minister in 1948. He graduated from Alabama State University in 1950, receiving a BA degree in mathematics. The next year, he graduated from Atlanta University with an MA degree in sociology. He married Juanita Jones and they had five children.

In 1951, he became the minister of the First Baptist Church in Montgomery, Alabama. On December 5, 1955, Rosa Parks violated a Montgomery city law when she refused to give up her seat on a municipal bus to a white man. She was promptly arrested. The black community sought to protest her arrest, and they turned to Abernathy for assistance. He met with another local minister, Dr. Martin Luther King Jr., and they formed the Montgomery Improvement Association to organize a boycott of the city's buses. The boycott lasted for 381 days and resulted in the desegregation of the municipal bus system. This protest is generally considered to have sparked the modern civil rights movement.

Abernathy helped to organize a meeting of civil rights groups in Atlanta, Georgia, in January 1957. During the meeting, Abernathy's home and church in Montgomery were bombed. Groups from 10 states attended the meeting, which culminated in the founding of the Southern Christian Leadership Conference (SCLC). King was elected president of the organization, and Abernathy was elected secretary-treasurer.

Abernathy, working on behalf of the SCLC, assisted in organizing 21 meetings in prominent southern cities as part of the "Crusade for Citizenship" in 1958. The goal of the meetings was to vastly increase the number of black voters throughout the South. In 1960, both Abernathy and King moved their families to Atlanta. The two men worked closely together for the remainder of King's career. Abernathy participated in the "Freedom Rides" of 1961, in which civil rights activists challenged segregation on buses and in public accommodations throughout the South. That same year he was elected vice president of SCLC.

In 1963, Abernathy, along with King, organized a massive protest in Birmingham, Alabama, which many considered to be the most segregated city in America. Both men were arrested for holding a demonstration without a permit and served eight days in jail. Later in 1963, Abernathy helped organize the "March on Washington for Jobs and Freedom," which brought an estimated 200,000 demonstrators to the nation's capital to protest racial discrimination. Abernathy also helped coordinate the "Freedom Summer" of 1964, in which numerous civil rights groups went to Mississippi to increase the number of black registered voters.

In 1965, Abernathy helped organize a large civil rights protest in Selma, Alabama. The protest turned violent when numerous activists were beaten and one was killed. This prompted Abernathy to lobby for passage of the Voting Rights Act to ensure that blacks had equal access to voting polls in the South. Later that year, Congress did pass the Voting Rights Act of 1965. After King's assassination in 1968, Abernathy was elected president of SCLC. In the late 1960s, he led several strikes on behalf of black workers. He resigned in 1977 and returned to Atlanta to serve as a church minister. He died on April 17, 1990.

Gene C. Gerard

Further Reading

Abernathy, Donzaleigh. *Partners to History: Martin Luther King, Jr., Ralph David Abernathy, and the Civil Rights Movement.* New York: Crown Publishing Group, 2003.

Abernathy, Ralph. *And the Walls Came Tumbling Down: An Autobiography.* New York: HarperCollins Publishers, 1989.

Affirmative Action

Affirmative action, one of the most contentious outcomes-oriented civil rights policies of the twentieth century, first entered the public lexicon on March 6, 1961, when President John F. Kennedy issued Executive Order 10925. Facing mounting pressure from civil rights activists, Kennedy called on employers to engage in "affirmative action" to address the race issue in the United States. Thus, the policy began with the stroke of the presidential pen. Kennedy's vision focused on the need for the federal government to foster and promote fairness and equal opportunity in federal employment practices. Given the expansiveness of government involvement with private employers, the initial efforts focused on businesses that received federal support through lucrative government contracts.

After Kennedy's death, President Lyndon B. Johnson strengthened affirmative action policy on September 28, 1965, when he reaffirmed the government's position in Executive Order 11246. The order prohibited discrimination on the basis of race, creed, color, and national origin, but not sex. At that time, women were not identified as an underrepresented group in need of legislative protection. In 1973, President Richard Nixon amended Executive Order 11246 with Executive Order 11375 in order to include sex as a protected class. This concluded the presidential initiatives that launched affirmative action policy. Over the next several decades, affirmative action's evolutionary process was marked by the passage of various legislative and regulatory acts, laws, executive orders, and Supreme Court decisions. Its early supporters argued that the concept of equal opportunity for all American citizens was grounded in legal mandates of the Constitution, the Four-teenth Amendment, and civil rights acts; and, if aggressively applied, affirmative action could become an important aspect of the nation's civil rights initiative.

In the 1960s, affirmative action was endorsed by many who lauded the govern-ment's efforts to increase minority participation in the workforce. Access to blue-collar positions was the primary target of the federal government's enforcement efforts. However, as businesses and unions began organized forms of resistance to affirmative action, they were rebuffed by liberal politicians and scholars who believed that strong governmental enforcement was an essential component of the policy. As the federal initiative expanded to include hiring and admission prac-tices at institutions of higher education, however, strong public opposition to the policy emerged.

Proponents argued that affirmative action was a morally justified approach to re-dress the nation's historic practices of racial and sexual discrimination. Opponents advanced the concept of "reverse discrimination," contending that whites, and more specifically white males, were being victimized by college and university efforts to include members of diverse groups on their campuses. Although many opposing voices acknowledged the devastating impact of past discrimination on African Americans and similarly situated groups, they posited that a "color-blind" approach was the only legitimate way to end centuries of social discrimina-tion and social injustice.

Supporters on both sides eagerly awaited the 1978 Supreme Court decision in *Regents of the University of California v. Bakke*. Allan Bakke, a 36-year-old, white male engineer, had been denied admission to the University of California at Davis's Medical School. He sued on the basis that the institution's affirmative action program, which used a quota system to guarantee minority inclusion, vio-lated his constitutional rights as an individual. In a split decision, the Supreme Court affirmed that quota systems were a violation of constitutional law; however, the court also affirmed its support for affirmative action, ruling that race could be used as a factor in the admission and selection process. Thus, the national debate on which criteria would be acceptable under the government's affirmative action policy began. And repeated legal challenges to affirmative action in both the public and private sectors made it difficult for institutions committed to diversity to con-tinue their efforts.

As popularity for affirmative action waned, many looked to the office of the president to help clarify the nation's direction. The Jimmy Carter administration (1976–1980) was supportive of affirmative action policy. By the early 1980s, how-ever, the Ronald Reagan administration's (1980–1988) open opposition to civil rights and race-sensitive solutions to the nation's social problems helped to usher in a new era of social resistance. And the George H. W. Bush administration's

(1988–1992) lack of enthusiasm for affirmative action was consistent with that of his predecessor Reagan. However, the Bill Clinton administration (1992–2000) offered hope that affirmative action initiatives would be strengthened, particularly as it related to the appointment of federal justices who shouldered primary responsibility for interpreting the nation's policy. Then, early in the administration of George W. Bush (2000–2008), the president indicated his opposition to affirmative action as policy, and decision makers continued to muddle through the legal morass. The legal challenge to the University of Michigan's affirmative action program, which finally made its way to the Supreme Court in 2003, was the most anticipated affirmative action ruling in the early twenty-first century. It was the first opportunity for the Supreme Court to rule on affirmative action policy in nearly 25 years.

In two closely related cases (*Grutter v. Bollinger* and *Gratz v. Bollinger*), conservative activists sued the University of Michigan hoping to strike down the school's race-sensitive admission programs at both the undergraduate college and the law school. Support for Michigan's affirmative action program was broad-based. Colleges, universities, Fortune 500 companies, and retired military personnel from throughout the nation filed *amici* briefs (friends of the court) supporting the university. In another split decision (5–4), the Supreme Court affirmed the Bakke ruling, noting that talented and qualified individuals of every race and ethnicity should be given opportunities, and that race could be considered. In a related decision, however, the court invalidated the school's undergraduate policy that used a point system to help diversify its student body, further weakening the institution's diversity efforts.

The debate on the merits of affirmative action continues. For many in the African American community, affirmative action is the unfinished business of the Black Power movement, the civil rights movement, Reconstruction, and the Freedmen's Bureau. It is a quest for redistributive justice and will remain a strategic path to equal opportunity until another viable policy option takes its place.

Patricia Reid-Merritt

Further Reading

Anderson, Terry H. *The Pursuit of Fairness: A History of Affirmative Action*. Oxford: Oxford University Press, 2004.

Curry, George E., ed. *The Affirmative Action Debates*. New York: Perseus Books, 1996.

Eisaguirre, Lynne. *Affirmative Action: A Reference Handbook*. Santa Barbara, CA: ABC-CLIO, 1999.

Kellough, J. Edward. *Understanding Affirmative Action: Politics, Discrimination, and the Search for Justice*. Washington, DC: Georgetown University Press, 2006.

Perry, Barbara A. *The Michigan Affirmative Action Cases*. Lawrence: University Press of Kansas, 2007.

Albany, Georgia Movement

The Albany, Georgia movement refers both to the campaigns to end racial segregation and the organization founded to achieve this goal. The Albany movement began in 1960 as an umbrella group composed of various civil rights organizations in Albany, a city in southwest Georgia. Some of the community groups involved included the Student Nonviolent Coordinating Committee (SNCC), the National Association for the Advancement of Colored People (NAACP), the Federation of Women's Clubs, the Negro Voters League, and various churches. Led by Dr. William G. Anderson and Slater King, the Albany movement sought to dismantle the system of racial segregation that excluded African Americans from full participation in the political, social, and business affairs of their city.

Undaunted by the arrest of some its members, the Albany movement held mass meetings in churches to plan strategies. During the meetings, members sang freedom songs that became a common feature of civil rights marches in the 1960s. These songs demonstrated the spirit and resolve of the protesters while also providing a cultural link between the present day and hundreds of years of African American suffering. SNCC members also instructed Albany residents nightly on nonviolent tactics.

Although the Albany movement had existed for almost a year, it was a demonstration at the city bus depot by five students on November 1, 1961 that served as a catalyst for the acceleration of protests. The Interstate Commerce Commission (ICC) had found racial segregation in interstate transportation facilities unconstitutional, with the order banning segregation to take effect on November 1. As the African American students attempted to enter the waiting room reserved for whites, Albany police blocked their way. Threatened with arrest, the students left the bus terminal but vowed to return another day.

Impressed by the demonstrations, Martin Luther King Jr. accepted a one-day invitation to speak at a mass meeting. On December 15, 1961, King spoke at Shiloh Baptist Church, urging Albany residents to continue their struggle. King eventually decided to stay and participate in a protest march at city hall planned for the next day, where Albany police arrested him along with more than 250 others. Initially claiming he would remain in jail over Christmas to highlight the treatment of African Americans in the South, King was released from jail on bail when city officials announced they had reached an agreement with the Albany movement. The city was to drop the charges levied against the 250 demonstrators and comply with the ICC ruling.

However, it was soon apparent that the city did not plan to keep its part of the bargain. The decision to leave jail helped Albany police chief Laurie Pritchett devise a strategy to defeat the demonstrations. Whenever King was arrested, Pritchett would find someone to bail him out, thus preventing King from publicizing the arrests.

In addition, Pritchett, who had read King's book on nonviolent direct-action campaigns, reserved jail space in surrounding counties so the media in Albany would not see African Americans jailed in overcrowded conditions. Also, he ordered the police force to remain peaceful while arresting demonstrators. In this regard, Pritchett downplayed the violence that lay at the root of racial segregation and appeared somewhat reasonable to the national media. While Pritchett continued to outmaneuver African American leaders, the Albany city government remained committed to racial segregation. In essence, the Albany campaign seemed a stalemate. African Americans would continue to protest, Chief Pritchett would quietly arrest them, and the city government would maintain racial segregation.

The lack of progress led to problems within the campaign. Racial violence erupted on a number of occasions in July 1962 when African American protesters threw stones, bottles, and other items at police. Upset by this turn of events, King called for a temporary halt in the marches and a day of penance to atone for the violent outbreaks. There was also dissension between the Southern Christian Leadership Conference (SCLC), led by King and other nationally prominent leaders, and the other civil rights groups involved in the Albany movement. Some had perceived of the desegregation campaign as a local initiative, only inviting King and the SCLC to help publicize the situation. Once they joined the Albany movement, however, SCLC leaders became assertive in a way that angered those who thought the Albany movement should remain in the hands of Albany citizens.

In the end, beset with internal problems and a strategy that seemed ineffective against Chief Pritchett, the campaign did not achieve the tangible goal of desegregating city facilities. Nevertheless, the Albany movement did become a sustained effort by local African Americans to end racial inequality. When the SCLC and King left the area in 1962, the Albany movement continued protesting against discrimination. Before this period, as was common in many communities, the various civil rights groups competed against each other for the allegiances of local African Americans. Under the Albany movement umbrella, there was unity among elites, professionals, and workers that had not existed previously.

David Kenneth Pye

Further Reading

Carson, Clayborne. *In Struggle: SNCC and the Black Awakening of the 1960s.* Cambridge, MA: Harvard University Press, 1981.

Chalfen, Michael. "The Way Out May Lead In: The Albany Movement beyond Martin Luther King, Jr." *Georgia Historical Quarterly* 79 (1995): 560–98.

Garrow, David. *Bearing the Cross: Martin Luther King, Jr., and the Southern Christian Leadership Conference.* New York: William Morrow, 1986.

Lewis, David L. *King: A Biography.* Urbana: University of Illinois Press, 1978.

Ali, Muhammad

Muhammad Ali was a three-time heavyweight boxing champion of the world. He was born Cassius Marcellus Clay Jr. (named after his father, Cassius Marcellus Clay Sr., who was named after the nineteenth-century abolitionist and politician Cassius Clay) in Louisville, Kentucky, on January 17, 1942. Ali's journey to superstardom began in 1954 when he was just 12 years old. The young Ali parked his bicycle in front of a Louisville department store. When he returned to retrieve his bicycle after leaving the store, it had been stolen. Angry, frustrated, and distraught, young Ali sought out a police officer named Joe Elsby Martin Sr. for help. He told Officer Martin that he wanted to "whoop" whoever stole his bicycle. Martin, the coach of the Louisville city boxing program, told Ali that if he planned to "whoop" someone, he needed to learn how to fight. The following day, Ali appeared at Louisville's Columbia Gym and began his first boxing lessons with Martin.

Ali first came into public consciousness when he won the gold medal at the Olympic Games in Rome in 1960. As an Olympic coach, Martin accompanied Ali to Rome in 1960, where Ali competed in the light heavyweight division. Ali's medal-winning performance quickly made him the golden boy of American sports. He had grown to 6'3" and developed an unconventional boxing technique for a heavyweight: he held his hands at his sides, rather than the standard boxing style

Three-time heavyweight boxing champion, Muhammad Ali wearing the 24-carat gold-plated championship belt, 1964. (Library of Congress)

of holding the hands high to defend the face. He relied on his height, tremendous quickness, and agility to avoid punches. Martin taught Ali to maximize his speed and grace in the ring. Ali credits Martin with teaching him how to "float like a butterfly, sting like a bee."

In Louisville on October 29, 1960, Ali won his first professional fight against Tunney Hunsaker. From 1960 to 1963, the young fighter amassed a record of 19–0, including 15 knockouts. The boxers he defeated included Tony Esperti, Jim Robinson, Donnie Fleeman, Alonzo Johnson, George Logan, Willi Besmanoff, Lamar Clark, Doug Jones, Henry Cooper, and Archie Moore, a boxing legend who fought over 200 previous fights and trained with Ali's trainer prior to Angelo Dundee.

Ali became the top contender for the heavyweight championship held by Sonny Liston. In spite of Ali's impressive record, few people expected him to beat Liston. The fight was scheduled for February 25, 1964. In the weeks that preceded the fight, Ali repeatedly mocked Liston, dubbing him "the big ugly bear." During the weigh-in on the day before the fight, Ali predicted that he would befuddle Liston with his boxing skills, wear him down with his quickness, and knock him out with underrated strength. In the opening rounds, Ali's speed enabled him to elude Liston's powerful head and body shots. He used his significant height advantage to beat Liston to the punch with his jab. By the third round, Ali was clearly winning the fight. Liston recovered somewhat in the fourth round, as Ali was temporarily blinded by a mysterious and controversial substance that was discovered on Liston's gloves. Many believe that the material was something that was used to close Liston's cuts near his eyes, or something intentionally smeared on Liston's gloves to harm Ali. Despite his impaired vision, Ali evaded Liston's punches until his eyes cleared up and his sight returned. Toward the end of the fifth, a reenergized Ali hit Liston with a barrage of combinations. He was in complete control of the fight by the sixth round. Liston had no answer for Ali's proficiency, agility, and endurance. Then, in a stunning turn of events, Liston refused to emerge from his corner at the beginning of the seventh round. He simply gave up. Liston later claimed that he could not continue because of an injured shoulder. Many believed that the fight had been "fixed" because of this inexplicable and shocking conclusion. Ali was victorious, however, having overcome overwhelming odds to win the heavyweight championship of the world.

Immediately after the fight, Ali stunned the world again by announcing that he had joined the highly controversial Nation of Islam (NOI) and changed his name to Cassius X, rejecting his surname as a remnant of colonialism and his ancestors' enslavement. He was mentored by the Black Nationalist leader and NOI minister Malcolm X, and directed by Elijah Muhammad, the leader of the NOI. Cassius X was soon given the name Muhammad Ali by Elijah Muhammad, who explained that the name *Muhammad* meant "worthy of all praise," and that *Ali* meant "most high."

Many people, particularly members of the media, rejected Ali's new name and snubbed his religious conversion. Howard Cosell, one of the most influential broadcast journalists in the twentieth century, was among the first prominent figures to accept Ali's transformation and new name. Ali and Cosell went on to forge a strong friendship based upon mutual respect and admiration. The adoption of Ali's new name, however, signified his new identity as a Muslim and presaged his emergence as a powerful spokesperson for and symbol of freedom, self-determination, and black pride.

Ali's conversion, coupled with his increasingly visible Black Nationalism, race consciousness, and boastful personality, quickly eroded his unsolicited "golden boy" image. When he refused to be inducted into the military and serve in Vietnam in 1966, the U.S. government and millions of Americans labeled him a "draft dodger," and the media was no less abusive. He was stripped of his title by boxing authorities in 1967, sentenced to prison, and fined $10,000. Freed on appeal, he was inactive as a boxer for over three years while his case dragged on. He remained in the spotlight and supported himself by giving many antiwar and antiracism speeches on college campuses in the United States and abroad. He began to more consciously and strategically cultivate and communicate his political and religious beliefs, as well as intensify and coordinate his humanitarian activities. Despite his separation from the boxing world, he remained true to his principles, and during his exile, he fashioned a new life. In 1970, Ali was finally able to get a boxing license. Due to a loophole (there was no state boxing commission in Georgia), he was granted a license to box in Georgia. Having won his case against the U.S. government, he returned to defeat Jerry Quarry in three rounds in October. Shortly after the Quarry fight, the New York State Supreme Court ruled that Ali was unjustly denied a boxing license. Once again able to fight in New York, he fought Oscar Bonavena at Madison Square Garden in December 1970. Ali beat Bonavena in 15 rounds, paving the way for a title fight against the awkward and highly efficient Joe Frazier.

Ali lost a thrilling contest with Frazier. He would later win two rematches with Frazier, including the legendary "Thrilla in Manila" in 1975. Ali made it clear that although he was devoting the majority of time to regaining the heavyweight crown, he would still be outspoken on issues of equality, religion, race, and representation. In the weeks leading up to his highly anticipated championship bout with the younger, presumably indestructible George Foreman (the "Rumble in the Jungle"), Ali responded to questions about his form by proclaiming his strength and agility: "I rassled an alligator, I done tassled with a whale, I handcuffed lightning, and threw thunder in jail." Few believed that an aging Ali would defeat Foreman on October 30, 1974, in Kinshasa, Zaire. Ali's cunning (including the introduction of his famous "rope-a-dope" strategy), however, triumphed over power as he knocked out Foreman in the eighth round.

Ali converted from NOI to orthodox Sunni Islam after he defeated Foreman in 1975. He attributed his conversion to the shift toward Sunni Islam made by W. D. Muhammad after he gained control of NOI upon the death of his father Elijah Muhammad in 1975. In 1975, Ali also fought Frazier in the last of their three confrontations. Ali's frequent insults, slurs, and belittling poems directed at Frazier increased the anticipation and excitement for the fight. The bout itself lasted 14 back-breaking rounds, which saw Frazier's trainer Eddie Futch refuse to allow Frazier to continue and Ali emerge victorious. Ali was so spent after the contest that he said, "This must be what death feels like." This fight has been called the greatest fight of all time by many. Ali won many of the early rounds, but Frazier staged a comeback in the middle rounds. By the late rounds, however, Ali had reasserted control, and the fight was stopped due to Frazier's eyes being closed.

Neither fighter was ever the same again. Frazier would permanently retire after two more fights, and a declining Ali would struggle with many opponents from then on, aided by some controversial victories. Ali retained his title until a February 1978 loss to 1976 Olympic champion Leon Spinks. Ali fought Spinks again in a rematch in September 1978 and won a highly controversial 15-round decision over his opponent. On June 27, 1979, Ali announced his retirement and vacated the title. His retirement was short-lived, however, and on October 2, 1980, he challenged Larry Holmes for the World Boxing Council's (WBC) version of the world heavyweight title. Looking to set another record, as the first boxer to win the heavyweight title four times, Ali lost by technical knockout in the 11th round.

Ali's health took a turn for the worse during the late 1970s and early 1980s. He was diagnosed with Parkinson's disease during this period; his motor functions then began a slow decline. He was ultimately diagnosed with pugilistic Parkinson's syndrome. Despite the apparent end of his boxing career and his deteriorating medical condition, Ali would fight one more time.On December 11, 1981, he fought rising contender and future world champion Trevor Berbick. Although Ali performed marginally better against Berbick than he had against Holmes 14 months earlier, he still lost a 10-round unanimous decision to Berbick, who at 27 was 12 years younger and in better condition. Following this loss, Ali retired permanently in 1981, with a career record of 56 wins (37 by knockout) and 5 losses. Ali beat almost every top contender of his era, an age that has been labeled the "Golden Age of Heavyweight Boxing." Ali was named Fighter of the Year by *Ring Magazine* more times than any other boxer, and participated in more *Ring Magazine* Fight of the Year matches than any other heavyweight. He is a member of the International Boxing Hall of Fame, and he tallied victories over seven other Hall of Fame inductees. He is regarded by many as the greatest heavyweight champion of all time, and one of the best pound-for-pound boxers in the history of the sport. Ali boxed with his mind in addition to his body. He is also one of only three boxers to be named Sportsman of the Year by *Sports Illustrated*, and he was a highly intelligent self-promoter, whose psychological tactics before, during, and after fights were very entertaining and effective.

Matthew C. Whitaker

Further Reading

Ali, Muhammad, and Richard Durham. *The Greatest: My Own Story*. New York: Random House, 1975.

Bingham, Howard L., and Max Wallace. *Muhammad Ali's Greatest Fight: Cassius Clay vs. The United States of America*. New York: M. Evans and Company, 2000.

Brunt, Stephen. *Facing Ali: 15 Fighters, 15 Stories*. New York: Lions Press, 2002.

Early, Gerald, ed. *The Muhammad Ali Reader*. Hopewell, NJ: Ecco Press, 1998.

Hauser, Thomas. *Muhammad Ali: His Life and Times*. New York: Simon & Schuster, 1991.

Lois, George, ed. *Ali Rap: Muhammad Ali, the First Heavy Weight Champion of Rap*. New York: ESPN Books, 2006.

Marqusee, Mike. *Redemption Song: Muhammad Ali and the Spirit of the Sixties*. New York: Verso Books, 2004.

Remnick, David. *King of the World*. New York: Vintage Books, 1998.

Ronney, John. "Muhammad Ali: He Fought with His Fists and his Words," *U.S. News and World Report*, August 20, 2001.

Anderson, William G.

African American physician W. G. Anderson presided over the Albany Movement in Georgia from the 1950s through the 1960s and is highly regarded as a civil rights leader for his endeavors and achievements in this role. Anderson drew national attention to the civil rights campaign in southwest Georgia when Martin Luther King Jr. accepted his invitation to assist local leaders in their desegregation efforts in late 1961.

Born in Americus, Georgia, on December 12, 1927, William Gilchrist Anderson graduated from Alabama State College in 1949 and later received his doctor of osteopathic medicine from the University of Osteopathic Medicine and Health Sciences in Des Moines, Iowa. Anderson taught in the Atlanta public school system and at the Atlanta School of Mortuary Science before starting a private osteopathic medical practice in Albany, Georgia.

In November 1961, the Student Nonviolent Coordinating Committee (SNCC) arrived in Albany and began testing the Interstate Commerce Commission's ban on racial segregation in interstate bus terminals. No arrests were made initially, but local leaders joined together to form the Albany Movement. Anderson was elected president of the organization, which consisted of members of SNCC, the local ministerial alliances, the Federation of Women's Clubs, the Negro Voters League, and other groups. As the movement in Albany assumed the daunting task of desegregating all public facilities in the city, local leaders sought assistance from a more experienced civil rights group. As a longtime friend and classmate of Southern Christian Leadership Conference secretary-treasurer Ralph Abernathy, Anderson and his wife were able to persuade King to lend his leadership and support to the Albany Movement.

In July 1962, Anderson attracted national attention with his performance on the television news show *Meet the Press*, where he successfully defended the movement to hostile white newsmen. Anderson was standing in for King, who was imprisoned at the time for his role in the Albany demonstrations. The following year, Anderson, with several other Albany leaders, was indicted on charges of conspiring to injure a juror. These charges stemmed from the 1963 picketing of an Albany grocery store owned by Carl Smith, a former juror who helped acquit a sheriff in the murder of a black man. While the Albany leaders maintained that they were picketing the store because of Smith's failure to promote black employees, Smith believed he was picketed in retaliation for his role in the verdict.

Living in Detroit, and no longer president of the Albany Movement, Anderson was extradited to Albany for a trial in October 1963 that resulted in a mistrial. After moving to Detroit, Anderson completed his training in general surgery at the Art Center Hospital and maintained a successful group medical practice until 1984. After leaving the practice, Anderson served as clinical professor of osteopathic surgical specialties at Michigan State's College of Osteopathic Medicine, executive vice president and chief medical officer of the Michigan Health Corporation, director of governmental affairs for the Detroit Osteopathic Hospital, and associate dean of Kirksville College of Osteopathic Medicine, among several other leadership positions. In 1994, Anderson was elected to be the first African American president of the American Osteopathic Association.

Clayborne Carson

Further Reading

Carson, Clayborne. *In Struggle: SNCC and the Black Awakening of the 1960s.* Cambridge, MA: Harvard University Press, 1981.

Carson, Clayborne. *The Martin Luther King, Jr., Encyclopedia.* Westport, CT: Greenwood, 2007.

Kellogg African American Health Care Project. "William G. Anderson." University of Michigan. http://med.umich.edu.

"Leaders Sentenced on Perjury Charge." *Student Voice*, December 30, 1963.

B

Baker, Ella

Ella Baker was one of the most influential African Americans in the civil rights movement of the twentieth century. She became a black activist long before the struggles of the 1950s and 1960s, and she worked throughout her 83 years of life to advance the position of African Americans. An African American herself, Baker worked as both an organizer and an activist in well-known civil rights organizations such as the National Association for the Advancement of Colored People (NAACP), the Southern Christian Leadership Conference (SCLC), the Student Nonviolent Coordinating Committee (SNCC), and the Mississippi Freedom Democratic Party (MFDP).

Baker was born in Norfolk, Virginia, on December 13, 1903, and moved to North Carolina as a child in 1911. She entered Shaw University in Raleigh, North Carolina, and in 1927, she graduated as valedictorian of her class. Although Baker wanted to enter graduate school, her financial situation would not allow it. She instead moved to Harlem, New York. While there, Baker became actively involved in organizing and promoting the advancement of African Americans. From 1929 to 1932, she was a member of the editorial staffs of the *American West Indian News* and the *Negro National News.* During the Great Depression, she accepted a position with the federal Works Progress Administration (WPA).

In 1938, Baker began working with one of the most renowned civil rights organizations in the country—the NAACP. By 1942, she was named national director of all the NAACP branches. It was in this position that Baker greatly expanded her contacts within the African American community. In 1946, however, she left the national office over a conflict of interests. Baker felt that the NAACP was overly concerned with the opinions and recognition of whites and middle-class blacks. She, on the other hand, thought more attention needed to be given to the lower-class black masses. Although Baker removed herself from the national office, she remained involved on the local level. In 1954, she became president of the New York City branch of the NAACP. As president, she aimed to bring the movement back to the masses.

In the mid-1950s, Baker, along with A. Philip Randolph, Bayard Rustin, and Stanley Levinson, formed In Friendship, a New York–based organization that provided economic assistance for disadvantaged blacks in the South. After the eruption of the Montgomery Bus Boycott (1955–1956), following Rosa Parks's refusal to give up her seat to a white man on a Montgomery, Alabama, city bus,

In Friendship worked to raise funds for the Montgomery efforts. When the boycott ended with the Supreme Court's decision that desegregated public transportation, In Friendship united with several other newly created civil rights organizations to form the Southern Christian Leadership Conference (SCLC), led by Dr. Martin Luther King Jr. Baker became the first full-time executive director of the SCLC. Her involvement in the organization, however, was short-lived. As with the NAACP, Baker did not feel she fit in with the SCLC. The organization was primarily composed of clergy. Baker, as a woman, and an older woman at that, knew she had little place within the organization for leadership roles. Furthermore, Baker disliked the leadership style of the SCLC. Baker believed that civil rights organizations should be group-centered. The SCLC, like the NAACP, was more individual-centered.

Baker's role with the SCLC allowed her to assist in the creation of the Student Nonviolent Coordinating Committee (SNCC). In 1960, the sit-in movement erupted among black college students throughout the South. Initially, many of the sit-ins were disconnected; Baker used the numerous contacts she had made through the NAACP and SCLC to bring the detached demonstrations together. In 1960, Baker convinced the SCLC to sponsor a meeting of student activists at her alma mater, Shaw University. The NAACP, SCLC, and Congress for Racial Equality (CORE) all sent representatives to the meeting, which culminated with the creation of SNCC, with Baker as its primary adviser. Other civil rights organizations, like the NAACP, SCLC, and CORE, all wanted in on the action, but Baker worked to keep the students in SNCC independent of other adult civil rights organizations. By 1961, SNCC had become the organization that Baker had been trying to create for several years. Unlike the SCLC, SNCC allowed for the active participation of women and young people. Unlike the NAACP, SNCC took civil rights back to the masses. Most important, SNCC's leadership, unlike either the SCLC or NAACP, was group-centered.

Baker will forever be remembered for her contributions to the progress of African Americans. More than anything else, she believed in the power of the masses to organize and demand change. Throughout her life, Baker was the organizational factor behind many of the civil rights organizations of the 1950s and 1960s. She never wanted to make a name for herself, but instead wished to enlarge the civil rights movement and bring freedom to her fellow African Americans. Baker's contributions to the advancement of African Americans are immeasurable. She worked with the NAACP in the 1940s, the SCLC in the 1950s, and SNCC and the MFDP in the 1960s. With each organization, she expanded the civil rights movement and advanced the African American struggle for freedom and equality.

Baker remained actively involved with SNCC over the years. In 1964, she helped to organize the Mississippi Freedom Democratic Party (MFDP), which sought to combat the disenfranchisement of African Americans in the South.

The organization forced the Democratic Party (at that time still dominated in the South by segregationists) to elect many black leaders in Mississippi. Baker remained involved in the advancement of civil rights until her death on December 13, 1986.

Mindy R. Weidman

Further Reading

Dallard, Shyrlee. *Ella Baker: A Leader behind the Scenes.* Englewood, NJ: Silver Burdett, 1990.

Grant, Joanne. *Ella Baker: Freedom Bound.* New York: John Wiley, 1998.

Ransby, Barbara. *Ella Baker and the Black Freedom Movement: A Radical Democratic Vision.* Chapel Hill: University of North Carolina Press, 2003.

Baldwin, James

Once regarded as the heir to Richard Wright, the preeminent African American novelist, James Baldwin (1924–1987) did not sustain his early achievement. Today, he may be most remembered as an essayist, in particular for several collections of essays published in the 1950s and 1960s that made him one of the most important literary spokespersons for the civil rights movement.

Born in Harlem, Baldwin was adopted by his stepfather, a factory worker named David Baldwin, when he was still very young. Although Baldwin would be much influenced by his stepfather's avocation as a street-corner evangelist, they had a very troubled relationship that left scars on Baldwin's sense of self-esteem. His experiences in school had a more salutary effect. From an early age, he had escaped into the local library and into the books that he read voraciously. At Frederick Douglass Junior High School, one of Baldwin's teachers and early mentor's was the poet Countee Cullen, who encouraged the thoughtful reader to become a committed writer. At Frederick Douglass and at DeWitt Clinton High School, Baldwin would publish his first stories and essays in the school newspapers.

During his teens, Baldwin also became a popular preacher at the Fireside Pentecostal Assembly. The leader of this storefront church in Harlem was Mother Horn, whose influence on Baldwin was profound. Whereas his stepfather had stressed the fear of divine retribution, Mother Horn emphasized the beneficent effects of divine love and Christian fellowship. In addition, Baldwin's experience as a preacher would show itself in the biblical cadences in much of his writing, especially his essays.

After high school, Baldwin moved to New Jersey, where he worked on a construction crew and, for the first time, was exposed for sustained periods to virulent racism. His stepfather's death in an asylum coincided with the outbreak of terrible rioting in Harlem, and this combination of family and public traumas compelled Baldwin to commit himself to his writing. He began living in Greenwich Village, where his exposure to the bohemian lifestyle and radical activism awakened hedonistic and political impulses in him that would be every bit as intense as his earlier religious fervor.

Baldwin's literary career really began with his receiving the Eugene F. Saxton Memorial Trust Award, on the recommendation of Richard Wright. As his first essays and stories began to appear in magazines, he started to work on his first novel. His progress was slowed by personal issues, primarily his struggle to accept his homosexuality after his relationship with a woman had led to their formal engagement. In the wake of the end of that relationship, Baldwin followed Wright to France. There, as he established relationships with all sorts of writers and artists, his relationship with Wright soured, and for much of his subsequent career, Baldwin would be very conscious of trying to step out of Wright's shadow.

Baldwin's first novel, *Go Tell It on the Mountain* (1953), was a pointedly auto-biographical coming-of-age story. Powerfully immediate and intimate, this debut effort is considered by many critics to be Baldwin's most fully realized novel. Set on a single day that provides a microcosm of a family's life together, the novel focuses on the strained relationship between a preacher with a hard temperament and his teenage stepson.

As the civil rights movement gathered momentum, Baldwin was inspired to write some of the seminal essays on race in America collected in *Notes of a Native Son* (1955), *Nobody Knows My Name: More Notes of a Native Son* (1961), and *The Fire Next Time* (1963). In these essays, Baldwin managed to combine eloquent and incisive insight with a deep sense of personal and communal rage as he exposed the pernicious causes and effects of the continuing social, economic, political, and cultural oppression of African Americans. He warned white America that the extended quest for equality had very nearly exhausted the patience of African Americans and had pushed them to a revolutionary edge.

In his second novel, *Giovanni's Room* (1956), Baldwin created a sensation with his unsparing exploration of issues of identity related to both race and sexual orientation. After Knopf refused to publish it, the novel was published first in the United Kingdom and then picked up by Dial in the United States. The novel draws on Baldwin's own complicated personal relationships before he immigrated to France, but it is set among expatriates in France and Spain.

Baldwin's later novels include *Tell Me How Long the Train's Been Gone* (1968), *If Beale Street Could Talk* (1974), *Just above My Head* (1979), and *Harlem Quartet* (1987). His short stories are collected in *Going to Meet the Man* (1965), and his best-known plays are *The Amen Corner* (1955) and *Blues for Mister Charlie* (1964).

Over the last two decades of his life, Baldwin continued to produce work in a variety of genres. But increasingly he seemed a prematurely anachronistic figure.

In the course of the social revolution of the 1960s, the political and sexual radicalism that he had given voice to in the 1950s suddenly seemed quite dated, even tame. Having spent much of his career trying to step out of Richard Wright's shadow, Baldwin now found himself in the uncomfortable position of seeing his later work overshadowed by his earlier work. Baldwin died on December 1, 1987.

Martin Kich

Further Reading

Balfour, Katharine Lawrence. *The Evidence of Things Not Said: James Baldwin and the Promise of American Democracy*. Ithaca, NY: Cornell University Press, 2001.

Bloom, Harold, ed. *James Baldwin*. New York: Chelsea House, 1986.

Bobia, Rosa. *The Critical Reception of James Baldwin in France*. New York: Peter Lang, 1997.

Campbell, James. *Talking at the Gates: A Life of James Baldwin*. Berkeley: University of California Press, 2002.

Clark, Keith. *Black Manhood in James Baldwin, Ernest J. Gaines, and August Wilson*. Urbana: University of Illinois Press, 2002.

Kollhofer, Jakob, ed. *James Baldwin: His Place in American Literary History and His Reception in Europe*. New York: Peter Lang, 1991.

Leeming, David Adams. *James Baldwin: A Biography*. New York: Knopf, 1994.

McBride, Dwight A., ed. *James Baldwin Now*. New York: New York University Press, 1999.

Porter, Horace A. *Stealing the Fire: The Art and Protest of James Baldwin*. Middletown, CT: Wesleyan University Press, 1989.

Baraka, Amiri

Amiri Baraka (1934–2014) was a writer who is perhaps best known as the founder of the black arts movement. Born as Everett LeRoi Jones on October 7, 1934, in a lower middle-class neighborhood of Newark, New Jersey, he attended predominately white public schools, then Rutgers University and Howard University, before beginning military service in the U.S. Air Force in 1954. After his release from the military in 1957, he attended graduate school and moved to New York's Greenwich Village, where he met and married a white woman, Hettie Cohen. The couple went on to have two daughters. Baraka lived in the Village from 1957 to 1965, working as an editor, poet, dramatist, and jazz critic. He befriended numerous beat writers, including Allen Ginsberg and Frank O'Hara, and established a beat magazine called *Yugen*. As part of the Village's bohemian, avant-garde crowd, he published his first major collection of poetry, *Preface to a Twenty Volume Suicide Note* (1961). Throughout these poems, Baraka drew on the styles of the beat poets to combine stream of consciousness, projective free verse, and dialect.

Amiri Baraka, essayist, playwright, poet, and leading figure in the Black Arts Movement. (Library of Congress)

By 1962, he was pulling away from Ginsberg and rejecting the otherworldly poetics of beat writers. In his early poetry, Baraka had meditated on the black man's loneliness. Excluded from white America, he was also disconnected from black Africa, and Baraka laid out that racial isolation. His focus on the existential isolation of African Americans would soon translate into the solution of Black Nationalism, a nation within a nation, and so a home for black people in white America. In 1964 and 1965, he shifted from introspective, semiautobiographical poetry to forge a collective voice in his work. No longer writing out of lyric self-consciousness, he produced poems of lyrical communism.

By 1965, Baraka was celebrating the African heritage of African Americans. Black Americans have African imaginations, are beautiful, and must embrace blackness, as he put it in 1966. He offered a shift from dislocated black American to proud African American, declared a hatred for the black middle class (equating its values with Euro-American values), and expressed one of the tenets of Black Nationalism: the assertion of black Americans' identity as a people of African ancestry.

Baraka began to seek out friendships with Black Nationalists including Stokely Carmichael. Moving to Harlem in the wake of Malcolm's death, he also married a black poet, Sylvia Robinson, in 1967, and the same year converted to Islam.

To express this transformation, he changed his name from LeRoi Jones to Imamu ("spiritual leader") Amiri ("warrior") Baraka ("sacrifice"). Becoming more and more engaged with Black Nationalist politics, Baraka assumed leadership of his own black Muslim organization, Kawaida. From 1968 to 1975, he also chaired the Committee for Unified Newark, a Black United Front organization, and he was a prominent figure in the National Black Political Convention of 1972.

The beat poet had become a Black Nationalist. Baraka believed that art could create this black "Nation," and he challenged black artists to create a "Black Poem" and a "Black World" in his 1966 poem "Black Art." Explaining that he wanted to go beyond mere poetry to achieve literature as action, he called for art that both described the situation of black people *and* showed how to change it. He also formulated a theory of the "theater of assault." Laying out his manifesto for a new kind of theater in 1965, Baraka explained that revolutionary theater should force change and be a political weapon. To its shocked audiences and dazzled critics, Baraka's play *Dutchman* (1964) perhaps seemed just that kind of revolutionary theater. The story of a deathly encounter between a white woman and a black college student, it depicted a seemingly unstoppable race war between black and white Americans. It went on to win an Obie Award, was proclaimed the best play in America by Norman Mailer, and in 2007, it was controversially revived in New York.

In July 1967, Baraka was arrested for unlawfully carrying a weapon during the Newark Rebellion. The trial judge read Baraka's poem "Black People" (1967) to the all-white jury. "I'm being sentenced for the poem. Is that what you are saying?" responded Baraka. Although not published until *after* the riots, "Black People" seemed a call to violence: "We must make our own World . . . and we cannot do this unless the white man is dead. Let's get together and kill him" (Harris 1991, 224). The poem was admitted as evidence of a plot to ignite violence, and on January 4, 1968, Baraka was sentenced to three years in New Jersey's state penitentiary and fined $1,000 (although the conviction was overturned on appeal).

This incident illustrates the long-standing fusion of politics and art at the center of Baraka's work, a canon that encompasses 14 books of poetry, 24 plays, 5 books of essays, 4 anthologies, and a novel. As he explained in a recent interview, "all art is political" and no literature exists in a vacuum. Any suggestion to the contrary is meant "only to have us look away from the real world so that . . . all's well in the big house while the great majority—slaves, serfs, the generally exploited—suffer out of sight" (Trodd 2006, 375).

In part because of this insistence on the political nature of art, Baraka is a controversial figure in American literature. Even more controversial is his use of art to advocate violence. As with "Black People," his poems often call for violent action. Not only using art to advocate violence, he also imagines art *as* violent: in numerous poems, he demands that writers be warriors, describes language as a weapon, and fashions poems themselves as daggers, fists, and poison gas.

These calls to violence echo the rhetoric of the black militant leader Malcolm X, as do Baraka's repeated critiques of nonviolence as a continuing with the status quo. In fact, Malcolm's influence on Baraka was profound. Malcolm was killed while speaking in Harlem, on February 21, 1965. Responding to the assassination, Baraka wrote "A Poem for Black Hearts" (1965). Here he celebrates and mourns Malcolm X. Also in response to the assassination, Baraka left his white wife, moved uptown to Harlem from his Greenwich Village home, and embraced Black Nationalism.

Emphasizing his transformation still further, Baraka published a series of Black Nationalist poems. His hostility toward all white people appears in numerous other poems from this period, and his rejection of any cross-racial collaboration was even more evident during an infamous encounter with a white woman. She stated her desire to help solve racial tensions, and Baraka replied that she can help by dying. As well, several of his poems discuss raping white women as a way to counterbalance the oppression of black men. Leading to further criticism of his gender politics, Baraka went on to demonstrate an apparent hostility to all women, black or white. For example, he controversially stated that the recovery of healthy African identities depended on distinct gender roles and a submissive femininity.

Another new aesthetic that Baraka explored was the jazz avant-garde. Musical freedom as social activism continued the work of Harlem Renaissance poets Langston Hughes and James Weldon Johnson, and, in a recent interview, Baraka observed that the black arts movement (BAM) was on a continuum with the Harlem Renaissance. But Baraka also noted in the same interview that BAM was a version of Mao's Cultural Revolution. Baraka's references to Mao are in fact representative of his worldview after a second major transformation: from a Black Nationalist to a third-world Marxist, in 1974. A trip to Cuba in 1960 had begun to radicalize his thinking about oppression in the third world, and in the mid-1970s, he proclaimed a complete identification with the artists he had met on his trip. Dissatisfied with Kenneth Gibson's black bourgeois leadership of their Newark organization and newly impassioned by theories of African socialism, he reformed the Congress of African People as the Revolutionary Communist League.

This final transformation came with an unexpected shift to humor. His early work, from the late 1950s and early 1960s, had focused on the themes of death and despair, of moral and social corruption, and of self-hatred. His Black Nationalist poems of 1965–1975 are militant in tone, and his later poems frequently exhibit a comic sensibility. Baraka's life and art, therefore, falls into these three periods: beat generation, Black Nationalism, and third-world Marxism. But the thread that runs throughout is his stated belief that "ethics and aesthetics are one" (Trodd 2006, 375). Baraka died at the age of 79 on January 9, 2014, in Newark, New Jersey.

Zoe Trodd

Further Reading

Baraka, Amiri. *Home: Social Essays*. New York: Morrow, 1966.

Baraka, Amiri. *Raise, Race, Rays, Raze: Essays since 1965*. New York: Random House, 1972.

Baraka, Amiri. *Selected Poetry of Amiri Baraka/LeRoi Jones*. New York: Morrow, 1979.

Harris, William J., ed. *The LeRoi Jones/Amiri Baraka Reader*. New York: Thunder's Mouth Press, 1991.

Trodd, Zoe, ed. *American Protest Literature*. Cambridge, MA: Harvard University Press, 2006.

Watts, Jerry Gafio. *Amiri Baraka: The Politics and Art of a Black Intellectual*. New York: New York University Press, 2001.

Bates, Daisy

Daisy Bates was an African American civil rights activist, journalist, author, and National Association for the Advancement of Colored People (NAACP) leader during the Little Rock desegregation crisis of 1957. As president of the Arkansas NAACP, Bates helped direct negotiations between the Little Rock School Board and state and federal authorities, while focusing primarily on the well-being of the nine black students who were integrating the high school.

Bates was born Daisy Lee Gatson in tiny Huttig, in southern Arkansas, on November 11, 1914. She grew up with friends of her parents after her mother was killed by whites and her father fled town. This background inspired Bates to fight for racial equality throughout her life. When she was 15 years old, she began dating L. C. Bates, and they were married three years later. He was an insurance salesman when they first met, but he studied journalism and worked for several black-owned newspapers.

The Bateses leased a struggling church-owned press and began printing the *Arkansas State Press*, a Little Rock newspaper focused on civil rights issues. Besides journalism, they worked for the NAACP. Bates was not a member of Little Rock's black upper crust. She never completed college, had no significant role in the African American church, and was not wealthy. Yet she still managed to rise in the NAACP, eventually becoming president of the state's confluence of local branches in 1952.

After the *Brown v. Board of Education* (1954) Supreme Court decision, school desegregation became the Arkansas NAACP's primary focus. Bates and the NAACP Legal Defense Fund brought a lawsuit against the Little Rock School Board in 1956. In *Aaron v. Cooper*, the U.S. Supreme Court established that Central High School would desegregate in the fall of 1957. Thereafter, more black students and schools would be integrated. On September 2, 1957, the day before school was scheduled to begin, Orval Eugene Faubus, Arkansas's segregationist governor, ordered the Arkansas National Guard to surround Central High School to keep the peace as an angry white mob had gathered to protest and harass the black students. Desegregation did not begin on September 3 as scheduled.

After more judicial activity, Faubus removed the National Guard, and city police took over on September 20. On September 23, the nine black students entered Central High through a side door. With a mob of angry whites growing larger and more unruly, police removed the black students from school. The next day, President Dwight D. Eisenhower sent the 101st Airborne Division to keep order in Little Rock. The following day, soldiers escorted the "Little Rock Nine" to school.

Throughout this period and during the school year, Bates served as a liaison between the students, NAACP lawyers, public officials, and the media. The NAACP's local lawyer, Wiley Branton, relied on Bates to communicate with the students and their families, who did not have legal representation of their own. The Bates home became an unofficial meeting place for members of the media from the North who descended on Little Rock and had also been attacked by segregationist protesters.

Bates continued to be harassed on a nightly basis, becoming a lightning rod for attack from white supremacists. The Bateses did not believe in the nonviolent tactics of Martin Luther King Jr.'s Southern Christian Leadership Conference and were heavily armed at home. Several crosses were burned on her lawn, her windows were shot out repeatedly, and threatening phone calls offered her little rest at night from 1956 until she moved to New York in 1960 to work on her memoir of the Little Rock crisis. *The Long Shadow of Little Rock* was published in 1962 with a foreword by former First Lady Eleanor Roosevelt. The account of her enduring work won much acclaim and later the American Book Award for a version republished by the University of Arkansas Press in 1982.

Bates lived in Washington, D.C., and worked with President Lyndon B. Johnson's War on Poverty initiative until she had a stroke in 1965. She moved back to Arkansas in 1968 but continued working on local poverty issues in Mitchellville. After the death of her husband, Bates focused on restarting the *Arkansas State Press*. The newspaper reappeared in 1984, with Ernest Green, one of the Little Rock Nine, working as its national marketing director. Also in 1984, Bates received an honorary law degree from the University of Arkansas–Fayetteville, where she is known for her unwavering devotion to fighting discrimination against African Americans. Her presence also challenged the domination by black male clergyman in the NAACP's leadership roles. She broke the mold of most female civil rights supporters and did not have the deep religious background of other women working in the movement. Unlike Ella Baker, Bates worked in the foreground, becoming a public face of activism. Most important, Bates did not permit the Little Rock Nine to become sacrificial lambs for the civil rights movement. The actions by Bates and President Eisenhower's federal intervention ensured that massive resistance never became an accepted practice and pushed the civil rights movement in new directions.

Peter Carr Jones

Further Reading

Bates, Daisy. *The Long Shadow of Little Rock*. Little Rock: University of Arkansas Press, 1986.

Jacoway, Elizabeth. *"Turn Away Thy Son": Little Rock, The Crisis That Shocked the Nation*. New York: Free Press, 2007.

Stockley, Grif. *Daisy Bates: Civil Rights Crusader from Arkansas*. Jackson: University Press of Mississippi, 2005.

Belafonte, Harry

Harry Belafonte is a prominent African American musician, actor, and social activist, known as the "King of Calypso" as well as a staunch advocate for civil rights and humanitarian issues. Harold (Harry) George Belafonte Jr. was born to West Indian parents in Harlem, New York, on March 1, 1927. After he graduated from high school, he joined the U.S. Navy. Following his military discharge, he worked at various jobs in New York City. Because of his interest in the performing arts, he studied acting at Stanley Kubrick's Dramatic School. He also studied at the New York School for Social Research. Two of his most recognized classmates were Walter Matthau and Marlon Brando.

Belafonte became successful in the early 1950s when he gained a great amount of recognition as a folk singer. His performance style was appealing and attracted a large following from across the United States. His signature calypso song was titled "Banana Boat Song." Other calypso songs he made popular include "Jamaica Farewell," "Matilda," "Brown Skin Girl," "Come Back Lisa," "Coconut Woman," and "Hold 'Em Joe."

Even though Belafonte was a fan favorite, he experienced racism on several occasions. Such negative experiences played a significant role in his decision to become a political activist. He played a significant role in Dr. Martin Luther King Jr.'s 1963 March on Washington and participated in the 1965 Selma March (which sparked Bloody Sunday).

Belafonte was able to maintain a balance between his career and his involvement in issues related to social injustices throughout the 1950s, 1960s, and 1970s. His production of the first integrated musical show on television gained him an Emmy Award in 1960. He was chastised by the network and corporate sponsors, however, because popular singer Petula Clark touched his arm. In fact, Belafonte was fired because of this particular incident. The firing clearly represented the racial divide in the United States.

Many achievements and career highlights establish Belafonte as a significant figure in the world of entertainment. He earned a Tony Award in 1953 as a cast member in John Murray Anderson's *Almanac*. In 1954, he performed in the revised version of Bizet's Opera *Carmen Jones* with costar Dorothy Dandridge. His other film appearances include *Bright Road* (1953), David Boyer's *Island in the Sun* (1957), *The Heart of Show Business* (1957), *The World, the Flesh, and the Devil* (1959), *Odds against Tomorrow* (1959), *Tonight with Belafonte* (1960), *The Angel Levine* (1970), *Buck and the Preacher* (1972), *Uptown Saturday Night* (1974), *Sometimes I Watch My Life* (1982), *Three Songs* (1983), *The Payer* (1992), *White Man's Burden* (1995), and *Kansas City* (1996).

The performing arts medium truly embraced Belafonte for his artistry within the profession and his marketability. He is the recipient of the Donaldson Award, 1953–1954; U.S. Department of State Award, 1958; an Emmy Award for the 1960 TV special, *Tonight with Harry Belafonte*; an honorary doctorate of humanities from Park College in Missouri; the Martin Luther King Jr. Nonviolent Peace Prize in 1982; the Thurgood Marshall Lifetime Achievement Award, 1993; the National Medal of Arts in 1994; and the Bishop John T. Walker Distinguished Humanitarian Service Award from Africa in 2002. He was inducted into the Black Filmmakers Hall of Fame in 1976. Belafonte continued to garner accolades, receiving the BET humanitarian award in 2006.

Belafonte became very active in addressing social issues around the globe in the 1980s. The concept behind the song "We Are the World" (1985) was the brainchild of Belafonte. The performance and sale of recordings of this song generated millions of dollars to assist in fighting famine in Ethiopia. In 1987, he was named UNICEF goodwill ambassador and was selected to chair the welcome committee for Nelson Mandela's visit to the United States after his release from prison in South Africa. He also performed in Monte Carlo at the Princess Grace Red Cross Ball in 1987 and became the first entertainer to serve on the Advisory Committee of the Peace Corps in 1989.

Belafonte had a prolific recording career, including *Calypso* (1956), *Mary's Boy Child* (1956), *Coconut Woman* (1957), *Love Is a Gentle Thing* (1959), *Mark Twain and other Folk Favorites* (1959), and *We Shall Overcome* (video recordings, 1989) by Harry Belafonte (1992). In addition to his involvement as a social activist, filmmaker, and recording artist, he found time to appear on talk shows as a performer and/or engage in intellectual dialogue related to political and social events. Belafonte appeared on diverse television shows including *The Dick Cavett Show* (1972), *The Mike Douglas Show* (1974), and *Paul Robeson (The People)* (1976).

Belafonte also represented the United States on the world stage in speaking of the disenfranchised and those persons or societies whose quality of life does not meet expected standards. He continued to offer commentary on politics and society and was most recently an outspoken critic of the George W. Bush administration.

Lemuel Berry Jr.

Further Reading

Estell, Kenneth. *African American: Portrait of a People*. Washington, DC: Visible Ink Press, 1994.

Hill, Early G., and James V. Hatch. *A History of African American Theater*. New York: Cambridge University Press, 2003.

Southern, Eileen. *Biographical Dictionary of Afro-American and African Musicians*. Westport, CT: Greenwood Press, 1982.

Southern, Eileen. *The Music of Black Americans*. New York: W. W. Norton, 1997.

Bethune, Mary McLeod

Mary McLeod Bethune (1875–1955), an educator, civil rights activist, and founder of a historically black college, was one of the most important black leaders of the early twentieth century. She played an important role in promoting education for blacks, led numerous African American organizations, and also worked as a member of the "black cabinet" in Franklin Delano Roosevelt's presidential administration. Although Bethune played such a significant role in high-level politics, she argued that she wanted to help ordinary African Americans. She fought for racial integration as a means for blacks to gain civil rights.

Mary McLeod was born in Maynesville, South Carolina, in 1875, the 15th of 17 children of former slaves. She was born and grew up in the South during the era of Jim Crow segregation and violence. Mary McLeod distinguished herself by her academic ability at a young age and attended a local school run by black educator Emma J. Wilson. In 1887, she won a scholarship to a boarding school— Scotia Seminary for Negro Girls—in Concord, North Carolina. Mary McLeod would play a prominent role in black education, in large part owing to her early experiences with schools. She believed that education was the key to advancement of African Americans and spent much of her career promoting schools for blacks.

In 1898, Mary McLeod married Albertus Bethune, a clothing salesman. The couple gave birth to their son, Albert, the next year. The family moved to Florida shortly thereafter and opened a school. In 1904, Mary McLeod Bethune founded the Daytona Literary and Industrial Training School for Negro Girls.

Like Booker T. Washington at the Tuskegee Institute, Bethune promoted industrial education. In 1907, Albertus left and went back to South Carolina. The couple never divorced, however, and Albertus died in 1918. Bethune struggled to raise funds to keep the school afloat, and the student population increased tremendously over the next two decades. The school was later renamed the Daytona Normal and Industrial School and, in 1923, it merged with the Cookman Institute of Jacksonville, Florida. The school ultimately became a four-year college, Bethune-Cookman College. Bethune served as the president of the college from 1923 to 1942 and again from 1946 to 1947.

Bethune also played a central role in women's political activities in the early twentieth century, where she focused on her goal of improving the lives of black women. She served as the head of the Florida Federation of Colored Women's Clubs from 1917 to 1925. In this capacity, she founded a home for delinquent black girls in Ocala, Florida. Bethune served as the president of the Southeastern Federation of Colored Women's Clubs from 1920 to 1925 and headed up the National Association of Teachers in Colored Schools from 1923 to 1924. Bethune was elected president of the National Association of Colored Women (NACW) from 1924 to 1928 after defeating Ida B. Wells-Barnett for the position. She served as the NACW president for two terms.

Bethune was recognized nationally for her work promoting education and political upliftment of African Americans. In 1930, President Herbert Hoover invited her to a conference at the White House to reward her active work within the Republican Party. When Franklin Delano Roosevelt was elected president on the Democratic ticket in 1932, however, Bethune aligned herself with the Democrats. In 1935, Bethune wanted to promote a more radical political agenda, so she formed the National Council of Negro Women (NCNW). Bethune sought to create an organization that would promote the interests of all black women and also make the entire nation recognize the struggles and triumphs of African American women.

Bethune moved to Washington, D.C., in 1936 when she joined the National Youth Administration (NYA), an agency within the Works Progress Administration. The NYA was founded to spread democratic ideas to American youth and to provide vocational training for youth struggling with the economic ramifications of the Great Depression. In 1939, Bethune's unit of the NYA was moved to the Division of Negro Affairs in the Federal Security Agency, making Bethune the highest-ranking African American woman in the federal government. In her role, she promoted college education for black students as well as training in skills necessary for the war effort.

In 1936, Bethune began to serve on the Federal Council on Negro Affairs, also known as the "black cabinet." The cabinet promoted civil rights for all blacks. In 1937, Bethune helped to organize the National Conference on the Problems of the Negro, a widely publicized conference. Attendees included Eleanor Roosevelt along with other important political figures. The conference promoted the goal of integration and publicized the struggles of African Americans.

After the attack on Pearl Harbor and the entrance of the United States into World War II, Bethune encouraged black Americans to support the war effort. She viewed the war as an opportunity for blacks to fight for their civil rights. She promoted war bonds and also worked to recruit black women to the army through the Women's Army Auxiliary Corps (WAC). She also agitated for equal treatment of black soldiers and protested against unfair treatment for black women in the WAC. As World War II drew to a close, Bethune assumed a role on the international stage. In 1945, the State Department reluctantly named her an associate consultant to the U.S. delegation to draft the UN Charter in San Francisco. She was the only black woman on the delegation. She also continued to play a prominent role in American politics. From 1936 to 1952, Bethune served as president of the Association for the Study of Negro Life and History, an organization founded by Carter G. Woodson.

Bethune left Washington, D.C., and returned to Florida in 1949, where she continued her work. In addition to taking trips to Haiti and Liberia, she also continued to promote equality for African Americans. She worked with black businessmen to develop beaches that blacks could use under the Bethune-Volusia Project. She also founded the McLeod Bethune Foundation, a charitable organization to house her papers and promote black education. In 1955, Bethune attended the World Assembly for Moral Re-Armament (MRA) conference in Switzerland. The MRA promoted honesty, purity, unselfishness, and love, all traits that appealed to Bethune and her political philosophy. Mary McLeod Bethune suffered a heart attack on May 18, 1955, and died at her home in Florida.

Jane E. Dabel

Further Reading

Collier-Thomas, Bettye, and V. P. Franklin. *Sisters in the Struggle: African American Women in the Civil Rights–Black Power Movement*. New York: New York University Press, 2001.

Hanson, Joyce Ann. *Mary McLeod Bethune and Black Women's Political Activism*. Columbia: University of Missouri Press, 2003.

Holt, Rackham. *Mary McLeod Bethune: A Biography*. Garden City, NY: Doubleday, 1964.

Bevel, James

Credited by Martin Luther King Jr. with initiating the Children's Crusade during the Birmingham Campaign of 1963, Reverend James Bevel emerged as a civil rights leader from the ranks of the Nashville, Tennessee, student movement. Bevel was at King's side during many of the major campaigns of the Southern Christian

Leadership Conference (SCLC) and was at the Lorraine Motel at the time of King's assassination in 1968.

James Luther Bevel was born in Itta Bena, Mississippi, on October 19, 1936, and was one of 17 children. He served in the U.S. Naval Reserve in 1954 and 1955 before entering the American Baptist Theological Seminary in Nashville, Tennessee. He was ordained as a Baptist minister in 1959 and went on to pastor the Chestnut Grove Baptist Church. During this period, Bevel joined with fellow seminarian John Lewis, Diane Nash from Fisk University, and Vanderbilt's James Lawson in the Nashville movement to initiate a local sit-in campaign in early February 1960. That same year, Bevel and the other Nashville activists attended the founding meeting of the Student Nonviolent Coordinating Committee (SNCC) at Shaw University. Bevel and Nash helped lead the Freedom Rides in 1961 and married later that year. In 1962, Bevel left the SNCC to become Mississippi field secretary for the SCLC.

Bevel and Nash moved to Alabama in the spring of 1963 and played leading roles, along with Dorothy Cotton, Andrew Young, Bernard Lee, Fred Shuttlesworth, and the Alabama Christian Movement for Human Rights, in the campaign to desegregate Birmingham. As the number of adult participants willing to go to jail dwindled, Bevel began recruiting black students from Birmingham's high schools, colleges, and churches to participate in the protests. Mass demonstrations by students triggered a violent police response that brought national attention to Birmingham. One week later, city leaders reached an accord with movement leaders.

As he prepared to work on the Alabama voter registration movement that would later culminate in the 1965 Selma March, Bevel informed King that more staff was needed to build a nonviolent movement in Alabama. Bevel feared that activists who were not committed to nonviolence were conducting "demonstration[s] for the sake of demonstrating," and that these tactics resulted in "rioting and deaths." He advised, "In order to off-set these trends, the non-violent must project and execute a program that will [allow] more Negroes to become convinced of the effectiveness of non-violence and the principles of it." Bevel further implored King to put "the whole non-violent staff" on the Alabama project. His pressure paid off, and at the May 1964 executive staff meeting, King recommended that SCLC increase its presence in Alabama. Bevel led this effort as the head of SCLC's Direct Action Department.

Bevel moved to Chicago in 1965 to begin laying the groundwork for a nonviolent northern civil rights drive. He went on to become national director of the Spring Mobilization Committee to End the War in Vietnam in 1967 and, the following year, joined King in the effort to win the Memphis sanitation workers strike. After King's assassination, Bevel publicly defended the innocence of King's accused killer, James Earl Ray, and even offered to defend him in court. The case's judge, however, refused Bevel's representation due to the fact that he was not a lawyer.

In 1969, Bevel left the SCLC and became involved in the Republican Party. He had two unsuccessful runs for political office: a run for Congress in 1984, and a bid for vice president alongside presidential candidate Lyndon LaRouche in 1992. He later co-initiated the Million Man March at Washington, D.C., in 1995, at which approximately 870,000 African American men gathered to bring the attention of politicians to the social and economic difficulties faced by African Americans and other minorities.

Before his death in December 2008, Bevel was convicted of incest with one of his teenage daughters and sentenced to 15 years in prison. After serving seven months, he was released on account of having terminal pancreatic cancer.

Clayborne Carson

Further Reading

Honey, Michael K. *Going Down Jericho Road*. New York: W. W. Norton, 2008.

Lewis, John. *Walking with the Wind: A Memoir of the Movement*. New York: Houghton Mifflin Harcourt, 1998.

Weber, Bruce. "James L. Bevel, 72, an Adviser to Dr. King, Is Dead." *New York Times*, December 23, 2008. http://www.nytimes.com/2008/12/23/us/23bevel.html?_r=0.

Birmingham Campaign

In April 1963, Martin Luther King Jr. and the Southern Christian Leadership Conference (SCLC) joined with Birmingham, Alabama's existing local movement, the Alabama Christian Movement for Human Rights (ACMHR), in a massive direct action campaign to attack the city's segregation system by putting pressure on Birmingham's merchants during the Easter season, the second-biggest shopping season of the year. As ACMHR founder Fred Shuttlesworth stated in the group's "Birmingham Manifesto," the campaign was "a moral witness to give our community a chance to survive."

The campaign was originally scheduled to begin in early March 1963 but was postponed until April 2, when the relatively moderate Albert Boutwell defeated Birmingham's segregationist commissioner of public safety, Eugene "Bull" Connor, in a runoff mayoral election. On April 3, the desegregation campaign was launched with a series of mass meetings, direct actions, lunch counter sit-ins, marches on city hall, and a boycott of downtown merchants. King spoke to black citizens about the philosophy of nonviolence and its methods and extended appeals for volunteers at the end of the mass meetings. With the number of volunteers increasing daily, actions soon expanded to kneel-ins at churches, sit-ins at the library, and a march on the county building to register voters. Hundreds were arrested.

On April 10, the city government obtained a state circuit court injunction against the protests. After heavy debate, campaign leaders decided to disobey the court order. King declared: "We cannot in all good conscience obey such an injunction which is an unjust, undemocratic and unconstitutional misuse of the legal process." Plans to continue to submit to arrest were threatened, however, because the money available for cash bonds was depleted, so leaders could no longer guarantee that arrested protesters would be released. King contemplated whether he and Ralph Abernathy should be arrested. Given the lack of bail funds, King's services as a fund-raiser were desperately needed, but King also worried that his failure to submit to arrests might undermine his credibility. King concluded that he must risk going to jail in Birmingham. He told his colleagues: "I don't know what will happen; I don't know where the money will come from. But I have to make a faith act."

On Good Friday, April 12, King was arrested in Birmingham after violating the anti-protest injunction and was kept in solitary confinement. During this time, King penned the "Letter from Birmingham Jail" on the margins of the *Birmingham News*, in reaction to a statement published in that newspaper by eight Birmingham clergymen condemning the protests. In addition, King's request to call his wife, Coretta Scott King, who was at home in Atlanta recovering from the birth of their fourth child, was denied. After she communicated her concern to the Kennedy administration, Birmingham officials permitted King to call home. Bail money was made available, and he was released on April 20, 1963.

In order to sustain the campaign, SCLC organizer James Bevel proposed using young children in demonstrations. Bevel's rationale for the Children's Crusade was that young people represented an untapped source of freedom fighters without the prohibitive responsibilities of older activists. On May 2, more than 1,000 African American students attempted to march into downtown Birmingham, and hundreds were arrested. When hundreds more gathered the following day, Commissioner Connor directed local police and fire departments to use force to halt the demonstrations. During the next few days, images of children being blasted by high-pressure fire hoses, clubbed by police officers, and attacked by police dogs appeared on television and in newspapers, triggering international outrage. While leading a group of child marchers, Shuttlesworth himself was hit with the full force of a fire hose and had to be hospitalized. King offered encouragement to parents of the young protesters: "Don't worry about your children, they're going to be alright. Don't hold them back if they want to go to jail. For they are doing a job for not only themselves, but for all of America and for all mankind."

In the meantime, the white business structure was weakening under adverse publicity and the unexpected decline in business due to the boycott, but many business owners and city officials were reluctant to negotiate with the protesters. With national pressure on the White House also mounting, Attorney General Robert Kennedy sent Burke Marshall, his chief civil rights assistant, to facilitate negotiations between prominent black citizens and representatives of Birmingham's Senior Citizen's Council, the city's business leadership.

The Senior Citizen's Council sought a moratorium on street protests as an act of good faith before any final settlement was declared, and Marshall encouraged campaign leaders to halt demonstrations, accept an interim compromise that would provide partial success, and negotiate the rest of their demands afterward. Some black negotiators were open to the idea, and although the hospitalized Shuttlesworth was not present at the negotiations, on May 8, King told the negotiators he would accept the compromise and call the demonstrations to a halt.

When Shuttlesworth learned that King intended to announce a moratorium, he was furious—about both the decision to ease pressure off white business owners and the fact that he, as the acknowledged leader of the local movement, had not been consulted. Feeling betrayed, Shuttlesworth reminded King that he could not legitimately speak for the black population of Birmingham on his own: "Go ahead and call it off . . . When I see it on TV, that you have called it off, I will get up out of this, my sickbed, with what little ounce of strength I have, and lead them back into the street. And your name'll be Mud." King made the announcement anyway but indicated that demonstrations might be resumed if negotiations did not resolve the situation shortly.

By May 10, negotiators had reached an agreement, and despite his falling out with King, Shuttlesworth joined him and Abernathy to read the prepared statement that detailed the compromise: the removal of "Whites Only" and "Blacks Only" signs in restrooms and on drinking fountains, a plan to desegregate lunch counters, an ongoing "program of upgrading Negro employment," the formation of a biracial committee to monitor the progress of the agreement, and the release of jailed protesters on bond.

Birmingham segregationists responded to the agreement with a series of violent attacks. That night, an explosive went off near the Gaston Motel room where King and SCLC leaders had previously stayed, and the next day, the home of King's brother Alfred Daniel King was bombed. President John F. Kennedy responded by ordering 3,000 federal troops into position near Birmingham and making preparations to federalize the Alabama National Guard. Four months later, on September 15, Ku Klux Klan members bombed Birmingham's Sixteenth Street Baptist Church, killing four young girls. King delivered the eulogy at the September 18 joint funeral of three of the victims, preaching that the girls were "the martyred heroines of a holy crusade for freedom and human dignity."

Clayborne Carson

Further Reading

Alabama Christian Movement for Human Rights. "Birmingham Manifesto." April 3, 1963. MLKJP-GAMK.

Brinkley, Douglas. "The Man Who Kept King's Secrets." *Vanity Fair*, April 2006.

Carson, Clayborne, David J. Garrow, Gerald Gill, Vincent Harding, and Darlene Clark Hine, eds. *The Eyes on the Prize: Civil Rights Reader: Documents, Speeches, and*

Firsthand Accounts from the Black Freedom Struggle, 1954–1990. New York: Penguin Books, 1991.

Eskew, Glenn T. *But for Birmingham: The Local and National Movements in the Civil Rights Struggle.* Chapel Hill: University of North Carolina Press, 1997.

Hampton, Henry, Steve Fayer, and Sarah Flynn. *Voices of Freedom: An Oral History of the Civil Rights Movement from the 1950s through the 1980s.* New York: Bantam Books, 1990.

King, Martin Luther, Jr. "Eulogy for Carol Denise McNair et al." September 18, 1963. Martin Luther King, Jr. Papers, 1950–1968, Martin Luther King, Jr. Center for Nonviolent Social Change, Atlanta, Georgia.

King, Martin Luther, Jr. *Why We Can't Wait.* New York: Harper & Row, 1964.

Black Arts Movement

In 1965, the passage of the Voting Rights Act ended one phase of the civil rights movement and, by October 1966, the emergent doctrine of Black Power had concrete political form in the Black Panther Party for Self-Defense. Black Power also had an artistic extension in the form of the black arts movement (BAM). Positioning themselves as an alternative to the mainstream civil rights movement, BAM poets and Black Power activists replaced the ideal of integration with that of black cultural particularism.

BAM was led by Amiri Baraka, Ed Bullins, Addison Gayle Jr., Hoyt Fuller, Larry Neal, Ishmael Reed, and James Stewart. It emerged out of Philadelphia, New York, and Oakland during the early 1960s, and by 1964, it had a literary center in the arts journal *Liberator*, founded by Neal and Askia Touré. In 1968, the publication of the *Black Fire* anthology, edited by Baraka and Neal, marked one of the major events in BAM's print culture. BAM reached the peak of its cultural influence in the late 1960s and early 1970s.

Central to the movement was a belief that political action would come through artistic expression. Art had a social value, and the artist had a role in political transformation. Black Nationalist cultural politics would help answer problems like poverty, police brutality, and substandard education, because imaginative culture could alter the reality of oppressed peoples.

The movement also stressed cultural heritage, the beauty of blackness, and a black aesthetic. It asked that black people no longer see through white eyes, and BAM poets therefore subverted traditional forms and accepted values. If "white" and "black" were signifiers for "good" and "bad," then BAM poets would use the terms differently, celebrating what Baraka frequently termed "black magic." In 1968, Neal described BAM as a cultural revolution, adding that a whole new system of ideas was needed. Neal's poem "Black Boogaloo" (1969) went on to instruct black poets, painters, and musicians: "Take care of business. All get together. . . . Combine energy. . . . Calling all Black People" (42).

As part of this revolution, BAM artists embraced the jazz avant-garde. They believed that music articulated an authentic black expression: "Negro music alone, because it drew its strengths and beauties out of the depth of the black man's soul, and because to a large extent its traditions could be carried on by the lowest classes of Negroes, has been able to survive the constant and wilful dilutions of the black middle class," wrote Baraka in 1966 (Mitchell 1994, 165). Musical freedom constituted another form of social activism, and BAM poets used the rhythms of black music in their verse. We were "drenched in black music and wanted our poetry to be black music ... its rhythms, its language, its history and struggle," remembered Baraka of BAM. "It was meant to be a poetry we copped from the people and gave them right back, open and direct and moving" (Baraka 1984, 237).

Alongside this interest in music as a language of the people, BAM poets stressed the orality of poetry, focused on vernacular speech as a communicative medium, and tried to make art accessible to the whole Harlem community. In 1965, Baraka founded the Black Arts Repertory Theatre/School (BART/S) in Harlem to assist the creation of a black culture. Focused on community art, BART/S produced plays that questioned core American values and provided African Americans with new meanings to their lives. BAM saw the artist-audience relationship as localized and collaborative, and when BART/S closed in 1966, Baraka opened Spirit House in Newark, New Jersey, guided by the same founding principles as BART/S.

Yet for all their efforts, BAM writers failed to resonate beyond a limited group of black urbanites. Nearly all of the movement's theater groups and journals were short-lived, and Gayle began preserving BAM for posterity as early as 1971. In an anthology titled *The Black Aesthetic,* he juxtaposed BAM writers with other major twentieth-century theorists of the black aesthetic (including W. E. B. Du Bois and Langston Hughes), as though to ensure BAM's place in the annals of literary history. Then in 1973, Bullins's book *The Theme is Blackness* offered a closing statement of BAM and also expressed admiration for the accomplishments of the mainstream civil rights movement. Increasingly criticized for its anti-Semitism and chauvinism, as well as its exclusion of liberal whites and its strident form of nationalism, BAM faded from public view by the mid-1970s.

Zoe Trodd

Further Reading

Baraka, Amiri. *The Autobiography*. New York: Freundlich Books, 1984.

Baraka, Amiri, and Larry Neal, eds. *Black Fire*. New York: Morrow, 1968.

Ed Bullins, *The Theme of Blackness: 'The Corner' and Other Plays*. New York: Morrow, 1973.

Gayle, Addison, Jr. *The Black Aesthetic*. New York: Doubleday, 1971.

Mitchell, Angelyn, ed. *Within the Circle: An Anthology of African American Literary Criticism from the Harlem Renaissance to the Present*. Durham, NC: Duke University Press, 1994.

Neal, Larry. "The Black Arts Movement." *Drama Review* 12 (Summer 1968): 29–39.

Neal, Larry. *Black Boogaloo*. San Francisco: Journal of Black Poetry Press, 1969.

Black Nationalism

Black Nationalism was an ideological movement that advocated the political autonomy of African Americans ranging from support of the empowerment and self-sufficiency of the black community within an integrated society to complete separation from white society. Black Nationalism did not emerge as a coherent movement focused on racial solidarity until the early twentieth century.

The origins of Black Nationalism lie in the philosophies of black abolitionists—namely Martin R. Delany, who advocated immigration to Africa. Explaining that African Americans were culturally and politically homeless, Delany proposed that they needed to build their own nation in Sierra Leone and Liberia. He also believed that this development would raise the social status of those who remained behind in the United States. Trying to move his plan forward, he led an immigration commission to West Africa in 1859 and explored potential sites.

By the 1920s, the Jamaican immigrant Marcus Garvey had developed radical abolitionist theories into a full-fledged Black Nationalist movement. In 1914, Garvey founded the Jamaica-based Universal Negro Improvement Association (UNIA), and, in 1917, he opened a first branch in the United States. UNIA advocated black unity and self-improvement, sponsored several educational institutions, convened international conventions, and opened more than 1,000 branches. Garvey had turned the ideas of abolitionists into a movement and developed the first major strand of Black Nationalism: black separatism through a Back-to-Africa ideology.

His movement also inspired a new Black Nationalist effort: Farrad Muhammad's Nation of Islam (NOI). Founded and developed during the early 1930s, and with many former Garveyites among its early members, the NOI represented a second major strand in Black Nationalism: black separatism within the United States. To prepare for this separate black nation, the NOI preached black racial superiority and focused on developing economic self-sufficiency within black communities. Led by Elijah Muhammad after 1934, it entirely rejected white society and demanded several American states—a nation within a nation—as compensation for slavery.

By the late 1950s, Malcolm X had become NOI's most prominent spokesperson. As a minister for the NOI, he defined land as the basis of freedom and equality, called for racial independence and a separate black identity, and advocated black self-defense. He also termed American history a *white* history. He aimed these Black Nationalist philosophies at a primary audience of young, urban African Americans, who were frustrated by what they saw as Martin Luther King Jr.'s embrace of white protest traditions (including civil disobedience) and futile gradualism.

In 1964, Malcolm X declared independence from the NOI and formed Muslim Mosque, Inc. He soon expanded his vision of Black Nationalism to include

Africans and made two trips to Africa in 1964 in an effort to solicit support from African leaders. On June 28, 1964, he called a press conference to announce his new project, the Organization of Afro-American Unity (OAAU). Rather than promoting a Back-to-Africa movement, like Garvey's, this would be an organization that sought to achieve a global African community, promote the interests of black people worldwide, fight white supremacy, and link African Americans with Africa.

Malcolm X was killed on February 21, 1965, before he could develop the OAAU program any further. But his ideas soon inspired a new Black Nationalist vision in the form of the Black Panther Party for Self-Defense (BPP). Bobby Seale and Huey P. Newton founded the BPP at a community center in North Oakland, California, in October 1966. Long frustrated with mainstream civil rights efforts, they were also galvanized by the defeat of the Mississippi Freedom Democratic Party in 1964, the Los Angeles Riot of 1965, and the Voting Rights Act of 1965. They believed that King and his supporters paid scant attention to the situation of urban African Americans, including the ongoing problems of high unemployment, substandard housing, and poor education.

Adopting Malcolm X's model of armed self-defense, they quickly formed a system of police patrols, aimed at countering police brutality against Oakland's black community. Their new members began to monitor and confront law enforcement officials and to advise Oakland residents of their rights. They began to use the term "black power" as a theory to explain their practices. This represented a new spin on Black Nationalism. Richard Wright had first used this phrase in his 1954 book of the same title, but it was Stokely Carmichael, the Student Nonviolent Coordinating Committee (SNCC) chair and eventually the BPP's honorary prime minister, who first developed the idea into a full movement ideology.

In 1966, he laid out a philosophy of Black Power that Newton and Seale adopted for their newly formed organization: black people needed to achieve racial pride and reclaim a black history, as well as build separate black communities, develop economic self-sufficiency, and collectivize their resources. Black Nationalism now meant not only political and economic control, but also psychic and historical control. Another part of this Black Power philosophy was to prohibit whites from joining the liberation movement. Carmichael explained that whites could not relate to the black experience and that an all-black project was needed in order for black people to achieve freedom. He rejected racial reconciliation, nonviolent civil disobedience, and any notion of the American dream as defined by white people.

Newton and Seale translated this philosophy of absolute self-determination into the formation of community programs, rather than into attempts to achieve an independent black colony. The BPP therefore represented a third major strand in Black Nationalism: the development of black community control over political and economic resources, or community nationalism. The BPP "survival programs" tried to combat the institutional racism at the heart of substandard housing, bad diets, poor health care services, and poor education for African Americans. They eventually offered breakfasts for schoolchildren, medical care, pest control, busing to prisons for the families of inmates, sickle cell anemia testing, clothing and shoes, community political education classes, and "liberation schools." In part because of this smaller-scale, practical application of Black Nationalist philosophy —improving existing black communities rather than reaching for a separate black nation—the BPP's membership had grown to around 5,000 by the end of 1968, with chapters in India, Israel, Australia, and England as well as 40 chapters in the United States.

But the organization was under attack. In August 1967, the Federal Bureau of Investigation (FBI) under J. Edgar Hoover had instructed its covert action program—COINTELPRO—to disrupt and neutralize "Black Nationalist Hate Groups," and by July 1969, the Panthers were COINTELPRO's primary focus (although it also targeted the Southern Christian Leadership Conference, the SNCC, the Revolutionary Action Movement, and the NOI). The program attempted to weaken BPP leaders, discredit the organization, and prevent the unification of Black Nationalist groups. They set other groups against the BPP and created rifts and factions within the BPP itself. A series of FBI raids and prosecutions, including the 1969 indictment and conviction of Seale for protesting during the Democratic National Convention of August 1968, weakened the BPP's national and regional leadership and diminished its local membership.

By the early 1970s, its leadership was also engaged in a series of internal conflicts over the primary focus of Black Nationalist activism. Newton wanted to emphasize community service, but another BPP leader, Eldridge Cleaver, believed armed confrontation was more important. Cleaver publicly criticized the BPP as "reformist" rather than "revolutionary," and Seale countered that the survival programs *were* "revolutionary." In early 1971, Newton expelled Cleaver from the Central Committee and stated that his focus on violence alienated the black community and inhibited his potential role in the Black Nationalist transformation of society.

Before long, the BPP was entirely crippled. Internal disputes, infiltration by covert government operations, and the deaths of party members during violent clashes with the police had diminished its energy and support. In March 1978, the membership of the BPP had declined to around 20. But the party's platform did offer a blueprint for other 1960s protest manifestos, including those by the Brown Berets, the Young Lords, the White Panther Party, the Red Guards, and the Gray Panthers.

The BPP represents the last truly influential Black Nationalist movement in the United States. But elements of Black Nationalism do persist. As late as 1995, the NOI attracted between 650,000 and 1.5 million people to its "Million Man March" in Washington, D.C. The Black Nationalism emphasis on racial pride and black history also influenced the emergence of hip-hop as a protest medium.

For example, Tupac Shakur embraced the doctrines of Black Nationalism in songs like "Panther Power" (1989). As well, elements of the Back-to-Africa movement influenced the development of pan-Africanism. Several former Panthers, including Carmichael, shifted direction to embrace pan-African pride, explaining that the only way forward for Black Nationalism was a socialist pan-African revolution.

As for the strand of Black Nationalism focused on community development, this persists in two new groups. In the early 1990s, activists inspired by the BPP pointed to new and continuing crises in African American communities: poverty, AIDS, infant mortality, drugs, high unemployment, and institutionalized racism. They announced the return of Black Nationalism and, in 1994, former members of the original BPP launched the Black Panther Collective. They began to document police brutality in New York and to raise public awareness about political prisoners. The New African American Vanguard Movement was also founded in 1994, with B. Kwaku Duren as its chair. It became the New Panther Vanguard Movement in 1997. The group develops community-based social and cultural institutions, also demanding sentencing reviews and reductions for black prisoners.

But the separatist strand of Black Nationalism was also taken up by a more high-profile contemporary Black Nationalist group: the New Black Panther Party (NBPP), founded in 1991. The party's literature references Garveyism and calls for independent African-centered schools, more trade with Africa, black tax exemption, and its own provisional government. The NBPP's ultimate aim is black national liberation and a black "liberated zone." But its strong anti-Zionist tendencies have led to accusations of anti-Semitism, and several members of the original BPP have condemned the NBPP, observing that the BPP had operated with love for blacks, not hatred of whites.

Zoe Trodd

Further Reading

Bracey, John, et al., eds. *Black Nationalism in America*. Indianapolis, IN: Bobbs-Merrill, 1970.

Essien-Udom, E. U. *Black Nationalism: A Search for an Identity in America*. Chicago: University of Chicago Press, 1962.

Gardell, Mattias. *In the Name of Elijah Muhammad: Louis Farrakhan and the Nation of Islam*. Durham, NC: Duke University Press, 1996.

Haines, Herbert H. *Black Radicals and the Civil Rights Mainstream, 1954–1970*. Knoxville: University of Tennessee Press, 1988.

Robinson, Dean E. *Black Nationalism in American Politics and Thought*. New York: Cambridge University Press, 2001.

Seale, Bobby. *Seize the Time: The Story of the Black Panther Party and Huey P. Newton*. Baltimore: Black Classic Press, 1991.

Ullman, Victor. *Martin R. Delany: The Beginnings of Black Nationalism*. Boston: Beacon Press, 1971.

Black Panther Party

The Black Panther Party (BPP) was a radical African American political organization. Originally called the Black Panther Party for Self-Defense, it was established in 1966 in Oakland, California, by Huey P. Newton, minister of self-defense, and Bobby Seale, chair. The BPP perceived itself as a vanguard party that mobilized the unemployed members of the African American working classes and addressed the needs and desires of poor, segregated, urban communities that had not benefited from the legal victories of the civil rights movement. Throughout their 16-year existence, from 1966 to 1982, the party's political perspective and activity were marked by ideological flexibility, adaptability, and hybridization—a fusion of ideas from post–World War II black liberation struggles in the United States and anticolonial struggles abroad.

The group's organizational beginnings can be traced to October 1966, with the creation of the "Black Panther Party Platform and Program," a manifesto outlining the group's ideological and political perspectives and goals with respect to housing issues, educational and economic opportunities, police violence, and African American disenfranchisement. Equipped with pistols, shotguns, and law books, Newton, Seale, and Bobby Hutton, the first member and treasurer of the organization, traversed Oakland to ensure that police officers did not violate residents' rights. Patrols had a threefold effect: they taught the community how to protect themselves from the police, they decreased the incidents of police brutality, and they increased the membership of the BPP. As the membership increased so did police patrols of other African American neighborhoods in the San Francisco Bay Area.

In 1967, the party gained recognition among San Francisco Bay Area communities after it investigated and publicized the fatal police shooting of Denzil Dowell. Eldridge Cleaver, the renowned ex-convict and writer for the leftist magazine *Ramparts*, became the organization's minister of information. His writing ability and connections with leftist activists were instrumental in attracting new members and helping the party create the Black Community News Service and the *Black Panther*, a weekly newspaper. By the end of the decade, the BPP had grown to be a national organization with 40 chapters, more than 5,000 members, and tens of thousands of supporters. By 1969, the BPP comprised individual chapters unified under one central committee.

To connect the work being done in the southern states by the Student Nonviolent Coordinating Committee (SNCC) with BPP work in western and northern urban areas, the two organizations attempted a merger. The merger was short-lived and the appointments were largely symbolic, as the union was destroyed by organizational mistrust. With the merger between the BPP and SNCC undermined, the BPP Central Committee set out to maintain a cohesive national unit. From 1967 to 1970, Newton was imprisoned. Concurrently, Cleaver and Seale were trying to gain popular support to "Free Huey" and were involved in their own court cases. But all chapters were unified around the survival programs, a willingness to re-envision the party platform and revolutionary activity, and government repression.

Survival programs were instituted with the primary objective of transforming social and economic relations within the United States. The party's survival programs supplemented ostensibly radical political activities (mainly armed protection of African American communities, rallying for self-determination, running political candidates, building interracial coalitions, and critiquing the intersection of racism and capitalism) with radical work that ensured the survival of African American communities. From 1967 to 1974, BPP chapters throughout the country instituted survival programs addressing the needs of urban communities.

In August 1967, the BPP was targeted by the Federal Bureau of Investigation's (FBI) Counter-Intelligence Program (COINTELPRO) for neutralization. In September 1969, J. Edgar Hoover, FBI director, declared that the BPP was a major threat to the domestic security of the United States. The FBI's repression of BPP chapters was nationwide in scope. Moreover, of the 295 counterintelligence operations in 1969, 233 were directed toward crippling the BPP.

After his release from prison in 1970, Newton became the sole authority in party matters from 1970 to 1974. Newton publicly censured and dismissed individuals. In 1973, at the behest of Newton, the BPP moved into the political arena with its attempt to get Seale elected mayor of Oakland. To ensure victory, Newton proposed that all state offices close and move to Oakland. With members refusing to submit to his decision, chapters across the country closed in protest and individuals resigned from the party. Some, however, moved to Oakland in 1972 and 1973 to assist in Seale's campaign. When Seale lost the election, many of the transplants resigned. The party's membership fell to 500. In the summer of 1974, after a disagreement with Newton, Seale resigned, followed by other key members of the deteriorating organization.

From 1974 to 1977, with Newton in exile, Elaine Brown assumed the party's leadership, decentralized power, appointed more women to leadership positions, obtained government funding to operate a school—the Oakland Community School—and ran for public office. Upon Newton's return in 1977 with fewer than 200 members, Newton again took the mantle of leadership until the party's demise in 1982. Survival programs were discontinued, funds were mismanaged, and the party's relationship with the community deteriorated. In 1980, the *Black Panther* was discontinued, and in 1982, the school was closed, marking the end of the organization.

Jamie J. Wilson

Further Reading

Brown, Elaine. *A Taste of Power: A Black Woman's Story.* New York: Pantheon Books, 1992.

Churchill, Ward. *Agents of Repression: The FBI's Secret War against the Black Panther Party and the American Indian Movement.* Boston: South End Press, 1988.

Jeffries, Judson. *Huey P. Newton: The Radical Theorist.* Jackson: University Press of Mississippi, 2002.

Jones, Charles E., ed. *The Black Panther Party Reconsidered.* Baltimore: Black Classic Press, 1998.

Newton, Huey P. *War against the Panthers: A Study of Repression in America.* New York: Harlem River Press, 1996.

Seale, Bobby. *Seize the Time: The Story of the Black Panther Party and Huey P. Newton.* New York: Random House, 1970.

Black Power

Black Power refers to a phase or extension of the civil rights movement beginning in the period after 1966 when individual activists and organizations began to articulate the need for black political empowerment and self-defense as a means of achieving a variety of goals.

In most historical accounts, Black Power began as a slogan during the James Meredith March against Fear in June 1966. After Meredith's shooting in Jackson, Mississippi, two activists in the Student Nonviolent Coordinating Committee (SNCC), Stokely Carmichael (Kwame Ture) and Willie Ricks (Mukasa Dada), used the slogan as an alternative to "We Shall Overcome," which had been an unofficial anthem of the civil rights movement. Although this may have been the genesis of the slogan as it became associated with the civil rights movement, it was not the first time that African American leaders or activist articulated a need for black empowerment. On the eve of Ghanaian independence, Richard Wright penned his 1954 book *Black Power* as a reflection on the possibilities of empowerment on the African continent. Both Paul Robeson and Adam Clayton Powell Jr. had articulated the specific need for Black Power, whereas others, including W. E. B. Du Bois, Malcolm X, Ida B. Wells-Barnett, and Robert F. Williams, epitomized its meaning and ultimate potential in earlier decades.

Pressed for a definition of Black Power, Ture, along with political scientist Charles V. Hamilton, published *Black Power: The Politics of Liberation* in 1967 as an answer to the many critics of the concept. In essence, Ture defined black power as mobilizing blacks to use their newfound political voice—as a result of the passage of the Voting Rights Act of 1965—to create semiautonomous communities in which black police officers patrolled black people, black businesses provided jobs, black elected officials and black-controlled political parties articulated the aspirations of blacks, and blacks used armed self-defense to protect their lives. Thus, Black Power can be seen as a "community-control" form of Black

Nationalism. In many ways, this definition of Black Power was shaped largely by Ture's organizing activities in Lowndes County, Alabama, in 1965, where he and other SNCC organizers had helped create the Lowndes County Freedom Organization (LCFO). In a region that was 97 percent black, voter registration, the creation of an all-black political party (the LCFO), and mass mobilization could potentially lead to a complete takeover of the county and, hence, real black empowerment. Using the Black Panther as the symbol of their political party, the LCFO had several candidates vying for political office in the election season of November 1966. Hoping to elect candidates for sheriff, coroner, tax assessor, and in the board of education, all of the LCFO's candidates lost in the general election. Despite this defeat, the idea of community-controlled Black Nationalism and the symbol of the Black Panther spread to black communities across the United States.

The example and potential of Lowndes County spread and was articulated by an ever-widening group of individuals and organizations after 1966. Among the many organizations espousing Black Power that grew between 1967 and 1974 were the Black Panther Party (BPP), the SNCC, the Congress of Racial Equality (CORE), the Republic of New Afrika, the Congress of African Peoples, and the Deacons for Defense and Justice. Although these organizations and their leadership differed vastly in goals and tactics, practically all of them were heirs of Malcolm X. In this sense, armed self-defense, as opposed to the nonviolent tactics of Martin Luther King Jr., were generally embraced. Malcolm X's life, his many speeches, and his 1965 posthumous autobiography became canonical texts for many Black Power advocates. In addition, Robert F. Williams's *Negroes with Guns* (1962) and Frantz Fanon's *Wretched of the Earth* (1961) were quite influential in giving definition and shape to Black Power. Although the Black Power movement was eventually split between cultural nationalist and socialist factions, the goal of achieving some semblance of black empowerment and autonomy were concepts that all Black Power activists continued to embrace.

Walter C. Rucker

Further Reading

Carmichael, Stokely, and Charles V. Hamilton. *Black Power: The Politics of Liberation in America*. New York: Random House, 1967.

Jeffries, J. L. *Black Power in the Belly of the Beast*. Urbana: University of Illinois Press, 2006.

Joseph, Peniel E. *Waiting 'til the Midnight Hour: A Narrative History of Black Power in America*. New York: Henry Holt, 2006.

Ogbar, Jeffrey Ogbonna Green. *Black Power: Radical Politics and African American Identity*. Baltimore: Johns Hopkins University Press, 2004.

Van Deburg, William L. *New Day in Babylon: The Black Power Movement and American Culture, 1965–1975*. Chicago: University of Chicago Press, 1992.

Black Power Salute at the 1968 Olympics

On the morning of October 16, 1968, the Black Power movement found expression at the XIX Olympiad in Mexico City. In the aftermath of the assassination of Martin Luther King Jr. and the rise of the Black Panther Party for Self-Defense, Tommie Smith and John Carlos of the U.S. Olympic track and field team provided a lasting, if controversial, image for the world stage after the 200-meter race. Teammates at California's San Jose State University, both men were initially influenced by calls for African American athletes to boycott the 1968 Summer Olympics as a means of bringing attention and focus to the civil rights movement in the United States and the movement against South African apartheid. Organized by sociologist Harry Edwards, a professor at San Jose State, this initial call for a boycott led to the establishment of an organization called the Olympic Project for Human Rights (OPHR). Although the call for a boycott was not successful, the OPHR did gain the support of several prominent athletes, intellectuals, and civil rights leaders, including Smith and Carlos.

Influenced by OPHR's goals and Edwards's leadership, Smith and Carlos planned a silent protest to occur during the medals ceremony after the 200-meter race. Although the most-discussed aspects of their protest were their black-gloved raised fists and bowed heads during the playing of the national anthem, the men were adorned with symbols of protest. Smith, who won the race in world-record time, wore a black scarf to represent African American pride. Carlos, who placed third, unzipped the top of his track suit to symbolize solidarity with blue-collar workers in the United States and wore beads around his neck in protest of the violence of the Middle Passage, slavery, and Jim Crow–era lynchings and race riots. Both men received their medals shoeless, wearing only black socks, to symbolize African American poverty. In solidarity with Smith and Carlos, Australia's Peter Norman, who placed second in the race, wore an OPHR badge and even suggested that Carlos put on Smith's left-handed black glove and wear it as a symbol of unity among African Americans. During the course of the protest, the crowd booed the two athletes, and this would be only the beginning of the backlash.

Avery Brundage, president of the International Olympic Committee, responded almost immediately to the protest. Brundage, who had served as the U.S. Olympic Committee president in 1936, raised no objections at that time to the Nazi salutes and symbols, including swastikas, adorned by German athletes during the XI Olympiad, but he was openly appalled by the actions of Smith and Carlos. Because the Nazi salute was considered the national salute of Germany at the time of the Berlin Olympics, it was not seen in the same light as the Black Power salutes of Smith and Carlos, which indeed were meant as protests against their sponsoring country.

Noting that the Olympic Games were to be apolitical and generally devoid of overt political statements, Brundage ordered the two athletes suspended from the

U.S. team and prohibited them from entering the Olympic Village. When the U.S. Olympic Committee initially balked, Brundage began maneuvering to ban the entire U.S. track team. With this threat and its implications, Smith and Carlos were formally expelled from the XIX Olympiad. Upon their return home, both men and their families received scores of death threats. Even Australian runner Peter Norman faced a backlash when he returned home after the Olympic Games. Australian Olympic authorities ostracized him and went as far as banning him from participating in the 1972 Summer Olympics despite the fact that he had officially qualified to participate.

The Black Power salutes in 1968 became one of the two most lasting images of the Olympic Games; the other, ironically, was the various depictions of Jesse Owens smashing the conceptualization of the superior Aryan athlete during the 1936 Summer Games. Both Smith and Carlos went on to brief stints in the National Football League and coached track and field teams at various levels. Between 1997 and 2008, both men individually and together received a number of honors in recognition of their courage and commitment to social justice, including the Courage of Conscience Award from the Peace Abbey and the Arthur Ashe Award for Courage, and a statue in their honor has been erected on the campus of San Jose State University.

Walter C. Rucker

Further Reading

Bass, Amy. *In the Game: Race, Identity, and Sports in the Twentieth Century.* New York: Palgrave Macmillan, 2005.

Bass, Amy. *Not the Triumph but the Struggle: The 1968 Olympics and the Making of the Black Athlete.* Minneapolis: University of Minnesota Press, 2002.

Hoffer, Richard. *Something in the Air: American Passion and Defiance in the 1968 Mexico City Olympics.* New York: Free Press, 2009.

Witherspoon, Kevin B. *Before the Eyes of the World: Mexico and the 1968 Olympic Games.* DeKalb: Northern Illinois University Press, 2008.

Zirin, Dave. *What's My Name, Fool? Sports and Resistance in the United States.* Chicago: Haymarket Books, 2005.

Zolov, Eric. "Showcasing the Land of Tomorrow: Mexico and the 1968 Olympics." *The Americas* 61 (2004): 159–88.

Bloody Sunday

Bloody Sunday was a brutal attack by members of the Alabama state and local police (using tear gas, nightsticks, and bullwhips) on 300 predominantly African American civil rights marchers that took place on Sunday, March 7, 1965, in Selma, Alabama.

Bloody Sunday took place within the larger context of the African American freedom struggle that has been ongoing before, during, and since the 1960s.

Although African Americans were guaranteed the right to vote long before the 1960s, through the Fifteenth Amendment to the U.S. Constitution (ratified March 30, 1870), southern states instituted a series of state and local restrictions abridging African American civil rights as bolstered by the Supreme Court decision in *Plessy v. Ferguson* (1896). The *Plessy* decision upheld the doctrine of "separate but equal" as well as the power of state and local agencies to maintain and regulate under the guise of their "police power" segregation policies—also called Jim Crow laws. In keeping with a long-standing "organizing tradition," African Americans created self-help agencies and civil rights organizations such as the National Association for the Advancement of Colored People (NAACP) in 1909, the National Urban League (NUL) in 1911, and the Congress of Racial Equality in 1942 to combat restrictions placed on black citizens' civil rights. Voting rights were of particular concern to African Americans because many southern municipalities had adopted obstacles that prevented African Americans from voting, such as the grandfather clause, the poll tax, and the literacy test.

Jim Crow laws were accompanied by regular acts of violence and brutality against African Americans. An estimated 82 percent of the lynchings that took place in the United States between 1890 and 1900 occurred in the American South, with an average of more than 150 lynchings per year. In the first decade of the twentieth century (1900–1910), southern lynchings increased by more than 10 percent. Although African Americans were not the only group subject to lynching, they were certainly the chief victims in overwhelming numbers. In response to continuous violence, disenfranchisement, and segregation in public facilities, African Americans challenged such measures through "sit-down" campaigns in the 1940s and boycotts and marching in the 1950s. The civil rights movement expanded and became a mass movement through the 1950s and 1960s to include such organizations as the Southern Christian Leadership Conference (SCLC), created in 1957, and the Student Nonviolent Coordinating Committee (SNCC), established by black student activists in 1960. In 1965, representatives from the aforementioned civil rights organizations felt it necessary to cross the Edmund Pettus Bridge in Selma, Alabama, on their march to the state capital, Montgomery, to secure voting rights for African Americans in the state.

Although the collective activism of African Americans secured important gains between 1960 and 1965, such as the Civil Rights Act of 1964—which guaranteed equal access to jobs and public facilities—26 civil rights workers were killed during this time period, and no major voting rights legislation was in place to guarantee black voting rights. Martin Luther King Jr. (1929–1968) declared that the most important civil right was the right to vote and actively incorporated voting rights as a central issue into his civil rights campaigns beginning between 1963 and 1965. From 1960 to 1965, SNCC students organized several voter registration projects (including the Freedom Summer of 1964) in places such as Mississippi and Alabama in an effort to increase the number of African American registered voters across the South. Only 1 percent of the black population eligible to vote in Mississippi was registered to vote before 1965, while 2 percent of the black population eligible to vote in Alabama before 1965 was registered to vote. Thus, African American civil rights activists such as John Lewis of SNCC (later a U.S. Congress member), along with Hosea Williams and eventually Martin Luther King Jr., decided to mount a voter's rights demonstration in Selma, Alabama, in the spring of 1965. These individuals sought to bring attention to the problems of disenfranchisement, segregation, and vigilantism (African American Jimmy Lee Jackson was shot on February 18, 1965, by an Alabama police officer) on the part of whites in Selma by organizing a 54-mile trek on U.S. Highway 80 across the Edmund Pettus Bridge toward Montgomery to demand redress for their grievances.

Bloody Sunday occurred as John Lewis and Hosea Williams led 300 silent marchers across the Edmund Pettus Bridge on March 7, 1965. The marchers were teargassed and charged by 200 state and local police officers—many on horseback—wielding nightsticks and whips. Lewis was beaten and fell bloodied to the ground. Five women marchers were beaten unconscious. Ultimately, several marchers were attacked and bludgeoned senseless. Seventeen marchers were hospitalized, including civil rights organizer Amelia Boynton, who was almost gassed to death. Because this incident was televised and people around the United States were able to see scenes of defenseless marchers attacked by police, it brought national support to the movement. Martin Luther King Jr. called for a continuation of the march on March 9, but decided instead to hold a short ceremonial march to the Edmund Pettus Bridge and then turn around until a court order was secured. A white Unitarian minister, James Reeb from Boston, who came to Alabama to join the second march, was attacked the same day by an angry mob and died on March 11. After Reeb's death, a federal judge ruled in favor of King and SCLC. The number of marchers completing the journey on March 25, 1965, eventually increased to an estimated 25,000.

Bloody Sunday led to the signing of the Voting Rights Act of 1965. This act invalidated any test or device to deny voting, including a poll tax, literacy test, and grandfather clause, and allowed federal examiners to enter states to ensure the registration of African Americans in any state with a history of discrimination. "And we shall overcome," stated President Lyndon B. Johnson in a speech supporting voting rights for African Americans and asking Congress to pass the Voting Rights Act following Bloody Sunday.

Hettie V. Williams

Further Reading

Branch, Taylor. *At Canaan's Edge: America in the King Years, 1965–1968*. New York: Simon & Schuster, 2006.

Fager, Charles. *Selma 1965: The March That Changed the South*. Boston: Beacon Press, 1985.

Garrow, David. *Protest in Selma: Martin Luther King, Jr. and the Voting Rights Act of 1965*. New Haven, CT: Yale University Press, 1979.

Bombingham

In 1963, Martin Luther King Jr. referred to Birmingham, Alabama, as the most segregated city in the United States. To the city's African American residents, it was simply "Bombingham," a place where they had suffered decades of reactionary violence, police brutality, and political emasculation. The city had earned such a sobriquet because of its high frequency of racially motivated bombings—no fewer than 50 between 1947 and 1965—and because its elected officials did little to impede the carnage. Nearly everyone who lived in or visited Birmingham in the years before the civil rights movement noted its oppressive climate and its glaring lack of concern for basic human rights. And it was for these reasons that King and the Southern Christian Leadership Conference (SCLC) targeted the city for their 1963 campaign, thus transforming Bombingham into the main battleground in the postwar struggle for civil rights.

Birmingham was founded in the 1870s, a scion of America's postwar industrial boom. By 1900, thousands of working-class whites and blacks called the city home, daily plying their trade in the iron and steel mills that dotted the bleak urban landscape. Few of the business and industrial leaders who controlled the local economy actually resided in Birmingham. Rather, they managed its affairs from New York or Pennsylvania, or they settled in the "over the mountain" communities of Mountain Brook, Homewood, and Vestavia Hills. Hence, the city's political power structure was controlled by working- and lower-middle-class whites, who composed a majority of the population and who enjoyed all the economic advantages residing with their race. African Americans made up about 40 percent of the population by the late 1950s, yet fewer than 20 percent could cast a vote. A majority of the black populace lived at or below the poverty level, and only a handful worked in trades not classified as unskilled or menial. A strict system of segregation determined the parameters of social interaction between the two races. And if blacks ever endeavored to step beyond the narrow confines of Jim Crow, whites would often react with violence.

After World War II, racial tensions escalated to unprecedented levels in Birmingham. Because of a postwar housing shortage in the city, African American families began moving into residences that either bordered on, or rested in, historically white neighborhoods such as North Smithfield (an area later designated as Dynamite Hill). This not only violated segregated housing ordinances; it drew the ire of working-class whites who wanted to maintain the racial integrity of their communities. As a result, a number of black residences were bombed by night-riding vigilantes in the latter half of the 1940s. The Birmingham Police

Department, headed by Public Safety Commissioner Eugene "Bull" Connor, failed to adequately investigate the attacks, much less arrest those responsible. Consequently, members of the African American community responded to the lack of police protection by posting armed guards in front of their homes and conducting nightly neighborhood patrols. Their actions probably saved dozens of homes from destruction. But the conflict raged on.

After the 1954 *Brown* decision, racial animosities heightened all over the city. This time, vigilantes began targeting civil rights activists, like the Reverend Fred Shuttlesworth, who headed the Alabama Christian Movement for Human Rights. Twice, in 1956 and 1962, terrorists bombed Shuttlesworth's church, Bethel Baptist, coming close to killing the fearless minister. Similar bombings targeted the homes of attorney Arthur Shores, A. G. Gaston, and A. D. King, the brother of Martin Luther King Jr. In September 1957, Shuttlesworth and his wife were attacked by a mob when they attempted to integrate Phillips High School. Shuttlesworth was severely lashed with bicycle chains and brass knuckles in the melee, and his wife received a stab wound to the hip. In May 1961, Klansmen, with Bull Connor's full blessing, savagely assaulted a busload of Freedom Riders in the downtown Trailways station. Photographs of the attack ran in newspapers around the world, shocking the international community and convincing many Birmingham businessmen that the continued maintenance of white supremacy was both impractical and immoral.

In the spring of 1963, King and the SCLC conducted widespread demonstrations in Birmingham, hoping, among other things, to end discriminatory hiring practices in downtown businesses, desegregate public facilities, and integrate the local school system. The campaign was only marginally successful in Birmingham itself, but it eventually influenced Congress and the White House to pass the Civil Rights Act of 1964.

The situation in Birmingham, however, seemed as volatile as ever. On September 15, 1963, days after area schools were desegregated, a bomb was detonated outside the Sixteenth Street Baptist Church, resulting in the deaths of four black children. Withdrawing into their familiar roles, local and state police did little to nab those responsible for the blast. In fact, it was not until the late 1970s that one of the bombers, Robert Chambliss, was brought to justice. More than two decades after Chambliss's conviction, two of his accomplices, Bobby Frank Cherry and Thomas Blanton, were tried and found guilty for their roles in the attack. Finally, and mercifully, Birmingham could begin the process of healing.

Gary S. Sprayberry

Further Reading

Eskew, Glenn T. *But for Birmingham: The Local and National Movements in the Civil Rights Struggle*. Chapel Hill: University of North Carolina Press, 1997.

McWhorter, Diane. *Carry Me Home: Birmingham, Alabama, the Climactic Battle of the Civil Rights Revolution*. New York: Simon & Schuster, 2001.

Nunnelly, William A. *Bull Connor*. Tuscaloosa: University of Alabama Press, 1991.

Thornton, J. Mills. *Dividing Lines: Municipal Politics and the Struggle for Civil Rights in Montgomery, Birmingham, and Selma*. Tuscaloosa: University of Alabama Press, 2002.

Brown, Elaine

Elaine Brown (b. 1943), a former chairperson of the Black Panther Party, redefined leadership roles during the 1970s. In 1974, she became the first woman to hold the party's highest honor. She clarified her intent to maintain a unified organization after the departure of Huey P. Newton for Cuba. Brown was born to Dorothy Clark, a factory worker, in a predominately black, low-income area of North Philadelphia on March 2, 1943. Her father, Horace Scott, was a prominent physician who cheated on his wife to conceive Brown with Clark. Scott refused to accept Brown as his daughter during her youth on York Street in North Philadelphia. As a child, Brown grew up singing in various choirs at the Jones Tabernacle African Methodist Episcopal Church and eventually recorded the Black Panthers' National Theme in 1969 called "The Meeting." Brown also recorded albums in the 1970s titled *Seize the Time* with Vanguard Records and *Until We're Free* with Black Forum Records, and she also appeared on a 2002 Black Panther record called *The Fugitives*.

During Brown's youth, Brown's mother often bought her pretty dresses and made her take ballet classes as a means to separate her from all things considered black. As a student at Philadelphia High School for Girls, Brown recalled when her mother stated that light skin and straight hair were better features than dark skin and tightly curled hair. Brown eventually would internalize bourgeois concepts as a child, particularly during a visit with her Aunt Francine in Los Angeles. Nevertheless, she persevered and briefly attended Temple University as a prelaw student. After leaving in 1965, Brown went to Los Angeles and taught piano at the Jordan Downs housing project. While working at the Pink Pussycat Club in West Hollywood, Brown met Jay Kennedy, her eventual mentor and lover. Kennedy, a screenwriter and wealthy patron who was 30 years her elder, introduced her to critical aspects of the civil rights movement. With the aid of Kennedy and other friends such as Beverlee and Tommy Jacquette, Brown furthered her interest in sociopolitical activism. While in Los Angeles, Brown began a Black Student Union newsletter and organized the Southern California College Black Student Alliance while at the University of California at Los Angeles.

In 1967, Brown became acquainted with the Black Panther Party, and by April of the next year, she joined the Southern California chapter. By 1969, Brown became the deputy minister of information and was elevated to the minister of information in 1971. As a result of heightened scrutiny by COINTELPRO of the FBI, many leaders in the Black Panther Party were jailed or killed by the early 1970s. Also in 1971,

Brown gave birth to her only child Ericka, whom she conceived with former party member Mesai Hewit. Similarly to her father, Horace Scott, Hewit left Brown during her fourth month of pregnancy and later remarried. Before Newton escaped murder charges for Cuba, Brown unsuccessfully campaigned for an Oakland (California) City Council position in 1973 and would try for the same position in 1976. During Brown's tenure as chairperson, she continued the free medical care, expanded the free breakfast program, and created the renowned Oakland Community Learning Center in the city's poorest neighborhood.

Brown also registered nearly 100,000 new voters and endorsed Governor Jerry Brown and Lionel Wilson, who later would become Oakland's first black mayor. Also, Brown provided jobs to thousands of blacks during the Grove-Shafter freeway expansion that revitalized downtown Oakland. In 1976, Brown was chosen as a delegate to the Democratic Party's national convention, and she also was involved in many Oakland-based community and civic organizations. In 1977, Brown was viewed as a pawn and when Newton returned, neither his cocaine habit nor pressures from the majority male party could save Brown's leadership role. In fact, once Brown witnessed the beating of a female counterpart, she fled with her daughter to Los Angeles. Once there, Suzanne de Passe befriended Brown and allowed her to read scripts and write songs for Motown Records.

Through de Passe, Brown met French industrialist Pierre Elby and later moved to France to write her autobiography and first book, *A Taste of Power*, which she began in 1985 and completed in 1994. In 2002, Brown wrote her second book, titled *The Condemnation of Little B*, which examines the high incarceration rate for black men in the prison-industrial complex. At the time of this writing, Brown maintained an active role in prisoner reform, as seen by her work with the Mothers Advocating Juvenile Reform and the National Alliance for Radical Prisoner Reform. Brown also lectured throughout the United States, wrote articles, and intended to coauthor a book on the life of Jamil Al-Amin. Also, *A Taste of Power* was being optioned for film. In November 2005, Brown ran for mayor of Brunswick, Georgia, as a member of the Green Party.

Jamal L. Ratchford

Further Reading

Bray, Rosemary. "A Black Panther's Long Journey: Elaine Brown's Life Is Comfortable Now, but the Passing Years Haven't Quelled the Anger." *New York Times Magazine* 142 (1993): 21–24.

Brown, Elaine. *The Condemnation of Little B: New Age Racism in America*. Boston: Beacon Press, 2002.

Brown, Elaine. *A Taste of Power: A Black Woman's Story*. New York: Anchor Books, 1994.

Perkins, Margo V. *Autobiography as Activism: Three Black Women of the Sixties*. Jackson: University Press of Mississippi, 2000.

Brown, H. Rap

Jamil Abdullah Al-Amin (b. 1943), also known as Hubert Gerold Brown and H. Rap Brown, was a civil rights activist and proponent of Black Power who served as the chair of the Student Nonviolent Coordinating Committee (SNCC) and the justice minister of the Black Panther Party. He is perhaps best known for his statement that "violence is as American as cherry pie." Born on October 4, 1943, in Baton Rouge, Louisiana, Al-Amin attended Southern University from 1960 until 1964 before becoming an active member of the Non-Violent Action Group (NAG) and SNCC. He became known as H. Rap Brown because of his mastery over playing the dozens and signifying. Al-Amin's quick wit and oratorical skills made him a legendary dozens player, and he often set his verbal jabs to rhymes, earning him the nickname "Rap." While Al-Amin was at Southern, his brother Ed encouraged him to read W. E. B. Du Bois, Frederick Douglass, Marcus Garvey, and Richard Wright; in many ways, this was the beginning of his political education. After joining NAG and then later SNCC, Al-Amin became involved in a series of protest activities including sit-ins, voting rights campaigns, and marches.

In 1965, Al-Amin's transformation into an advocate of Black Power began when he, along with several other African American leaders, were called to the White House to meet with President Lyndon Baines Johnson. As Al-Amin would later reflect in his book *Die Nigger Die!* Johnson's impatient arrogance coupled with the passivity of the group of African American leaders meeting with him led Al-Amin to personally engage President Johnson in his typically brash manner. It was after this exchange that Al-Amin would claim that he became a marked man. In rapid succession after this meeting, he would be called up for the draft, he was involved in a shootout with police in Cambridge, Maryland, and he was arrested twice in Virginia. Al-Amin was certainly one of many targets in the FBI's COINTELPRO campaign, particularly after he ascended to the chair of the SNCC in 1967. Shortly thereafter, he joined the Black Panther Party to serve as their justice minister in 1968. The potential coalition of two of the most prominent Black Power organizations—SNCC and the Black Panthers—was actively disrupted by the FBI, and both Al-Amin and his close friend and associate, Stokely Carmichael (Kwame Ture), found themselves in a precarious situation.

In 1970, Al-Amin went underground for 18 months during the course of a trial in Maryland on the charges of inciting riot and carrying a gun across state lines. As a direct result, he appeared on the FBI's Ten Most Wanted List. By 1972, Al-Amin resurfaced and was arrested for attempted robbery of a bar in New York City. Released from prison in 1976, Al-Amin moved to Atlanta, Georgia, to open a grocery store. Having converted to Islam in prison, he became leader of the National Ummah and worked to eradicate drugs, gambling, and prostitution in Atlanta's West End. On March 16, 2000, when two sheriff's deputies attempted to serve an arrest warrant, both men were shot and one died the next day from his wounds. The surviving deputy identified Al-Amin as the shooter and, on March 9, 2002, he was convicted of 13 criminal charges including murder. At the time of this writing, Al-Amin was serving a life sentence at the ADX Super Maximum Security Prison in Florence, Colorado.

Walter C. Rucker

Further Reading

Al-Amin, Jamil. *Die, Nigger, Die!* New York: Dial Press, 1969.

Al-Amin, Jamil. *Revolution by the Book: The Rap Is Live.* Beltsville, MD: Writers' Inc.-International, 1993.

Heineman, Kenneth J. *Put Your Bodies upon the Wheels: Student Revolt in the 1960s.* Chicago: I. R. Dee, 2001.

Thelwell, E. M. "H. Rap Brown/Jamil Al-Amin: A Profoundly American Story." *Nation* 274 (2002): 25–35.

Brown v. Board of Education

Brown v. Board of Education (1954) is the landmark Supreme Court decision that declared segregated educational institutions illegal. Even before the Supreme Court upheld the separate-but-equal doctrine decree in *Plessy v. Ferguson* (1896), individual parents challenged separate educational facilities via the courts, mostly because separate schools were rarely equal. Pursuant to their goal of eliminating segregation in all public facilities, the National Association for the Advancement of Colored People (NAACP) began the process of challenging segregation by laying the groundwork for *Brown*. To do so, the NAACP tried cases dealing with desegregation in graduate and professional schools. Two of the most significant cases include *Sweatt v. Painter* (1950), which found that segregated law schools deprived black students of certain intangible qualities, and *McLaurin v. Oklahoma State Regents* (1950), which mandated that black graduate students be treated the same as white graduate students.

The Kansas segregation statute permitted cities with a population greater than 15,000 to maintain separate elementary schools despite the fact that high schools, except in Kansas City, were desegregated. The Topeka Board of Education decided to operate segregated elementary schools, which provided the NAACP with an opportunity to take legal action. The District Court ruled that while segregated schools did have a detrimental effect on African American children, the schools were substantially equal and therefore compliant with *Plessy*.

The NAACP lawyers, including Thurgood Marshall, Robert L. Carter, and Jack Greenberg, originally argued the case before the Supreme Court in 1952, but a decision was not reached because there were similar cases pending. As a result, the *Brown* case is actually an amalgam of four class-action school segregation cases in Kansas, South Carolina (*Briggs v. Elliott*), Virginia (*Davis v. County School Board of Prince Edward County*), and Delaware (*Gebhart v. Belton*), representing approximately 200 plaintiffs. The NAACP legal team argued that segregated schools violated the equal protection clause of the Fourteenth Amendment. Using evidence supplied by Kenneth Clark and Mamie Phipps's doll experiments, the legal team also argued that segregated schools deprived black students of the opportunity to learn to adjust personally and socially in an integrated setting, lowered black children's level of aspiration, instilled feelings of insecurity and inferiority in them, and hampered their mental and educational development.

The unanimous *Brown* decision, written by Chief Justice Earl Warren, declared that to separate children from others of similar age and qualifications solely because of their race generates a feeling of inferiority as to their status in the community that may affect their hearts and minds in a way unlikely ever to be undone. Most important, the court found that maintaining separate educational facilities violated the equal protection clause of the Fourteenth Amendment and therefore declared that in the field of public education, the doctrine of "separate but equal" has no place. Separate educational facilities are inherently unequal.

Although the 1954 *Brown* decision overturned *Plessy v. Ferguson*, it did not provide guidance as to how the schools should desegregate. The court decided that because the situations were so diverse, the remedies were best decided at the local level. *Brown II* (1955) mandated that the district courts should oversee the desegregation process "with all deliberate speed." Without a specific timeline in place, desegregating public schools was a slow-moving process. Only two southern states, Texas and Arkansas, began desegregation in 1954. Some other school districts circumvented the ruling by closing all the public schools. The process was so sluggish that it was 1957 when children attempted to desegregate schools in Little Rock, Arkansas, only to be met by angry mobs and National Guard troops. In other areas of the country, it was more than a decade before schools and school districts began the arduous process of desegregation. The most immediate success of the *Brown* ruling was that it set the stage for civil rights groups to challenge segregation in other public arenas, including public transportation.

Lisa Doris Alexander

Further Reading

Bell, Derrick. *Silent Covenants:* Brown v. Board of Education *and the Unfulfilled Hopes for Racial Reform.* Oxford: Oxford University Press, 2004.

Ogletree, Charles J., Jr. *All Deliberate Speed: Reflections on the First-Half Century of* Brown v. Board of Education. New York: W. W. Norton, 2004.

Patterson, James T. Brown v. Board of Education: *A Civil Rights Milestone and Its Troubled Legacy.* Oxford: Oxford University Press, 2001.

Robinson, Mildred Wigfall, and Richard J. Bonnie, eds. *Law Touched Our Hearts: A Generation Remembers* Brown v. Board of Education. Nashville, TN: Vanderbilt University Press, 2009.

Whitman, Mark. *Removing a Badge of Slavery: The Record of* Brown v. Board of Education. Princeton, NJ: Markus Wiener, 1993.

Bunche, Ralph

Ralph Johnson Bunche (1904–1971) was born in Detroit, Michigan, the son of a barber. He moved from Detroit to Toledo, Ohio, with his parents as his father searched for work. He attended elementary school in Ohio. In 1917, when his mother died, Bunche, then 13 years old, and his sister became orphans. His maternal grandmother, Lucy Taylor Johnson, took charge of the children, who went to live with her in Los Angeles, California.

After graduating in 1922 from a Los Angeles high school, where he excelled in academics and sports, Bunche attended the University of California at Los Angeles (UCLA). He continued to be an outstanding student. He was both a Phi Beta Kappa and summa cum laude graduate at UCLA. In 1927, he received an undergraduate degree in political science. Based on his academic prowess, he was awarded a fellowship to attend Harvard University to study political science in the Department of Government.

Ralph Bunche, United Nations official and first African American to win the Nobel Peace Prize in 1950, led peacekeeping efforts throughout his career. (Carl Van Vechten Collection/Library of Congress)

In 1928, Bunche graduated from Harvard University with a master's degree in political science. He then took a position as an instructor at Howard University in Washington, D.C., where he founded and became chair of its political science department. At Howard, Bunche played a major role as both an academic and a quasi-university administrator when he served as assistant to the university president. Bunche's work at Howard was rewarding, but he wanted to pursue his terminal degree. He enrolled in a PhD program in political science at Harvard and began working on his doctoral studies during summers from 1929 through 1934. While at Harvard, Bunche met Ruth Harris, whom he married in 1930. One year later, Ruth gave birth to Joan, the first of his three children. The Bunche family would include two additional children, Jane and Ralph Jr. In 1934, five years after he began his formal doctoral studies, Bunche fulfilled all the requirements for his PhD degree in the Department of Government, when the faculty accepted his dissertation "French Administration in Togoland and Dahomey." He had the unique distinction of receiving the William Toppan Prize, an annual award bestowed on doctoral students who submitted the best dissertation in political science. Bunche was also the first African American to receive a PhD from Harvard, or from any institution of higher education in political science. With his newly minted PhD, Bunche was identified as a rising star in the academic community. He was considered someone who could make a major contribution to the field. But Bunche opted to publish a few short articles from his research instead of turning his dissertation into a major book.

Bunche held some interesting views about poverty and political powerlessness. At the outset of his career, he believed that capitalism was the root of poor political and economic conditions for blacks. He advocated the position that blacks and whites should work together for "economic and political justice," which would ultimately result in the creation of a new, more equal society. In 1939, Bunche had the unique opportunity to work part time with Gunnar Myrdal, the noted Swedish economist and sociologist, on the issue of race in the United States. This field of research culminated in the 1944 landmark publication *The American Dilemma: The Negro Problem and Modern Democracy.*

Bunche left academic life to embark on a new career. In 1941, President Franklin Delano Roosevelt created the Office of Coordination of Information, later renamed the Office of Strategic Service or OSS. Needing a specialist on Africa, Roosevelt reached out to his alma mater Harvard University for a recommendation; Bunche was recommended, and Roosevelt accepted him.

Over the next three decades, Bunche would play a significant role in shaping government and international affairs. In 1942, Bunche moved from OSS to the U.S. State Department. In addition, he participated in preparing those chapters of the United Nations Charter that dealt with colonial territories. In 1946, Bunche became the director of the UN Trustee Division, to help monitor the progress of autonomy in the UN Trust Territories, and thus began his illustrious career at the UN.

In 1948, UN secretary general Trygve Lie appointed Bunche his representative in Palestine, but Bunche soon became acting mediator for the crisis. His diplomatic skills were instrumental in hammering out an armistice agreement on Palestine between Israel and several Arab countries. For his efforts in defusing the conflict and in brokering a deal in the Middle East, on December 10, 1950, Bunche became the first African American to receive the Nobel Peace Prize.

In the 1950s, the economic plight of African Americans was still very much on his mind. At this time, Bunche changed his political philosophy about capitalism, as he no longer blamed capitalism for economic disparity. He now believed that economic inequities were based on racism. In 1953, UN secretary general Dag Hammarskjold appointed Bunche the undersecretary general for special political affairs. For more than a decade, Bunche participated in peacekeeping missions in the Middle East and Africa.

In the 1960s, Bunche believed strongly in civil rights and sought integration and equality for African Americans. He supported Dr. Martin Luther King Jr. and participated in the 1963 March on Washington and the 1965 march from Selma to Montgomery, Alabama. In 1963, President Lyndon B. Johnson presented Bunche with the Medal of Freedom. The urban unrest of the 1960s, starting with the 1965 Watts riots in particular, solidified his views on the need for integration; as a result, black radicals of the time called him an "Uncle Tom." Bunche was also vehemently against the Vietnam War. He saw irony in the fact that African American soldiers were fighting for the rights of the South Vietnamese, yet they had limited rights in their own country.

In the later part of the 1960s, Bunche suffered a number of personal tragedies. In October 1966, one of his two daughters committed suicide. In addition to this devastating event, his personal health began to fail. He was diagnosed with diabetes, which had an impact on his eyesight. In early 1967, Bunche wanted to resign from his UN position, but Secretary General U Thant refused to accept his resignation. His career and his family obligations were at odds; his wife accused him of deserting his family for his career. He resigned from the UN on October 1, 1971, because of ill health.

Slightly two months later, on December 9, 1971, Bunche died in New York Hospital from complications connected with diabetes. As a lasting tribute to Bunche, in 1980, a park facing the UN building in New York City was named "The Ralph Bunche Park for Peace" in his honor.

Joseph C. Santora

Further Reading

Henry, Charles P. *Ralph Bunche: Model Negro or American Other?* New York: New York University Press, 1999.

Holloway, Jonathan Scott. *Confronting the Veil: Abram Harris, Jr., E. Franklin Frazier, and Ralph Bunche, 1919–1941.* Chapel Hill: University of North Carolina Press, 2002.

Keppel, Ben. *The Work of Democracy: Ralph Bunche, Kenneth B. Clark, Lorraine Hansberry, and the Cultural Politics of Race.* Cambridge, MA: Harvard University Press, 1995.

Lindsay, Beverly. *Ralph Johnson Bunche: Public Intellectual and Nobel Peace Laureate.* Urbana: University of Illinois Press, 2007.

Rivlin, Benjamin, ed. *Ralph Bunche: The Man and His Times.* New York: Holmes & Meier, 1990.

Urquhart, Brian. *Ralph Bunche: An American Life.* New York: W. W. Norton, 1993.

Busing

Busing, the act of moving students outside of their school district to end de facto segregation of public schools, became a controversial integration strategy ordered by the Supreme Court during the 1960s and 1970s. In 1954, the court determined in *Brown v. Board of Education* that de jure segregation violated the Fourteenth Amendment. Despite the court's ruling to end segregation, whites resisted desegregation in the North and in the South.

In 1968, the Supreme Court, unsatisfied with the slow pace of desegregation, ruled in *Green v. County School Board of New Kent County* that open enrollment desegregation programs did not comply with the *Brown* decision. School districts were required to take affirmative steps to achieve racial balance. Three years later, in *Swann v. Charlotte-Mecklenburg,* the court ordered busing as a valid means to reach racial integration.

The public responded in protest. In June 1974, U.S. district judge W. Arthur Garrity ordered the Boston public school system to begin busing several thousand students between predominantly white South Boston, Hyde Park, and Dorchester and mostly black Roxbury. White opponents of busing demonstrated to prevent black children from entering white schools and withheld their own children from being bused into black schools. For weeks, violence and hostilities ensued.

Integration efforts were damaged further when white parents moved their families to the suburbs, leaving behind overwhelmingly black urban enclaves. A month after Garrity's decision, the court assessed the consequences of "white flight" on urban schools and overturned a Detroit busing plan in *Milliken v. Bradley.* In the 1990s, the Supreme Court redefined school desegregation, prohibiting racial discrimination, but relieved school districts of integration requirements.

John Matthew Smith

Further Reading
Dimond, Paul R. *Beyond Busing: Inside the Challenge to Urban Segregation.* Ann Arbor: University of Michigan Press, 1985.

Graglia, Lino A. *Disaster by Decree: The Supreme Court Decisions on Race and the Schools.* Ithaca, NY: Cornell University Press, 1976.

Schwartz, Bernard. *Swann's Way: The School Busing Case and the Supreme Court.* New York: Oxford University Press, 1986.

Wolters, Raymond. "From *Brown* to *Green* and Back: The Changing Meaning of Desegregation." *Journal of Southern History* 30 (May 2004): 317–26.

C

Carmichael, Stokely

Stokely Carmichael was a charismatic and controversial leader of the civil rights movement in the 1960s and 1970s. He is best known as an activist and chair of the Student Nonviolent Coordinating Committee and a leader in the Black Power movement, which marked a turning away from the nonviolent tactics of leaders like Martin Luther King Jr. in favor of a more militant brand of activism.

Carmichael was born in Port of Spain, Trinidad, on July 29, 1941, to Mabel and Adolphus Carmichael. Carmichael's parents moved to New York City when he was three years old, and in 1952, he and his three sisters joined them there. The family first settled in Harlem before relocating to the Bronx, where Adolphus worked as a cab driver and carpenter and Mabel worked as a maid. Carmichael attended the Bronx High School of Science, one of the most prestigious schools in New York City, where he was one of only two African American students, and graduated in 1960.

Before graduating from high school, Carmichael experimented with political activism by participating in a sit-in sponsored by the New York chapter of the Congress of Racial Equality (CORE). He was beaten up during the sit-in, which only fueled his desire to further participate in the civil rights movement. Through CORE, he participated in boycotts of Woolworth stores in New York, which the organization targeted because of the company's policy of segregating their southern locations. Although Carmichael received scholarship offers from a number of universities, including Harvard University, he chose to attend Howard University, an all-black institution in Washington, D.C. Because he did not receive a scholarship, Carmichael's parents had to pay his tuition.

While at Howard University, he continued to work closely with CORE, as well as the Nonviolent Action Group (NAG), a local organization that planned demonstrations and sit-ins in the Washington, D.C., area. In 1961, Carmichael expanded his involvement in the civil rights movement by joining the Freedom Riders, a group of protesters who traveled to southern cities via bus (with whites riding in the back and African Americans in front), challenging segregation and attempting to integrate public places that upheld the practice. He and his fellow riders were arrested for these actions in Mississippi and spent 53 days in Parchman Penitentiary, a notoriously brutal state prison. During this period of incarceration, the prison guards subjected the prisoners to terrible food, dirty mattresses, and constant harassment.

Stokely Carmichael, leader of the Student Nonviolent Coordinating Committee (SNCC), brought the concept of black power into the U.S. civil rights movement. Later, in 1967, Carmichael broke with SNCC and joined the Black Panther Party. (Library of Congress)

The prisoners sang protest songs as a way of keeping up morale, but their songs only brought more harsh punishment from the guards.

Carmichael was released from prison in time for his second year at Howard University, where he changed his major from premed to philosophy. He continued his education while also constantly participating in civil rights demonstrations. Carmichael finally finished his degree in the spring of 1964, and, although he received a scholarship offer from Harvard University for graduate school, he passed in favor of joining the Mississippi Freedom Summer Project (MFSP), which aimed to increase black voter registration, organize a legal Democratic Party that included African Americans, establish schools for teaching basic literacy skills to African American children, and open community centers where poor families could receive legal and medical assistance.

Carmichael left the MFSP at the end of the summer in search of a new project that would allow him to work solely with other African Americans. He did not like that the MFSP encouraged alliances with whites and felt there needed to be an all-black political party in order to achieve real political power. Carmichael also believed that leaders like King, who advocated peaceful resistance, were too focused on integration and were getting in the way of establishing strong and independent African American communities. Carmichael preferred more militant leaders such as Malcolm X, who encouraged African Americans to defend themselves, through violence if necessary, and to learn about and embrace their African heritage.

In 1965, Carmichael went to Lowndes County, Alabama, in the hopes creating a strong, all-black resistance movement there. The number of blacks in Lowndes

County outnumbered the whites, yet whites held all the positions of power, and the intense racial oppression there left African American citizens living in fear. Carmichael felt that this town provided the ideal setting for incubating a black rights movement. Dressed in overalls so that he fit in with his surroundings, the charismatic Carmichael convinced black citizens in the county that they should vote, despite violent resistance from local whites, and managed to register nearly 300 African American voters. Once registered, however, these African American voters did not know who to vote for. There were no African American members of either the Republican or the Democratic Party in Lowndes County, and black voters did not trust any white politicians to protect their interests. Carmichael decided to create a new party, the Lowndes County Freedom Organization, which soon became known as the Black Panthers because of its mascot. Several members of the Black Panthers ran for office in the next election, and although none of them won, the African American community in Lowndes felt they had more power and were better organized to protect their rights in the future.

After his success in organizing Lowndes County, Carmichael ran for and won the chair of SNCC in 1966. His election marked the beginning of a new, more militant chapter of the organization's history. Like Carmichael, many members of the SNCC felt that nonviolent protest had not achieved any results and that stronger action was necessary. Shortly after his election, Carmichael found a national platform for his ideas. In June 1966, James Meredith was shot during his solitary "March against Fear." While Meredith recuperated from his wounds, Carmichael joined King, National Association for the Advancement of Colored People (NAACP) president Roy Wilkins, and other civil rights activists to finish the march. At the end of the march, Carmichael gave a rousing speech in which he invited African Americans to embrace "Black Power," meaning that they should be prideful of their race while also striving to achieve socioeconomic independence from the white community. The term became a rallying cry for young African Americans across the country, with the most public example being the 1968 Olympics, when two African American track-and-field medalists raised their fists in the Black Power salute while standing on the award podium. SNCC, which valued a group ethic over individual merit, became displeased with Carmichael's growing celebrity, and, in response, he stepped down from his position of leadership in 1967. He traveled the country, becoming more closely identified with the Black Panther Party and writing a book entitled *Black Power* (1967).

In 1968, Carmichael married South African singer Miriam Makeba, and the following year, the two moved to Guinea, where he became an aide to Prime Minister Ahmed Sekou Toure and a student of exiled Ghanaian president Kwame Nkrumah. Shortly after his arrival in Guinea, Carmichael published a formal rejection of the Black Panther Party, citing their increasing willingness to form alliances with whites. In 1970, he returned to the United States in order to appear before the Subcommittee to Investigate the Administration of the Internal Security Act and

Other Internal Security Laws. The subcommittee asked him to provide information on organizations and people that might be trying to overthrow the U.S government, including the Black Panthers and SNCC. They also asked Carmichael to provide details of his activities while outside the United States. He pleaded the Fifth Amendment throughout the hearing.

In 1971, Carmichael published another book entitled *Stokely Speaks: Black Power Back to Pan-Africanism*, which contained many of his speeches during his years with the SNCC and the Black Panther Party. In 1978, he divorced his wife and changed his name to Kwame Ture in honor of his two new patrons, although many people continued to refer to him by his birth name. He then married Marlyatou Barry, a doctor whom he divorced several years later. He became a member of the All African People's Revolutionary Party (AAPRP), a group that advocated Pan-Africanism, or the uniting of all African peoples inside and outside of Africa to form a single political entity. Ture traveled the world organizing new chapters of AAPRP for nearly a decade.

After the death of Ahmed Sekou Toure in 1984, the military regime that took his place arrested Ture several times on suspicion of trying to overthrow the government, although the reasons behind these allegations remain a mystery. He was jailed for several days for these charges, marking his final encounter with the law. By the mid-1980s, Ture grew disillusioned with the civil rights movement. Although there were 255 African American mayors in the United States by 1984, he felt that African Americans had never truly organized effectively enough to gain real political power. Even so, he continued to visit the United States several times a year in efforts to promote Pan-Africanism. After receiving treatments for prostate cancer over a period of two years, Kwame Ture died on November 15, 1998, in Conakry, Guinea, at the age of 57.

Sara K. Eskridge

Further Reading

Carmichael, Stokely. *Stokely Speaks: Black Power Back to Pan-Africanism*. New York: Random House, 1971.

Carmichael, Stokely, and Charles V. Hamilton. *Black Power: The Politics of Liberation in America*. New York: Random House, 1967.

Carmichael, Stokely, and Ekwueme Michael Thelwell. *Ready for Revolution: The Life and Struggles of Stokely Carmichael (Kwame Ture)*. New York: Scribner, 2003.

Dittmer, John. *Local People: The Struggle for Civil Rights in Mississippi*. Urbana: University of Illinois Press, 1994.

Johnson, Jacqueline. *Stokely Carmichael: The Story of Black Power*. Englewood Cliffs, NJ: Silver Burdett Press, 1990.

Wayne, Bennett, ed. *Black Crusaders for Freedom*. New York: Garrard, 1974.

Chicago Campaign

On January 7, 1966, Martin Luther King Jr. and the Southern Christian Leadership Conference (SCLC) announced plans for the Chicago Freedom Movement, a campaign that marked the expansion of their civil rights activities from the South to northern cities. King believed that "the moral force of SCLC's nonviolent movement philosophy was needed to help eradicate a vicious system which seeks to further colonize thousands of Negroes within a slum environment." King and his family moved to one such Chicago slum at the end of January so that he could be closer to the movement.

Groundwork for the Chicago Campaign began in the summer of 1965. In July, Chicago civil rights groups invited King to lead a demonstration against de facto segregation in education, housing, and employment. The Coordinating Council of Community Organizations (CCCO), convened by Chicago activist Albert Raby, subsequently asked SCLC to join them in a major nonviolent campaign geared specifically at achieving fair housing practices. King believed that turning SCLC's attention to the North made sense: "In the South, we always had segregationists to help make issues clear. . . . This ghetto Negro has been invisible so long and has become visible through violence." Indeed, after riots in Watts, Los Angeles, in August 1965, it seemed crucial to demonstrate how nonviolent methods could address the complex economic exploitation of African Americans in the North.

CCCO had already organized mass nonviolent protests in the city and was eager to engage in further action. In addition to tapping into this ready-made movement, Chicago politics made the city a good choice for a northern campaign. Mayor Richard Daley had a high degree of personal power and was in a position to directly mandate changes to a variety of racist practices. In addition to targeting racial discrimination in housing, SCLC launched Operation Breadbasket, a project under the leadership of Jesse Jackson, aimed at abolishing racist hiring practices by companies working in African American neighborhoods.

The campaigns had gained momentum through demonstrations and marches, when race riots erupted on Chicago's West Side in July 1966. During a march through an all-white neighborhood on August 5, black demonstrators were met with racially fueled hostility. Bottles and bricks were thrown at them, and King was struck by a rock. Afterward, he noted: "I have seen many demonstrations in the south but I have never seen anything so hostile and so hateful as I've seen here today."

Throughout the summer, King faced the organizational challenges of mobilizing Chicago's diverse African American community, cautioning against further violence, and working to counter the mounting resistance of working-class whites who feared the impact of open housing on their neighborhoods. King observed, "Many whites who oppose open housing would deny that they are racists. They turn to sociological arguments ... [without realizing] that criminal responses are environmental, not racial."

By late August, Mayor Daley was eager to find a way to end the demonstrations. After negotiating with King and various housing boards, a summit agreement was announced in which the Chicago Housing Authority promised to build public housing with limited height requirements, and the Mortgage Bankers Association agreed to make mortgages available regardless of race. Although King called the agreement "the most significant program ever conceived to make open housing a reality," he recognized that it was only "the first step in a 1,000-mile journey."

Following the summit agreement, some SCLC staff stayed behind to assist in housing programs and voter registration. King himself stayed in Chicago until taking time off in January 1967 to write *Where Do We Go from Here: Chaos or Community?* Jackson also continued his Chicago branch of Operation Breadbasket with some success, though city officials failed to take concrete steps to address issues of housing despite the summit agreement. King, in a March 24, 1967, press conference, said, "It appears that for all intents and purposes, the public agencies have [reneged] on the agreement and have, in fact given credence to [those] who proclaim the housing agreement a sham and a batch of false promises."

Clayborne Carson

Further Reading

"Dr. King Is Felled by Rock." *Chicago Tribune*, August 6, 1966.

Halvorsen, David. "Cancel Rights Marches." *Chicago Tribune*, August 27, 1966.

Hampton, Henry, and Steve Fayer, eds. *Voices of Freedom: An Oral History of the Civil Rights Movement from the 1950s through the 1980s.* New York: Bantam Books, 1990.

King, Martin Luther, Jr. "Press Conference at Liberty Baptist Church." March 24, 1967. Martin Luther King, Jr. Papers, 1950–1968, Martin Luther King, Jr. Center for Nonviolent Social Change, Atlanta, Georgia.

King, Martin Luther, Jr. *Where Do We Go from Here: Chaos or Community?* Boston: Beacon Press, 1967.

Chisholm, Shirley

Best known as the first African American woman to run for president of the United States, Shirley Chisholm (1924–2005) was also the first African American woman to be elected to the U.S. Congress. She served seven terms as a representative from New York's 12th District, from 1969 until her retirement in 1982.

Originally named Shirley Anita St. Hill, she was born on November 30, 1924, in Brooklyn, New York, in the notoriously impoverished neighborhood of Bedford-Stuyvesant. Her parents were both immigrants to the United States; her father, Charles Christopher St. Hill, was born in British Guiana and arrived in New York in 1923 in New York City; her mother, Ruby Seale, was born in Barbados and arrived in New York City in 1921. Although young Shirley lived her early life in Brooklyn, she was sent, at age three, to live with her maternal grandmother in Barbados. Her parents, who were struggling to save money for their children's education, sent Shirley and her three sisters to live in Barbados for nearly eight years. At the age of 11, however, she returned to New York City and was enrolled in an all-girls high school in Brooklyn.

After graduating from high school, she won tuition scholarships to Oberlin, Vassar, and Brooklyn College; she ultimately decided to remain at home and attend Brooklyn College, where she pursued a degree in sociology. Young Shirley had been exposed to politics throughout her life, especially since her father was a reputed follower of activist Marcus Garvey, who advocated black pride and unity among blacks to achieve economic and political power. As a result, during her years in college, she became active in many black organizations including the Harriet Tubman Society, the Urban League, the National Association for the Advancement of Colored People (NAACP), and Delta Sigma Theta Sorority, Inc. As her participation in the black community expanded, she began to attend city meetings, which eventually prompted her to raise questions about the conditions plaguing her predominantly black neighborhood. Even so, Shirley did not immediately consider becoming a politician.

Shirley Chisholm was an important civil rights leader and the first African American woman to run for Congress in the United States, representing the 12th New York District from 1969 to 1983. Chisholm became the first African American to run for president, running for the Democratic Party nomination in 1972. (Library of Congress)

Instead, in 1946, she graduated cum laude from Brooklyn College and began working as a teacher. For the next few years, she worked in a nursery school and pursued a graduate degree in elementary education at Columbia University. In 1949, she married Conrad Chisholm, and two years later, she earned her master's degree. Upon graduating from Columbia, Chisholm continued to work in the educational sector; she served as the director of the Friends Day Nursery in Brownsville, New York, and, from 1953 to 1959, as the director of the Hamilton-Madison Child Care Center in Lower Manhattan. For the next several years, from 1959 to 1964, she worked as an educational consultant in New York City's Bureau of Child Welfare.

Yet despite her important work in the field of education, Shirley Chisholm never lost her interest in community and political matters. She served on the board of directors of the Brooklyn Home for Aged Colored People and became a prominent member of the Brooklyn branch of the NAACP. She likewise volunteered for various political organizations, including the Democratic Women's Workshop, the League of Women Voters, and the Bedford-Stuyvesant Political League, an organization formed to support black candidates.

By 1964, Chisholm had earned a name in Brooklyn's political scene, which inspired her to consider a run for the New York State Assembly. To the surprise of many in the Democratic political machine, Chisholm won the election and served as an assemblywoman from 1964 to 1968. During her time in office, Chisholm sponsored 50 bills, most of which reflected her interest in the cause of blacks and the poor, women's rights, and educational opportunities. Although most of the bills failed to gain sufficient support, at least eight of them became law and made significant changes in her community. One of the successful bills provided an opportunity for poor students, particularly students of color, to gain financial support to pursue higher education. Another provided employment insurance coverage for personal and domestic employees. Still another reversed a law that caused female teachers in New York to lose their tenure while they were out on maternity leave.

In 1968, Chisholm made the bold decision to campaign for a seat in Congress. Ironically, she ran against seasoned civil rights leader James Farmer, but she easily won the election and became the first African American woman to earn a seat in the U.S. Congress. Ultimately, she spent 13 years in the halls of Congress; she was a member of the U.S. House of Representatives from the 91st through the 97th Congress (1969–1982). As she had in the New York State Assembly, Chisholm fought persistently to represent the needs of her community. Perhaps the most famous demonstration of her commitment came when she was assigned to the Forestry Committee, an appointment she strongly opposed on the grounds that she would rather serve on a committee that would allow her to grapple with issues of racism, social justice, and poverty. During her years in Congress, Chisholm served on several House committees, including Agriculture, Veterans'

Affairs, Rules and Education, and Labor. More specifically, she supported bills that sought to address tangible issues such as housing, education, discrimination, and abortion. She became a particularly outspoken advocate of women's rights, and, in 1971, she joined other feminists such as Gloria Steinem to establish the National Women's Political Caucus.

Perhaps Chisholm's most bold political decision came on January 25, 1972, when she announced her candidacy and became the first African American woman to run for president of the United States. Her platform encompassed a wide variety of issues including civil rights, prison reform, economic justice, gun control, and opposition to police brutality and drug abuse. Even so, the primary issue that drove her campaign was her vehement opposition to the Vietnam War and President Richard M. Nixon's policies nationally and abroad. As a result, Chisholm gained only limited support. Many black leaders were hesitant to endorse her, and although she received significant encouragement from women and young people, Chisholm struggled from insufficient funding. In the end, George McGovern won the presidential nomination at the Democratic National Convention, but Chisholm managed to capture 10 percent of the delegates' votes, particularly after Hubert H. Humphrey released his black delegates to vote for her.

Although Chisholm lost her bid for the presidency, she was reelected to her position in the House of Representatives in 1972 and faithfully served in that role for the next 10 years. In the early 1980s, however, the political climate in the United States changed dramatically. With the election of Ronald Reagan in 1980, liberals and the Democratic Party steadily lost their foothold in Congress. Thus, when Chisholm announced her retirement in February 10, 1982, she openly expressed her frustration with the rise of the Reagan era and President Reagan's domestic and international policies and lamented the decline of progressive politicians. Chisholm's decision to retire, however, was also motivated by personal considerations. After divorcing her first husband in 1977, she married Arthur Hardwick, a businessman from Buffalo, New York. After Hardwick was seriously injured in a car accident, Chisholm wanted to spend more time assisting with his recovery; Hardwick died several years later in 1986.

Even after her retirement from Congress, Chisholm remained publicly active. She joined the faculty at Mount Holyoke College, the oldest women's college in the United States, where she taught courses in political science and women's studies until 1987. She also spent a year as a visiting scholar at Spelman College in 1985 and, in that same year, she became the first president of the newly formed National Political Congress of Black Women. She also campaigned for Jesse Jackson when he sought the Democratic Party's presidential nomination in 1984 and 1988.

Even after Chisholm moved to Florida in 1991, she remained outspoken on political matters, particularly her strong opposition to the Persian Gulf War.

In 1993, President Bill Clinton nominated Chisholm as ambassador to Jamaica, but because of declining health, she withdrew her name from further consideration. After suffering many strokes, Chisholm died on January 1, 2005, at the age of 80.

Leslie M. Alexander

Further Reading

Chisholm, Shirley. *The Good Fight*. New York: HarperCollins, 1973.

Chisholm, Shirley. *Unbought and Unbossed*. New York: Houghton Mifflin, 1970.

Gill, Laverne McCain. *African American Women in Congress: Forming and Transforming History*. Piscataway, NJ: Rutgers University Press, 1997.

Scheader, Catherine. *Shirley Chisholm: Teacher and Congresswoman*. Berkeley Heights, NJ: Enslow Press, 1990.

Civil Rights Act of 1960

The Civil Rights Act of 1960 advanced the struggle for African American freedom by responding, albeit in limited form, to the "massive resistance" of southern segregationists. The legislation criminalized the obstruction of federal (desegregation) court orders (Title I) and the crossing of state lines to engage in racially motivated violence against religious and civic institutions (Title II). For the children of military personnel living on federal property, the act provided for their education if public schools closed to avoid racial integration (Title V). The legislation also mandated the preservation of registration and voting records in federal elections (Title III), the judicial appointment of "voting referees" to compile evidence of voting rights violations (Title VI), and the authority for the Commission on Civil Rights to take sworn testimony.

The legislation had symbolic and strategic implications for subsequent, landmark legislation (the Civil Rights Act of 1964 and the Voting Rights Act of 1965). President Dwight Eisenhower's enactment of the legislation symbolized a critical juncture in American federalism. Henceforth, the national government's authority would be deployed against efforts by states to deny citizenship rights to racial minorities.

The strategic acumen developed by (congressional) civil rights proponents during the act's passage neutralized southern obstructionism in subsequent civil rights legislation. Congress also invoked its authority to regulate interstate commerce as the constitutional basis for prohibiting racial violence by private individuals (Title II), thereby insulating the act from the sort of constitutional challenge that invalidated the Civil Rights Act of 1875. The legislation therefore prefigured a significant broadening of Congress's authority to ban racial discrimination in public accommodations in 1964.

Michael S. Rodriguez

Further Reading

Berman, Daniel. *A Bill Becomes A Law: The Civil Rights Act of 1960.* New York: Macmillan, 1962.

Civil Rights Act of 1964

The Civil Rights Act of 1964 ushered in a relatively brief period (1964–1968) of progressive legislation that rectified the post-Reconstruction evisceration of statutory and constitutional protections for African Americans. The act (and subsequent amendments), the Voting Rights Act of 1965, the Immigration Act of 1965, and the Fair Housing Act of 1968 established the statutory and bureaucratic enforcement mechanisms that substantially expanded the national government's authority to protect the civil rights of African Americans and other groups who endured historical patterns of discrimination on the basis of race, national origin, language, religion, disability, age, or sex. This era of landmark legislation is often characterized as the Second Reconstruction because it dismantled the (Jim Crow) system of racial hierarchy and privilege and produced unprecedented levels of federal intervention into areas of social relations traditionally within the jurisdiction of state governments.

President Lyndon B. Johnson demonstrated extraordinary political courage and prescience for understanding that his signature on the act (July 2, 1964) would exacerbate the fracturing of the New Deal coalition. The act also marked the nadir of legislative obstructionism by southern Democrats on proposed civil rights legislation. For the first time in the Senate's history, a successful cloture vote by a coalition of northern Democrats and Republicans defeated a civil rights filibuster by southern Democrats. In the subsequent presidential elections of 1968 and 1972, the Democratic nominee won the electoral votes of only one of the former states of the Confederacy (Texas in 1968).

Although President Johnson demonstrated exceptional leadership and moral conviction in championing the act (and voting rights legislation a year later), the Johnson administration was also responding to an emerging national consensus that meaningful civil rights legislation was an urgent national priority. A "window of opportunity" for a major breakthrough in civil rights legislation was precipitated by several factors: the paroxysms of racial violence against African American churches, civic organizations, and civil rights activists; the moral urgency President John F. Kennedy attached to civil rights legislation before his assassination; urban unrest in northern cities often triggered by incidents of police brutality; and the increasing unease in the national security establishment that the international status of the United States was severely undermined by government repression of nonviolent civil rights protesters.

The act also indirectly corrected a long-standing Supreme Court precedent that invalidated congressional authority to prohibit racial discrimination in public accommodations. In the Civil Rights Cases (1883), the court ruled that the Fourteenth Amendment was limited to prohibitions against racial discrimination by state governments (the state action doctrine). Congress anticipated similar challenges and instead anchored the act's constitutional authority on the Interstate Commerce Clause. That approach was affirmed by the Supreme Court in two companion cases decided just five months after the passage of the act (on December 14, 1964). In a concurring opinion for both cases, Justice William O. Douglas signaled a potential willingness by the court to revisit Congress's Fourteenth Amendment authority to protect civil rights through enabling legislation.

In its initial formulation and subsequent amendments, the Civil Rights Act of 1964 constituted a substantial expansion of federal authority in protecting civil rights by prohibiting differential standards for voter eligibility in federal elections (Title I); prohibiting discrimination in public accommodations (Title II); empowering the attorney general to bring lawsuits against states that maintained racially segregated public school systems (Title III); outlawing discrimination in federally funded programs (Title VI); prohibiting employment discrimination on the basis of race, color, national origin, language, religion, age, sex, and disability (Title VII); establishing the Equal Employment Opportunity Commission to investigate employment discrimination and mandate the collection of workforce demographic data (also Title VII); and banning gender-based discrimination in educational programs that receive federal funding (Title IX).

Enactment of the Civil Rights Act of 1964 contained several far-reaching implications for the development of civil rights policy in American society. The act underscored the necessity for congressional legislation and executive branch action (enforcement mechanisms) to fully implement landmark judicial opinions such as *Brown v. Board of Education*. It established the legislative and bureaucratic framework for the subsequent promulgation of affirmative action policies and programs in federal contracting, public sector employment, and higher education. The act's inclusion of prohibitions against discrimination on the basis of sex, age, language, and disability suggests that the national government's responsiveness to civil rights claims is not exclusively predicated on mass mobilization by historically marginalized groups. For instance, key policy entrepreneurs within government contributed significantly to the adoption of Section 504 of the Rehabilitation Act of 1973 and the Americans with Disabilities Act, two major achievements of the disability rights movement. Perhaps the most enduring legacy of the act is the proposition that the full legislative, administrative, and judicial authority of the national government can be deployed to dismantle long-standing patterns and practices of discrimination in civil society and state and local governments.

Michael S. Rodriguez

Further Reading

Berry, Mary Frances. *Black Resistance/White Law: A History of Constitutional Racism in America*. New York: Penguin Press, 1994.

Skrentny, John D. *The Minority Rights Revolution*. Cambridge, MA: Harvard University Press, 2002.

Walton, Hanes, Jr., and Robert C. Smith. *American Politics and the African American Quest for Universal Freedom*. 2nd ed. New York: Longman Press, 2003.

Civil Rights Act of 1968

The Civil Rights Act of 1968, often referred to as the Fair Housing Act, was designed to prohibit discrimination in the sale, rental, advertising, and financing of housing. President Lyndon B. Johnson signed it into law on April 11, 1968, but the bill was delayed for several years before it was eventually passed in Congress. The original legislation was intended to extend federal government protection to civil rights workers, many of whom had been injured or killed in the struggle to obtain basic civil rights, but it was later amended to provide for fair housing throughout the United States regardless of one's race, color, religion, or national origin. It stands as one of the last major civil rights statues passed in the United States during the 1960s.

The act came in the wake of other key civil rights legislation, the most widely known of which is the Civil Rights Act of 1964. Of its many provisions, this act created an equal employment commission, required businesses that wanted federal business to have a pro–civil rights charter, enforced the constitutional right to vote, and barred discrimination in federally assisted programs. It was evident, however, that housing was an issue that had otherwise been insufficiently addressed by prior legislation, despite provisions outlawing discrimination in public places and venues. The segregation existing in many parts of the country, the failure of banks to provide loans to African Americans, and the refusal of landlords to rent to individuals and families on the basis of race helped create a hostile housing climate that severely limited most African Americans' fair access to housing.

It is argued that the Civil Rights Act of 1968 had its roots in President John F. Kennedy's Executive Order 11063, which he set out in 1962. This order directed all departments and agencies of the U.S. government to take necessary action to prevent discrimination on the basis of one's race, creed, or national origin in the sale, rental, or leasing of federally owned or operated residential property. It also prohibited racial discrimination in public housing built with federal funds and in new housing built with loans from federal agencies. Kennedy's order notwithstanding, it remained clear that the legislation needed to be strengthened and broadened in its chief aims if it was to substantially alter the lack of parity African Americans faced when trying to purchase real estate and secure housing.

Clarence Mitchell Jr., the Washington director of the NAACP, is credited with spearheading the effort to secure the 1968 bill. Mitchell, dubbed by some as the "101st Senator," was a leading force in the battle to obtain civil rights legislation, and his efforts to ensure that this particular bill would become law were critical. A conservative legislative branch used several procedural tactics to delay the passage of the bill for a number of years, but it gained increasing support when Senate Republican minority leader Everett Dirksen strongly backed its enactment. Dirksen generally had a conservative position on domestic legislation and held weekly broadcast news conferences to voice Republican opposition to Kennedy's administration. Yet he had previously been a designer and supporter of civil rights bills and firmly backed the 1968 fair housing bill. After Dirksen announced his support, the Senate voted to pass the bill by a tight 65–32 margin on March 4, 1968, but it was thought to be impassable in the House unless it was amended, and likely weakened, in committee.

The assassination of Martin Luther King Jr. on April 4, 1968, just one month after the bill was voted on in the Senate, contributed to mounting pressure to pass the bill in its entirety. The riots, burnings, and looting occurring in the wake of his assassination in more than 100 cities across the United States marked 1968 as a particularly tumultuous year and served as a powerful indication that advocates of racial justice would continue to resist social, judicial, economic, and political inequalities under the law. The House Rules Committee voted to send the fair housing bill straight to the House floor, permitted only one hour of debate without any further amendments, and the bill went on to pass swiftly the day after King's funeral. President Johnson signed it into law the next day as the nation continued to mourn the loss of a renowned civil rights leader.

The act was amended in 1974 to include sex as a protected class in fair housing, and, in 1988, disability and familial status were added to make it more comprehensive in its aims and scope. The U.S. Department of Housing and Urban Development, state and local governmental agencies, and nonprofit fair housing advocacy organizations now exist throughout the country to assist those who feel they have been subjected to housing discrimination. This network of agencies and organizations also exists to help ensure that housing does in fact remain fair to African Americans and all those who seek to establish a residence.

Amanda J. Davis

Further Reading

Carson, Clayborne, David J. Garrow, Gerald Gill, Vincent Harding, and Darlene Clark Hine, eds. *The Eyes on the Prize: Civil Rights Reader: Documents, Speeches, and Firsthand Accounts from the Black Freedom Struggle, 1954–1990*. New York: Penguin Books, 1991.

Klarman, Michael. *From Jim Crow to Civil Rights: The Supreme Court and the Struggle for Racial Equality.* New York: Oxford University Press, 2004.

Lawson, Steven F., and Charles Payne. *Debating the Civil Rights Movement: 1945–1968.* Lanham, MD: Rowman & Littlefield Publishers, 1998.

Clark, Septima

Septima Clark was an important African American educator and major civil rights activist who fought for equality for African Americans and women. Septima Poinsette Clark was born in 1898 in Charleston, South Carolina. Her father, Peter Porcher Poinsette, was a caterer, and her mother, Victoria Warren Anderson, was a washerwoman. Clark attended private and public schools for African Americans in Charleston, including Avery Normal Institute. She claimed that she always wanted to be a teacher, a desire nurtured by her parents' strong emphasis on education.

After graduating from 12th grade with a teaching certificate in 1916, Clark took her first job teaching on Johns Island, near Charleston. There she earned $30 a month teaching 132 children with only one other teacher, while in comparison, white teachers on the island averaged $85 for teaching approximately 10 students. Clark then taught at various schools in North and South Carolina, eventually moving to Columbia, South Carolina, where she taught for 18 years.

In 1920, Clark married Nerie Clark, a sailor from Hickory, North Carolina, with whom she had one surviving son, Nerie Clark Jr. Clark's husband died from kidney failure five years later, and her son spent much of his youth living with her in-laws in Hickory while she worked in South Carolina.

Clark first contributed to organized civil rights when she participated in a movement demanding that black teachers be allowed to teach in black public schools in Charleston. Clark argued that the white teachers assigned to black schools were of poor quality and were not interested in African American achievement. She helped gather more than 10,000 signatures for the victorious National Association for the Advancement of Colored People (NAACP) petition drive. In Columbia, she continued her activism by participating in a successful legal challenge to force the school system to equalize salaries for similarly qualified black and white teachers. Clark also resumed her education, earning her BA from Benedict College in Columbia and her MA from Hampton Institute in Virginia. She returned to Charleston to teach from 1947 to 1956, after which her teaching contract in the public schools was not renewed because of her membership in the NAACP.

Through the encouragement of Anna Kelly, executive secretary of the Charleston African American YWCA, Clark attended a workshop on desegregation at the Highlander School, in Monteagle, Tennessee, in 1954. Highlander Folk School, founded by Miles Horton in the 1930s, initially trained southern labor organizers and then turned its attention to civil rights, holding a series of workshops in 1953 and 1954 on strategies for peaceful school desegregation. Clark then took Esau Jenkins and other community members from Johns Island to Highlander, which ultimately resulted in the establishment of the first citizenship school on the island in January 1957. Clark and the first citizenship school teacher, Bernice Robinson, designed the curriculum and materials based on what participants asked to learn on the first day. They taught students how to sign their names, fill out money orders, and to read and write using lessons on citizenship and democracy. This model for citizenship schools quickly expanded, and Clark assisted other communities in designing their own citizenship schools.

Clark was asked to become director of education at Highlander School, where, in addition to establishing citizenship schools, she ran workshops designed to help community leaders address illiteracy, desegregation, and other issues. When the Tennessee General Assembly tried to revoke the school's tax-free charter on trumped-up charges of alcohol possession, the Southern Christian Leadership Conference (SCLC), the civil rights organization founded by Martin Luther King Jr., took over the citizenship school program, and Clark moved to Atlanta. As supervisor of teacher training, Clark traveled around the South recruiting teachers to attend a five-day workshop at the Dorchester Cooperative Community Center in McIntosh, Georgia. Clark also spent time in various communities assisting local volunteers with setting up citizenship schools, forming 897 schools between 1957 and 1970. In 1962, the SCLC joined with the NAACP, the Congress of Racial Equality (CORE), the Student Nonviolent Coordinating Committee (SNCC), and the National Urban League to form the Voter Education Project. Between 1962 and 1965, this project trained about 10,000 teachers for citizenship schools, resulting in about 700,000 black voters registering in the South. After passage of the Voting Rights Act of 1965, more than one million black voters registered before 1970. Civil rights leader Andrew Young credited the citizenship schools as being the basis on which the entire civil rights movement was built.

Clark's activism was driven by her belief that one had to empower local leaders to organize their own communities. She wrote to King, suggesting that he allow more local activists to lead marches so as to facilitate grassroots leadership. Clark later recalled that the executive staff laughed at her suggestion because she was a woman. As the first woman on the executive staff of SCLC, she and Ella Baker faced opposition from the mostly male ministers who dominated SCLC and did not respect the contributions of women, according to Clark. In 1966, at the invitation of white civil rights activist Virginia Foster Durr, Clark attended the organizational meeting of the National Organization for Women. Clark argued that both black and white southern women were constrained by the authority of their husbands. Notwithstanding her differences with King regarding women's roles, Clark respected and admired him deeply and strongly believed in his philosophy of non-violence. King came to think so much of her and her work on behalf of civil rights that he wanted her to come with him to Stockholm, Sweden, to accept the Nobel Peace Prize in 1965. Despite the dangers of arrest, violence, harassment, and threats to her ability to earn a living, Clark always insisted that she was not afraid because she understood the importance of the work she did.

In addition to her work in the NAACP and SCLC, Clark was also involved in the South Carolina Federation of Colored Women's Clubs, the Charleston Tuberculosis Association, the YWCA, and her sorority, Alpha Kappa Alpha, with whom she worked on a health campaign for Johns Island. After retiring from the SCLC in 1970, she volunteered for the American Field Service, helped organize day care facilities, and was elected a member of the Charleston school board, the same board that had fired her for her political beliefs years earlier. In 1979, President Jimmy Carter presented Clark with a Living the Legacy Award for her dedication to civil rights and to the nation. She died on December 15, 1987.

Joan Marie Johnson

Further Reading

Brown, Cynthia Stokes, ed. *Ready from Within: Septima Clark and the Civil Rights Movement*. Navarro, CA: Wild Trees Press, 1986.

Clark, Septima. *Echo in My Soul*. New York: E. P. Dutton, 1962.

Crawford, Vicki L., Jacqueline Anne Rouse, and Barbara Woods, eds. *Women in the Civil Rights Movement: Trailblazers and Torchbearers, 1941–1965*. Brooklyn, NY: Carlson Publishing, 1990.

Ling, Peter. "Local Leadership in the Early Civil Rights Movement: The South Carolina Citizenship Education Program of the Highlander Folk School." *Journal of American Studies* 29 (1995): 399–422.

McFadden, Grace Jordan. *Oral Recollections of Septima Poinsette Clark*. Columbia: University of South Carolina Instructional Services Center, 1980.

Cleaver, Eldridge

Eldridge Cleaver was a writer, an advocate of Black Power, and a member of the Black Panther Party for Self-Defense (BPP), serving in the capacity of minister of information in the organization for several years.

Leroy Eldridge Cleaver, the son of a nightclub piano player, was born on August 31, 1935, in Wabbaseka, Arkansas, and moved with his family to Phoenix and, by 1946, Los Angeles. While in California, Cleaver began to have early encounters with law enforcement as a teenager, with arrests for stealing a bicycle and selling marijuana. After a brief stint in a reform school, he was arrested again for selling marijuana and was sentenced to 30 months in Soledad Prison. After his release in 1957, Cleaver again turned to a life of crime, committing a series of rapes, and, by 1958, he was convicted of assault and attempted murder and was sentenced to serve an indeterminate sentence of 2 to 14 years in San Quentin Prison. Before leaving prison in 1966, Cleaver read a number of books on African American history and the civil rights struggle. He became an ardent supporter of the late Malcolm X, and he wrote a series of articles for *Ramparts* magazine.

Upon his release from San Quentin, Cleaver did a number of things in rapid succession. He published his *Ramparts* magazine articles as a book entitled *Soul on Ice*; he married Kathleen Neal in December 1967; he joined the newly formed BPP and was appointed as the minister of information; and, in 1968, Cleaver was a presidential candidate for the Peace and Freedom Party. He is most famous for his actions after the assassination of Dr. Martin Luther King Jr. On April 6, 1968, Cleaver, along with Bobby Hutton and David Hilliard, were involved in an altercation with Oakland, California, police that left Hutton dead and Cleaver injured. Apparently, Cleaver led this small group in a purposeful attempt to initiate a violent altercation with police. He was subsequently arrested and charged with attempted murder. Fearing a lengthy stay in prison, Cleaver skipped bail and fled the country. His escape route took him through Mexico to Cuba, although he also spent time in exile in Algeria and France.

While in exile, Cleaver continued to write for *Ramparts*, the *Black Scholar*, and other publications. Because of a series of disagreements between him and Huey P. Newton, Cleaver was expelled from the Black Panther Party in 1971. After seven years in exile, he returned to the United States, immediately renouncing the BPP and experiencing a profound religious and political transformation. Not only did Cleaver renounce the Panthers and their philosophy, he rejected socialism, communism, and radicalism. He became an evangelical Christian and later a Mormon, and even endorsed Republican politician Ronald Reagan, a former archenemy of the Panthers, for president in 1980 and 1984. In 1986, Cleaver even made an unsuccessful run for the Republican Party nomination for a Senate seat in California. Throughout the 1980s and early 1990s, Cleaver was an ardent and dedicated conservative Republican and evangelical Christian, in diametric opposition to his prior activities as a Black Panther. He was also addicted to crack cocaine during this period and was arrested on at least two occasions for burglary and cocaine possession. At the time of his death in May 1, 1998, Cleaver was a diversity consultant for the University of La Verne in Southern California.

Walter C. Rucker

Further Reading

Cleaver, Eldridge. *Soul on Ice*. New York: McGraw-Hill, 1967.

Cleaver, Eldridge, and Robert Scheer. *Eldridge Cleaver: Post-Prison Writings and Speeches*. New York: Random House, 1969.

Jones, Charles E., ed. *The Black Panther Party (Reconsidered)*. Baltimore: Black Classic Press, 1998.

Otis, George. *Eldridge Cleaver: Ice and Fire*. Van Nuys, CA: Bible Voice, 1977.

Cleaver, Kathleen Neal

Kathleen Neal Cleaver became the first woman member of the Black Panther Party's Central Committee. As the party's communication secretary, Cleaver was a key figure in the early development of the Black Panther Party and a significant figure in the black liberation struggle since the mid-1960s.

Cleaver's father, Ernest Neal, was a professor of sociology at Wuley College in Marshall, Texas, when she was born on May 13, 1945, in Dallas, Texas. In 1948, the Neals moved to Tuskegee, Alabama, where Cleaver's father taught sociology and served as director of the Rural Life Council at Tuskegee Institute. In 1954, Cleaver's father joined the Foreign Service, which took the family to India, Liberia, Sierra Leone, and the Philippines. In 1958, Cleaver began attending high school in the United States. After high school, she attended Oberlin College, transferred to Barnard College, and, in 1966, left Barnard to join the New York office of the Student Nonviolent Coordinating Committee (SNCC). In January 1967, Cleaver began working at the SNCC headquarters in Atlanta, Georgia.

While organizing a student conference at Fisk University in Nashville, Tennessee, in April 1967, Kathleen met Eldridge Cleaver, minister of information for the Black Panther Party. The Black Panther Party was cofounded in Oakland, California, in 1966 by Huey P. Newton and Bobby Seale. The party advocated a comprehensive agenda for black liberation detailed in their 10-point program, "What We Want, What We Believe." Eldridge Cleaver had just recently been paroled from Soledad Prison, where he had written the bestselling book *Soul on Ice*. In November 1967, Kathleen left SNCC and moved to California to join the Black Panther Party, becoming its first female member. In December 1967, Eldridge and Kathleen were married.

As the Black Panther's Central Committee communication secretary from 1967 to 1971, Cleaver provided press releases, delivered public speeches, wrote articles about the party, and was the assistant editor of the party newspaper, the *Black Panther*. With the imprisonment of the party's minister of defense, Huey Newton, in 1968, on charges of killing an Oakland police officer, Cleaver crusaded for Newton's release through the "Free Huey Campaign." In late 1967, the Black Panther Party formed a coalition with the Peace and Freedom Party to run alternative candidates to the Democrats and Republicans in California. In 1968, Cleaver ran for the 18th District seat in the California State Assembly as a Peace and Freedom

Party candidate on a ticket that included other prominent Black Panther Party members and peace activists.

In 1968, Eldridge Cleaver was wounded by San Francisco police and arrested and charged with parole violation. He was subsequently to return to prison. However, in November 1968, he fled to Cuba and then Algeria. In the summer of 1969, Kathleen and Black Panther Party minister of culture Emory Douglas joined him in Algeria, where they organized and led the International Section of the Black Panther Party. In July 1969, Kathleen gave birth to a son, Maceo, in Algeria. In 1970, Joju, a girl, was born in North Korea while the Cleavers served on the American Peoples Anti-Imperialism Delegation to the International Conference of Revolutionary Journalists.

In 1971, as a result of a dispute between Huey Newton and Eldridge Cleaver, the International Section was expelled from the Black Panther Party. Following their expulsion, the International Section members reorganized to form the Revolutionary Peoples Communications Network (RPCN). In 1971, Kathleen established the organization's headquarters in New York and traveled throughout the United States building support for the RPCN.

In January 1973, the Cleavers moved to Paris. From Paris, Kathleen returned to the United States to arrange for the safe return of her husband and to coordinate his legal defense. In November 1975, Eldridge Cleaver returned to the United States, surrendered to authorities, and served eight months in prison before being released on bail.

In 1981, the Cleavers separated and Kathleen moved with her children to New Haven, Connecticut, where she attended Yale University. She graduated Phi Beta Kappa and summa cum laude with a degree in history in 1984 and entered Yale Law School. In 1987, the Cleavers were divorced; the next year, Cleaver earned her law degree.

Cleaver became an associate at the law firm Cravath, Swaine, and Moore in New York City and, in 1991, was a law clerk in the U.S. Third Circuit Court of Appeals in Philadelphia. Cleaver also served on the Georgia Supreme Court Commission on Racial and Ethnic Bias in the Courts and as a board member of the Southern Center for Human Rights. She has taught at several universities, including Emory University and Yale University, and has received numerous fellowships at leading institutions including the Bunting Institute of Radcliffe College, the W.E.B. Du Bois Institute of Harvard University, and the Schomburg Center for Research in Black Culture in New York. In addition to teaching, Cleaver continued her activism for human rights and justice and for the release of political prisoners.

Kenneth S. Jolly

Further Reading

Cleaver, Kathleen, and George Katsiaficas, eds. *Liberation, Imagination, and the Black Panther Party: A New Look at the Panthers and Their Legacy.* New York: Routledge, 2001.

Foner, Philip S., ed. *The Black Panthers Speak*. New York: De Capo Press, 1995.

Jones, Charles E., ed. *The Black Panther Party Reconsidered*. Baltimore: Black Classic Press, 1998.

Seale, Bobby. *Seize the Time: The Story of the Black Panther Party and Huey Newton*. Baltimore: Black Classic Press, 1991.

COINTELPRO

Between 1956 and 1971, the Federal Bureau of Investigation (FBI) conducted a series of domestic covert action programs, COINTELPROs (for Counter Intelligence Program), which discredited, disrupted, and neutralized leaders, members, and supporters of social movements that threatened the social, political, and economic status quo. Developed in the context of Cold War anxieties, COINTELPROs were designed to thwart the infiltration of communist influence but were used to justify FBI policy against organizations and activists involved in the civil rights,Black Power, and antiwar movements.

Launched in 1961, COINTELPRO–Socialist Worker's Party (SWP) singled out African American SWP political campaigns for disruption and attempted to block a developing political alliance with Malcolm X's Organization of Afro-American Unity. Launched on August 25, 1967, the COINTELPRO–Black Nationalist Hate Group (BNHG) operation formally institutionalized covert operations that had targeted groups such as the Nation of Islam (NOI) and the Southern Christian Leadership Conference (SCLC). These operations had aggravated factionalism in the NOI, exposed "links" between SCLC activists and the Communist Party, and attempted to expose Martin Luther King Jr.'s sexual affairs to induce him to commit suicide. Consisting of 360 documented operations, COINTELPRO-BNHG targeted groups that engaged in civil disobedience, picketing, or antiwar activity; advocated separatism, self-defense, or revolution; or associated with other COINTELPRO targets. This included the Student Nonviolent Coordinating Committee (SNCC), the Revolutionary Action Movement (RAM), the Junta of Militant Organizations, the Black Liberators, the Invaders, Black Student Unions, and the US Organization; 79 percent of all operations targeted the Black Panther Party (BPP).

FBI agents used surreptitious entry, electronic surveillance, and informants to acquire and covertly distribute material to police, Congress, the media, elected officials, landlords, college presidents and the Internal Revenue Service (IRS). By covertly distributing intelligence information and mailing derogatory and scurrilous communications, agents prevented activists from gaining respectability among white liberals, moderate blacks, and other social movement activists. To discredit activists and organizations, agents alerted local police to targets' plans and activities so that they could arrest activists on pretext. To disrupt personal lives, agents sent anonymous communications to spouses alleging infidelity with traveling companions and coworkers. These operations thwarted fund raising, recruiting, organizing, and favorable publicity; prevented coalition building; and harassed movement leaders.

To capitalize on ideological, organizational, and personal conflicts, create factionalism, and provoke conflict between organizations, FBI agents made anonymous telephone calls and created counterfeit movement literature, cartoons, and other notional communications. Alleging misconduct, provoking ridicule, snitchjacketing activists as informants, and alleging the existence of assassination plots, such communications framed effective movement leaders as embezzlers, charlatans, informants, and provocateurs. Such tactics exacerbated divisions among white leftists and black revolutionaries, between moderates and radicals, and between advocates of public positions on nonviolence versus self-defense. COINTELPRO operations also exacerbated and provoked violent conflicts such as those between the Huey P. Newton and Eldridge Cleaver factions of the BPP, and between the BPP and Jeff Fort's Chicago-based Blackstone Rangers. Similar operations provoked internecine violence in the streets of New York and San Diego. COINTELPRO operations even helped to provoke members of Maulana Karenga's Los Angeles–based US Organization to kill four Panthers.

FBI informants raised controversial issues, led factional fights, embezzled funds, provoked violence, and supplied information to justify police raids. A provocateur set up an African American man named Larry Ward, offering him money to commit a bombing, and Seattle police killed him in an ambush. BPP FBI-informant William O'Neal facilitated the police killings of Chicago Panthers Fred Hampton and Mark Clark, and George Sams engineered the torture-murder of Alex Rackley by labeling him an informant. FBI and police operations are responsible for perhaps 25 other killings. Informants also committed perjury, even as the FBI suppressed exculpatory evidence, enabling convictions and incarcerations on trumped-up charges. Some African American activists fled overseas or went underground; BPP members Dhoruba bin Wahad and Geronimo Ji Jaga Pratt were incarcerated for decades before their lawyers exposed the police and FBI misconduct that underlay their convictions. COINTELPROs led to the devolution of some Black Power organizations into terrorist cells in the 1970s.

John Drabble

Further Reading

Blackstock, Nelson. *COINTELPRO: The FBI's Secret War on Political Freedom.* New York: Pathfinder, 1988.

Churchill, Ward, and Jim Vander Wall. *The COINTELPRO Papers: Documents from the FBI's Secret Wars against Dissent in the United States.* Boston: South End Press, 1990.

Garrow, David J. *The FBI and Martin Luther King, Jr.: From "SOLO" to Memphis.* New York: W. W. Norton, 1981.

O'Reilly, Kenneth. *Racial Matters: The FBI's Secret File on Black America, 1960–1972*. New York: Free Press, 1989.

Theoharis, Athan, ed. *COINTELPRO: The FBI's Counterintelligence Program*. Wilmington, DE: Scholarly Resources, 1978.

Cold War and Civil Rights

The Cold War greatly influenced U.S. race politics and the African American quest for civil rights. On one hand, the struggle with the Soviet Union brought questions of racial equality to the forefront and improved the government's civil rights record. It provided the civil rights movement with leverage with the government. On the other hand, it restrained the civil rights movement in its activities.

With the victory in World War II, the alliance between the United States and the Soviet Union ended and developed into a stalemate between the two new superpowers. They both longed to fill the new power vacuum. Europe was weakened. The colonial empires of Europe in Asia and Africa disintegrated and new nations evolved. The Soviet Union and the United States struggled for zones of influence throughout the world. Their views of and plans for the world and its future were seemingly irreconcilable. The Soviet Union aspired to expand communism and combat capitalism. The United States feared this expansion and sought instead to spread democratic capitalism in the world. Within the contest for allegiance against communism, the question for civil rights and racial equality became of great importance to the U.S. government. The Cold War made civil rights an international issue—the world audience became a great factor in shaping American domestic race relations and politics.

The war and the disclosure of the horrors of the Holocaust had discredited ideas of racial superiority, such as eugenics and Social Darwinism. Racism in any form grew to be less acceptable around the world. The assurance of equal human rights for all that was included in the UN Charter turned into a major principle of world and domestic politics. In the escalating struggle for world leadership and allegiance in the destabilized or newly evolving nations, propaganda and image played an ever-growing role.

To influence emerging nations in Asia and Africa, the Soviet Union attempted to spread distrust of the United States and its claim of world leadership of freedom and democracy. Because of their colonial past, these contested nations were already distrustful of the West. The Soviet Union disseminated America's persistent human rights violations. According to the State Department, in the early 1950s, half of the Soviet propaganda pieces were on racist practices in the United States. The spread of racial violence and the mounting numbers of lynchings after the war were living proof of the American disregard for people of color within and outside the United States.

Not only did the Soviet Union tout the appalling position of African Americans, but newspapers all over the world reported on racial violence in the United States. Foreign countries were appalled by the cruelty and the U.S. government's reluctance to intervene. U.S. racist practices became a worldwide embarrassment for the United States and called into question its legitimacy as a world leader. In late 1947, the report *To Secure These Rights* by the President's Committee on Civil Rights pinpointed the negative influence of American racial inequality on American diplomatic endeavors and image in foreign countries. It underscored the international significance of ending domestic segregation and racism. The Cold War and growing international interest in American domestic policy pressured the United States to adapt its aspired image as the paradigm and bearer of democracy and equality.

As a result of these developments, the White House, the State Department, and the Justice Department turned to pro–civil rights and desegregation policy reform to improve its standing in the world and prove its superiority to the Soviet Union. From President Harry S. Truman through President Lyndon B. Johnson's term, the link between the Cold War and international interest in American equal rights and civil rights is most visible. With the Vietnam War, the attention shifted away from the image of domestic racial equality. Although not downplaying the essential importance of the civil rights movement and the black vote, foreign policy considerations also undeniably influenced the government's civil rights agenda during the Cold War. Despite the protest of southern whites, the United States began to advance its record on civil rights regulations and launched an image campaign in an effort to counter Soviet propaganda.

The White House pressed for governmental action on civil rights. The State Department, in particular, was aware of the importance of international opinion in the success of U.S. Cold War foreign policy. Its officials all over the world in their meetings with international audiences, especially at the United Nations, called increased attention to the precarious standing of the United States in the world with respect to race relations. They sought to change the record. The responsible forces, however, also knew that a majority in Congress would not be willing to embrace these plans. Southern congressional representatives, who had enormous power in Congress, used the Cold War as a reason for opposing equal rights for minorities. Explaining their opposition to civil rights reform, southerners primarily argued that a change of race relations was a threat to national security and a hindrance to the aims of American foreign policy. Civil rights reform had to be accomplished mainly without the help of Congress.

Beginning with President Truman, the civil rights record of the federal government improved. Truman issued executive orders restricting segregation in the United States. The integration of the U.S. military, accelerated by the Korean War, was internationally one of his most visible civil rights reforms. Truman began to increase the number of African Americans in the State Department and Foreign

Service, a development continued by all subsequent presidents. The State Department also regularly financed trips of African American activists to spread a positive outlook on American race relations and politics.

During Dwight D. Eisenhower's presidency, the decision in *Brown v. Board of Education* officially ended school desegregation. *Brown* and the following Little Rock desegregation crisis were international issues and stories that highly affected the American image of race relations. Before *Brown,* the Justice Department had already decided in some cases that racial segregation violated the UN Charter and seriously hurt American foreign policy. Its *amicus curiae* briefs displayed concern for the global implications of the American race problem. The racial integration of Washington, D.C., as representative of the nation, took on a special role and would soon be implemented.

The civil rights reforms undertaken during the Cold War, especially early on, contained a considerable amount of tokenism and window dressing. Although the civil rights reforms were issued and celebrated as a proof of change, their implementation lagged. The government claimed their success in improving civil rights and used it as proof of continuous racial progress, but did not force implementation. Political civil rights advocacy and activism was often designed more for impressing the international audience than for revolutionizing domestic race relations.

Propaganda and communication were key elements in the international endeavor to gain supporters for the United States in the Cold War struggle. The propaganda was intended to influence the world audience. It was to counter Soviet propaganda that constantly played on the chasm between the American claim of freedom and the situation of African Americans. American propaganda constructed a story of constant racial progress. The government argued that only in a democracy could these changes come about. The newly founded United States Information Agency (USIA) had primary responsibility for spreading information of American racial progress internationally. Civil rights progress was also examined for its propaganda value. The continued existence of segregation and the recurring protest and violence against African American civil rights, particularly in the South, created problems with the constructed image of racial change and progress. These incidents, however, were incorporated into the image of America's constant change for the better. It was argued that these were individual cases in restricted areas that proved racial progress was only possible in a democracy.

Although the world audience was the main aim of American propaganda, the domestic audience was also to be convinced of the necessity of civil rights reforms and improvements with the Cold War discourse. Civil rights advocates argued that civil rights were essential to a successful fight against communism, although individual states and people were often not too interested in the claim that civil rights advocacy could support the anticommunist struggle.

As much as segregationists used the Cold War as a tool to protest civil rights reform, the African American civil rights movement also attempted to use the Cold

War and the international attention as leverage for racial progress. Many African Americans believed that supporting U.S. anticommunist foreign policy would result in the government fighting domestic discrimination. In their civil rights activism, the African American community felt connected to the emerging third-world nations' struggle against colonialism that simultaneously took place. The African American civil rights movement was well aware of the international interest in and importance of American race relations. The creation of the United Nations was of service to the African American civil rights movement. Although the United Nations would not interfere in U.S. domestic affairs, and the U.S. government did not intend to justify its domestic race relations in front of the UN, the civil rights movement used it as a multiplier of information on the African American situation. Petitions on U.S. segregation and racial discrimination to the UN furthered the internationalization of racial issues in the United States. The documents were widely published and discussed in the world press, augmenting the pressure on the American government to improve its standing on racial issues.

In its activism, the civil rights movement attempted to make use of the Cold War discourse to pressure for civil rights actions of the government. From Walter White and the National Association for the Advancement of Colored People (NAACP) to Martin Luther King Jr., major civil rights leaders made use of the Cold War discourse to influence the domestic audience on issues of civil rights. They argued for the necessity of racial reform if the United States wanted to win the support of the international community, the newly emerging nations of Asia and Africa in particular, and effectively contain the international and national spread of communism.

As much as the Cold War might have informed the civil rights movement and its goals, it also seriously restricted it. Anticommunist hysteria, fear of communist conspiracy, and McCarthyism constrained the leeway for civil rights activism. The infringement of constitutional rights during the Cold War seriously affected the African American civil rights movement in particular. Suspecting a communist threat, the Federal Bureau of Investigation (FBI) put all civil rights organizations under close scrutiny. As a result of these political and societal pressures, the successful use of mass movement activism and any cooperation with left-leaning organizations were suspicious and nearly impossible. The civil rights movement had to spend considerable effort and money to fight any public association with communism assigned to them, a serious allegation that slowed down, seriously weakened, and divided the civil rights movement. Only with the decline of the Cold War in the late 1960s could the civil rights movement radicalize and step up its activism.

Christine Knauer

Further Reading

Anderson, Carol. *Eyes Off the Prize: The United Nations and the African American Struggle for Human Rights, 1944–1955*. Cambridge: Cambridge University Press, 2003.

Borstelmann, Thomas. *The Cold War and the Color Line: American Race Relations in the Global Arena.* Cambridge, MA: Harvard University Press, 2001.

Dudziak, Mary L. *Cold War Civil Rights: Race and the Image of American Democracy.* Princeton, NJ: Princeton University Press, 2000.

Horne, Gerald. *Black and Red: W. E. B. Du Bois and the African Response to the Cold War, 1941–63.* Albany: State University of New York Press, 1986.

Plummer, Brenda Gayle. *Rising Wind: Black Americans and U.S. Foreign Affairs, 1935–1960.* Chapel Hill: University of North Carolina Press, 1996.

Skrentny, John David. "The Effect of the Cold War on African-American Civil Rights: American and the World Audience, 1945–1968." *Theory and Society* 27 (1998): 237–85.

Von Eschen, Penny M. "Commentary: Challenging Cold War Habits: African Americans, Race, and Foreign Policy." *Diplomatic History* 20 (1996): 627–38.

Congress of Racial Equality

The Congress of Racial Equality (CORE) was an early pioneer of nonviolent direct-action campaigns that took place during the civil rights movement during the 1950s and 1960s. The organization grew out of the Christian pacifist student organization, the Fellowship of Reconciliation (FOR), which was started in 1942. At the outset, the group's goal was to foster improvement in race relations. CORE's nonviolent, direct-action ideology was used a number of times within urban African American communities during the era in their struggle against racial discrimination. These protests developed out of a long-established protest tradition that ranged from the "Don't Buy Where You Can't Work" Campaign in Chicago and New York City during the 1930s, A. Philip Randolph's March on Washington Movement of the 1940s, and the more militant mood among African Americans over the obvious contradictions between America's democratic war propaganda and its violation of democratic principles at home. Each of these campaigns came in response to inadequate housing opportunities, job segregation, and discrimination in public accommodations and public spaces. This discrimination resulted from white resistance to the growing number of black migrants moving north in search of better economic and social opportunities in the early twentieth century, and during World War II and the postwar period.

The first CORE chapter, the Chicago Committee of Racial Equality, was formed in 1942 at the University of Chicago. The leaders of this new, interracial organization, which included future national directors James Farmer and James A. Robinson, were skeptical and critical of conservative actions of older civil rights groups like the National Association for the Advancement of Colored People (NAACP) and the National Urban League, which often insisted on lengthy court battles to fight Jim Crow. The first CORE chapter instead embarked on campaigns that directly

James Farmer, national director of the Congress of Racial Equality (CORE), leads a demonstration at New York World's Fair, 1964. (Library of Congress)

confronted discrimination in housing, employment, and public accommodations. In March 1942, for instance, the group chose the White City Roller Rink as its first site to test Illinois's civil rights law. Here, 24 CORE members sought entry into the facility. When the African Americans in the group were denied entry, the group negotiated with the manager to end segregation at the location. Later that same year, the group targeted discrimination in housing at the University of Chicago Hospital and Medical School and at the university barbershop.

After changing its name to the Congress of Racial Equality in 1943, CORE expanded its operations and affiliated with other civil rights groups across the country. This proved difficult, because CORE affiliates resisted centralized leadership out of the belief that a central structure would deprive local chapters of valuable, and often limited, financial resources. Moreover, problems in northern urbanized areas transcended mere segregation and encompassed a myriad of other issues—in particular, residential and employment discrimination. Many chapter leaders believed that creating a bureaucracy unfamiliar with local issues would severely limit the type of activism that could be used.

Despite this resistance, throughout the late 1940s and early 1950s, local CORE groups managed some substantial victories. In 1949, St. Louis CORE, operating in a locale whose African American populace had increased during wartime migration, launched a successful campaign to desegregate Woolworth's lunch counters through sit-ins and picketing. In another example, CORE operations in Omaha, Nebraska, successfully pressured a local Coca-Cola plant to agree to more equitable hiring practices. Unfortunately, the successes of these campaigns were not enough to maintain morale and activism among CORE affiliates across the nation. By 1954, while the NAACP was enjoying success as a result of the *Brown v. Board of Education* case; and 1955, when Martin Luther King Jr. and the Montgomery Bus Boycott gained national attention, CORE suffered from organizational disarray and growing anticommunist investigations.

In 1961, CORE reached an important point in its organizational history when James Farmer, after a brief time working for the NAACP, became its national director. Farmer's influence on CORE's activism developed after he attended Howard University's Divinity School. Farmer refused ordination as a Methodist minister, saying he could not preach in a church that practiced discrimination. Subsequently, he began work for a number of pacifist and socialist groups, applied for conscientious objector status, and was deferred from the draft during World War II because of his divinity degree. During his early career as an activist, Farmer worked for two Chicago organizations—a pacifist group, the Fellowship of Reconciliation (FOR), in 1941, and later, CORE from 1942 to 1945. With FOR, Farmer helped draft responses to such social ills as war, violence, bigotry, and poverty. With CORE, where he served as the group's first chair, Farmer proposed a new strategy based less on religious pacifism and more on the principle of nonviolent direct action that was used in northern urban areas during the Great Migration and World War II eras as African Americans increasingly questioned the contradictions between American racism and the nation's war for democracy.

Before Farmer (whose charisma proved invaluable in strengthening CORE's ability to increase its profile within the African American community), CORE had begun to develop a reputation as being a predominantly white organization. With Farmer as its leader, the group moved into a more influential position among African American protest organizations because of its willingness to directly confront racial inequality.

On May 4, 1961, CORE brought its confrontational style to the Deep South when 13 CORE members departed via bus from Washington, D.C., in two interracial groups as part of the Freedom Rides. The endeavor was modeled after the 1946 Journey of Reconciliation, which tested the limits of a Supreme Court ruling banning discrimination in interstate travel sponsored by CORE and FOR. The Freedom Rides, a demonstration that Farmer had long pushed the NAACP to undertake, was a new effort to challenge southern segregation in interstate travel and to test a recent Supreme Court ruling, *Boynton v. Virginia*, that extended nondiscrimination to bus terminal accommodations. The Freedom Rides were a dangerous undertaking, and on May 13, outside Birmingham, Alabama, an armed mob attacked buses carrying a group of Freedom Riders and firebombed one of the buses. These incidents prompted CORE activists to abandon the remainder of their trip, and the riders were transported to New Orleans under the protection of the Justice Department. These actions, although initially disappointing, inspired other Freedom Rides throughout the South and demonstrated how a protest strategy, tested and proven in northern states, could be implemented in the South. In the end, the Freedom Rides and voter registration drives in the South succeeded in moving CORE into a better position to fight racism throughout the North and South.

The visceral hatred demonstrated by southern whites and the extreme racial violence aimed against the Freedom Riders made national news and thrust CORE into the national spotlight. The events surrounding the Freedom Rides transformed the national profile of the group in civil rights circles. During Farmer's tenure, CORE and Farmer soon developed a reputation of being one of the "Big Four" in the civil rights movement—along with Roy Wilkins of the NAACP, Whitney Young of the National Urban League, and Martin Luther King Jr. of the Southern Christian Leadership Conference—and was considered by many to be the spiritual leader of the movement.

In 1964, CORE, the Student Nonviolent Coordinating Committee (SNCC), and the NAACP organized its Freedom Summer campaign. The primary objective was to end the political disenfranchisement of African Americans in the Deep South. Volunteers from these three groups concentrated efforts in Mississippi, where, in 1962, only 6.7 percent of African Americans in the state were registered to vote, the lowest percentage in the country. This activism included the formation of the Mississippi Freedom Democratic Party (MFDP). CORE, along with SNCC and NAACP, also established 30 Freedom Schools in towns throughout Mississippi. Volunteers taught in the schools, and the curriculum now included black history and the philosophy of the civil rights movement. During the summer of 1964, more than 3,000 students attended these schools, and the experiment provided a model for future educational programs such as Head Start.

White mobs frequently targeted the Freedom Schools but also attacked the homes of local African Americans involved in the campaign. During the summer months, 30 black homes and 37 black churches were bombed, and more than 80 volunteers were beaten by white mobs or racist police officers. In addition, the murder of three voting rights workers—James Chaney, Andrew Goodman, and Michael Schwerner—by the Ku Klux Klan on June 21, 1964, created nationwide publicity for the Freedom Summer campaign.

The year 1963 ushered in a new philosophy in the civil rights movement: "Freedom Now!" For many activists within CORE, the achievements won between 1960 and 1963 brought only token success. This new philosophy brought organizations like CORE into more substantial debates with the NAACP and Urban League, which were devoting much of their resources to ending segregation in public spaces and less attention to economic freedom. Nowhere was this more important than in the 1963 March on Washington. In the initial planning of the march, CORE was approached by A. Philip Randolph to cosponsor the event. As the event grew and more organizations agreed to participate, however, the original impetus of the march—jobs—became a secondary focus behind the passage of the 1964 Civil

Rights Act. Moreover, the NAACP, the Urban League, and the Southern Christian Leadership Conference (SCLC) openly argued against militant direct action or sit-ins in exchange for CORE's participation. This conflict accentuated an already contentious relationship between CORE and these other groups over such issues as membership, funding, and prestige.

By 1964, civil rights activists found it increasingly difficult to coordinate activities with other groups. For CORE, this cooperation was made more difficult, as the organization developed a more militant critique of the Vietnam War and promoted Black Nationalism. This conflict gained growing momentum within CORE when Floyd McKissick succeeded James Farmer in 1966. McKissick's ascension marked a shift from an adherence to Gandhian principles of nonviolent direct action to a philosophy of Black Nationalism.

CORE's nationalist shift was modeled on that of other groups of the period, particularly SNCC. For CORE, this position not only was a marked departure from the group's origins, but it also alienated white members and financial support. Although during McKissick's tenure, whites were not expelled from the organization, during the 1967 CORE convention, McKissick's opponents within the group demanded the dismissal of all white members from the organization. In 1968, Roy Innis became national director, and the transition of CORE into a Black Nationalist body was complete. White financial support virtually disappeared, and CORE found itself at the brink of bankruptcy.

After 1968, political developments within the organization caused CORE to create a more politically conservative platform. For example, CORE supported the presidential candidacy of Richard Nixon in 1968 and 1972. More recently, CORE commented on same-sex marriage and black health, calling the issue not something that is a civil right, but a human one. Moreover, COREcares, an HIV/AIDS advocacy, education, and prevention program for black women, was dismantled; and Innis remained on the board of Project 21, a conservative public policy group that provides broadcasters and the print media with prominent African American conservative commentators as columnists and guests. At the time of this writing, the organization referred to itself as "The National Leadership Network of Black Conservatives."

Lionel Kimble Jr.

Further Reading

Farmer, James L. *Freedom, When?* New York: Random House, 1966.

Farmer, James L. *Lay Bare the Heart: An Autobiography.* New York: Arbor House, 1985.

Meier, August, and Elliott Rudwick. *Core: A Study in the Civil Rights Movement, 1942–1968.* Urbana: University of Illinois Press, 1975.

Noble, Phil. *Beyond the Burning Bus: The Civil Rights Revolution in a Southern Town.* Montgomery, AL: New South Books, 2003.

Rachal, John R. " 'The Long, Hot Summer': The Mississippi Response to Freedom Summer, 1964." *Journal of Negro History* 84, no. 4 (1999): 315–39.

Council of Federated Organizations

The Council of Federated Organizations (COFO) was a coalition of national and regional organizations engaged in civil rights activities in Mississippi. Established in 1962 with the goal of maximizing the efforts of the Student Nonviolent Coordinating Committee (SNCC), the Congress of Racial Equality, and the National Association for the Advancement of Colored People (NAACP), the organization focused on voter registration and education.

Under the leadership of SNCC activist Robert Moses, and staffed primarily by SNCC activists, COFO launched the Mississippi Freedom Summer Project in 1964. In describing the difficulties faced by COFO and Freedom Summer workers, Martin Luther King Jr. said: "Our nation sent out Peace Corps Volunteers throughout the under-developed nations of the world and none of them experienced the kind of brutality and savagery that these voter registration workers have suffered here in Mississippi."

One of COFO's first efforts in Mississippi was the fall 1963 Freedom Vote, a mock election for Mississippi governor and lieutenant governor held to protest the mass disenfranchisement of black citizens in the state. COFO sought to demonstrate that without discriminatory registration procedures and fear of white reprisals, blacks would vote in large numbers. With the help of northern students, more than 80,000 ballots were cast for COFO president and NAACP state president Aaron Henry and Minister Edwin King. This success led to COFO's organization of the Mississippi Freedom Summer project, which brought hundreds of northern white college students to the state to assist COFO. The project opened on a tragic note when three civil rights workers, James Chaney, Michael Schwerner, and Andrew Goodman, disappeared in late June 1964. When they were found murdered in early August, Martin Luther King, Jr. called the killings "an attack on the very concept of a democratic society." Confronting ongoing violence and harassment, Freedom Summer volunteers canvassed neighborhoods, registered voters, developed public health programs, and taught literacy and civics in "Freedom Schools."

Freedom Summer included the formation of the Mississippi Freedom Democratic Party (MFDP), an interracial political party that challenged the all-white official state delegation at the 1964 Democratic National Convention in Atlantic City, New Jersey. COFO hoped to generate national party pressure to change state election practices but garnered little support from national officials of the Democratic Party. President Lyndon B. Johnson approved offering the MFDP a compromise of two seats as at-large delegates, which MFDP rejected.

Conflicts over the rejection of Johnson's compromise increased existing tensions among COFO's member organizations. Most of the summer's volunteers returned to college in the fall, and COFO director Moses resigned at the end of 1964. Weakened by substantial losses in its leadership, workforce, and funding, COFO disbanded in 1965.

Clayborne Carson

Further Reading

Bankston, Carl L. *Racial and Ethnic Relations in America*. Vol. 1. Pasadena, CA: Salem Press, 2000.

Carson, Clayborne. *In Struggle: SNCC and the Black Awakening of the 1960s*. Cambridge, MA: Harvard University Press, 1981.

King, Martin Luther, Jr. "Statement in Support of Mississippi Freedom Democratic Party." July 22, 1964. Martin Luther King, Jr. Papers, 1950–1968, Martin Luther King, Jr. Center for Nonviolent Social Change, Atlanta, Georgia.

King, Martin Luther, Jr. "Statement on the Deaths of Michael Henry Schwerner, Andrew Goodman, and James Earl Chaney." August 4, 1964. Martin Luther King, Jr. Papers, 1950–1968, Martin Luther King, Jr. Center for Nonviolent Social Change, Atlanta, Georgia.

McAdam, Doug. *Freedom Summer*. New York: Oxford University Press, 1988.

D

Davis, Angela

Angela Davis is a well-known lecturer, writer, academic, former member of the Communist Party, and political activist who advocates for the abolishment of the prison-industrial complex. She is a major icon of the Black Power era. In the early 1970s, Davis became a cause célèbre as a result of her radical political affiliations and activism.

Angela Yvonne Davis was born on January 26, 1944, to B. Frank and Sallye E. Davis in Birmingham, Alabama. Her parents were schoolteachers, but her father became an automobile mechanic to earn more money and bought a gas station. He was thus able to provide a comfortable lifestyle for his family in a middle-class neighborhood. It had been zoned for whites and was eventually referred to as Dynamite Hill because the Ku Klux Klan frequently bombed it. Davis's mother taught her to read, write, and do arithmetic before the first grade, and Davis took dance, piano, and clarinet lessons.

Davis had ample opportunity to observe the interplay and impact of classism, sexism, and racism as a child. Her maternal grandmother instilled in her a sense of outrage over slavery, and her activist parents instilled an appreciation for humanity and a desire for a more humane society. In college, her parents were members of the Southern Negro Youth Congress, a civil rights organization. In 1931, they participated in the campaign to free the nine teenage boys in the Scottsboro Boys Case, who were wrongly sentenced to the electric chair for the rape of two white girls. Davis developed a lift-up-the-race mentality. In elementary school, Davis attended civil rights demonstrations with her mother. In high school, she helped to organize interracial study groups that were disbanded by the police.

Davis often spent summers in Manhattan while her mother worked toward a master's degree at New York University. At age 15, Davis earned a scholarship from the American Friends Service Committee to attend the Elizabeth Irwin High School, a progressive private school in Greenwich Village. Many teachers there were banned from working in the public schools because of their radical political ideology. During this time, Davis was introduced to socialist ideology and joined the Marxist-Leninist group Advance. This school was more challenging than Parker High School in Birmingham, where Davis was an A student. She had to struggle to achieve the same grade point average. She lived with the family of William Howard Melish, an Episcopalian minister. In 1961, Davis graduated and enrolled at Brandeis University in Waltham, Massachusetts, on a scholarship.

Davis was an excellent student, majoring in French literature. Her junior year was spent at the Sorbonne in Paris, where she met Algerian students who were involved in the struggle against French colonialism. Their interpretations of discrimination in their homeland and the 1963 Birmingham church bombing killing of four girls whom Davis knew enhanced her commitment to social change. In her senior year, she studied under the philosopher Herbert Marcuse. His analysis of modern Western industrial society and suggestion that individuals were responsible for resisting and rebelling against the oppression of capitalism impressed her. Davis wrote in *Angela Davis: An Autobiography* (1974) that she was particularly impressed with the idea that emancipation of the proletariat would set the foundation for the freedom of all oppressed groups in society.

Davis graduated magna cum laude from Brandeis with Phi Beta Kappa membership in 1965. Until 1967, she attended graduate school at the Institute for Social Research at the Johan Wolfgang von Goethe University in Frankfurt, West Germany. This was the most prestigious center for the study of Marxism and German idealism. Philosophy professors Oskar Negt and Theodor Adorno were impressed with her scholarship, and Davis spoke both French and German. In Frankfurt, she became a member of a socialist student group that opposed the Vietnam War.

In 1967, Davis returned to the United States to complete her master's degree and study again under Marcuse, now at the University of California at San Diego. She joined several organizations, among them Maulana Karenga's group called "US," the Black Panther Party, and the Student Nonviolent Coordinating Committee (SNCC), and resumed her participation in the civil rights movement. That same year, she attended an "Economics and the Community" workshop sponsored by SNCC. There she met Franklin Alexander and his wife, Kendra, who were active in SNCC, the Black Panthers, and the Communist Party.

Alexander's sister Charlene was the leader of the Che-Lumumba Club, an all-black collective of the Communist Party of Southern California. This organization was focused on the third world. In 1969, Davis moved to Los Angeles and joined Che-Lumumba because she was disappointed with the sexism in SNCC, the Black Panthers, and US. In 1969, Davis earned her master's degree, made a pilgrimage to communist Cuba, and was hired by the University of California at Los Angeles (UCLA) as an assistant professor of philosophy. She taught courses in literature, philosophy, and political theory. A graduate student in anthropology and a paid FBI informer published a letter in the UCLA *Daily Bruin* announcing that there was a communist on the faculty. A *San Francisco Examiner* article named Davis as the communist.

At the insistence of Governor Ronald Reagan, the university regents fired Davis, even though she had strong support at the university. Davis challenged the dismissal in court and was reinstated because of violation of her constitutional right to teach regardless of political affiliation. The UCLA administration continued to monitor her courses; students rated the instruction as excellent and unbiased. In 1970, the board refused to renew her contract because of her inflammatory speeches in the community and because she had not completed her doctorate.

Davis had become active in the cause of the so-called Soledad Brothers, prisoners who had been treated harshly because they organized a Marxist group among the inmates at Soledad State Prison in Soledad, California. She delivered speeches and led demonstrations calling for their parole. On January 13, 1970, 15 militant black and racist white inmates started fighting on the exercise yard. A guard killed one white and three black convicts to stop the fight. The district attorney ruled the action justifiable homicide, and the grand jury confirmed this verdict. On that same day, another guard was beaten and thrown over a railing, falling to his death. All 137 convicts in the wing where the murder occurred were confined to their cells. The prison authorities assumed that only the militants could have organized the killing and blamed the Soledad Brothers. Because of Davis's defense of the Soledad Brothers, she received anonymous death threats. She purchased several weapons and secured them in the Che-Lumumba Club headquarters. A brother of one of the Soledad Brothers became her bodyguard.

On August 7, 1970, Davis's bodyguard, Jonathan Jackson, used these weapons to rescue James McClain, who was on trial for assaulting a San Quentin prison guard, from California's Marin County Courthouse. Jackson, McClain, and two inmate witnesses took hostages: three jurors, Assistant District Attorney Gary Thomas, and Judge Harold Harley. Jackson intended to trade the hostages for the Soledad Brothers. The effort was stymied by a barrage of shooting by the San Quentin guards, in defiance of the sheriff's instructions not to shoot. The judge, two prisoners, and Jackson were killed. A federal warrant was issued for Davis because the weapons were registered in her name. She fled rather than surrender to the authorities.

The state of California charged Davis with kidnapping, conspiracy, and murder; the Federal Bureau of Investigation placed her on the "Ten Most Wanted Fugitives" list and undertook a massive two-month search for her. She was arrested in New York, extradited to California, and placed in jail without bail. An international "Free Angela" movement ensued. On February 23, 1972, a judge released Davis on $102,000 bail, which was paid by singer Aretha Franklin. The subsequent trial received worldwide attention. Acting as cocounsel, Davis explained that she had been involved in the liberation struggle of minority groups, in the opposition to the Vietnam War, in the fight to raise the status of women, and in the defense of academic freedom. She went underground because of fear. Her chief counsel, Howard Moore, an Atlantan who defended the Black Power leaders H. Rap Brown and Stokely Carmichael, argued that there was insufficient evidence to prove Davis was part of the murder plans, as she was not at the scene. Her defense committee was renamed the National Alliance against Racism and Political Repression. Davis was acquitted of all charges.

Davis remained politically active. She delivered speeches on behalf of the National Alliance against Racism and Political Oppression and led demonstrations on numerous issues over the years. Ronald Reagan and the California State Board of Regents voted in 1972 that she would never teach at a state-supported university because of her militant activities. However, Davis went on to teach at a number of California universities. In 1980 and 1984, she ran for vice president of the United States on the Communist Party ticket.

Davis's several books include *Women, Race, and Class* (1983), *The Angela Y. Davis Reader* (1998), and *Are Prisons Obsolete?* (2003). She has continued to speak out on all forms of oppression and against racism and classism in the criminal justice system. She became professor emerita of History of Consciousness and Feminist Studies at the University of California, Santa Cruz.

Marva Strickland-Hill

Further Reading

Aptheker, Bettina. *The Morning Breaks: The Trial of Angela Davis.* Ithaca, NY: Cornell University Press, 1999.

Davis, Angela Y. *Angela Davis: An Autobiography.* New York: Random House, 1974.

Nadelson, Reggie. *Who Is Angela Davis? The Biography of a Revolutionary.* New York: P. H. Wyden, 1972.

Perkins, Margo V. *Autobiography as Activism: Three Black Women of the Sixties.* Jackson: University Press of Mississippi, 2000.

Deacons for Defense and Justice

The Deacons for Defense and Justice (DDJ) was an African American self-defense organization that protected civil rights activists against racist terrorism during the mid-1960s. The history of the Deacons began in the small town of Jonesboro, Louisiana. In June 1964, organizers of the Congress of Racial Equality (CORE) and local African American activists launched nonviolent protest campaigns and voter registration drives to challenge the town's tradition of white supremacy. When white residents and the area's Ku Klux Klan (KKK) responded with a wave of violence and intimidation, a group of armed black men began to guard the CORE office against white attacks. Although Jonesboro's police department deputized five African American men, ostensibly to provide more security, the new police officers could do little to stop white violence. When Klansmen staged a nightly parade through Jonesboro's African American neighborhood in late July 1964, members of the informal protective squad decided to establish an official defense unit to halt the Klan's terrorism. This organization came to be known as the DDJ.

In the following months, the DDJ evolved into a highly sophisticated and disciplined protection agency. The Deacons consisted mostly of working-class military veterans who had to conform to strict membership criteria. The organization's president, a stockroom worker named Percy Lee Bradford, and cofounder Earnest Thomas, a mill worker and handyman, accepted only American citizens who were at least 21 years old. They preferred married men and registered voters. Applicants who had a reputation for being hot-tempered were quickly rejected. In this strictly defensive spirit, the new organization continued to guard the CORE headquarters and began to patrol the African American neighborhood with rifles and shotguns. Armed men also guarded civil rights meetings and provided escorts for white and black activists who were canvassing in the dangerous areas of the surrounding Jackson parish. Walkie-talkies facilitated the coordination of guard duties. When Jonesboro's police department disbanded the group of black deputies in October 1964, the Deacons remained the only protection against white violence. Ultimately, the DDJ's activities put an end to Klan intimidation in Jonesboro and effectively stemmed the tide of white harassment.

The formation of another Deacons chapter in Bogalusa, Louisiana, marked the beginning of the defense unit's rise to national fame and notoriety. Located 60 miles north of New Orleans, the city was a stronghold of the Ku Klux Klan. As in Jonesboro, segregationists resorted to violent terror when, in January 1965, local African Americans sought the assistance of CORE to challenge Jim Crow. In February, the necessity of protecting the African American community and CORE's field workers from KKK violence prompted several men to organize a DDJ branch in Bogalusa. The Jonesboro Deacons assisted in the formation and, after receiving a charter from the state of Louisiana in March 1965, granted the new branch an official certificate of affiliation. Although protection was the key rationale behind its activities, the defense group also became an enormous source of pride among black activists. Defying the southern myth of the submissive and contented "Negro," the Deacons powerfully asserted African American dignity and their legitimate claim to the rights of American citizenship. Its members considered their armed actions an important affirmation of African American manhood.

In April 1965, when a new round of nonviolent demonstrations exacerbated racial tensions in Bogalusa, a shootout between Klansmen and a group of Deacons catapulted the defense squad into the national spotlight. By that time, the Federal Bureau of Investigation (FBI) had launched a large-scale investigation into the activities of the defense squad. Although FBI agents and white journalists tended to regard the militant group as the harbinger of racial warfare, the Bogalusa Deacons worked side by side with CORE, complementing its nonviolent protest campaigns and ultimately enhancing its effectiveness in Bogalusa. In part, white concerns stemmed from the defense unit's strategy to exaggerate its actual strength to deter white terrorists. Media accounts put the Deacons' membership at several thousand in 59 chapters across the South, but the real number of members was never larger than several hundred, and the Deacons established only three official chapters in Louisiana. Despite its hyperbole, the Deacons did have expansionist ambitions and inspired the formation of loosely affiliated groups in 14 southern and four northern cities. Amidst the media frenzy about the defense unit, CORE was hard-pressed to justify its alliance with the Deacons. CORE's leadership accepted self-defense but reassured the concerned media of the organization's unwavering commitment to nonviolence.

By 1968, however, as segregation and disenfranchisement were on the wane and state and local authorities in the South finally appeared to take seriously their responsibility to protect civil rights protest, African American self-defense groups such as the Deacons had outlived their usefulness. Until the summer of 1967, the Bogalusa Deacons continued to patrol the city's black neighborhood and guarded a last round of nonviolent demonstrations. By November 1967, the Bogalusa Deacons no longer held official meetings. Four months later, the FBI ascertained that the Deacons and affiliated chapters had ceased their activities.

Simon Wendt

Further Reading

Hill, Lance E. *The Deacons for Defense: Armed Resistance and the Civil Rights Movement.* Chapel Hill: University of North Carolina Press, 2004.

Honigsberg, Peter Jan. *Crossing Border Street: A Civil Rights Memoir.* Berkeley: University of California Press, 2000.

Wendt, Simon. " 'Urge People *Not* to Carry Guns': Armed Self-Defense in the Louisiana Civil Rights Movement and the Radicalization of the Congress of Racial Equality." *Louisiana History* 45, no. 3 (Summer 2004): 261–86.

Du Bois, W. E. B.

Dr. William Edward Burghardt Du Bois (1868–1963) was a scholar, civil rights activist, editor, and novelist. Born February 23, 1868, to Alfred Du Bois and Mary Silvina Burghardt, Du Bois grew up in Great Barrington, Massachusetts, where less than 1 percent of the predominantly Dutch and English population was of African descent. After graduating from high school, Du Bois earned an AB from Fisk University and a BA in philosophy and an MA in history from Harvard University. In 1892, he continued graduate studies at the University of Berlin, Germany, as a Slater Fund fellow. He returned to the United States in 1894 and taught classes at Wilberforce University. In 1895, Du Bois became the first African American to receive a doctorate from Harvard. During the next 65 years, he was a professor of history, economics, and sociology at the University of Pennsylvania and Atlanta University, a leader of the NAACP, and an advocate of peace and civil rights. He also wrote two novels, edited several periodicals, and received numerous awards and honorary degrees. He died in 1963 as a citizen of Ghana.

Analyses of race and racism were prominent themes throughout Du Bois's career and were shaped by his education, worldwide travels, and experiences of the effects on African Americans of race riots, lynching, war, imperialism, and capitalism. His evolving racial consciousness impacted the scholarship he produced and the professional and political activities in which he participated. Du Bois made significant contributions to African American and American history, culture, politics, and scholarship. He developed ways to understand African Americans' racial identity, established the field of sociology, elucidated the historical significance of race, and fought internationally for freedom, equality, and peace.

Du Bois's most famous scholarly contributions were his interpretations of African American racial identity. In *The Souls of Black Folk*, published in 1903, Du Bois described African Americans' spirituality and history from 1861 to the early twentieth century to explain the peculiar character of their identity as a race. He identified this race identity as "double consciousness," or the simultaneous presence in African Americans' minds of two conflicting "souls"—a longing to be a part of mainstream American society coupled with an equally strong feeling of kinship with African and African American culture. In this book, he discussed how double consciousness colored African Americans' contributions to American labor, music, economics, and religion. As a continuation of *The Souls of Black Folk*, Du Bois wrote *Darkwater*—a mixture of poetry, autobiography, and prose published in 1920—in which he described the effects of racism, imperialism, economic greed, sexism, and war on African Americans' racial identity.

Du Bois also contributed to academic research through pioneer sociological studies. In *The Philadelphia Negro*, he examined the economic and health statistics, education, and social experiences of black Americans in Philadelphia in the late 1890s. From 1897 to 1911, Du Bois directed the Atlanta University Studies of the Negro Problem, the only scientific social studies of aspects of African American life and culture in the world during the late nineteenth and early twentieth centuries. During the 1940s, he founded and edited *Phylon*, a journal published by Atlanta University that interpreted racial and cultural issues from the perspectives of the social sciences.

Du Bois made major contributions to historiography by interpreting American history through the lens of race relations, particularly as pertained to Africans and African Americans. Du Bois's historiography challenged historians' refusal to acknowledge facts regarding the significance of Africans' achievements and struggles in America and the world. *The Suppression of the African Slave-Trade*, published in 1896, and *Black Reconstruction in America, 1860–1880*, published in 1935, clarified and scrutinized two misconstrued and overlooked epochs in

American history. *The World and Africa*, published in 1947, expanded the work of the aforementioned publications to a global scale, emphasizing Africans' crucial roles in the history of humankind from prehistoric times through modernity.

By editing mass-circulated publications, Du Bois extended his scholarship into African American communities. He created the NAACP's official monthly news magazine, the *Crisis*, and edited it from 1910 to 1934. In the early 1920s, Du Bois founded and edited *Brownie's Book*, a magazine for African American children containing visual images and literature.

Civil rights activism was integral to Du Bois's life. In 1905, he established the Niagara Movement to organize black intellectuals committed to black freedom. In 1909, he helped found the NAACP, a civil rights organization consisting of black and white liberals of various professions. On behalf of the NAACP, Du Bois investigated black American troops' experiences of racism in Europe during World War I and presented to the United Nations *An Appeal to the World*, denouncing American segregation.

Ultimately, Du Bois epitomized his idea of the "talented tenth" and was one of the earliest practitioners of American studies and Africana studies. As a member of the talented tenth, or the top 10 percent of African Americans responsible for training and serving the masses of black communities, Du Bois devoted his professional career, scholarship, and political activism to the causes of racial uplift and equality. Decades before the establishment of an American studies discipline, Du Bois conducted interdisciplinary research to illuminate various aspects of American culture. He incorporated physiology, psychology, sociology, economics, history, and philosophy into analyses of the significance of race in America. Du Bois's interpretations of the experiences of members of the African diaspora created ways to understand black American identity and culture that remain among the premier scholarship of Africana studies.

Kimberly M. Curtis

Further Reading

Bruce, Dickson D., Jr. "W. E. B. Du Bois and the Idea of Double Consciousness." *American Literature* 64 (June 1992): 299–309.

Du Bois, W. E. B. *The Autobiography of W. E. B. Du Bois*. New York: International Publishers, 1968.

Du Bois, W. E. B. *The Souls of Black Folk*. New York: Penguin Books, 1996.

Lewis, David Levering. *W. E. B. Du Bois: Biography of a Race, 1868–1919*. New York: Henry Holt, 1993.

Lewis, David Levering. *W. E. B. Du Bois: The Fight for Equality and the American Century, 1919–1963*. New York: Henry Holt, 2000.

E

Evers, Medgar

Medgar Evers was a prominent Mississippi civil rights leader who pushed for black equality without confrontation. Assassinated in June 1963, at the age of 37, Evers became a national hero for African Americans across the United States.

Medgar Wiley Evers was born on July 2, 1925, in Decatur, Mississippi. He was born into a typical southern farming family. His father James and his mother Jessie raised him and his six brothers and sisters to be proud, self-sufficient, and hardworking. Throughout his younger years, Evers was taught the importance of education. Although most southern farming families took their children out of school during the harvesting season, Evers's parents did not. In 1942, Evers dropped out of Newton High School to join the army. After spending a few years in the service, he returned to Newton in 1947 to complete his high school degree. During the same year, Evers successfully voted in the local county election. He had attempted to vote the year before, but was blocked because of white opposition.

After completing high school, Evers enrolled in Alcorn State University, one of only two black universities in Mississippi. Although many African Americans chose a path to the teaching profession, Evers decided to take a different and more radical route, as a business major. At Alcorn, Medgar met his future wife, Myrlie Beasley. On Christmas Eve 1951, the two married. The next year, Evers graduated from Alcorn. He was instantly hired by a newly created black business—Magnolia Mutual Insurance Company.

While employed by the insurance company, Evers spent most of his time visiting poor black sharecroppers and other southern black families in an attempt to sell them insurance. Evans always defied the white power structure, but it was not until his experience with the poor blacks of Mississippi that he became more directly involved in the civil rights struggles of southern blacks. Seeing the dreadful conditions of many of these poor southern blacks, Evers joined the National Association for the Advancement of Colored People (NAACP). The NAACP, founded in 1909, was one of the most prominent civil rights organizations in the country. The NAACP, however, did not have a Mississippi branch. Evers's efforts changed this. By 1953, the NAACP had 21 branches in Mississippi.

Mississippi was a rigidly segregated southern state. Even after the 1954 *Brown v. Board of Education* decision, in which the U.S. Supreme Court ruled school segregation unconstitutional, segregation remained in Mississippi. To test the

Brown decision, Evers applied to the University of Mississippi Law School, but was denied admission on the basis of his race. Evers fought for admission but was unsuccessful, and the university remained segregated. Despite this setback, the NAACP, impressed with Evers's actions, awarded him the newly created position of field secretary for the state of Mississippi. In this position, Evers became the national NAACP's representative for the state of Mississippi.

On behalf of the NAACP, Evers worked emphatically to educate blacks and helped them to register to vote. When segregation continued to run rampant in Mississippi, Evers encouraged blacks to patronize only black-owned businesses. This angered many whites throughout the state. In 1962, James Meredith applied to the University of Mississippi Law School. Meredith was originally denied admittance, but he continued to fight the racial ban—with the support of Evers and the NAACP—and Meredith was awarded admission in September, a privilege denied to Evers eight years earlier.

Evers's leadership position with the NAACP and his support of black equality decreased his standing within the state's white community. Whites in Mississippi were becoming more and more hostile to him. In May 1963, Evers's home was firebombed. Evers was at a nearby church when the firebombing occurred, but his wife Myrlie and their three children, Darrell, Rena, and Van, were at home. The firebombing was deemed an assassination attempt on Evers's life. Nevertheless, he continued in his civil rights efforts. The next month, on June 12, 1963, Medgar Evers was shot in front of his home after returning home from a civil rights rally. He died within the hour.

More than 4,000 people came to Evers's funeral to honor and remember the activist, who died for the civil rights battles he fought. He was buried at Arlington National Cemetery in Virginia. Eleven days after Evers's assassination, Byron de la Beckwith was arrested and charged with Evers's murder. Beckwith was tried twice by all-white juries and both cases ended in mistrial. Despite strong evidence incriminating Beckwith, neither jury could unanimously decide Beckwith's guilt or innocence. The case was dropped and Beckwith was released. Decades later, in 1989, evidence surfaced indicating that the juries of the first two trials were tampered with. Consequently, in February 1994, a third trial was held with a biracial jury. This time Beckwith was found guilty of the murder of Medgar Evers.

Evers may not have lived to see the civil rights advances for which he had long fought, but he played a major role in bringing them to fruition. His untimely death increased support for the civil rights movement. Furthermore, as one of the first martyrs of the cause, his death angered many blacks in the South. No longer would African Americans be afraid to stand up against their white counterparts. Instead, many blacks decided to stand up against their opposition and demand equality. On July 2, 1964, the Civil Rights Act of 1964 was passed. Similarly, in August 1965, the Voting Rights Act of 1965 was passed. With these two acts,

Evers's battle had been won. Blacks in Mississippi and across the nation were legally awarded the civil rights for which they had long fought.

Mindy R. Weidman

Further Reading

Brown, Jennie. *Medgar Evers.* Los Angeles: Melrose Square Publishing, 1994.

Nossiter, Adam. *Of Long Memory: Mississippi and the Murder of Medgar Evers.* Reading, MA: Addison-Wesley, 1994.

F

Farrakhan, Louis

Louis Farrakhan was the principal architect of the Million Man March and is the current leader of the African American religious organization, the Nation of Islam (NOI). While at the center of various controversial public statements and stances, Farrakhan has been a prominent leader in the African American community and a key figure in public debates regarding polemic African American issues.

Farrakhan was born Louis Eugene Walcott on May 11, 1933, in Bronx, New York. His mother raised him in Roxbury, Massachusetts. He adopted the surname Farrakhan after his conversion to Islam. In his youth, Farrakhan's greatest ambition was to attend New York's Juilliard School of Music. Although he was a talented singer, he was denied admission to the prestigious institution. As an alternative, he enrolled at a teachers college for African Americans located in Winston-Salem, North Carolina. Within a few years, he withdrew from the college and became a calypso singer in a Boston nightclub. He was nicknamed "The Charmer."

Throughout the earlier part of his life, Farrakhan was a devout member of the Episcopal Church. In 1955, however, having grown disillusioned with the presumed hatred that white Christians showed toward black Christians, he severed his church affiliation. Frustrated with the racial inequality that persisted throughout the United States during this period, Farrakhan began seeking an alternative religious and spiritual outlet. During the early twentieth century, many African Americans began aligning themselves with the Black Nationalist movement. The movement was chiefly designed to eradicate the "race problem" of the twentieth century. Some Black Nationalists, including members of NOI, purported that abolition of white supremacy would include the defrayal of a separate space whereby African Americans could control their economic, social, and political fate through "external emigration" (colonization) to Africa or by disconnecting from the white masses in the United States. Farrakhan's initial reaction to the Black Nationalist agenda, and specifically NOI, was one of disinterest.

At first glance, Farrakhan regarded the NOI as a peculiar and undesirable resolve to his animosity for the prejudice and discrimination persistent in American Christianity. On meeting Malcolm X, then NOI spokesperson and influential religious leader, in 1955, however, his feelings changed. Farrakhan was immediately drawn to Malcolm X's rhetorical abilities and within a short time, he enlisted in the NOI. Malcolm X began to train minister Farrakhan and, after Malcolm X's assassination in 1965, Farrakhan ascended as the NOI's primary representative and became minister of New York's Temple Number Seven where Malcolm X preached.

After the death of Elijah Muhammad, the original leader of the NOI from 1934 to 1975, the organization fell to the leadership of his son, Wallace Muhammad. Wallace Muhammad was a Sunni Muslim who sought to integrate the organization with orthodox Islamic values. To revitalize and reform the original precepts of the NOI, and to refurbish the socialization process that the organization was noted for, Farrakhan broke away from Muhammad's "new nation" in 1978. He subsequently began establishing another branch of the NOI modeled after the teachings of Elijah Muhammad and Farad Muhammad, the original founder of the NOI. Elijah Muhammad had been trained by Farad Muhammad who believed that African Americans were the original members of the Tribe of Shabazz, wrongfully exploited and enslaved in the United States. Farad is revered by NOI members as a prophet sent by God to teach African Americans a thorough and "true" knowledge of themselves and God.

With the NOI physically and ideologically splintered, Farrakhan assumed the arduous task of attempting to rebuild the NOI as it existed before the break. He successfully secured a large following and gained the interest of members of the African American community, just as his predecessors had attempted to do. Throughout his career, he has enjoyed monumental successes. His newspaper, *The Final Call*, was established in 1979 and modeled after Elijah Muhammad's *Muhammad Speaks*. The newspaper has a circulation of more than 500,000 per edition. Farrakhan has participated in numerous political, religious, and civic organizations and has become an international voice to promote peace and enfranchisement for marginalized groups in the United States and abroad. The building of the Salaam restaurant in Chicago in 1995 and the expansion of Muhammad Farms, a black-owned independent agricultural system, are also included among his achievements.

Farrakhan continued to add to his achievements, most notably the 1995 Million Man March. The march represented one of the largest assemblies of African Americans in U.S. history. It was designed to inspire African American men about atonement, reconciliation, hard work, and responsibility, bringing them together to make solemn oaths to be better husbands, fathers, sons, and citizens. After the march, there was a tremendous increase in voter registration among African Americans as well as in church and mosque memberships. In 2000, Farrakhan organized the Million Family March to fulfill similar objectives as the Million Man March and to bring African American families together. However, both marches were intended to be different from the civil rights demonstrations of the 1950s. NOI officials purposefully designed the marches to focus on African Americans helping themselves without interracial cooperation.

Much like Elijah Muhammad, Farrakhan is considered one of the most controversial African American religious leaders to date. Holding fast to the tenets of

Black Nationalism, much of Farrakhan's vision is geared toward racial solidarity, uplift, and self-efficacy. He is often scrutinized for his radical beliefs and charged with being anti-Semitic by his critics due to polemic statements made in the national press or public appearances.

Talitha L. LeFlouria

Further Reading

Alexander, Amy, ed. *The Farrakhan Factor: African American Writers on Leadership, Nationhood, and Minister Louis Farrakhan.* New York: Grove Press, 1998.

Banks, William, Jr. *The Black Muslims.* Philadelphia: Chelsea House Publishers, 1997.

Gardell, Mattias. *In the Name of Elijah Muhammad: Louis Farrakhan and the Nation of Islam.* Durham, NC: Duke University Press, 1996.

Levinsohn, Florence Hamlish. *Looking for Farrakhan.* Chicago: Ivan R. Dee, 1997.

Van Deburg, William L., ed. *Modern Black Nationalism: From Marcus Garvey to Louis Farrakhan.* New York: New York University Press, 1997.

Faubus, Orval Eugene

Orval Faubus served as governor of Arkansas during the heated civil rights movement years and is best known for blocking the desegregation of Little Rock's Central High School, as mandated by the Supreme Court decision in *Brown v. Board of Education.* Orval Eugene Faubus was born on January 7, 1910, in Greasy Creek, Arkansas. A rural schoolteacher from 1928 to 1938, he then served as county recorder from 1939 to 1942 and acting postmaster from 1946 to 1947, and later postmaster during 1953–1954 for Huntsville, Arkansas, while owning and running a newspaper. From 1949 to 1953, he served as assistant to the governor and director of highways.

Faubus was elected governor of Arkansas and served from 1954 to 1967. He was generally considered a southern populist who supported New Deal policies. After he was elected governor, he named six black men to the Democratic State Committee. This led to a 1956 campaign charge that he was "soft" on racism by his opponent, former state senator Jim Johnson. Faubus had boasted that he had put African Americans on the Democratic State Committee and that his son was attending an integrated school.

According to federal judge J. Harvie Wilkinson III, Arkansas, "though opposed to integration, was not the Deep South." African Americans had attended the University of Arkansas, and by 1955, 10 school districts had school desegregation plans. Little Rock had not had racial troubles and had a progressive mayor, congressional representative, and newspaper.

By 1957, Faubus, known as urbane and a personable governor rather than as a "redneck," saw his political future, which included a third gubernatorial term, tied to stopping school desegregation. Thus, he precipitated a constitutional crisis by blocking the token school desegregation of Central High School in Little Rock, Arkansas, in 1957 by calling out the Arkansas National Guard to "prevent violence." The Guard proceeded to block the entrance of the nine black students (known as the Little Rock Nine) poised to enter and desegregate the school. He received much publicity for his antidesegregation efforts, including great national television exposure.

As a result of these actions, President Dwight D. Eisenhower ordered Faubus to remove the Arkansas Guard. Faubus did not comply, and Eisenhower was forced to send in 1,000 federal troops. The act of federal interference sparked a mob at the high school, which became hostile to any African Americans on the scene. Once they arrived, federalized National Guardsmen protected the nine black students that day and for the remainder of the school year from repeated violent acts.

After leaving office in 1967, Faubus worked as a bank clerk and ran three more times, unsuccessfully, for the governorship. He died on December 14, 1994, in Conway, Arkansas.

Jeffrey A. Raffel

Further Reading

Duram, James. *A Moderate among Extremists: Dwight D. Eisenhower and the School Desegregation Crisis.* Chicago: Nelson-Hall, 1981.

Raffel, Jeffrey A. *Historical Encyclopedia of School Segregation and Desegregation: The American Experience.* Westport, CT: Greenwood, 1998.

Wilkinson, J. Harvie, III. *From Brown to Bakke: The Supreme Court and School Integration, 1954–1978.* New York: Oxford University Press, 1979.

Forman, James

James Forman was an important African American leader in the civil rights movement. From 1961 to 1966, his charisma and skills as an organizer transformed the ragtag student organization—the Student Nonviolent Coordinating Committee (SNCC)—into a vibrant, potent force in the struggle for equal rights for black Americans. He was also an author of a number of books on the civil rights movement and the black experience in the United States. He remained a political activist and organizer throughout his life and still participated in demonstrations in the last year of his life at the age of 75.

Forman was born in Chicago on October 4, 1928. Until the age of six, he was cared for by his grandmother on a farm in Mississippi because of his parents' poverty. His family then brought him back to Chicago. He attended Chicago's Englewood High School and graduated with honors in 1947. He then joined the

U.S. Air Force, serving in Okinawa, during the Korean War. Upon his discharge, he studied at the University of Southern California. Unfortunately, in 1953 during his second semester at the university, he personally experienced police brutality. One late night, as he was leaving a study session at the university library, two Los Angeles police officers drove up, accused him of robberies in the area, and hauled him down to the downtown police station. There he was beaten. He was released three days later but did not recover from the experience; he suffered a mental breakdown, spent time at the Veteran's Hospital in Los Angeles, and then returned to his family in Chicago.

Forman continued his studies at Roosevelt University in Chicago and graduated in 1957. His aspiration was to be a writer or journalist. That year, he commenced graduate work in French literature at Boston University. However, the dramatic events of the Little Rock desegregation crisis grabbed Forman's attention, and in 1958, he secured a job with the black newspaper, the *Chicago Defender*, to report on the violent white resistance to school integration in Arkansas.

He began to search for opportunities to engage in civil rights activities in the South. Soon, after working as a substitute elementary school teacher, he found a position in Fayette County, Tennessee, not far from his childhood home with his grandmother. Seven hundred sharecropping farmers and families had been forced from their land and homes for having dared to register to vote. Forman worked among those evicted families in a program subsidized by the Congress of Racial Equality (CORE). He distributed food, registered voters, and also traveled to Chicago to draw attention to their suffering.

In the summer of 1961, Forman became involved with SNCC (pronounced "snick") after being held along with SNCC activists in a North Carolina jail for protesting segregation. Almost immediately, SNCC made Forman their executive secretary, a position he held from 1961 to 1966. Within a week of his arrival, he began systematizing and reforming SNCC's administration. As executive secretary, he expanded the staff, raised the funds necessary to keep the organization running, and managed much of the nitty-gritty administration of the organization. He organized the logistics for SNCC's direct action campaigns in Mississippi, Georgia, Alabama, and other southern states, ensuring that SNCC activists were fed and housed and raising the bail to get them out jail.

At the height of the civil rights movement, SNCC was one of the big four black organizations that pushed for social change—including CORE, National Association for the Advancement of Colored People (NAACP), and the Southern Christian Leadership Conference. As befitting its more youthful membership, SNCC tended to be the most radical organization, pushing the most aggressively for the end of racial terror and inequality in the South.

Beyond his role in support activities for the organization, Forman was in his own right an important leader and influenced the direction of SNCC. In 1961, as a respected elder, Forman proposed a solution to a disagreement within SNCC that threatened to tear apart the student organization. At the 1963 March on Washington, Forman was front and center in the negotiations with Martin Luther King Jr. to tone down the supposedly too-radical speech of SNCC leader John Lewis.

Forman's experiences in the movement radicalized him. He began to lose his faith that nonviolent tactics would gain blacks an equal place in American society. He stated, "accumulating experiences with Southern 'law and order' were turning me into a full-fledged revolutionary." But it was not just Forman and others being jailed, harassed, and beaten by southern police while they engaged in activities guaranteed by the U.S. Constitution; it was also the response of the federal government that radicalized him. In 1963, the Federal Bureau of Investigation (FBI) refused to protect the lives and safety of young black and also white activists from southern violence. FBI director J. Edgar Hoover declared, "We don't guard anybody. We are fact-finders. The FBI can't wet-nurse everybody who goes down and tries to reform or educate the Negroes in the South." In 1964, despite Forman's strenuous efforts, the Democratic Party refused to seat a black delegation representing Mississippi—the Mississippi Freedom Democratic Party—at the party's national convention, despite evidence that the regular Mississippi party delegation excluded all black participation.

In the fall of 1964, Forman and other SNCC leaders went to Guinea, Africa, and returned with a more radical ideology. Forman argued that African Americans should create Marxist communities, join with black peoples around the globe to defend against white attack, and develop a black cultural identity. He viewed African Americans as like Africans—as former colonial subjects adjusting to a new life of freedom.

Forman became increasingly militant. However, in 1966, SNCC replaced Forman and director Lewis as insufficiently radical. Under the leadership of Stokely Carmichael (Kwame Ture), SNCC embraced some of the ideals of the Black Power movement. This reflected, in part, the recognition that the movement's old tactics and goals would not meet the needs of poor blacks living in the North. In addition to dismantling the laws that discriminated against African Americans, there needed to be economic changes—indeed, a redistribution of such resources as wealth and jobs—before blacks could emerge from generations of enforced poverty and claim an equal place in American society.

Forman too in many ways embraced the ideas of the Black Power movement. In 1969, he was among the first to issue a call for "reparations" from whites to blacks to help repair the economic damages and psychological trauma suffered by generation upon generation of African Americans. On a Sunday morning at New York City's Riverside Church, he interrupted services to issue his "Black Manifesto." The manifesto called for $500 million in reparations from white churches and temples to pay for a detailed program aiming to increase black economic and cultural resources and autonomy. To back up his call for payments, Forman threatened demonstrations and disruptions.

Forman's later years were filled with efforts at reforming and bettering American society. He founded a nonprofit organization called Unemployment and Poverty Action Committee. In 1981, he launched a Washington, D.C., newspaper that lasted only briefly. He also started the Black American News Service, and he continued to write and publish. He was the author of a number of works on civil rights movements and the predicaments of blacks in America: *Sammy Younge, Jr.: The First Black College Student to Die in the Black Liberation Movement* (1968); *The Making of Black Revolutionaries* (1972); and *Self Determination: An Examination of the Question and Its Application to the African American People* (1980).

On January 11, 2005, Forman died after a long struggle with colon cancer.

ABC-CLIO

Further Reading

Carson, Clayborne. *In Struggle: SNCC and Black Awakenings of 1960.* Cambridge, MA: Harvard University Press, 1981.

Forman, James. *The Making of Black Revolutionaries: A Personal Account.* New York: Macmillan, 1972.

Greenberg, Cheryl Lynn. *A Circle of Trust: Remembering SNCC.* New Brunswick, NJ: Rutgers University Press, 1997.

Freedom Rides

The Congress of Racial Equality (CORE) organized the Freedom Rides as a bus journey through the South to test the enforcement of laws banning segregation. The Freedom Riders, an interracial group, decided to test specifically President John F. Kennedy's commitment to enforce two Supreme Court decisions banning segregated interstate travel by forcing Kennedy to take a public stand against segregation. To achieve their goal, the Freedom Riders would travel throughout the South, stopping at various bus stations, with white riders going into "colored only" areas and black riders going into "white only" areas. On May 4, 1961, two buses left Washington, D.C., en route to New Orleans. Their route would take them New Orleans in a little less than two weeks.

The Freedom Riders faced little resistance at the start of the trip compared to what they would face in the Deep South. From Atlanta, Georgia, to Birmingham, Alabama, the riders were met by violent white mobs. Outside of Anniston, Alabama, with riders still aboard, their bus was firebombed. As riders fled through the back of the bus, they were attacked by a white mob. Many were injured and several were left with permanent injuries, including white riders.

A second bus headed from Atlanta to Birmingham was also met with violence. On their way to Birmingham, the Freedom Riders hoped they would be protected

A bus carrying civil rights Freedom Riders is fire-bombed during a caravan to advocate black voting rights in 1961. The Freedom Riders were civil rights advocates, both black and white, who traveled to the South from the North on buses in 1961 as volunteers for the Congress of Racial Equality. (Library of Congress)

by local police or even the Federal Bureau of Investigation (FBI). However, the riders were unaware that the FBI knew of Ku Klux Klan activity in Birmingham and did nothing to prevent the violence. Furthermore, the local police had received the riders' itinerary ahead of time and passed it on to the Klan, knowing an attack would occur. A white mob was waiting for the riders and attacked them as they got off the bus. Several minutes later, the attackers dispersed and police appeared.

To prevent further violent incidents, the U.S. Justice Department flew the riders to New Orleans, as buses proved to be too dangerous. The Student Nonviolent Coordinating Committee (SNCC) decided to take over for CORE riders despite the immense risk of violence and even death. According to Stokely Carmichael, one of the Freedom Riders, SNCC felt "if the freedom rides were stopped because of violence, and only because of violence, then the nonviolent movement was over. We might as well disband SNCC. Our movement is over. Give the racist this victory and it sends the clear signal that at the first sign of resistance, all they have to do is mobilize massive violence, the movement will collapse and the government won't do a thing. We can't let that happen."

A new group of Freedom Riders left Nashville and headed to Birmingham, where they were arrested. They were then driven to the state line and dropped off, having to fend for themselves. After making their journey back to Nashville, they again decided to head back to Birmingham. Attorney General Robert F. Kennedy wanted assurances from Alabama that they would protect the riders; if Alabama would not make those assurances, the federal government would have to intervene. Robert Kennedy sent in his assistant, John Seigenthaler, to negotiate with state officials, and after intense discussions, Alabama officials decided they would provide protection. Thus, Alabama placed state police cars every 10–15 miles along the highway toward the state capital, Montgomery. In addition, a plane followed overhead and two officials from Greyhound Lines were on each bus. Despite the protection, about 40 miles outside of Montgomery, all protection disappeared. As the bus entered the Montgomery bus station, it was eerily quiet.

Without warning, whites rushed the bus with "sticks and bricks." The first to come off the bus was a white man, Jim Zwerg. The mob took him and severely beat him, allowing other riders to disembark the bus, going unnoticed. Riders and whites sympathetic to the riders were beaten, including Seigenthaler. Later that evening, Dr. Martin Luther King Jr. spoke at a local church when a white mob surrounded the church. Federal marshals had been sent in by Attorney General Kennedy, but Governor John Patterson declared martial law, and National Guardsmen were sent in to control rioters and help federal marshals.

On May 24, the Freedom Riders continued to Jackson, Mississippi, with adequate and constant protection. Once in Jackson, the riders were allowed to walk through the white sections of the bus station but were subsequently arrested for trespassing. The local court was not sympathetic to the Freedom Riders, and they were sentenced to 60 days in a maximum-security prison. Hundreds were arrested and sentenced as more Freedom Riders came into Jackson. Some riders, including Carmichael, spent more than a month in jail before having their bonds posted. Jail had halted the Freedom Riders, but their goals had been achieved.

Robert Kennedy petitioned the Interstate Commerce Commission to pass a regulation making segregation illegal in interstate travel. In September 1961, the commission complied, and the Freedom Riders had their victory. This victory was important not only because it showed what direct-action protest could achieve, but also because it signaled the importance of student organizations in the freedom movement.

Cristy Casado Tondeur

Further Reading

Carmichael, Stokely. *Ready for Revolution: The Life and Struggles of Stokely Carmichael.* New York: Scribner, 2003.

Carson, Clayborne, et al., eds. *Eyes on the Prize.* New York: Penguin Books, 1987.

Payne, Charles. *I've Got the Light of Freedom: The Organizing Tradition and the Mississippi Freedom Struggle.* Berkeley: University of California Press, 1995.

Freedom Schools

Freedom schools were created in 1964, during the Student Nonviolent Coordinating Committee's (SNCC) Mississippi Freedom Summer Project. One of SNCC's goals during this incredibly ambitious civil rights campaign was to create a homegrown movement among African American youths in Mississippi. To achieve this goal, SNCC organized more than 40 Freedom schools throughout the state, which ran from late June through mid-August, and was staffed by hundreds of volunteers who were mostly white, female college students.

A young African American SNCC worker named Charlie Cobb initially proposed the Freedom school idea in November 1963. When observing black Mississippi schools, Cobb noticed that there was a complete absence of academic freedom. African American students in Mississippi were not allowed to openly discuss the situation facing them, despite how poverty-stricken and disenfranchised their parents were. There were multiple instances where black teachers were fired for telling students about the National Association for the Advancement of Colored People (NAACP) or discussing the nationwide battle for civil rights. Furthermore, it was frowned on to teach black children anything about the functions of the U.S. government or the world outside of Mississippi. During the first days of Freedom schools, many of the volunteer teachers recorded that their students did not know basic things such as the nation's capital, or how many states comprised America. This lack of access to education, Cobb observed, created an intellectual vacuum among black students and often fulfilled its goal in rendering them powerless.

After leaders of SNCC accepted Cobb's Freedom school proposal, a conference was held in New York City to discuss the curriculum to be taught in these schools. Veteran civil rights activists such as Myles Horton, Septima Clark, Bayard Rustin, and Ella Baker, combined with young SNCC leaders and academics such as Stoughton Lynd to create an impressive and comprehensive core curriculum for the schools. The group decided that the Freedom schools should be based on a model of participatory education. This structure called for a great deal of classroom discussion during which students would raise questions and provide answers. Teachers would merely provide background information and facilitate conversations. The conference also called for the development of remedial programs to fill basic educational gaps, and leadership training exercises that taught the students not only how to lead, but how to conduct civil rights protests by writing letters, organizing, and using modern nonviolent tactics.

As the Summer Project began in late June, volunteers noticed an incredible response to Freedom schools. Community members of all ages helped SNCC workers construct the schools, and men stood guard outside their doors at night. When a school would be bombed or burned by racist local whites, entire communities would turn out to construct another building while school sessions continued under the shade of an old tree or inside someone's house. Within two weeks, Freedom school attendance surpassed all estimations, and by the time the summer was over, Freedom schools had more than 2,000 attendees. The Freedom schools were incredibly successful. Toward the end of the Freedom Summer, Freedom school students had started canvassing potential black voters, conducting nonviolent protests, and forming their own organizations. Freedom school students remained the most important legacy of the Freedom Summer, and they would continue the fight for civil rights in the state long after the SNCC summer project ended.

William Mychael Sturkey

Further Reading

Carson, Clayborne. *In Struggle: SNCC and the Black Awakening of the 1960s.* Cambridge, MA: Harvard University Press, 1981.

Dittmer, John. *Local People: The Struggle for Civil Rights in Mississippi.* Urbana: University of Illinois Press, 1994.

G

Garvey, Marcus

Marcus Garvey, the charismatic black leader of the early twentieth century, led the world's largest movement of people of African descent in history. His Pan-African movement, called Garveyism, generated racial pride, uplift, economic independence, and, most importantly, a return to Africa. To that end, Garvey was influential in establishing black businesses and the first black-run international organization for blacks, the Universal Negro Improvement Association and African Communities League (UNIA), established in 1914. UNIA was formed to draw blacks across the world to promote racial pride, worldwide industry, the development of Africa, and educational opportunities.

Marcus Mosiah Garvey was born on August 17, 1887, in St. Ann's Bay, Jamaica, to Marcus and Sarah. He was the youngest of 11 children. Garvey's parents were Jamaicans of unmixed African stock, descendants from the Maroons, a group of slaves who escaped the Jamaican slave regime. The Maroons established independent communities after being rewarded with a treaty of independence from Britain in 1739. Marcus Garvey was raised in St. Ann's Bay on the northern coast of Jamaica. Trained as a printer's apprentice, he attended elementary school but was forced to drop out at the age of 14 to help with his family's finances. His activism started early in life. While working as a foreman printer, the union went on strike and Garvey was elected as their leader. However, the strike failed and Garvey was blacklisted. It was at this time that he became skeptical about the use of labor unions and socialism as a form of government to assist blacks.

After his first opportunity to become active, Garvey traveled extensively to find that black people throughout the world were being treated unfairly. From Costa Rica to Venezuela, everywhere Garvey traveled, he was able to observe firsthand the harsh conditions of black people around the world. As a result of this new knowledge and his desire to right the injustices of black people, Garvey used his skills to publish several newspapers. The first newspaper was started in 1910, *Garvey's Watchman*, with a weekly circulation of 3,000 copies. He founded his second paper in Costa Rica, *La Nacion*. Garvey used his papers to attack the British consul for its indifference to the conditions of blacks. In Panama, he published *La Prensa*.

Garvey solicited support from the British, but they were indifferent to his initial concerns; thus he concluded that black people could not rely on whites

Portrait of Marcus Garvey, publisher and founder of the Universal Negro Improvement Association and African Communities League. (Library of Congress)

to provide equality. The lack of support from the British government prompted Garvey to travel to Europe. He settled in London, where he met Duse Mohammed Ali, who sparked his interest in pursuing African freedom. The turning point in Garvey's life during this time was his exposure to Booker T. Washington. After reading Washington, Garvey's quest to become a race leader began.

In 1914, Garvey returned to Jamaica, where, on August 1, 1914, he established the UNIA, whose motto was "One God! One Aim! One Destiny!" though the UNIA had several objectives. As defined by Garvey, these objectives were to unify the race, inspire a spirit of pride and love, attend to the needs of the poor, undermine imperialism on the African continent, and help facilitate commerce and industrial development throughout the African world. Much like Booker T. Washington, who heavily influenced him, Garvey argued that although blacks are handicapped by circumstances, they are keeping themselves back, which causes other races to refuse to notice them. In an effort to deal with these handicaps, Garvey sought to begin an industrial and technical school in Jamaica similar to the Tuskegee Institute. In an effort to begin the school, Washington extended an invitation to Garvey to meet with him in Tuskegee. The meeting never took place, because Washington died in November 1915.

By 1916, at the age of 28, Garvey set up a UNIA chapter in New York's Harlem to recruit members. To keep up with the growing membership of the UNIA throughout the world, Garvey began to publish the *Negro World,* the official newspaper of the UNIA, his greatest publishing venture. It quickly became one of the leading American black weeklies, with a regular circulation around the world of about 200,000. The *Negro World* refused to accept any advertisement that would degrade the black race, such as hair-straightening or skin-whitening compounds. On the first page of each issue was an editorial by Garvey in which he reminded blacks of their rich history. The remaining parts of the newspaper carried articles on black history and culture, UNIA activities, and racial news. The program of the UNIA was communicated in an eight-point platform in the *Negro World.*

1. To champion Negro nationhood by redemption of Africa.
2. To make the Negro race conscious.
3. To breathe ideals of manhood and womanhood into every Negro.
4. To advocate self-determination.
5. To make the Negro world-conscious.
6. To print all the news that will be interesting and instructive to the Negro.
7. To instill racial self-help.
8. To inspire racial love and self-respect.

Much to the fascination of whites, Garvey was a force to be reckoned with. He was a dominant power with a rapidly growing movement. His message of uplift, international solidarity, and support for Irish, Indian, and Egyptian independence was a threat to international order. As such, British and American intelligence agencies began to accuse Garvey of fomenting racial strife.

By 1919, there were UNIA chapters chartered in most American cities with large black populations. The headquarters of UNIA was established in Harlem. The organization had saved enough money to purchase an auditorium, which Garvey named Liberty Hall, which was used for various purposes including meetings, dances, and feeding the hungry. The UNIA also established the Negro Factories Corporation (NFC), a black business that produced a variety of commodities and provided jobs to black people, ultimately employing 300 people.

Garvey's business ventures expanded and also included the Black Star Line (BSL), a fleet of black-owned and operated steamships. The BSL was incorporated in Delaware and capitalized at $500,000—with 100,000 shares at $5 per share to be sold only to blacks, with no individual able to purchase more than 200 shares. The BSL was authorized to own, operate, and charter ships and to carry freight, passengers, and mail. The line was different from the NFC. It offered blacks three distinct opportunities: to invest in a black-owned business, to make money, and to make history. Although many laughed at the idea of the BSL, it was able to purchase several ships—the SS *Yarmouth*, the SS *Shadyside,* and the *Kanawha.* Blacks everywhere marveled at the accomplishment of Garvey's BSL.

At UNIA's pinnacle, Garvey called for the First International Convention of the Negro Peoples of the World, which was held in Liberty Hall on August 1, 1920. The delegates attending the convention represented 48 states, 25 countries, and three continents. Dignitaries at the convention included an African prince; the mayor of Monrovia, Liberia; and tribal chiefs. The event was a momentous occasion where the various units of the UNIA were amassed together. In a parade through Harlem, the Black Cross Nurses, ready to come to the aid of black people, were dressed in white. The African Legion, which included many World War I veterans dressed in dark blue uniforms with red stripes, were mounted on horseback and marched with precision, indicating to the world that the organization would be prepared to use force to gain black redemption. The white press took notice of the pageantry, which displayed the might and organization of Garvey's group.

Flying high in the midst of the crowd were the crimson, black, and green banners of the delegates, who welcomed Garvey with a five-minute standing ovation. His opening statement preached Black Nationalism, calling for the freedom of Africa. Garvey stated:

> We are the descendants of a people determined to suffer no longer. We shall now organize the 400,000,000 Negroes of the world into a vast organization to plant the banner of freedom on the great continent of Africa. . . . We do not desire what has belonged to others, though others have always sought to deprive us of that which belonged to us . . . If Europe is for the Europeans, then Africa shall be for the black peoples of the world. We say it; we mean it . . . The other races have countries of their own and it is time for the 400,000,000 Negroes to claim Africa for themselves.

The convention designated Garvey as the provisional president of the African Republic, an exile government. Other officers in this government included the titles of supreme potentate, supreme deputy potentate, and an entire cabinet. The Declaration of Rights of the Negro Peoples of the World, a statement of protest and plan of action for blacks, was also adopted at the convention.

By 1922, however, Garvey's momentum took an incredible turn downward. The black establishment waged mounting attacks against the UNIA's business activities because of the large sums of money it had collected from blacks. A few disgruntled stockholders also lodged complaints and accused the BSL of mismanagement. As a result, Garvey and several associates were arrested and charged with 12 counts of mail fraud in promoting the stock of the BSL. Shortly after his arrest, with an operating budget of merely $31.12, Garvey announced that BSL's operational activities would end. The trial was delayed and Garvey was released on bond.

While awaiting trial, Garvey promised to return to the UNIA. Much to the dismay of America's black elite, Garvey maintained a faithful following; however, disgruntled BSL stockholders and employees sued him. At his trial, Garvey denied overstating the profits of the BSL. He did admit that there were no assets and the corporation had more than $600,000 in operating expenses. The trial also revealed that the BSL never paid dividends to stockholders. The judge stated that Garvey had preyed on his own people. In addition to the business troubles faced by Garvey, there were also domestic troubles that became the center of attention for the black elite in mounting attacks against Garvey.

By 1922, when the third annual convention of the UNIA met in Harlem, Garvey's opposition had mobilized and called its own meeting. A group called Friends of Negro Freedom, organized by the editors of *The Messenger* magazine, Chandler Owen, and A. Philip Randolph, adopted the slogan "Garvey Must Go!" This group also called for his immediate deportation. Another major argument against Garvey were various rumors that he had made an agreement with the Ku Klux Klan (KKK). The opposition's most fatal move against Garvey was a letter written to the U.S. attorney general in 1923 protesting the delay of Garvey's trial.

Although no one knows the influence of the letter, Garvey's trial began within six months after the letter was written. Garvey mounted his own defense by blaming his critics and competitors for BSL's demise. The trial revealed that Garvey had used the BSL for promoting the sale of stock rather than using it as a business enterprise. It also revealed that funds were transferred between the BSL and other UNIA business ventures without proper accounting methods. Garvey was found guilty of promoting the sale of BSL stock knowing the company was in financial trouble. He was sentenced to five years in prison and a $1,000 fine. The codefendants were acquitted. Garvey's attorneys made plans for appeals as he was remanded to the Tombs prison in New York.

Garvey was released on bail in September 1923. While waiting appeal, he pursued another maritime venture, the Black Cross Navigation and Trading Company, which purchased one ship, the *General G. W. Goethals.* At the 1924 convention, Garvey declared the ship to be named the *Booker T. Washington.* He hoped it would be the vessel to carry blacks back to Africa. The UNIA sent machinery and technical experts to Liberia to claim the land that had been promised them for colonization, only to find that the goods had been confiscated by the shipping company for lack of payment. The experts were also immediately deported amid fears from Liberians that they would be a domestic threat. Garvey's hopes for the *Booker T. Washington* never came to fruition.

By 1925, Garvey's appeals were rejected, and the Supreme Court refused to hear the case. On February 8, 1925, he entered the Atlanta, Georgia, penitentiary to begin serving a five-year prison term. Although efforts were made to continue the work of the UNIA, they fell short because of a lack of a flamboyant leader. Surprisingly, during Garvey's time in prison, even those who had never supported him became increasingly aware that he had fallen victim to a contentious America. After supporters (including Earl Little, the father of Malcolm X) urged clemency for Garvey, President Calvin Coolidge commuted his sentence in 1927. As an alien, U.S. law required nonresidents convicted of a felony to be deported. So on release, without having an opportunity to visit UNIA headquarters in New York, Garvey was taken to New Orleans and put aboard the SS *Saramacca*, where he delivered a farewell address before heading for Panama and the West Indies.

Even in his homeland of Jamaica, Garvey continued the work of the UNIA by visiting local chapters. *Negro World* also continued to publish editorials to be sent to his American following. With the support of his wife, in 1928, he traveled to Europe and established new UNIA headquarters in London and Paris. He also presented a petition to the League of Nations at Geneva and urged them to create a "free Negro state in Africa."

By 1929, Garvey issued a call for the Sixth International Convention of Negro Peoples of the World to be held in Kingston, Jamaica. Similar to the first international convention, this was the last major UNIA convention that garnered great attention. Most of the discussion at the conference involved improving the conditions of blacks around the world. The delegates established a Department of Health and Public Education to improve the health conditions of blacks through the world, and it also sought to establish UNIA consulates in black population centers and to publicize grievances and protect the rights of blacks. Much to the dismay of critics, even after serving jail time and being deported, Garvey continued to be a force among blacks.

Garvey also seemed to become a dominant force in Jamaican politics by organizing the Jamaican People's Political Party. He ran in an unsuccessful bid for the Jamaican legislature, which could have been derailed by the lawsuits and complaints by American chapters of the UNIA when he moved the headquarters to Jamaica. By the 1930s, the Garvey movement slowed significantly because the Great Depression left black Americans in disarray. Just as conditions in the United States supported Garvey's elevation as a race leader, later conditions in America accompanied his decline.

The seventh convention proved to be a disappointment, and Garvey moved the headquarters to London in 1935. Although small meetings of the UNIA were held in the mid-1930s, Garveyism had declined. By the late 1930s, Garvey's health was failing after suffering with pneumonia and a stroke that left him paralyzed. On June 10, 1940, Garvey died in London. In England, Garvey's death went unnoticed, but in the United States, black and white newspapers paid tribute to him. With mixed reviews on his triumphs and setbacks, they all agreed, it was unlikely that black America would see another Marcus Garvey.

On November 10, 1964, decades after his death, Garvey's body was returned to Jamaica. The next day, he was declared the country's first national hero.

Angela K. Lewis

Further Reading

Cronon, E. David., ed. *Black Moses: The Story of Marcus Garvey and the Universal Negro Improvement Association.* Madison: University of Wisconsin Press, 1955.

Garvey, Amy Jacques. *Garvey and Garveyism.* New York: Collier, 1970.

Garvey, Amy Jacques. *The Philosophy and Opinions of Marcus Garvey, or Africa for the Africans.* Dover, MA: Majority Press, 1986.

White, John. "Marcus Garvey: Jamaican Messiah." In *Black Leadership in America*, edited by John White, 75–108. New York: Longman, 1985.

Wintz, Cary D., ed. "Marcus Garvey." In *African American Political Thought 1890–1930: Washington, Du Bois, Garvey and Randolph*, edited by Carl D. Wintz, 167–242. Armonk, NY: M. E. Sharpe, 1996.

Gray, Fred

Martin Luther King Jr. once described lawyer and activist Fred Gray as "the brilliant young Negro who later became the chief counsel for the protest movement." Gray provided legal advice to Rosa Parks, King's Montgomery Improvement Association, the local branch and state conference of the National Association for the Advancement of Colored People, and the Montgomery Progressive Democratic Association.

Gray was born on December 14, 1930, in Montgomery, Alabama. He was ordained a Christian minister as a teenager and, following high school, he received a BS from Alabama State College for Negroes (1951) and an LLB from Case Western Reserve University in Cleveland, Ohio (1954). Gray then returned to Montgomery to open his private law practice while also serving as minister to the Holt Street Church of Christ. Gray recalled that he was anxious to return to Montgomery to "destroy everything segregated."

During the Montgomery Bus Boycott of 1955–1956, Gray's leadership and legal counsel played a crucial role in the successful desegregation of Montgomery city buses. He defended Claudette Colvin and Rosa Parks against charges of disorderly conduct for refusing to give up their seats to white passengers. Gray also filed the petition that challenged the constitutionality of Alabama state laws mandating segregation on buses (*Browder v. Gayle*). In November 1956, the Supreme Court affirmed the lower-court ruling that racial segregation on public transportation was unconstitutional.

Gray recalled that he and King occasionally had differences of opinion on what action should be taken to ensure that rights were protected: "There were times when Dr. King said, 'Fred, I understand what you say the law is, but our conscience says that the law is unjust and we cannot obey it. So, if we are arrested we will be calling on you to defend us.' "

Gray was involved in many other civil rights cases, including *Gomillion v. Lightfoot*, which challenged the Alabama legislature after it redrew the boundaries of the city of Tuskegee, Alabama, to exclude black neighborhoods, thereby denying African Americans the right to vote in municipal elections. Gray also fought for African American rights to education, the freedom to march peacefully, and the right to participate in juries; and he opposed injustices like the infamous Tuskegee Experiment—a syphilis study that purposely left affected black men untreated.

In 1970, Gray was elected to the Alabama legislature as a representative from Tuskegee. With this election, he became one of the first two African American officials to serve in the legislature since the Reconstruction era. In 1979, President Jimmy Carter nominated Gray to the U.S. District Court for the Middle District of Alabama, but Gray withdrew his name in August 1980, after opposition from conservative opponents. Gray received the American Bar Association's Equal Justice Award (1977), the Southern Christian Leadership Conference's Drum Major Award (1980), and the World Conference of Mayors' Legal Award (1985). He was elected president of the Alabama State Bar Association in 2001. In 2007, Gray became president of the Tuskegee Human and Civil Rights Multicultural Center, a permanent memorial honoring the participants of the Tuskegee syphilis study.

Clayborne Carson

Further Reading

Gray, Fred D. *Bus Ride to Justice: The Life and Works of Fred Gray.* Montgomery, AL: NewSouth Books, 1995.

Jones, James H. *Bad Blood: The Tuskegee Syphilis Experiment.* New York: Free Press, 1981 (revised 1992).

King, Martin Luther, Jr. *Stride toward Freedom: The Montgomery Story.* Boston: Beacon Press, 1957.

Hamer, Fannie Lou

African American civil rights activist Fannie Lou Hamer is known for her work in securing the inclusion of African Americans as a part of the delegation of the Democratic Party from the state of Mississippi, among her political involvement in the creation and establishment of various antipoverty programs.

Fannie Lou Townsend was born October 6, 1917, in Ruleville, Mississippi. She was the last of 20 children of Lou Ella and James Townsend. Residing in the Mississippi delta, the Townsend family consisted of descendants of Mississippi's enslaved population. Like most African American families of the era, they were sharecroppers. Sharecropping generally bound most workers to the land and characterized their poverty. At the age of six, Fannie Lou joined her parents in the cotton fields. By the time she was 12, she was forced to drop out of school and work full time to help support her family. She endured hard labor throughout her teens and young adult years. At age 27, she married another sharecropper named Perry "Pap" Hamer and went to work on the plantation that employed her husband. Later, Hamer and her husband adopted two children, Dorothy Jean and Virgie Lee.

In August 1962, Hamer attended a meeting of the Student Nonviolent Coordinating Committee (SNCC) in her hometown of Ruleville. Inspired by the youthful enthusiasm of the student organizers there, she made the decision to attempt to register to vote. Her earlier attendance at several conferences sponsored by the Regional Council of Negro Leadership had prepared her to move forward in her own personal struggle for civil rights. She had become part of the movement that would later lead to her activism as a civil rights worker and organizer.

Upon learning of Hamer's decision to register to vote, her landlord forced her to leave the plantation and denied her further opportunity to work. Undeterred, Hamer traveled to local communities to help spread the word about voter registration. African Americans who attempted to vote or who were involved in voter registration efforts were threatened with violence, loss of job, harassment, and murder. In June of the following year, Hamer and several SNCC colleagues traveled to Charleston, South Carolina, to participate in voter registration and literacy workshop activities. On their return home, they stopped in Winona, Mississippi. Here, they were jailed and violently beaten by law enforcement officers. This beating left her blind in her left eye and her kidneys permanently damaged.

As a leader and organizer of the Mississippi Freedom Democratic Party (MFDP) that was formed in April 1964, Hamer was selected as a delegate to attend

Fannie Lou Hamer, a Mississippi field hand for most of her life, became a prominent advocate of civil rights. Since Mississippi's Democratic Party refused African American members, Hamer helped form the Mississippi Freedom Democratic Party (MFDP) whose members attempted to unseat the regular party delegation at the Democratic National Convention in 1964. (Library of Congress)

the 1964 Democratic National Convention in Atlantic City, New Jersey. It was here, during her testimony before the convention's credentials committee that she emerged to national prominence as she sought to prohibit the seating of the all-white Mississippi delegation. An attempt at compromise, which would offer the MFDP two delegate seats, was rejected by the party. The overall effort to seat the MFDP failed, but the Democratic Party agreed that, in the future, no delegation would be seated from a state where anyone was illegally denied the vote. The Democratic Party and the country took note. Roughly a year later, the Voting Rights Act of 1965 was passed.

After her memorable experience in Atlantic City, Hamer turned her attention to building strong institutions for addressing problems at the local level. She continued her work in Mississippi, ran for Congress in 1964 and 1965, and was seated as a member of Mississippi's legitimate delegation to the Democratic National Convention in 1968 in Chicago. She played an active role in antipoverty programs, especially Head Start, and in 1969, she founded the Freedom Farms Corporation, designed to help poor farming families—black and white—become economically self-sufficient. In addition, she was a local leader in Dr. Martin Luther King Jr.'s Poor People's Campaign. In 1971, she sought, unsuccessfully, to become a Mississippi state senator as an independent.

The last six years of Hamer's life were marked by severe health and financial problems, but during this time she received numerous honors and awards that recognized a lifelong role in the civil rights movement. She died on March 14, 1977. The official cause of death was breast cancer. Her funeral in Ruleville drew a cross section of national dignitaries who came to sing her praises. In July, 2008, a coalition of local civil rights activists led by Alderwoman Hattie Jordan and Patricia Thompson, national scholars, and concerned citizens dedicated the Fannie Lou Hamer Memorial Garden in Ruleville, marking the final resting place of Mrs. Hamer and her husband.

Patricia Reid-Merritt

Further Reading

Lee, Chana Kai. *For Freedom's Sake: The Life of Fannie Lou Hamer.* Athens: University of Georgia Press, 1999.

Mills, Kay. *This Little Light of Mine: The Life of Fannie Lou Hamer.* New York: Dutton, 1993.

Nies, Judith. *Nine Women: Portraits from the American Radical Tradition.* Berkeley: University of California Press, 2002.

Wright, Giles R. *40th Anniversary Celebration: Fannie Lou Hamer, Atlantic City and the Democratic National Convention.* Pomona, CA: Richard Stockton College, 2004.

Hampton, Fred

Fred Hampton was one of the greatest young political activists to emerge during the Black Power movement. Hampton, chairman of the Illinois Black Panther Party for Self-Defense (BPP), was brutally murdered in his prime by the Chicago police and the Federal Bureau of Investigation (FBI).

Fred Hampton Sr. was born in Blue Island, Illinois, on August 30, 1948. He started his political career while he was a student at Proviso East High School. He helped found the Maywood chapter of the National Association for the Advancement of Colored People and was admired by both blacks and whites as an influential youth leader. He attended Triton Junior College in 1966, and, by the fall of 1967, Hampton attended Crane Junior College on Chicago's West Side. Crane Junior College, later known as Malcolm X College, was a central meeting place for black activists.

In 1968, Hampton founded the Illinois and Chicago chapters of the BPP. The BPP was a national organization dedicated to the liberation of black people. He was a gifted leader who made the Chicago BPP one of the most prominent branches in the country. Hampton strove to alleviate the oppression of black people and improve their living conditions. He established several community service programs that included free breakfasts for children, a free medical clinic, and political education classes.

Hampton was a charismatic public speaker who instilled hope and pride in many Chicagoans throughout the city. He spoke out against police brutality and advocated that members of the community defend themselves. Hampton created coalitions with other socially active groups such as the Students for a Democratic Society (SDS). He also reached across racial boundaries to build coalitions between black, white, and Latino street gangs.

Hampton and other BPP members gained national attention because they publicly advocated the use of weapons for self-defense and patrolled the community in an effort to prevent abuse by the police. J. Edgar Hoover, director of the FBI, stated that the BPP was "the greatest threat to the internal security of the country." The FBI's COINTELPRO (counterintelligence program) was established to neutralize black political activists and destroy their organizations. Many activists were killed or unjustly incarcerated as a result of COINTELPRO. Hampton was sent to Menard Prison for an alleged theft charge but was released on appeal after only a few months.

As a result of COINTELPRO, the Chicago BPP headquarters, located at 2350 West Madison, was ransacked several times by the police. On December 4, 1969, Chicago police raided a nearby apartment at 2337 West Monroe, where many BPP members slept. The police fired shots into the apartment to deliberately kill BPP leaders. Mark Clark, BPP defense captain of the Peoria, Illinois, branch, was killed first with a single shot to the heart. Hampton was killed next. Fellow BPP members heard two shots immediately before the police confirmed that Hampton was dead. There were seven survivors of the raid, including Hampton's beloved Deborah Johnson, who was pregnant with their son. Johnson was uninjured, but four other members sustained gunshot wounds. All of them were arrested and charged with attempted murder.

Thousands of community members visited the crime scene and were appalled by the apparent slaughter of these young leaders. Many concerned citizens demanded an investigation. The initial investigation, however, exonerated the police. Although no law enforcement officials were ever convicted of the crimes, subsequent investigations established that the raid was in fact a successful assassination attempt that was approved and sanctioned by the FBI. Eventually, 25,000 pages emerged that confirmed that FBI involvement had been suppressed from the evidence.

The investigations also proved that FBI informant William O'Neal was paid handsomely for his efforts and avoided incarceration for prior criminal activity. O'Neal infiltrated the Chicago BPP and served as the chapter chief of security and Hampton's bodyguard. O'Neal supplied the FBI with a floor plan of the apartment that was critical in the assassination plot because it indicated where members slept. Many BPP members believed that O'Neal drugged Hampton so that he would be unable to defend himself during the raid.

Ballistics evidence proved that the police shot at least 200 bullets into the apartment. BPP members were ambushed and therefore unable to successfully defend themselves. As a result of the findings, the murder charges against the BPP members were dismissed. The Clark and Hampton families filed a multimillion-dollar lawsuit that was eventually settled for $1.85 million.

At the time of this writing, Deborah Johnson, who became known as Akua Njeri, and Fred Hampton Jr. were working together with the December 4th committee to keep Fred Hampton's legacy alive.

Claudette L. Tolson (Ayodele Shaihi)

Further Reading

December 4th Committee. *Fred Hampton 20th Commemoration.* Chicago: Salsado Press, 1989.

Hampton, Fred. *We Don't Want You Coming Here Clapping and Leaving Here Not Doing Nothing—You've Got to Make a Commitment!* Chicago: Peoples Information Center, 1979.

Hampton, William E., and Templeton, Rini. *The Essence of Fred Hampton.* Chicago: Salsado Press, 1994.

Madhubuti, Haki R. *One Sided Shoot-out (for Brothers Fred Hampton and Mark Clark, Murdered 12/4/69 by Chicago Police at 4:30 AM While They Slept).* Detroit, MI: Broadside Press, 1969.

Harlem Youth Opportunities Unlimited (HARYOU)

Harlem Youth Opportunities Unlimited (HARYOU), founded in 1962 by members of the Harlem community and led by Kenneth Clark, was a program dedicated to alleviating the distressed conditions of black youth in Harlem, New York. HARYOU was well supported by the federal and state governments. Clark, best known for his extensive studies on the effects of racism on black youth, was an ambitious HARYOU leader. During his undergraduate years at Howard University, Clark protested racial segregation inside the nation's capital. He was later denied admission to Cornell University because of his color, but went on to Columbia University to receive a PhD in psychology. He then got a job as a research assistant working for Gunnar Myrdal on his book, *An American Dilemma* (1944). He worked closely with his wife, Dr. Mamie Phipps Clark, on pioneering research that used dolls to analyze the damage done to blacks' self-image due to racism and segregation. These studies, and Clark's direct involvement, were pivotal to the Supreme Court decision in *Brown v. Board of Education* (1954) to outlaw segregation in public schools.

In 1961, the concept of a social program to help Harlem youth was first reported in the *New York Times.* The New York City Youth Board and the Community Mental Health Board planned to work together with the Jewish Board of Guardians to establish programs to assist three communities in New York City. Members from the community, particularly the Harlem Neighborhoods Association (HANA), jumped at the chance to participate. HANA members put together a grant proposal and generated the ideas and objectives for HARYOU. The President's Committee on Juvenile Delinquency contributed $230,000, to be used to cover the costs for the 18-month planning period. The city of New York granted the group $100,000. Individuals on all levels genuinely supported and encouraged programs to assuage the mounting problems in Harlem.

The issues that beset Harlem youth—poverty, broken families, crime, drugs, unemployment, and poor housing conditions—were not that different from those in ghettos across the nation. Racism and racial segregation also took their toll. Police brutality and racist white gangs, which caused many young blacks to form their own gangs, were rampant. Racial profiling and racism in the judicial system put a disproportionate number of blacks in jails.

The HARYOU planning committee produced a comprehensive plan of action. It detailed their objectives, the issues concerning black youth to be addressed, the structure of the organization, the programs to be implemented, and the analysis to be used to evaluate the effectiveness of these programs. The plan formed a template for many similar programs used across the country.

The HARYOU programs were categorized as follows: community action, community services, arts and culture, and business enterprises. The group planned to train and employ Harlem youth to be leaders in each of these areas. Participants in the community action programs were responsible for organizing activities alongside such organizations as the National Association for the Advancement of Colored People (NAACP), the Community Council on Housing, the Student Nonviolent Coordinating Committee (SNCC), the Congress of Racial Equality (CORE), and local neighborhood boards.

Participants in the community service programs were employed as assistants with organizations such as the Junior Academy, the Senior Academy, the After-School Center, and the Neighborhood Board (Health Services). Participants in the arts and culture program performed at venues within HARYOU, the Harlem community, and beyond. Participants in the business enterprise programs worked to establish coffee shops, cultural centers, and a film and sound laboratory. They also helped to develop renovation projects within the community. In 1963, the HARYOU committee implemented its plan of action and published its findings in *Youth in the Ghetto* (1964).

In 1964, Harlem erupted in an urban rebellion after a white police officer fatally shot a 15-year-old black youth. Demonstrators, largely black youths, attacked their own community. Although HARYOU continued to promote its programs, it never did recover, nor did it achieve the results the organizers had intended.

Gladys L. Knight

Further Reading

Clark, Kenneth B. "An Architect of Social Change: Kenneth B. Clark." In *Against the Odds*, edited by Benjamin P. Bowser and Louis Kushnick, with Paul Grant, 147–57. Amherst: University of Massachusetts Press, 2002.

Clark, Kenneth B. *Dark Ghetto: Dilemmas of Social Power.* New York: Harper & Row, 1965.

HARYOU. *Youth in the Ghetto: A Study of the Consequences of Powerlessness and a Blueprint for Change.* New York: Harlem Youth Opportunities Unlimited, Inc., 1964.

Tyson, Cyril Degrasse. *Power and Politics in Central Harlem, 1862–1964: The HARYOU Experience.* New York: Jay Street Publishers, 2004.

Height, Dorothy

Dorothy Height devoted her life to the cause of civil rights for African Americans. She worked for both the National Council of Negro Women (NCNW) and the Young Women's Christian Association (YWCA), where she served as associate director of leadership training services and director of the Office for Racial Justice. She was a key figure in the civil rights movement, embracing the goals of "full freedom and first-class citizenship and participation for all."

Dorothy Irene Height was born on March 24, 1912. The family moved to Rankin, Pennsylvania, when she was four. Height attended integrated schools but went to church services at a segregated Baptist church, where her father was the choirmaster and Sunday school superintendent. Height was an active student in high school, where she became involved in both academic and sports activities, winning a $1,000 scholarship after graduation during a national oratory contest.

Height applied to Barnard College in New York City but was told that the school already had two African American students and that she would have to wait at least one more term and try again. She applied and was accepted to New York University, which received her reluctantly because of her superior academic record. Height received a bachelor's degree in three years, followed by a master's degree the following year.

After college, Height served as a case worker for the New York City Welfare Department for two years. In 1937, she traveled to Oxford, England, as one of 10 young people representing the United States at an international youth conference. The experience inspired her to seek a broader base for her life and career. Height quit her job and joined the staff of the YWCA's branch in Harlem. In 1938, she testified before the New York City Council on the plight of domestic workers in the Bronx and Brooklyn. In what Height described as a "slave market," young black women would bargain with passing motorists for a day's work at what turned out to be subsistence wages.

In 1944, Height moved to a Harlem apartment, where she made her home for several years while serving as director of the Emma Ransom House in New York City and the Phillis Wheatley YWCA in Washington, D.C. She also continued to work with the NCNW, which functioned as an organization and coordination center for anything from professional associations to campus women's organizations. The NCNW had observer status in the United Nations and a representative on the United Civil Rights Leadership.

Height became president of the NCNW in 1957. Beginning in the early 1950s, she had been called upon to extend her sphere of influence outside her normal job duties at the NCNW and YWCA. In 1952, she had served as a visiting professor in the School of Social Work of the University of Delhi, in India. From 1952 to 1955, she had worked in the advisory committee on women in the services for the U.S. Defense Department. In 1958, she was appointed to the New York Social Welfare Board. Height spent some time in Africa studying women's organizations in five African nations, an experience that allowed her to become a consultant on African affairs with the State Department. She used her influence to secure U.S. aid for new and struggling African nations.

The NCNW contributed to the civil rights movement of the 1960s with money and womanpower, organizing voter registration drives in the South and helping students who interrupted their studies to become involved in the movement's effort. Height also worked as a mediator between black and white women in Alabama and reported on abuses and intimidation of voters. The NCNW set up workshops to organize civil rights issues and put pressure on Midwestern congressmen who sought to avoid issues of racial justice because the movement was not yet active in their districts.

Despite her dedication and support for the civil rights movement and the plight of African Americans in the United States, Height was initially critical of the new Black Power movement led by young militants. After some years, however, she changed her mind, deciding that talk alone was not enough to change society.

In 1963, Height undertook a restructuring of the YWCA, focusing on racial integration. She eventually became director of the YWCA's Office for Racial Justice. At the 1970 triennial YWCA convention, however, some of the stresses of the civil rights era became apparent. Different views on women's liberation issues divided some white and black delegates. There were also disagreements in how both black and white delegates understood the sources of social unrest in the United States.

The Ford Foundation made a $300,000 grant available to the NCNW, which was used to set up Operation Black Woman, a vocational training and business start-up program to help African American women. The NCNW also ran a program set up by the Department of Health, Education, and Welfare, which also offered young black women job training. Teams of black and white women from 11 states traveled to Mississippi to reach local women who needed help but did not know how to get it. Similar programs to spark African American community action were set up in other states.

Height also worked as a member of the President's Committee for the Employment of the Handicapped, the President's Commission for the Status of Women, and many other organizations. She was a recipient of the John F. Kennedy Memorial Award, which recognized her efforts as a civil rights activist, and in 1989, she received the Freedom Medal.

Height died on April 20, 2010, in Washington, D.C., at the age of 98. She was still serving as chair and president emerita of the NCNW at the time of her death.

Jose Valente

Further Reading

Gates, Henry Louis, and Cornel West. *The African-American Century: How Black Americans Have Shaped Our Country.* New York: Free Press, 2000.

Height, Dorothy. *Open Wide the Freedom Gates: A Memoir.* New York: PublicAffairs, 2003.

Houston, Charles Hamilton

Attorney and educator Charles Hamilton Houston (1895–1950) was born in the District of Columbia, to William LePre Houston, a lawyer and part-time professor, and Mary Ethel Hamilton, an accomplished hairdresser and former schoolteacher. A bright youngster, Houston enjoyed a middle-class upbringing and had great pride in his heritage. He attended the racially segregated Washington, D.C., public school system, where he graduated from M Street High School at the age of 15, before enrolling at Amherst College in Massachusetts in 1911.

Houston graduated with a BA degree, magna cum laude, as one of Amherst's six valedictorians. He was the only black student in the Amherst class of 1915 and was elected to Phi Beta Kappa. After briefly teaching English at Howard University, Houston enlisted in the army in 1917 and was sent to Camp Fort Des Moines in Iowa in June 1917. While there, he sought training in the artillery corps, but black officers were trained to serve only in the infantry. Thus, Houston was commissioned first lieutenant of infantry, a position he resigned in June 1918 to attend artillery school. Later he reported to Camp Meade, Maryland, where he won his commission as a second lieutenant of artillery. Houston and other black officers were sent to France, where they encountered racism and segregation in the army.

After being honorably discharged from the army in 1919, Houston returned to Washington, D.C. Disturbed by the discrimination he and other black officers encountered and experienced in the army, he decided to follow in the footsteps of his father, who was then a leading member of the Bar of the District of Columbia.

Charles Hamilton Houston was the special counsel for the NAACP who led the judicial fight for civil rights from 1929 until his death just four years before the historic decision in *Brown v. Board of Education* (1954). (Library of Congress)

Houston entered Harvard Law School in the fall of 1919, and, after his first year, distinguished himself among his fellow students and was honored by becoming the first black to serve as editor of the *Harvard Law Review*. Houston earned a bachelor of law degree (cum laude) in 1922, and made history again in 1923, when he became the first black person to be awarded a doctor of juridical science at Harvard.

Houston was then awarded a one-year fellowship to study law in Europe at the University of Madrid in Spain, from which he earned a doctor of civil law degree (1924), before returning to Washington, and was admitted to practice law in the District of Columbia that same year. After a short period, he began a lifelong law partnership with his father in Washington, D.C., while also teaching at Howard University Law School. During his distinguished legal career, Houston answered numerous calls, but he remained closely associated with his father. On August 23, 1924, he married his first wife, Margaret Gladys Moran, but they were divorced in 1937. In August of that same year, he married his second wife, Henrietta Williams, with whom he had one child.

In 1929, Houston was appointed vice dean of Howard University Law School, where he also served as a professor of law. He directed the work of the law school as the chief administrative officer until 1935, and during his administration, Howard Law School trained most of the nation's blacks who entered the legal profession. The law school, however, lacked national recognition, and Houston worked tirelessly and provided leadership that helped transform Howard into a nationally distinguished legal training ground with a mission of racial advancement. His hard work paid off by 1931, when Howard University Law School was fully accredited by the American Bar Association and had gained membership in the Association of American Law Schools. During his tenure, Howard University Law School graduated and trained almost three-fourths of the nation's black law students. Many of the lawyers Houston mentored and trained carried on the struggle for equal justice and won numerous important cases after his death. Thurgood Marshall, the first black Supreme Court justice, Oliver Hill, and William Bryant, all of whom were distinguished civil rights litigators and later federal jurists, are examples of the national litigators that Howard Law School produced. In 1935, Houston left Washington, D.C., to become the first full-time paid special counsel for the National Association for the Advanced of Colored People (NAACP), headquartered in New York City. As head of the legal department, Houston launched a campaign against racial segregation in public schools that would later help to dismantle segregation.

Houston handled and won numerous important cases during the 1930s and 1940s, some of which helped to lay the groundwork for the landmark cases of the 1950s. For example in 1938, Houston won his first case for equality in educational opportunity, *Missouri ex rel. Gaines v. Canada* (1938). To protect the rights of persons accused of crimes, Houston litigated *Hollins v. Oklahoma* (1935) and *Hale v. Kentucky* (1938), in which the U.S. Supreme Court overturned the convictions and death sentences of African Americans who had been tried by juries from which African Americans were excluded on the basis of their race. As the major architect and the dominating force behind the NAACP's legal program, Houston aimed high and made heavy inroads. In 1940, he left the organization and returned to private practice in Washington, D.C., but he remained involved in the fight for the rights and welfare of African Americans including discrimination in education, labor, and housing. He was succeeded as NAACP special counsel by his former student, Thurgood Marshall.

Thereafter, he rejoined his father and formed the firm of Houston & Houston, later known as Houston, Houston, Hastie, & Bryant. His work in the firm covered many areas including discrimination in employment, housing, the rights of the accused, and other aspects of discrimination. Houston also won victories as a civil rights litigator in private practice, successfully arguing and winning cases before the U.S. Supreme Court, including *Steel v. Louisville & Nashville Railroad Co.* and *Tunstall v. Brotherhood of Locomotive Firemen and Enginemen* (1944), when he challenged discriminatory actions by government negotiators and contractors with regard to fair representation regardless of race or union affiliation. In 1948, Houston assisted the NAACP in preparation for a housing discrimination case, *Shelley v. Kraemer*, and was the chief counsel before the Supreme Court in *Hurd v. Hodge* (1948), in which the Supreme Court ruled against judicial enforcement of racially restrictive covenants in the District of Columbia. Throughout his career, Houston was involved in numerous civic duties, including the National Legal Aid Committee (1940–1950); he was vice president of the American Council of Race Relations (1944–1950), vice president of the National Lawyer Guild, a member of the National Board of Directors, and chairman of the national Legal Committee of the NAACP; for two years a member of the Board of Education in the District of Columbia; and a member of the President's Committee on Fair Employment Practices (1944), before resigning the next year. An active participant in the civil rights struggle beyond academia, Houston was also engaged in political activism during his lifetime, including marching in the 1930s for the freedom of the Scottsboro boys and testifying before Congress against lynching and other forms of racial inequality. An incredibly high-energy educator and lawyer, Houston inspired faculty and students with his philosophy of social engineering.

Historically, Houston's most important impact was his strengthening of Howard University Law School, as well as his tireless work as a civil rights litigator for the NAACP. Houston's extensive work and dedication to improving legal education at Howard is notable, and achieving accreditation for the law school was one of the greatest accomplishments for Houston and those who shared his vision. During his administration, Houston commanded and encouraged the legal army to fight and seek equality for African Americans, and many of the cases that Houston argued were instrumental in setting precedents that were later used in the Supreme Court's landmark decisions of *Brown v. Board of Education* (1954) and *Bolling v. Sharpe*, which declared racial segregation in public schools unconstitutional.

Houston muddled through the forests of oppression and discrimination seeking equal protection and justice for those who could not fight for themselves. Among the early builders of the road to freedom that later activists such as Martin Luther King Jr. significantly expanded and strengthened, no one played as major a role as Houston. He was the chief engineer and the dominant force on the civil rights legal scene. One of the greatest civil rights activists in American history, Houston was the primary force behind the ultimate success of the long struggle that led to an end of the legalized discrimination and in particular, the notion of "separate but equal."

Houston was instrumental in training a generation of fearless civil rights lawyers throughout the country, who carried on the struggle and remained an inspiration to those dedicated to social justice today. Aside from training Thurgood Marshall, he was also a close adviser to Marshall. The magnitude of Houston's contributions toward the quality of justice in American society today is tremendous. This civil rights icon was a giant of a man who dedicated his life to the cause of freedom that all Americans enjoy today. Houston made marked contributions to the civil rights movement and the struggle against oppression of African Americans, for which he was posthumously awarded the coveted Spingarn Medal by the NAACP. In 1958, Howard University renamed its law school building in Houston's honor.

Throughout his legal career Houston was a pillar for African Americans. For three decades, Houston's civil rights advocacy focused on achieving recognition of equal rights and opportunities, legal guarantees, and elimination of legalized racial discrimination. In spite of the increasing prominence of black scholars, legal academia does not recognize the Houstonian intellectual heritage. This deeply committed strategist, legal counsel, educator, mentor, and adviser in the struggle against racial discrimination remains a model for activists in the cause for justice and equality.

Houston's fast pace in the struggle for racial justice and equality was eventually cut short by a heart ailment. He was first hospitalized for exhaustion and suffered a severe heart attack in 1948, but he never recovered. Houston died on April 20, 1950, in Washington, D.C., four years before fully realizing his struggle against "separate but equal." He left behind his second wife, Henrietta Williams Houston, and their only child, Charles Hamilton Houston Jr. The death of this civil rights icon brought an irreparable loss to the black community and to America. Houston was buried in Lincoln Memorial Cemetery in Suitland, Maryland.

Njoki-Wa-Kinyatti

Further Reading

Carter, Robert L. "In Tribute: Charles Hamilton Houston." *Harvard Law Review* 11, no. 8 (1998): 2149–79.

Hastie, William H. "Charles Hamilton Houston." *Journal of Negro History* 35, no. 3 (1950): 355–58.

Klebanow, Diana, and Franklin L. Jonas. *People's Lawyers: Crusaders for Justice in American History.* New York: M. E. Sharpe, 2003.

McNeil, Genna R. *Ground Work: Charles Hamilton Houston and the Struggle for Civil Rights.* Philadelphia: University of Pennsylvania Press, 1983.

J

Jackson, Jesse

The Reverend Jesse Louis Jackson Sr. (b. 1941) emerged as a leader during the civil rights movement. In a long career alternately marked by success and controversy, Jackson founded economic justice organizations, ran for president twice, and negotiated with a host of foreign leaders. Jackson's distinctive and powerful speaking style is characterized by wordplay, rhyming couplets, and the phrase "I am somebody," a refrain aimed at cultivating the self-worth of dispossessed youth.

Jackson was born Jesse Louis Burns in Greenville, South Carolina, on October 8, 1941. His mother, Helen Burns, was an unwed 16-year-old. Her pregnancy dashed the hope of her mother, Matilda "Tibby" Burns, that Helen, born when she herself was only 13, would attend college on a singing scholarship. Jesse's biological father, Noah Robinson, was a married man who lived next door with his wife and stepchildren. In 1943, Jesse's mother married Charles Jackson, who later adopted Jesse when he was about 15. They had one child, Charles Jackson Jr.

Robinson, a former boxer and a well-known figure in Greenville's black community, acknowledged his paternity. He had little contact with Jesse, however, who has since said that as a child he would stand staring at the Robinsons' house hoping for a glimpse of his father. Subsequently, Robinson's wife gave birth to three sons, the eldest of whom, Noah Robinson Jr., went on to earn an MBA and become a young standout in the business world but was imprisoned for defrauding the IRS and being an accessory to attempted murder. Questions about these convictions dogged his half-brother on the 1988 campaign trail.

Jackson graduated from Sterling High School in Greenville in 1959. A distinguished student leader and athlete, he chose a football scholarship to the University of Illinois at Champaign-Urbana over a professional baseball contract. Jackson traced his first integration protest to his attempt to take books out of the Greenville library over winter break. He left Illinois after one year and transferred to the historically black North Carolina Agricultural and Technical College in Greensboro. Jackson maintained he was not allowed to play quarterback at Illinois because he was black. This comment caused controversy when it came to light that the school's starting quarterback that year was also black. At his new school, Jackson became student body president and met Jacqueline (Jackie) Lavinia Brown, who became his wife. The two participated in sit-in movements to

Rev. Jesse Jackson, founder of Operation PUSH (People United to Save Humanity), addresses supporters of the Humphrey-Hawkins Bill for full employment, January 1975. (Library of Congress)

integrate public facilities in Greensboro. Jackson graduated with a sociology degree in 1964.

Jackson had five children with his wife Jackie: Santita, Jesse Jr., Jonathan, Yusef DuBois, and Jacqueline Lavinia. Santita attended Howard University and sang in a backup group for Roberta Flack. Jesse Jr. attended his parents' alma mater, as did Jonathan and Jacqueline, and in 1995 was elected to the U.S. Congress representing the second district of Illinois. Yusef attended the University of Virginia on a football scholarship and became a lawyer. In 2001, it came to light that Jackson had fathered a sixth child, Ashley Laverne Jackson, in an affair with Karin Stanford, a former staffer who was being paid through Jackson's organizations.

After a stint with the Congress of Racial Equality (CORE), Jackson moved his growing family north to attend Chicago Theological Seminary. He became increasingly interested in the civil rights movement, participating in the 1965 march on Selma, Alabama, and dropped out of seminary in 1966 six months shy of graduating to become a member of the Southern Christian Leadership Conference (SCLC) staff under Martin Luther King Jr. He was later ordained a Baptist minister by Clay Evans and C. L. Franklin, Aretha's father. Chicago Theological Seminary awarded him a master of divinity degree in 2000 based on credits plus experience.

In 1966, King named Jackson the head of SCLC's Chicago branch of Operation Breadbasket, an organization founded to persuade businesses such as grocery stores and bakeries to hire more blacks and carry more products from black businesses. Under Jackson's leadership, the organization struck deals with several businesses that resulted in hundreds of jobs for blacks.

In April 1968, Jackson was traveling with King's retinue in Memphis to support a garbage workers' strike when King was gunned down outside his hotel room. There seems little dispute that Jackson was at the hotel when the shooting happened, but some of the tales told about the event were contested. Other civil rights leaders present became angry when Jackson claimed he cradled the dying leader's head in his arms and when he appeared on television the next day in a blood-spattered sweater. To many, Jackson's attempt to emerge as a major black leader after King's death was an insensitive grab for power. Jackson stayed with SCLC for three and a half years but left after a suspension resulting from his independent incorporation of the first Black Expo, which was meant as an SCLC fund-raiser.

In the early 1970s, Jackson founded his own organization, Operation PUSH, or People United to Save Humanity ("Save" later became "Serve"). He also began speaking at high schools to African American youth to promote hard work, education, and responsibility. Jimmy Carter's administration rewarded Jackson's school ministry, named PUSH for Excellence, with grants that later dried up under Ronald Reagan's presidency. Jackson also began to travel abroad, developing a vision that incorporated all the world's oppressed poor. In 1972, he initiated such travel with a trip to Liberia. In 1979, he spoke in South Africa against apartheid. The same year, he traveled to the Middle East and compared the conditions of the Palestinians to African Americans' plight in the United States. A picture of Jackson hugging PLO leader Yasser Arafat caused a major controversy and became for many American Jews a lingering source of distrust of Jackson. During that visit, the Israeli government refused to see him, but he made several return trips in which he met with both governments and attempted to spread the civil rights movement's concepts of nonviolent resistance and radical love as a political weapon to the Palestinian-Israeli conflict.

Although he had never held public office, Jackson made two noteworthy bids for the Democratic Party nomination for president in the 1980s. In 1967, King had proposed the Poor People's Campaign, a movement that would bring together the country's economically dispossessed regardless of ethnicity. The idea foundered after King's assassination but later found new life as Jackson's Rainbow Coalition, an organization he later merged with PUSH. Jackson's economic populism made substantial inroads with white farmers and factory workers. He also toured the country promoting voter registration and likely can be credited with the registration of millions of new voters in the 1980s. These new voters provided the margin that elected a contingent of black congresspeople and mayors in that decade. Jackson's first presidential bid got a boost from his negotiation to release Robert O. Goodman Jr., a black U.S. Navy lieutenant captured by Syria after his plane was shot down. Jackson accused the government of working less assiduously for Goodman's release than they would have if he were white. The Reagan administration decried his trip as reckless, but Jackson succeeded in obtaining the release.

Nation of Islam leader Louis Farrakhan traveled with Jackson to Syria, where his status as an American Muslim impressed the Syrians. Before Jackson received Secret Service protection as a presidential candidate, Farrakhan supplied him with Fruit of Islam guards from his organization. Not long after the Syria trip, Jackson's close relationship with Farrakhan fed into the black-versus-Jew controversy that seemed to haunt Jackson's career. Jackson's growing support and appeal following Goodman's release came to an abrupt halt when he referred to Jews as "Hymies" and called New York "Hymietown" in an off-the-record conversation with *Washington Post* reporter Milton Coleman, creating possibly the most intractable controversy of Jackson's entire career. Farrakhan, already an unpopular associate given his organization's association with a theology of the intrinsic evilness of the white race, threatened to have the black journalist who reported on the conversation killed. Setting aside Farrakhan's militance and black-supremacist theology, however, he and Jackson shared a platform of economic justice, self-reliance, and education, and both surprised white observers in the 1980s with their ability to draw large black crowds. Jackson only reluctantly distanced himself from Farrakhan after Farrakhan called Judaism a "dirty" religion.

Jackson tried to bounce back from the Hymietown affair with a trip to Cuba and South America. The highlight was an eight-hour session with Fidel Castro in which he persuaded the Cuban leader to release 22 Americans held on drug charges and 27 Cubans held for political activities. Jackson finished third in the 1984 primary season behind eventual nominee Walter Mondale and Gary Hart. He garnered just over three million votes.

Hart's 1988 bid met an early demise after an affair came to light. Jackson, often rumored to have had a series of amorous relationships, risked a similar disclosure but nevertheless entered the race with polls showing him to be a leading prospect for the nomination. The crowds he drew wherever he went seemed to indicate the same. When 800 townspeople in Greenfield, Iowa, forewent the Super Bowl to hear Jackson speak, he made Greenfield his Iowa headquarters and soon was running second only to Richard Gephardt in the 97 percent–white state. He won about 10 percent of the caucus share in that state and 10 percent of the votes in the New Hampshire primary. Jackson did better than expected on Super Tuesday, ending the day with more of the popular vote than any other Democrat. He followed that performance by claiming 55 percent of the vote in Michigan and briefly looked like the frontrunner. Ahead of the New York primary, New York City mayor Ed Koch resurrected the Hymietown comments and the Arafat hug, which hurt Jackson in that state even though he had spent the previous four years repairing relationships with the Jewish community. Jackson eventually lost the nomination to Michael Dukakis, but along the way, he finished second with almost seven million primary votes, about two million of them from whites. Jackson was disappointed not to be offered the vice presidential slot. Nevertheless, he threw himself into the Democratic campaign, logging more miles on Dukakis's behalf during the general election campaign than the candidate did.

Jackson declined to run in subsequent elections and was often critical of Democratic candidates. In March 2007, he endorsed Barack Obama, who went on to be the first African American to become a major party's nominee. Despite the endorsement, Jackson made headlines for grumbling that Obama did not give enough attention to racial issues, and in a particularly fraught incident, he was caught wearing an open mike and making a vulgar comment about Obama because of the way he talked about African Americans.

Jackson's commitment to global diplomacy long outlasted his official political career. In 1990, Jackson traveled to meet with Iraqi president Saddam Hussein after his invasion of Kuwait and negotiated the release of hundreds of captives during the run-up to war between Iraq and a U.S.-led coalition. In 1999, he negotiated the release of three U.S. military personnel captured by Slobodan Milosevic's regime. In 2004, he traveled to Libya and Sudan in an effort to end the Sudanese civil war. In 2005, Jackson met with the president of Venezuela, Hugo Chavez, and condemned evangelist Pat Robertson's comment that Chavez should be assassinated.

From 1991 to 1997, Jackson served in his only elected office, as one of two District of Columbia statehood senators, often known as "shadow senators," a position created to lobby for the district's statehood. In 1997, President Bill Clinton and Secretary of State Madeleine Albright gave Jackson the title "Special Envoy for the President and Secretary of State for the Promotion of Democracy in Africa." In 2000, Clinton honored Jackson with the Presidential Medal of Freedom, the country's highest civilian honor, for his lifetime of work on behalf of the poor and minority communities.

Brooke Sherrard

Further Reading

Clemente, Frank, and Frank Watkins, eds. *Keep Hope Alive: Jesse Jackson's 1988 Presidential Campaign*. Boston: South End Press, 1989.

Frady, Marshall. *Jesse: The Life and Pilgrimage of Jesse Jackson*. New York: Simon & Schuster, 1996.

Hertzke, Allen D. *Echoes of Discontent: Jesse Jackson, Pat Robertson, and the Resurgence of Populism*. Washington, DC: CQ Press, 1993.

Jackson, Jesse L. *Straight from the Heart*. Philadelphia: Fortress, 1987.

Jim Crow

"Jim Crow" was the American social practice of racial segregation, most prevalent from the 1880s to the 1960s, that robbed African Americans of their basic civil and civic rights and assaulted black people's humanity. This method of segregation allowed African Americans and whites to live within the same cities and towns, while still maintaining white economic, political, and social superiority. Through a series of social customs and state and federal laws, white Americans created "white only" public spaces designed to link free African Americans to their previously enslaved status. For example, the practice of Jim Crow required that newly freed African Americans ride in separate sections of public transportation vehicles and sit in separate sections of church, and that black children attend different schools from those of their white counterparts. By 1896, a racist Louisiana state law, requiring that white and black people sit in separate compartments on trains was upheld by the U.S. Supreme Court in the case of *Plessy v. Ferguson,* which institutionalized the doctrine of "separate but equal" accommodations and embedded Jim Crow segregation into southern culture and law for the next 60 years.

Although the term Jim Crow is most frequently associated with racial segregation in the twentieth century, it was first harnessed as a racial and spatial epithet in 1830s antebellum Massachusetts. A white actor, Thomas Dartmouth Rice, performing with black cork makeup on his face, made Jim Crow—the likeable yet derogatory African American slave he played on northern stages—a national and international sensation. The cultural impact of the show was so great that by 1834, northerners from all classes—from street urchins to congressional politicians to newspaper editors—alluded to Jim Crow's oft-quoted refrain: "Weel about and turn about and do jis so, Eb'ry time I weel about and jump Jim Crow." The popularity of both the tune and the character prompted Massachusetts's railroad conductors, when segregating black travelers on the newly minted trains, to name the dirty, drafty, and unkempt compartments reserved for drunken men, poor whites, and African Americans as the "Jim Crow car." The first record of this usage is 1838.

As early as the 1820s, free people of color vigorously protested segregation on public transportation in newspaper editorials. They further organized their protest strategies against the Jim Crow car and launched a concerted battle against the Massachusetts railroads from 1838 to 1843. African American abolitionists such as Charles Lenox Remond, Frederick Douglass, and David Ruggles refused to move from first-class seats, prompting violent confrontations between themselves and the railroads' cronies. These abolitionists and their white advocates demanded equal accommodations and argued that receiving equal treatment on public transportation was a right of citizenship.

Furthermore, black activists developed a sophisticated analysis of such racial segregation. They debunked the notion that African American travelers were set apart from whites because they smelled or were disrespectful to white women. Pointedly, black abolitionists highlighted the fact that during the antebellum period, white American men and women traveled alongside enslaved African Americans frequently and never made complaints. Instead, activists argued that what whites found so odious about black travelers in the antebellum North was not their skin color or their mere presence, but the social implications of their freedom. They argued that whites feared black political and economic success and imagined that black men sought sexual liaisons with white women because for so long, white men had exploited enslaved African American women in the South. Black freedom threatened social order. Segregation in public spaces such as the Jim Crow car was a way for Anglo-Americans to minimize the impact of African American freedom and to cripple black citizenship.

After four million African American slaves were freed in the South in 1865, it took just decades for the southern states to produce laws that echoed the customs of the antebellum North. In the decades after enslavement, and throughout the twentieth century, a new generation of black activists, emboldened by a legacy of African American activism against Jim Crow, believed that segregation threatened the meaning of freedom and citizenship and fought to overturn *Plessy v. Ferguson* through multiple protest strategies, including the courts.

In 1954, through a series of protracted legal battles, the legal arm of the National Association for the Advancement of Colored People (NAACP) successfully overturned *Plessy* in the public schools. The famous U.S. Supreme Court case, *Brown v. Board of Education*, is largely considered the first victory of the modern civil rights movement. Soon after, a grassroots movement to desegregate public transportation in Montgomery, Alabama, culminated in the successful Montgomery Bus Boycotts of 1956. Even as white supremacists in the South resisted Jim Crow's demise through deadly violence against African American and other activists, President Lyndon B. Johnson signed into law the Civil Rights Act of 1964, which outlawed racial segregation and gender discrimination in public schools, public places, and employment. These laws profoundly changed the face of Jim Crow in the United States, but many argue that the process of racial equality and integration is not yet complete. Jim Crow may no longer be an explicitly legal practice of racial exclusion, but socioeconomic factors that relegate African Americans and other Americans of color to poorer neighborhoods with less well-equipped schools and less chance for economic opportunity have fostered a reincarnation of Jim Crow into the twenty-first century.

Elizabeth Stordeur Pryor

Further Reading

Lhamon, W. T., Jr. *Jump Jim Crow: Lost Plays, Lyrics and Street Prose of the First Atlantic Popular Culture*. Cambridge, MA: Harvard University Press, 2003.

Litwack, Leon F. *Trouble in Mind: Black Southerners in the Age of Jim Crow*. New York: Knopf, 1998.

Medley, Keith Weldon. *We as Freemen:* Plessy v. Ferguson. Gretna, LA: Pelican Publishing, 2003.

Packard, Jerrold M. *American Nightmare: The History of Jim Crow*. New York: St. Martin's Press, 2002.

Woodward, C. Vann. *The Strange Career of Jim Crow.* 1955. Rev. ed., London: Oxford University Press, 2002.

Johnson, Lyndon B.

Lyndon B. Johnson, popularly known as LBJ, was the 36th president of the United States. He ascended to the presidency on November 22, 1963, when President John F. Kennedy was assassinated while on a political trip in Dallas, Texas. Johnson completed Kennedy's term and, in 1964, was elected to his own full term in a landslide.

Lyndon Baines Johnson was born on August 27, 1908, one of five children in Stonewall, Texas, to Samuel Ealy Johnson Jr. and Rebekah Baines in a farmhouse located on a poor section near the Pedernales River. His father served in the Texas legislature, and young Lyndon was steeped in politics from the time he was a small boy. The family was impoverished, however, and by the time Lyndon was a teenager, his father was trapped in debt and lost the family home. The elder Johnson struggled financially for the rest of his life. Family, friends, and biographers agree that this is when Johnson developed his affinity for the poor and disadvantaged, regardless of race.

President Lyndon B. Johnson meets with civil rights activists at the White House on August 6, 1965. (LBJ Library)

Johnson did poorly in school and was unable to get into college. He worked odd jobs for a few years after high school and was finally admitted to Southwest Texas State Teachers College, later renamed Texas State University–San Marcos, in 1927. Miserable there, he left college and went to Welhausen School, where he taught fifth through seventh grades and served as the principal to a student body made up of poor Mexicans and blacks. He returned to Southwest Texas State Teachers College and graduated in 1930. He later took a job at Pearsall High School, where he taught public speaking and advised the district championship debate team.

A gregarious person, Johnson gained the attention of U.S. Congress member Richard Kleberg, who asked him to be the secretary in his Washington, D.C., office. It was here that Johnson blossomed; he learned the arcane rules of Congress and was elected speaker of an organization of congressional workers known as the Little Congress. Johnson also caught the eye of his political idol, President Franklin D. Roosevelt, who appointed him as the Texas director of the National Youth Administration (NYA). Johnson was a most energetic NYA director and was very helpful to African Americans caught in the vice grip of the Great Depression. He was described as "warmly disposed to giving disadvantaged blacks opportunity for education and work" so that they could help themselves. While he blocked the representation of African Americans to the Texas NYA, he did appoint a black advisory board and enjoyed great success in the black community. He resigned from the NYA in 1937 to run in a special election for the 10th Congressional District to the House of Representatives.

After the bombing of Pearl Harbor in December 1941, Roosevelt helped Johnson obtain a commission to the U.S. Naval Reserve, where he won a Silver Star. Johnson left the military after Roosevelt ordered members of Congress to leave active service, and he won a second run for the U.S. Senate in 1948 by a mere 87 votes. There were allegations of voter fraud, and for the rest of his life, he could not shake the ironic nickname "Landslide Lyndon."

Johnson eventually became one of the most powerful Senate majority leaders in history. He did this by prodigious hard work, developing powerful alliances, mastering the byzantine rules of the Senate, and knowing his colleagues as well as they knew themselves. He understood their ambitions, remembered their families, and kept track of their strengths, weaknesses, and peccadillos. He used this information to develop what came to be called the *Johnson treatment*. Through the use of flattery, cajolery, intimidation, doublespeak, humility, and the sheer force of his personality, Johnson so overwhelmed people he was almost always able to enlist them to further his goals.

While in Congress, he was an ardent supporter of Roosevelt yet typically voted, as did his southern colleagues, against the federal antilynching bill, and for eliminating the poll tax, denying federal funds for lunch programs at black schools, and denying the federal government the right to send absentee ballots directly to soldiers stationed overseas. This effectively disenfranchised thousands of African American servicemen and servicewomen. He explained that his votes were based not on racial prejudice, but on upholding states' rights.

Johnson held the conventional views of his time as they applied to blacks. He was not above repeating racist jokes, and he routinely called blacks, including those who worked for him, "nigger," especially when he was in the company of other southerners. On the other hand, he often helped his black constituents or individual blacks he happened to meet. For example, he hired Zephyr Wright, a college graduate who could not find a job, as the Johnson family cook and spoke sorrowfully about how difficult it was for her to travel with the Johnsons when there were virtually no public accommodations available to blacks.

Privately, Johnson often supported the concept of equal opportunity. Although he refused to support a federal antilynching bill, on occasion he publicly expressed his horror of the crime. He opposed the poll tax, seeing it not as a racial issue, but something that hurt all those who were disadvantaged, regardless of race. Johnson also supported the civil rights plank in the 1948 Democratic platform, and he refused to ally himself with the Dixiecrats, white segregationists who bolted the Democratic Party and formed the States' Rights Party. Nevertheless, he repeatedly made the distinction between passing civil rights laws and attacking poverty, which he thought more helpful to minorities.

Events of the 1950s, however, forced civil rights matters to the forefront of American politics. In the case of *Brown v. Board of Education* (1954), the U.S. Supreme Court declared segregated schools unconstitutional. In 1955, Emmett Till, a black teenager from Chicago, was murdered for allegedly whistling at a white women when he was visiting relatives in Money, Mississippi, sparking an international outcry. In 1955, blacks in Montgomery, Alabama, led by a young minister named Dr. Martin Luther King Jr., protested against segregated seating on city buses by boycotting the bus company for more than a year, and the Supreme Court supported their position by declaring segregation in public transportation unconstitutional.

Johnson also recognized earlier than most of his southern colleagues that there was a shift in the public perception regarding racial equality; he knew that the South as a region would never prosper if it continued to focus on the old bugaboo of race. Furthermore, by the late 1950s, his own political ambitions were such that he began to think of running for the presidency, and he knew it would require him to prove that he was not just a southern leader, but a national one. To this end, he determined that his political fortunes would be advanced by helping to pass a civil rights bill.

In 1956, the administration of President Dwight D. Eisenhower sent a sweeping civil rights bill to Congress. It provided for creation of a bipartisan U.S. Commission on Civil Rights that would be empowered to investigate racial discrimination and recommend remedies for its eradication; aimed to turn the small civil rights section of the Department of Justice into a full-fledged division led by an assistant attorney general; proposed that the U.S. attorney general be given the power to obtain injunctions in civil rights cases and that those cases be moved from state courts to federal courts; and sought to expand the power of the Justice Department to ask for injunctions against those who threatened or interfered with the right to vote.

After some pruning by members of Congress, a weaker bill passed in the House and moved over to the Senate, where it faced a buzzsaw of criticism in the chamber long dominated by segregationist Democrats. As majority leader, Johnson knew that the bill could tear apart the Democratic Party for years to come, as it pitted anti– and pro–civil rights supporters against each other. Flexing his parliamentary muscles, he sent the bill to the Judiciary Committee, where Democrat and segregationist senator James O. Eastland of Mississippi eviscerated and then buried it in committee. Legislators who supported civil rights eventually agreed to drop their request for moving cases from state to federal courts, and enough southern senators grudgingly agreed to support the bill. Still, Senator Strom Thurmond, an ardent segregationist, conducted what was then the longest filibuster ever undertaken when he spoke for more than 24 hours straight against the bill. Greatly weakened and watered down, the bill finally passed both chambers on August 29 and was signed into law by President Eisenhower on September 9. Through it all, Johnson proved he could rise above partisan, sectional interests and think of the nation as a whole.

In 1959, Eisenhower sent another civil rights bill to Congress. This bill aimed to allow the federal government to inspect local and state voter registration polls and levy penalties against anyone who interfered with the right to register or vote. Once again, Johnson aimed for a bill that was narrowly focused so as to protect the rights of African American voters but would not alienate his southern colleagues. The bill passed the House and moved to the Senate. The Senate began debate on February 29, 1960; however, a group of 18 southern Democrats split into three teams of six each so as to create a continuous filibuster. By using this method, each senator would be required to speak for only four hours every three days. To blunt the impact of the filibuster, Johnson began requiring the Senate to meet in 24-hour sessions. A 15-minute break was allowed before the Senate sat for another 82 hours on March 2. The filibuster was then broken, and Congress passed the bill. President Eisenhower signed the bill into law on May 6, 1960. Both bills had been so weakened in the process that they were more symbolic than substantive. They did, however, prove that Congress could deal with such a volatile issue as civil rights without tearing the nation asunder, and Johnson again demonstrated his prowess as a national leader.

Emboldened by his success, Johnson began actively seeking the 1960 Democratic nomination for the presidency. He was outmaneuvered, however, by Senator John F. Kennedy, the junior senator from Massachusetts and a man

Johnson felt to be unqualified for the presidency, particularly in the field of civil rights. In a somewhat surprising move, Kennedy offered Johnson the post of vice presidential running mate, and even more surprisingly to some, Johnson accepted. It is certain that Kennedy could not have won the presidency without Johnson; his presence on the ticket ensured that several southern states that had gone over to the Republican Party during the Eisenhower years returned to the Democratic fold.

Civil rights activity bubbled to the surface from the beginning of the Kennedy administration. The president had raised expectations during the campaign by implying that civil rights reform could be achieved in part through vigorous activity by the executive branch. Thousands of demonstrations in favor of racial equality took place across the country. In 1961, the Freedom Rides tested compliance with the Interstate Commerce Commission's directive against segregation in interstate travel. The violence unleashed against the Freedom Riders drew the personal intervention of Robert F. Kennedy, the U.S. attorney general.

In 1962, the administration sought to enforce a federal court order requiring the University of Mississippi to admit James Meredith as its first African American student. When it was clear that the local and state police would not maintain order, Kennedy federalized the Mississippi National Guard. A riot ensued and two people were killed. On June 11, 1963, Alabama governor George Wallace fulfilled a campaign promise to stand in the schoolhouse door to prevent the admittance of two black students, Vivian Malone and James Hood, to the University of Alabama. President Kennedy reacted by federalizing the Alabama National Guard, and both students were admitted without violence or bloodshed. Then, on June 12, Medgar Evers, field secretary for the National Association for the Advancement of Colored People (NAACP), was assassinated in the driveway of his Jackson, Mississippi, home. On August 28, the March on Washington, which focused on civil rights and economic justice, brought 200,000 people to the nation's capital. These events appear to have been tailor-made for a man with the ambition and legislative skills of Johnson. Yet Kennedy rarely sought the advice of his vice president on civil rights.

Kennedy did recognize, however, that his administration could no longer rely on ad hoc solutions to individual civil rights crises. On June 19, he sent a far-reaching civil rights bill to Congress. The Kennedy civil rights bill was a multipronged attack on racial discrimination designed to outlaw discrimination in public accommodations, expand and protect the right to vote, and bar employment discrimination. It also contained a provision to cut off government funding to institutions that engaged in racial discrimination. In a nationwide television address, he labeled civil rights a moral issue and urged Congress and the American people to act to ensure equal rights for all Americans.

Several months after Kennedy was assassinated in November 1963, President Johnson told a joint session of Congress that passage of the Kennedy civil rights bill would be the most fitting memorial to the slain president. As president,

Johnson placed his reputation on the line and worked tirelessly to get the Civil Rights Act passed. The success of his career in Congress was of great benefit in this area, and he relished using the Johnson treatment at the presidential level. In the House, the bill had been bottled up in the Rules Committee by segregationist chair Howard W. Smith, who refused to release it. Over the course of the winter recess, public opinion moved toward support of the bill, and Smith finally released it from the Rules Committee. On February 10, 1964, the House passed the bill 290–130 and sent it to the Senate. Parliamentary maneuvers on the part of Democratic majority leader Mike Mansfield sent the bill to the full Senate for debate, bypassing the Judiciary Committee where it was sure to be stalled by southern segregationists. Southern Democrats launched a 54-day filibuster, but the liberal Democratic whip Hubert Humphrey led the movement to invoke, breaking the filibuster. The bill passed the Senate by a vote of 73–27, and Johnson signed the bill on July 2, 1964. He was said to have predicted that the Democratic Party had lost the southern vote for years to come. The impact of the bill was such that racial discrimination in public accommodations was virtually wiped out.

The right to vote, however, was still in question. Several civil rights organizations had been leading voter registration activities in Alabama and Mississippi since 1963, but demonstrators and activists were met with violence perpetrated by law enforcement officials and white citizens. In response to the situation, the Johnson administration sent to Congress a voting rights bill prohibiting states from interfering with or denying the right to vote in March 1965. The act also proposed to outlaw literacy tests and extend federal oversight of elections.

On February 18, 1965, an Alabama state trooper had shot a young black man named Jimmie Lee Jackson, who was trying to protect his mother and grandfather from the police. Jackson died on February 24, and civil rights worker James Bevel suggested a march from Selma to Montgomery to confront Governor George Wallace about Jackson's death. Instead, the march became an outlet for black anger and a memorial to Jackson. Wallace declared the march a threat to public safety and vowed to prevent it. On March 7, about 600 marchers made their way across Selma's Edmund Pettus Bridge, where they were met by local and state police officers who charged into the crowd on foot and horseback, beating demonstrators. The scene, referred to as Bloody Sunday, was captured by the media and beamed throughout the world.

King organized a second march, but federal district judge Frank M. Johnson issued a restraining order until additional hearings could be held. On March 9, King led a ceremonial march to the Edmund Pettus Bridge, stopped to pray and then turned back. That same evening, three white ministers who had traveled to Selma for the march found themselves in front of the Silver Moon Café, a gathering point for segregationist whites. The three were brutally attacked by several whites, and James Reeb, a Unitarian minister from Boston, died of his injuries. Judge Johnson lifted the restraining shortly thereafter, and a third march was planned for March 21–24. Citizens, college students, civil rights activists, religious leaders, and celebrities joined the three-day effort. After reaching Montgomery, on March 25, King dazzled the crowd of 25,000 with a speech beside the state capital. Later that night, Viola Liuzzo, a white Chicago wife and mother of five, was murdered by members of the Ku Klux Klan (KKK) as she transported Alabama volunteers to their homes. Her passenger, a young black man named Leroy Moton, was not hurt, and played dead while Klansman searched the car.

It is widely believed that the murders of Reeb and Liuzzo, both of whom were white, forced Congress to act quickly on the voting rights legislation. After a Senate filibuster, cloture was invoked, and the bill passed on May 11; the House passed the bill on July 10. Conference committees resolved the differences in the two bills and sent it to President Johnson, who signed the act on August 6, 1965. The impact of the law was immediate; the number of black registered voters in the 11 states of the Old Confederacy soared.

The Civil Rights Act of 1964 and the Voting Rights Act of 1965 did not resolve the persistent poverty, police brutality, overcrowding, poor health care, and a lack of public transportation for millions of African Americans, especially in the urban North. Beginning in the summer of 1965, a series of rebellions broke out in inner cities across America. The first major riot was in the East Los Angeles neighborhood of Watts in August 1965. That rebellion lasted almost a week, and California governor Pat Brown was forced to call out the National Guard. Thirty-four people were killed, and property damage was estimated at more than $30 million. Major disturbances also erupted in Newark, New Jersey, and Detroit, Michigan, as well as 57 other cities in 1967. President Johnson ordered about 5,000 troops from the 82nd and 101st Airborne units into Detroit when Governor George Romney reported that the Michigan Guard was unable to restore civil order.

In the wake of the rebellions, Johnson formed the National Advisory Commission on Civil Disorders, chaired by Illinois governor Otto Kerner. The so-called Kerner Commission issued a bleak report on American race relations, stating that the root causes of the rebellions were poverty, discrimination, and injustice, and recommended that the federal government mount a vigorous attack on those fronts. The Commission also famously reported that America was splintering into two societies, one black and one white.

The racial rebellions that occurred in the latter part of the 1960s caused a severe backlash among white Americans who thought that Johnson had moved too quickly on racial equality, and endangered his most important program, the War on Poverty, the foundation of what he called the Great Society. Johnson had signed the Economic Opportunity Act in 1964. The act created the Office of Economic Opportunity, which was the administrative arm of several programs. Head Start was designed to help disadvantaged preschoolers, Volunteers in Service to America (VISTA) was a domestic Peace Corps whose purpose was to help the poor across America, and Upward Bound sought to prepare poor teenagers for college. The Education Act funneled more federal money to colleges and universities and provided low-interest loans to financially strapped students. Funding for the first stage of the act was a modest $1 billion.

The War on Poverty was the first government program to involve poor communities in planning and implementing the programs that served them. In this respect, it taught leadership and organizing skills and gave meaningful paid work to hundreds of thousands of poor Americans. Increasingly, however, it was buffeted by disagreements among politicians, anger from white Americans who thought that the program rewarded shiftless and lazy blacks, and ever-rising expectations by African Americans. The biggest obstacle to the program, however, was increased spending on the Vietnam War, where 25 percent of frontline troops were African American.

In 1968, a presidential election year, it was assumed that President Johnson would run for a second term. The United States, however, was mired in an increasingly unpopular war in Vietnam; thousands of young people took to the streets in demonstrations. The Tet Offensive in January 1968 showed that the administration had not been truthful about the war, and for the first time, it seemed to be admitting that the war was unwinnable. Urban rebellions continued, and many young people seemed to be members of a counterculture that was a maze of sex, drugs, and rock 'n' roll. Senator Eugene McCarthy, the liberal Democrat from Minnesota, had come out against the war and entered the presidential race, and hundreds of college student volunteers cut their hair, shaved their beards, and became "Clean for Gene." Although he lost the New Hampshire primary to Johnson by 42 percent to 49 percent, he was able to show how vulnerable the sitting president was. After McCarthy's strong showing, Robert F. Kennedy, now junior senator from New York, announced his antiwar candidacy. On March 31, in a televised news conference, Johnson announced that he would neither run for nor accept the nomination of the Democratic Party for a second presidential term.

On April 4, civil rights leader and Nobel Prize winner Martin Luther King Jr. was assassinated in Memphis, Tennessee, where he had gone to support sanitation workers in their fight for better wages and working conditions. As a result, riots broke out in dozens of cities as angry and frustrated blacks sought to avenge King's death. On June 4, Robert F. Kennedy was assassinated in Los Angeles after he had claimed victory in the California primary. Kennedy had been one of the few whites in public life who understood the plight of minorities and the underclass. The country was spinning out of control.

The death of King heightened a sense of urgency in Congress as it debated a third piece of civil rights legislation. On April 11, Johnson signed the Civil Rights Act of 1968, which prohibited racial discrimination in the advertisement, sale, or rental of housing. It was the last piece of civil rights legislation he would sign. When Johnson turned the White House over to Republican Richard Nixon on

January 20, 1969, he was one of the most unpopular presidents in history. Johnson died on January 22, 1973, at his ranch in Texas.

Marilyn K. Howard

Further Reading

Caro, Robert A. *Master of the Senate*. Vol. 3 of *The Years of Lyndon Johnson*. New York: Knopf Publishing Group, 2003.

Dallek, Robert. *Lone Star Rising: LBJ and His Times, 1961–1973*. New York: Oxford University Press, 1998.

Goodwin, Doris Kearns. *Lyndon Johnson and the American Dream*. New York: St. Martin's Griffin, 1991.

Kotz, Nick. *Judgment Days: LBJ, MLK, Jr. and the Laws That Changed America*. Boston: Houghton Mifflin, 2005.

Mann, Robert. *The Walls of Jericho: Lyndon Johnson, Hubert Humphrey, Richard Russell and the Struggle for Civil Rights*. New York: Harcourt Brace, 1996.

K

Kennedy, John F.

John F. Kennedy served as the 35th president of the United States from 1961 until his assassination in 1963. Kennedy was a critical figure in U.S. history as it related to the experience of African Americans during the pivotal years of the civil rights movement. Although many have called Kennedy a reluctant participant in the civil rights movement, he was an essential participant nonetheless—he helped push civil rights legislation through Congress, supported the integration of schools and universities throughout the South, and collaborated extensively with leaders of the civil rights movement.

Born May 29, 1917, in Brookline, Massachusetts, John Fitzgerald "Jack" Kennedy grew up in a large, Roman Catholic family. Illness kept him indoors, reading, for most of his childhood and even hindered his graduation from both the London School of Economics and Princeton University as a young man. However, he eventually graduated from Harvard in 1940 and then enlisted in the U.S. Navy during World War II. In 1946, he began his political career when he was elected a Democratic representative of Massachusetts. Six years later, as the civil rights movement was building in momentum, he was elected to the U.S. Senate.

In 1954, the U.S. Supreme Court ruled that racial segregation in public schools was unconstitutional in the federal court case *Brown v. Board of Education.* However, this ruling was widely ignored throughout the South, and schools as well as restaurants, theaters, bathrooms, and many other public facilities remained segregated. As a result, the struggle for civil rights and social justice became an issue that necessitated action. Led by individuals such as Martin Luther King Jr. and by organizations such as the Southern Christian Leadership Conference (SCLC), the civil rights movement began to take action in the form of a series of sit-ins and nonviolent protests. As early as 1957, astute congressional leaders began to recognize that civil rights legislation would eventually become inevitability.

In 1956 and 1957, as the junior senator from Massachusetts, Kennedy designed a strategy for how to accommodate African Americans as well as a wide variety of Democrats in regard to civil liberties. However, this strategy was hardly the position of a stanch civil rights advocate. Instead, it was a political maneuver and calculated with thoughts of a campaign for the presidency in 1960. Kennedy engaged in debates on the Senate floor regarding Titles III and IV of a bill that would give the U.S. attorney general the power to intervene in school desegregations with military force. He was able to support this bill without upsetting northern liberals or southern conservatives, both constituencies that he would need in his bid for the presidency in 1960. Indeed, Kennedy walked a very thin line, which brought criticism from several stanch civil rights advocates.

This legislation culminated in the Civil Rights Act of 1957, which created a commission to monitor violations of civil liberties, especially as it applied to voting. It also upgraded the Civil Rights office to the Justice Department and gave that office the power to commence civil measures against states that discriminated based on race. Further, many saw Kennedy's support of a bill carrying an amendment guaranteeing the right of all Americans to serve on federal juries as a fake bill with no real substantive power to change the status quo. However, the Civil Rights Act of 1957 was the first time since Reconstruction that the U.S. Congress had acted in any way to protect the civil liberties of African Americans. Thus, Kennedy's journey down the path of civil rights began, and public sentiment held that he was trying to press forward with equal treatment of African Americans, but that he was most concerned with securing national unity through a legality course.

In Kennedy's bid for the White House in 1960 against Richard Nixon, he chose the tenuous position to advance civil rights. This position was politically expedient, as it secured the African American vote as well as consolidated the votes of northern liberals in favor of desegregation. However, Kennedy was taking a political gamble in losing the support of southern Democrats such as A. Willis Robertson and Harry F. Byrd of Virginia, who were pro-segregation. Kennedy began to add many leaders of the civil rights movement to his staff, including Marjorie Lawson, William Dawson, and Frank Reeves, who advised him on how to espouse an aggressive civil rights agenda. The Kennedy campaign also encouraged the creation of a national organization to create a nationwide voter registration drive within African American communities.

Throughout the campaign, Kennedy applauded the peaceful nonviolent strategies of civil rights activists; he spoke at several engagements at predominantly African American conferences and criticized the inaction of previous presidents who failed to bring integration sooner. Further, he promised to support civil rights legislation, including a pledge to see more African Americans hired in the highest levels of the federal government. Kennedy also cultivated favor among African Americans when he telephoned Coretta Scott King in regard to the jailing of her husband, Martin Luther King Jr. Indeed, not only did Kennedy sympathize with Mrs. King, but also his phone calls, as well as those of his brother Bobby, convinced Georgia's governor, Ernest Vandiver, to set King free. This multifaceted strategy landed Kennedy the support of African Americans in his bid for the presidency in 1960. Given the slim margin of victory (about 100,000 votes), African American voters played a significant role in sealing the victory for Kennedy. Nixon's attempt to strengthen his support among southern voters, as well as his silence about issues surrounding civil liberties, caused many African

American voters to reconsider their old ties to the Republican Party, which went back to the party's pro–civil rights record during Reconstruction in the mid-to-late 1860s.

Upon winning the presidency, Kennedy grew increasingly concerned about the violence surrounding the civil rights movement, particularly the Freedom Rides. His interests in civil liberties continued to display this concern, as his policies addressed the prevention of further disorder and violence. Because of his stance during the election, Kennedy was in a fixed position among southern democrats. However, it actually freed him to aid the civil rights movement in several ways. His first act as president toward support of the movement was the issuance of Executive Order 11063. This order obliged government agencies to discontinue discriminatory practices in federal housing. Kennedy also named Vice President Lyndon B. Johnson to be the chair of a newly appointed Committee on Equal Employment. In addition, nominating African Americans to a number of posts including Thurgood Marshall to the Second Circuit Court of Appeals, Carl Rowan to deputy assistant of the secretary of state, and George L. P. Weaver to assistant secretary of labor, further ingratiated Kennedy to African Americans.

One of the defining moments of the Kennedy administration in regard to civil rights was on June 25, 1962. James Meredith had applied to the University of Mississippi, had been rejected based on his race, and thus filed a complaint for racial discrimination in the U.S. Circuit Court of Appeals. The Fifth Circuit ruled that the university should admit Meredith, but Mississippi governor Ross Barnett stated that he would physically stand in the way of integration. As a result, Kennedy sent 300 federal marshals to enforce the court's decision. There were riots on campus that yielded the deaths of two individuals and over 200 arrests, and many federal marshals sustained serious injuries. Kennedy then put the Mississippi National Guard under federal jurisdiction and made sure that Meredith was admitted. Later, in June 1963, Kennedy took the same action against George Wallace in the desegregation of the University of Alabama.

In August 1963, Kennedy proposed to Congress the strongest civil rights bill yet seen in U.S. history. However, the strong bloc of southern voters in the House and Senate were able to keep the bill from passing. In support of Kennedy's bold new legislation, a coalition was formed between several civil rights organizations, including the Southern Christian Leadership Conference, the National Association for the Advancement of Colored People, the Congress of Racial Equality, and the Student Nonviolent Coordinating Committee, which organized a massive march in Washington. Later that August, about 250,000 marchers gathered near the Lincoln Memorial in support of equality in the job market, freedom, and civil justice through the passage of Kennedy's legislation. This is the context for Martin Luther King Jr.'s famous "I Have a Dream" speech. Using television images, many Americans witnessed this important protest of racial discrimination, and there was no doubt that the March on Washington helped pave the way toward the passage of the Civil Rights Act of 1964. However, in an act that became a double-edged sword for the civil rights movement, the assassination of Kennedy in November 1963 proved to be a tremendous loss, but also perhaps a tremendous gain for the movement.

The legacy of Kennedy as it related to the civil rights movement was fully realized by the passage of the Civil Rights Act of 1964. After the death of Kennedy, Vice President Johnson was inaugurated as the 36th president of the United States. Johnson, having taken the oath of office only four days prior, disclosed to the nation that he planned to support Kennedy's civil rights bill as a testament to Kennedy's work toward civil justice. A southerner from Texas, many leaders of the civil rights movement feared that Johnson would only buttress the southern voting bloc in the legislature that had kept such a bill from previous passage. However, with years of legislative experience at work, Johnson was able to push the bill through Congress despite massive resistance in the form of southern filibusters. The act banned segregation and racial discrimination in public facilities such as restaurants, hotels, schools, libraries, and swimming pools.

The Civil Rights Act of 1964 also called for a ban of racial discrimination in the American workforce. No longer could employers discriminate based on race, religion, ethnicity, or sex when considering a hire, promotion, or termination. To enforce these positions, the federal government was granted the power to withhold federal funding to any organization that was discriminating in any way. Finally, the Civil Rights Act of 1964 led to the desegregation of many public schools, it created the Employment Opportunity Commission to oversee practices of racial prejudice in employment, and it gave the attorney general the power to initiate prosecution on behalf of those who had been the victims of unfair injustice. This is perhaps one of the greatest legacies of the Kennedy administration as it related to the civil rights movement. Unfortunately, it was not until after Kennedy's premature death that the dream was fully realized.

In August 1965, Congress passed another act that augmented the 1964 legislation. The Voting Rights Act of 1965, although signed into law by Johnson, was also a part of the Kennedy civil rights legacy. This act outlawed the educational requirements throughout many states in the South that called for the reciting of the constitution or for the "proper" interpretations of various sections of the constitution in order to vote. Many of these requirements had kept African Americans from voting and therefore had a tremendous effect on the racial bias of state and local elections. The Voting Rights Act of 1965 also gave the attorney general the power to assign federal voter registrars to record African American voters. This had a tremendous influence on the numbers of the African American electorate. For instance, in Mississippi alone, the number of enrolled African American voters grew from 28,000 in 1964 to over 250,000 in 1968.

Otis Westbrook Pickett

Further Reading

Dallek, Robert. *An Unfinished Life: John F. Kennedy, 1917–1963*. New York: Little, Brown, 2003.

O'Brien, Michael. *John F. Kennedy: A Biography*. New York: Thomas Dunne Books, an imprint of St. Martin's Press, 2005.

Rorabaugh, W. J. *Kennedy and the Promise of the Sixties*. Cambridge: Cambridge University Press, 2002.

Rosenberg, Johnathan, and Zachary Karabell. *Kennedy, Johnson, and the Quest for Justice: The Civil Rights Tapes*. New York: W. W. Norton, 2003.

Stern, Mark. *Calculating Visions: Kennedy, Johnson, and Civil Rights*. New Brunswick, NJ: Rutgers University Press, 1992.

Kennedy, Robert F.

Robert Kennedy was a leading and influential political figure during the struggles for racial and economic equality of the 1960s. Formally trained as a lawyer and experientially as a politician, Kennedy served as attorney general of the United States from 1961 to 1964, during some of the most pivotal years of the civil rights movement. From 1965 until his assassination in 1968, he served as U.S. senator from New York, using his position and his political expertise to champion for racial, social, and economic equality.

Born the seventh of nine children into the prominent, powerful, and wealthy Kennedy family on November 20, 1925, Robert Francis "Bobby" Kennedy graduated from Harvard University in 1948 with a degree in government and earned a law degree from the University of Virginia Law School in 1951. Throughout the 1950s, Kennedy worked as a lawyer for the U.S. Department of Justice and for various Senate committees. In 1952, he served as campaign manager for his brother, John F. Kennedy, during his run for senator of Massachusetts. And in 1959, he managed another campaign for John: his bid to become the 35th president of the United States.

Elected to the presidency in 1960, John appointed Robert as his attorney general. Robert's job was to ensure the constitutional rights of the American people, and nowhere was he called to do so more than in the southern struggles for racial equality. Initially, Robert believed that the most necessary gain in these struggles would be unhindered access to the ballot box. African American citizens in the South often faced harassment for exercising their right to vote, so Robert dispatched federal marshals into these southern states to investigate and begin prosecuting counties that condoned voter intimidation.

While Robert tried to contain the Justice Department's policies to legislation, students and civil rights leaders opted for a different strategy. Lunch counter sit-ins, freedom rides, protest marches, school integration, and many other varieties of nonviolent direct action proliferated across the South. Robert provided Justice Department support wherever possible. He dispatched federal marshals to pacify angry mobs during the first Freedom Rides of May 1961. He encouraged President Kennedy to provide armed protection for endangered persons, such as for James Meredith, who in September 1962 integrated the University of Mississippi in Oxford. Robert also negotiated with segregationist southern leaders—such as Alabama governor John Patterson, who opposed the integration of the University of Alabama at Tuscaloosa—to enforce federal law.

By this time, Robert understood that although enfranchisement was certainly important, only a more comprehensive guarantee of civil liberties could ensure the rights of U.S. citizens. He urged his brother to draft a comprehensive civil rights bill to send to Congress, and he insisted that President Kennedy publicly address the civil rights issue. Thus, on June 11, 1963, President Kennedy became the first president to publicly declare the struggle for racial equality a moral issue. Immediately thereafter, civil rights leaders began planning a national March on Washington for Freedom, Jobs, and Justice to advocate for quick passage of this legislation. Robert's Justice Department guaranteed the marchers federal protection.

The March on Washington took place on August 1963, but John did not live to see the passage of the civil rights legislation. He was assassinated on November 22, 1963. His vice president, Lyndon B. Johnson, assumed the presidency and asked Robert to remain attorney general. In July 1964, Robert witnessed the signing of his brother's civil rights bill into law as the Civil Rights Act of 1964. The next month, Robert resigned his post as attorney general in order to campaign in New York for a U.S. Senate seat.

As a U.S. senator, Robert continued to fight for racial equality as well as for economic and social equality. In the latter half of the 1960s, nonviolent protest gave way to more confrontational methods. Riots erupted in urban centers around the country, but rather than condemn the rioters, Robert encouraged people to consider the conditions that might engender such actions. He called attention to inequities in education, housing, employment, and living wages. He took steps to mitigate against such injustices—for example, supporting the United Farm Workers and forming the Senate Subcommittee on Indian Education. He visited the impoverished Mississippi Delta in 1967, and afterward, he actively pursued food assistance for the area. Such community rehabilitation endeavors, the most famous of which revitalized the Bedford-Stuyvesant community in Brooklyn, occupied his Senate career. He implemented community development corporations, programs that combined residents' needs and energies with federal grants and private sector investment in community improvement.

In March 1968, Robert announced that he would challenge Johnson for the presidency. Over the next few months, Robert stormed the primary race, bolstered by the overwhelming support of those to whom he reached out most: African Americans, Hispanics, student protesters, the poor, the dispossessed, and the suffering. On June 4, 1968, celebrating an important primary win in California, Robert was shot at the Ambassador Hotel. He died two days later.

Aghigh Ebrahimi

Further Reading

Branch, Taylor. *Parting the Waters: America in the King Years, 1954–63*. New York: Simon & Schuster, 1988.

Huevel, Vanden, and Milton Gwirtzman. *On His Own: Robert F. Kennedy*. New York: Doubleday, 1970.

Kennedy, Robert F. *To Seek a Newer World*. New York: Doubleday, 1967.

Palermo, Joseph A. *Robert F. Kennedy and the Death of American Idealism*. New York: Pearson Education, 2008.

Schlesinger, Arthur M., Jr. *Robert Kennedy and His Times*. Boston: Houghton Mifflin, 1978.

Thomas, Evan. *Robert Kennedy: His Life*. New York: Simon & Schuster, 2000.

Kerner Commission Report

In the aftermath of the so-called Long Hot Summer of 1967, the nation was convulsed by major outbreaks of racial violence in Newark, Detroit, Cleveland, and numerous smaller cities. The official response to the riots was President Lyndon B. Johnson's Executive Order 11365, issued on July 29, 1967, which established a National Advisory Commission on Civil Disorders. Two days earlier, Johnson appointed the 11-member commission during a presidential address to the country. In essence, the commission would investigate civil disorders and would make recommendations to the president, Congress, governors, and mayors for implementing measures to help contain race riots in the future.

After seven months of investigation, the commission completed and submitted a report on February 29, 1968, named after its chairman, Illinois governor and later federal judge Otto Kerner Jr. Kerner was, in many ways, a prototypical member of the commission. Like New York mayor John Lindsay, vice chair of the commission, Senator Edward Brooke of Massachusetts, and Roy Wilkins of the National Association for the Advancement of Colored People (NAACP), Kerner was a political moderate.

The Kerner Commission Report was issued as a 426-page book, which, ironically, became a national bestseller, with more than two million copies in print. Charged by Johnson to investigate what happened, why it happened, and what could be done to prevent it from happening again, the commission issued findings that were surprisingly progressive given the embrace of moderate political ideology by most of its 11 members. According to the commission, white racism was the cause of race riots between 1965 and 1967, and the country was becoming "two societies, one black, one white—separate and unequal." The Kerner Commission Report dispelled a number of myths embraced by President Johnson and Federal Bureau of Investigation (FBI) director J. Edgar Hoover. The principal misconception corrected by the Kerner Commission Report was that race riots were not the product of black extremists or white radicals. Instead, they were the result of a suffocating mix of high unemployment (and underemployment), chronic poverty, poor housing conditions, poor schools, lack of access to affordable health care, police brutality, and harassment faced by millions of African Americans living in inner cities. The formation of the racial ghetto, the Kerner Commission Report claimed, was the fault of white America, and as white America was a factor in its creation, whites were also responsible for the conditions that made race riots possible.

The Kerner Commission Report recommended fundamental changes in federal policy to ameliorate the oppressive conditions faced by African Americans. Specifically, the commission called for federal initiatives directed at improving public services, schools, employment opportunities, and housing in predominantly African American inner-city neighborhoods. In addition, it called for a complete restructuring of the welfare system and for a national system of income supplementation that would address underemployment and single-parent households. By 1968, the political winds had shifted considerably. With the election of Richard Nixon as president, many of the Kerner Commission Report's recommendations would be ignored or greatly delayed.

Walter C. Rucker

Further Reading

Blaustein, Albert P., and Robert L. Zangrando. *Civil Rights and African Americans: A Documentary History.* Evanston, IL: Northwestern University Press, 1991.

Boger, John Charles, and Judith Welch Wegner. *Race, Poverty, and American Cities.* Chapel Hill: University of North Carolina Press, 1996.

Harris, Fred R. *Locked in the Poorhouse: Cities, Race, and Poverty in the United States.* Lanham, MD: Rowman & Littlefield, 1998.

Meranto, Philip J. *The Kerner Report Revisited.* Urbana: Institute of Government and Public Affairs, University of Illinois, 1970.

King, Coretta Scott

Coretta Scott King (1927–2006) was the wife of civil rights leader Martin Luther King Jr., an author, and a civil rights leader in her own right. Born on April 27, 1927, in Heiberger, Alabama, she was raised on a farm owned by her parents,

Bernice McMurry Scott and Obadiah Scott. The second of three siblings, King's family was not wealthy despite her father's entrepreneurial spirit. Obadiah Scott owned a truck, ran a barbershop, and owned a lumber mill, all while growing cotton on the family's own land. In the midst of the Great Depression, Coretta and her siblings picked cotton to supplement the meager family income. As a school-age child, King walked five miles each day to attend the Crossroad School, a segregated, one-room school in neighboring Marion, Alabama.

Owing to her parents' emphasis on education and King's own innate academic skills, she excelled in her studies, graduating from Lincoln High School as class valedictorian in 1945. She entered Antioch College in Yellow Springs, Ohio, the following autumn on an academic scholarship. During her time as an undergraduate, she joined the Antioch chapter of the NAACP and the Race Relations and Civil Liberties Committees. After receiving word that the Yellow Springs school board would not allow her to do required practice teaching, she continued her education at the New England Conservatory of Music in Boston with a scholarship to study concert singing.

Shortly after transferring to the New England Conservatory, King met Martin Luther King Jr., who, after his graduation from Morehouse College, was enrolled as a divinity student at Boston University. A year after their first meeting, the two were married on June 18, 1953. She completed her degree in voice and violin and moved with her husband in September 1954 to Montgomery, Alabama. Within a few short months of becoming pastor of the Dexter Avenue Baptist Church, King and his wife became involved in the Montgomery Bus Boycott. Between 1955 and 1968, King would often be with her husband at the front lines of various struggles against segregation and injustice. The couple would have four children: Yolanda (b. 1955), Martin Luther III (b. 1957), Dexter (b. 1961), and Bernice (b. 1963). After her husband's assassination on April 4, 1968, King was involved in organizing a commemorative service at Ebenezer Baptist Church in Atlanta every January 15 to mark his birth and honor his life. This commemoration was expanded to serve as the basis for calls for a national holiday. By an act of Congress, national observances of the holiday began in 1986. King also played a pivotal role in establishing the King Center for Nonviolent Social Change in Atlanta, which opened its doors to the public in 1981.

Between the 1970s and 1990s, King was actively involved in a number of movements seeking equality, justice, and civil rights. She had been an ardent opponent of the apartheid regimes of South Africa, working tirelessly with Winnie Mandela and the African National Congress (ANC) as well as politicians in the United States, including President Ronald Reagan, to combat the racist policies and denial of liberties to the black majority in the beleaguered nation. In addition to her opposition to apartheid, King was actively involved in addressing capital punishment; HIV/AIDS prevention; and lesbian, gay, bisexual, and transgender rights, and she was a staunch critic of the 2003 invasion of Iraq and various policies of

President George W. Bush, including the push to propose a marriage amendment. In honor of her continuing role as a voice for justice, she was awarded the Gandhi Peace Prize in 2004 by the government of India. After a lifetime of struggle, King's health began to fail in 2005 when she suffered a stroke and a mild heart attack. On January 30, 2006, King died at the age of 78 in Rosarito Beach, Mexico, of complications from ovarian cancer. On November 20, 2006, her remains were laid to rest next to her husband's at the King Center in Atlanta.

Walter C. Rucker

Further Reading

"Coretta Scott King: The First Lady of the Civil Rights Movement (1927–2006)." *Journal of Blacks in Higher Education* 50 (Winter 2005–2006): 60.

McCarty, Laura T. *Coretta Scott King: A Biography.* Santa Barbara, CA: ABC-CLIO, 2009.

Vivian, Octavia B. *Coretta: The Story of Coretta Scott King.* Minneapolis, MN: Fortress Press, 2006.

King, Martin Luther, Jr.

African American civil rights leader Martin Luther King Jr.'s emergence, notoriety, evolution, and demise paralleled that of the civil rights movement itself. He became the nation's preeminent spokesperson for the strategy of nonviolent direct action, the dismantling of Jim Crow laws in the South, and the creation of a larger "beloved community." He negotiated between the push of political expediency and the pull of militant black activists, all the while combating enemies who perceived him as a dangerous radical.

Born in Atlanta, Georgia, on January 15, 1929, King was raised in relative privilege. His father was pastor at the Ebenezer Baptist Church, which served a middle-class clientele. The second of three children, he enjoyed a comfortable home life, material security, and the attention of a loving family. However, he periodically experienced segregation in the Jim Crow South. He mostly thrived, however, within the institutions of the black middle class, especially the black church. He graduated from high school at age 15 and attended Morehouse College. Before his senior year, he decided to enter the ministry.

King attended Crozer Theological Seminary in Chester, Pennsylvania, from 1948 to 1951. At this liberal, predominantly white institution, he read the classics of Western philosophy, the key texts of Hinduism and Islam, and the writings of Mohandas Gandhi. He also questioned the liberal, optimistic belief in progress influenced by Reinhold Niebuhr. From 1951 to 1953, King attended Boston University, from which he received his doctorate in theology in 1955. In Boston,

Dr. Martin Luther King, Jr., President of the Southern Christian Leadership Conference, and Mathew Ahmann (center, wearing eyeglasses), Executive Director of the National Catholic Conference for Interracial Justice, in the Civil Rights March on Washington, D.C. on August 28, 1963. (National Archives)

he met Coretta Scott, a student at the New England Conservatory of Music. They married in 1953.

In 1954, King took the pastorship at Dexter Avenue Baptist Church in Montgomery, Alabama, that catered to a small congregation of African American professionals. In December 1955, the Montgomery police arrested Rosa Parks, a seamstress and National Association for the Advancement of Colored People (NAACP) secretary, for refusing to vacate her seat on the segregated city buses. The African American leadership recognized the political opportunity, declared a bus boycott, and formed the Montgomery Improvement Association; they elected the 26-year-old King president only because he had avoided the rivalries among the older ministers. King urged nonviolent protest, which not only placed the protesters on higher moral ground, but also engendered support from white liberals. For more than a year, Montgomery's African American citizens walked and established carpools, and King endured arrests and a bombing of his home. The national media paid King and the Montgomery Bus Boycott significant attention. In November 1956, the Supreme Court ruled Montgomery's bus segregation unconstitutional.

In the public mind, King had become the preeminent African American leader. He founded and led the Southern Christian Leadership Conference (SCLC), a political network for civil rights activism. Along with Roy Wilkins and A. Philip Randolph, he led a 1957 mass meeting in Washington, D.C., known as the prayer pilgrimage, but it failed to attract much attention from the media or the federal government. In 1959, he resigned from Dexter Avenue Baptist Church and based himself at SCLC headquarters in Atlanta.

The student sit-in movement campaigns of 1960, starting in Greensboro, North Carolina, and spreading through much of the South, energized the civil rights movement. In April 1960, King spoke at the organizing meeting of the Student Nonviolent Coordinating Committee (SNCC). During the next year's Freedom Rides, when activists from the Congress of Racial Equality (CORE) and SNCC encountered violence while desegregating bus terminals in the South, King again offered encouragement and political clout, but he declined to place himself on the dangerous frontlines of the Freedom Rides. In October 1960, King began a four-month sentence in an Atlanta prison on a trumped-up traffic violation. The Republican presidential candidate, Vice President Richard Nixon, had been Dwight D. Eisenhower's point man on civil rights, and he had worked behind the scenes to get King released. But Democratic presidential candidate John F. Kennedy, distant from African American protesters and quiet on King's arrest, placed a concerned telephone call to King's spouse Coretta Scott King. The Kennedy campaign publicized the gesture in African American newspapers and in pamphlets distributed to African American churches, helping deliver a close election over Nixon.

However, the Kennedy administration resisted any alliance with King. Kennedy feared King's capacity to stir up disorder, and he first invited to the White House more established African American leaders such as the NAACP's Roy Wilkins. U.S. attorney general Robert F. Kennedy sanctioned Federal Bureau of Investigation (FBI) surveillance of King and his associates. FBI director J. Edgar Hoover considered King a disloyal radical. King's trusted white adviser, Stanley Levison, moreover, once had financially supported the American Communist Party. Hoover's agents, who offered little protection to the civil rights demonstrators in the South, tapped the telephones of King and Levison. However, the FBI tapes reveal nothing politically incriminating about King. However, in private, he offered the occasional crude comment. He enjoyed bawdy late-night drinking sessions and smoked cigarettes, although never in public. His sexual indiscretions were not public knowledge, although friends warned him of the dangers to his image, and elements of the African American community whispered rumors. Hoover regarded him a moral degenerate and maintained FBI surveillance.

In December 1961, King arrived in Albany, Georgia, at the behest of the Albany, Georgia Movement, a coalition of community civil rights groups. His involvement gradually escalated from a speech, to a protest march, to an arrest, and finally to a longer commitment for the city's desegregation. King brought media attention and SCLC resources to this civil rights campaign, but the Albany Movement faltered. The NAACP fretted about militant SNCC tactics; local leaders resented the condescension of SCLC deputies; SNCC feared that King would leave Albany with a symbolic victory but little change to the substance of racial patterns. Police chief Laurie Pritchett also defused the demonstrators' tactics of moral theater by avoiding crude violence before television cameras and by arranging to jail demonstrators outside the city. King was arrested twice, but city leaders paid his fine and suspended his sentence, so that he could not become a media martyr. King left Albany in 1962 with few public facilities desegregated.

Unlike in Albany, in the 1963 SCLC campaign in Birmingham, Alabama, King and SCLC gave direction to the entire series of protests, and "Project C" began with specific targets: the desegregation of three downtown department stores, leading to broader desegregation, the hiring of African Americans for city jobs, and the formation of a biracial council. They trained volunteers in nonviolent resistance and raised reserves of money. Through early April, SCLC held sit-ins, marches, and mass meetings. After a state court injunction barring further protests, King led another march and was arrested. While in prison, he read that liberal white clergymen had condemned his campaign for "extremism" from "outsiders." King's response, referred to as "Letter from Birmingham Jail," outlined King's basic philosophies. He defied state law, he wrote, because of a higher moral law. He rejected the plea that African Americans must be patient, arguing that freedom for the oppressed arrives only when the oppressed demand freedom. Nonviolent direct action, moreover, did not promote racial ill will so much as bring it to the surface.

When King emerged from jail on Easter Sunday, Project C was floundering. In May, SCLC began using children for their protest marches. Thousands marched from the Sixteenth Street Baptist Church, singing freedom songs and clapping their hands. Commissioner of Public Safety Eugene "Bull" Connor responded with violence, unleashing police on African American demonstrators with billy clubs, electric cattle prods, attack dogs, and high-pressure fire hoses—images that circulated throughout the country. The protesters maintained the demonstrations, pressuring the city's business community and gaining a settlement that met SCLC's original demands. Birmingham's violence continued, but a corner had been turned. Civil rights protests again spread throughout the South, and national attention focused on the plight of African American southerners. President Kennedy now proposed a civil rights bill desegregating public accommodations.

The momentum continued in late August with the March on Washington. An interracial throng of 250,000 congregated at the Lincoln Memorial to hear speeches from assorted civil rights, labor, and religious leaders on live television. King began his speech solemnly, with a measured pace, using the metaphor of a promissory note to recall the U.S. government's unfulfilled commitment to protect the constitutional rights of its African American citizens. The "I Have a Dream" speech, broadcast in America's living rooms, proved an iconic moment in the country's history. *Time* magazine named him Man of the Year in 1963. In 1964, he won the Nobel Peace Prize. In June 1964, Congress also passed the Civil Rights Act of 1964, prohibiting the segregation of public facilities and backing it with significant enforcement mechanisms.

Nevertheless, King could no longer embody any consensus of black political thought. SCLC's 1964 campaign in St. Augustine, Florida, featured white mobs so vicious that any progress was seemingly impossible; only a King oration kept the city's African Americans from responding with violence in kind. For some activists, King had become too moderate. SNCC members mocked him as "De Lawd" for his preachy ego. When the interracial Mississippi Freedom Democratic Party tried to obtain delegate seats at the 1964 Democratic Convention, King urged acceptance of a compromise proposal, alienating him from militants. Malcolm X countered King's values of nonviolence and integration with calls for eye-for-an-eye justice and Black Nationalism.

In 1965, King and SCLC came to Selma, Alabama. President Lyndon B. Johnson urged patience as the Civil Rights Act went into effect. Not wishing to antagonize Johnson, King left for Atlanta in early March, before a planned march to the state capital of Montgomery. The march began without him, and television cameras captured the violence of Bloody Sunday on the Edmund Pettus Bridge, as the Selma police turned back the marchers with clubs and tear gas. King returned to Selma. By accepting Johnson's compromise to halt a second march upon reaching the bridge, he angered SNCC and other civil rights supporters. The Selma campaign nevertheless succeeded. The violent police response led Johnson to propose a voting rights bill on national television. The march to Montgomery was accomplished with the protection of federal marshals. In August, Congress passed the Voting Rights Act of 1965, eliminating the procedures that had long disenfranchised most southern African Americans.

In urban neighborhoods outside the South, African Americans faced police harassment, possessed little political power, lived in substandard public housing, and suffered the economic and social dislocations of poverty. King visited Chicago in 1965 and launched the Chicago Campaign for open housing in 1966. Leading protest marches and lobbying city leaders for the elimination of de facto segregation in housing, King faced resistance as stiff as that in the South. By 1967, he was an outspoken critic of the Vietnam War. He called for a "revolution of values" in the United States that transcended the greed governing American involvement in Vietnam. His stance alienated many liberals and infuriated Johnson, but King, beyond the political mainstream, upheld his principles. In 1967, King also announced an interracial crusade called the Poor People's Campaign. The movement would be highlighted by an encampment on the Washington Mall, designed to force the federal government to more deeply address the concerns of the poor. Some of the SCLC staff doubted the political wisdom of such a radical call, but again King forged beyond liberal reform.

In March 1968, in the midst of planning the Poor People's Campaign, King arrived in Memphis to lend support to striking sanitation workers in the Memphis Sanitation Workers' Strike. On April 4, 1968, stepping onto his motel balcony, King was struck by assassin James Earl Ray's bullet and died. His death sparked 130 separate instances of racial violence, leading to the deaths of 46 people.

Aram Goudsouzian

Further Reading

Ansbro, John J. *Martin Luther King, Jr.: The Making of a Mind*. Maryknoll, NY: Orbis Books, 1982.

Branch, Taylor. *Parting the Waters: America in the King Years, 1954–63*. New York: Simon & Schuster, 1988.

Branch, Taylor. *Pillar of Fire: America in the King Years, 1963–65*. New York: Simon & Schuster, 1998.

Carson, Clayborne, et al., eds. *The Papers of Martin Luther King, Jr.: Symbol of the Movement, January 1957–December 1958*. Berkeley: University of California Press, 2000.

Carson, Clayborne, et al., eds. *The Papers of Martin Luther King, Jr: Threshold of a New Decade, January 1959–December 1960*. Berkeley: University of California Press, 2005.

Dyson, Michael Eric. *I May Not Get There with You: The True Martin Luther King, Jr.* New York: Free Press, 2000.

Garrow, David J. *Bearing the Cross: Martin Luther King, Jr. and the Southern Christian Leadership Conference*. New York: Vintage, 1986.

Garrow, David J. *The FBI and Martin Luther King, Jr.* New York: Penguin Books, 1981.

King, Martin Luther, Jr. *The Autobiography of Martin Luther King*. New York: Intellectual Properties Management in association with Warner Books, 1998.

King, Martin Luther, Jr. *A Testament of Hope: The Essential Writings and Speeches of Martin Luther King, Jr.* San Francisco: HarperSanFrancisco, 1990.

Oates, Stephen B. *Let the Trumpet Sound: The Life of Martin Luther King, Jr.* New York: Harper & Row, 1982.

Posner, Gerald L. *Killing the Dream: James Earl Ray and the Assassination of Martin Luther King, Jr.* New York: Random House, 1998.

L

Lafayette, Bernard

A student activist in the Nashville, Tennessee, sit-in campaign of 1960, and a long-time staff member of the Student Nonviolent Coordinating Committee (SNCC), Bernard Lafayette gained a reputation as a steadfast proponent of nonviolence before Martin Luther King Jr. offered him the position of program director of the Southern Christian Leadership Conference (SCLC) in 1967.

Lafayette was born in Tampa, Florida, on July 19, 1940. In 1958, he moved to Nashville to attend American Baptist Theological Seminary. As a freshman, Lafayette began attending weekly meetings arranged by James Lawson, a representative of the Fellowship of Reconciliation who had contacted King during the Montgomery bus boycott. Throughout 1958 and 1959, in partnership with Nashville's SCLC affiliate, Lawson taught nonviolence techniques to Lafayette and his fellow Nashville students, including John Lewis, James Bevel, and Diane Nash. Energized by Lawson's classes and a weekend retreat at the Highlander Folk School, Lafayette and his friends began conducting sit-ins at segregated restaurants and businesses in 1960. When Ella Baker, under the auspices of SCLC, organized a conference of students on Easter weekend in 1960, Lafayette attended this conference that gave birth to SNCC.

Prior to the Supreme Court's 1960 ruling in *Boynton v. Virginia* declaring segregation in interstate travel facilities unconstitutional, Lafayette and Lewis integrated an interstate bus on their way home from seminary by sitting at the front and refusing to move. Months later, in 1961, he answered a Congress of Racial Equality (CORE) announcement recruiting students to participate in the Freedom Rides. Although unable to join the first ride because his parents refused to permit him to participate, Lafayette and other Nashville students volunteered to continue the rides after the first group of freedom riders was attacked in Alabama.

In Montgomery, Lafayette's group was attacked by members of the Ku Klux Klan. King met with Lafayette, Nash, and Lewis and then negotiated on their behalf with the White House and the Department of Justice to ensure their protection in Montgomery and a military escort on their continued journey to Mississippi. In Mississippi, Lafayette was arrested and served 40 days in Parchman Penitentiary, only to be rearrested upon his release for contributing to the delinquency of minors because the students he recruited to ride the buses were all under 18 years of age.

In 1962, Lafayette became the director of SNCC's Alabama Voter Registration Project. The following February, he and his wife, Colia, began running voter registration clinics in Selma, Alabama. In the summer of 1963, the pair was hired by the American Friends Service Committee to begin testing nonviolent methods in Chicago. When King launched SCLC's Chicago Campaign, he appointed Lafayette, still there in 1966, to help plan and execute the campaign's direct action program.

After King hired him as SCLC's program coordinator in 1967, Lafayette took on responsibility for the 1968 Poor People's Campaign. Following King's assassination, Lafayette continued to work on the campaign with Ralph Abernathy. Lafayette received his MEd from Harvard University in 1972 and a doctorate in 1974. He served as a scholar in residence at the King Center. After teaching at several universities, he was named president of his alma mater, American Baptist Theological Seminary, in 1993. He later became the director of the Center for Nonviolence and Peace Studies at the University of Rhode Island.

Clayborne Carson et al.

Further Reading

Arsenault, Raymond. *Freedom Riders: 1961 and the Struggle for Racial Justice.* New York: Oxford University Press, 2006.

Lewis, John. *Walking with the Wind: A Memoir of the Movement.* New York: Houghton Mifflin Harcourt, 1998.

Last Poets

The Last Poets arose from the American civil rights movement and consisted of a shifting group of poets, musicians, and activists. The group was founded in the late 1960s, when many African Americans had lost hope in the peaceful message of assimilation of Martin Luther King Jr., and had come to believe Black Nationalism and violent confrontation might be necessary. The group's combination of the spoken word and sparse musical accompaniment, as well as its political and social message, can be viewed as a forerunner to hip-hop and rap music as the group conveyed its message through poetry and song.

On May 19, 1968, three young poets, David Nelson, Abiodun Oyewole, and Gylan Kain, walked onto a stage in Harlem, New York, now referred to as Marcus Garvey Park. It was Malcolm X Day, and the group had come with hundreds of others to honor the memory of Malcolm X on what would have been his 43rd birthday. The impact of the first performance of the Last Poets was explosive. But the group needed a name to symbolize the hope and commitment they wanted to communicate.

Nelson read a poem by revolutionary black South African poet Keorapetse Kgositsile, "Towards a Walk in the Sun." The last line read: "The only poem you will hear will be the spear point pivoted in the punctured marrow of the villain." Nelson amended it to read: "Therefore, we are the 'last poets' of the world." This apocalyptic vision became part of the message of the Last Poets. The group also sang about the beauty of black people of all the shades from yellow and beige to black, with a love as "sweet as scuppernong wine."

The Last Poets were deeply influenced by the Black Arts Movement, whose purpose was African American liberation. Because of the group's militant message, they earned the title "bards of Black pride and revolution." Militant messages decrying the state of society and African Americans were first vocalized by the Last Poets. The Last Poets released several albums during their career. The first two, *Last Poets* and *This Is Madness*, are considered classics, not just because of the originality of the music, but also because of the powerful compositions, which articulated the feelings of an oppressed people. However, during this period, the group experienced irreparable conflicts that destroyed their unity. The change in personnel was considerable. Members of the group left and rejoined and others died.

The group continued to release albums, and in 1996, the two principal members of the Last Poets released *On a Mission: Selected Poems and a History of the Last Poets*, still determined to deliver their message, "We're no more godfathers of the spoken word than the man in the moon; it comes in a package from the motherland. But we accept that there is work out there that we can do. People need to see a focal point, a beacon, and we don't have no problem with shining, we don't walk away from the fight."

John Greer Hall

Further Reading

Gonzalez, David. "A Poet Warns about a Waste of Black Rage." *New York Times*, September 18, 1996, B1.

McConnell, Stacy A. *Contemporary Musicians: Profiles of the People in Music*. Vol. 21. Detroit, MI: Gale Research, 1998.

Lawson, James

A founder of the Student Nonviolent Coordinating Committee (SNCC), James Lawson participated in many of the significant civil rights initiatives of the 1960s, including the Nashville sit-ins, the Freedom Rides, and the Memphis Sanitation Workers' Strike.

Born on September 22, 1928, in Uniontown, Pennsylvania, to the Reverend James M. Lawson Sr. and Philane Cover, James Morris Lawson Jr. grew up in

Massillon, Ohio, where his father was pastor of a Methodist church. After graduating from high school, Lawson studied sociology at Baldwin Wallace College in Berea, Ohio. While at Baldwin Wallace, he received notice to report for military service. Because he was a committed pacifist, Lawson refused to serve. As a result, he was convicted of draft evasion and sentenced to two years in prison. Lawson returned to Baldwin Wallace to finish his sociology degree after serving 13 months of his sentence.

After graduation, Lawson traveled to India as a missionary for the Methodist Church. While in India, he was exposed to the nonviolent teachings of Mohandas K. Gandhi. As Lawson studied nonviolence, the philosophy was being applied in the American South by Martin Luther King Jr. in the Montgomery Bus Boycott. When he returned to the United States, Lawson met with King while he was a student at Oberlin College's school of theology. Profoundly moved by the struggle to dismantle segregation in the South, Lawson was determined to play a role in it. He was appointed southern regional director for the Fellowship of Reconciliation (FOR), an organization devoted to nonviolence.

After one year of study at Oberlin, Lawson enrolled in Nashville's Vanderbilt Divinity School. While in Nashville, Lawson married Dorothy Wood, and they had three sons: John, Morris, and Seth. In addition to his position with the Fellowship of Reconciliation, Lawson was also appointed projects director for the Nashville chapter of King's Southern Christian Leadership Conference (SCLC). In these roles he conducted workshops on Christian nonviolence for students from Nashville's African American colleges: American Baptist, Fisk, Meharry Medical, and Tennessee A&I.

Several of Lawson's students, inspired by his commitment to nonviolence, launched sit-in demonstrations at several downtown Nashville lunch counters on February 13, 1960. The demonstrations continued until May 10, when government and businesses leaders agreed to desegregate downtown stores. Lawson's leadership during the Nashville sit-ins made him one of the leading civil rights figures in the American South. But there was a cost. Angered over Lawson's leadership of the sit-ins, Vanderbilt chancellor Harvie Branscomb expelled him in March 1960. Undeterred, Lawson completed his divinity degree at Boston University and continued to spread the gospel of Christian nonviolence.

As the Nashville sit-ins reached their climax, Lawson traveled to Raleigh, North Carolina's Shaw University in April 1960 to attend a gathering of students committed to the civil rights struggle. At this meeting, SNCC was formed to expand civil disobedience throughout the South. In May 1961, the Congress of Racial Equality (CORE) adopted nonviolence with its Freedom Ride demonstrations. The rides were designed to pressure President John F. Kennedy and the Interstate Commerce Commission to enforce a 1960 Supreme Court decision declaring segregated bus terminals unconstitutional. When demonstrators were attacked by an angry white mob in Montgomery, Alabama, Lawson joined the effort. Boarding a bus at Montgomery, Lawson and several other Nashville sit-in veterans journeyed to Jackson, Mississippi, where they were arrested and sentenced to 30 days in the state penitentiary at Parchman. When Lawson was released from prison, he returned to divinity school in Boston.

After graduation from Boston University, Lawson was appointed pastor of Scott Church in Shelbyville, Tennessee, and in 1962, he was assigned to Centenary Methodist in Memphis. Although the elimination of racism and segregation was Lawson's primary focus, he did look beyond the struggle in the South. The Memphis pastor also expanded his promotion of Christian nonviolence to include the controversial Vietnam War. In 1965, he traveled to Southeast Asia as a representative of the Fellowship of Reconciliation's Clergymen's Emergency Committee on Vietnam. While in Southeast Asia, the committee met with a cross section of people including students, U.S. and South Vietnamese government leaders, North Vietnamese soldiers, and labor leaders. Upon their return, Lawson and the other committee members issued a report calling on the United Nations to intervene in the conflict to bring peace to the region. Although Lawson remained concerned about the war in Vietnam, events in Memphis led him to again confront American racism.

In February 1968, sanitation workers, poorly paid and forced to endure unsafe conditions, spontaneously walked off the job. When Memphis mayor Henry Loeb refused to negotiate, the strike became much more than a labor dispute. Because workers were predominately African American and desperately poor, Lawson joined their struggle and emerged as the most eloquent civil rights leader in Memphis. Drawing on his involvement in SNCC, Lawson and other leaders formed the Committee on the Move to Equality (COME). Lawson extended an invitation to King to speak in Memphis, which led to King's assassination in April 1968. Lawson continued to agitate for social change in Memphis until he moved to Los Angeles in 1974 to pastor Holman United Methodist Church. In 1982, he chaired the Peace Sunday Movement, which staged a large demonstration at the Rose Bowl. Lawson retired from the pulpit in 1999 but remained one of America's most eloquent leaders in the ongoing struggle to achieve social progress by just and peaceful means.

Gerald Wayne Dowdy

Further Reading

Alexander, Leslie M., and Walter C. Rucker. *Encyclopedia of African American History.* Santa Barbara, CA: Greenwood, 2010.

Beifuss, Joan Turner. *At the River I Stand: Memphis, the 1968 Strike, and Martin Luther King.* Memphis, TN: B&W Books, 1985.

Branch, Taylor. *At Canaan's Edge: America in the King Years, 1965–68.* New York: Simon & Schuster, 2006.

Halberstam, David. *The Children.* New York: Random House, 1998.

League of Revolutionary Black Workers

The League of Revolutionary Black Workers was officially launched in Detroit, Michigan, in October 1967 after the Detroit Rebellion of that same year. It was the final outcome of a combination of independent black industrial labor-related movements in the Detroit metropolitan area. The league grew as a result of the United Auto Workers (UAW) failure to address the racist and inhumane working conditions of black people employed in Detroit's manufacturing sector. It consisted of radical, prolific, blue-collar black workers with strong organizational skills. Historic and heroic struggles of black people provided the movement's strengths, inspiration was garnered by the revolutionary struggles of the developing world, and their convictions were guided by a Marxist-Leninist ideology. The league's goal was to unify black workers across Detroit.

In the 1960s, the UAW began to lose touch with minority members whose weekly organizational fees were deducted from their wages, although they had little representation on the organization's board of directors. Black workers held the view that the UAW was racist, oppressive, and not representative of their needs. The league developed out of the frustration of black workers who grew weary of the UAW's failure to meet their demands about improving their working conditions. Their demands were not unfounded, as the historical record reveals factory owners' productivity strategies that center on forced labor of black workers to work harder and faster in unsafe and unhealthy conditions. Throughout the late 1960s and early 1970s, conditions at the plants continued to deteriorate. Management hid these problems from outsiders, projecting plant life as harmonious and well paid. Unions were often loosely organized and too polarized to project to outsiders a real picture of what was actually happening in the plants. The league arose in response to these conditions.

The League of Revolutionary Black Workers united radical black organizing activists in Detroit's factories, neighborhoods, high schools, and colleges and university campuses against the horrendous racially charged circumstances that dominated life for black workers in the 1960s and 1970s. Revolutionary Union Movements (RUMs), built by ordinary black workers from Detroit's auto factories, were at the heart of the league. The RUMs effectively organized black workers to resist the racist and exploitive conditions in these factories and within the white-dominated UAW that officially represented the workers.

General Gordon Baker, John Watson, John Williams, Luke Tripp, Kenneth Cockrel, Mike Hamlin, and Chuck Wooten sat on the league's seven-man executive committee. Hamlin, Watson, and Cockrel held leadership positions and provided different but equal strengths to the mission of the organization. Hamlin embodied the stance that favored community building and student support, which enabled the league to carry out demonstrations when court injunctions stopped workers from protesting. Watson advocated the power of and need for an independent newspaper that would educate the public and challenge the ruling elite's power structure. In 1967, he actualized his vision through his editorial position on Wayne State University's student paper, the *South End*. Watson used the paper as a political arm for all radical revolutionary groups throughout the Detroit metropolitan area. He supported the equal publication of all views, and the paper was widely distributed to segments outside the university, including automobile factories. Cockrel provided legal expertise; he served the league by filing for a nonprofit status and keeping league activities within the law to avoid convictions from criminal and civil actions. The league's awareness of the reality of this aspect of organizing is how they differed from the Black Panther Party.

In 1971, the league began to take a different form and merged with the Black Workers Congress, whose manifesto centered on worker's rights, worker's demands, the elimination of racism, the liberation of women, and foreign policy questions. The Black Workers Congress had a strong beginning but petered out, as it was unable to put its ideology into practice and spent the majority of its time in meetings and setting up, but not applying, potential agendas. Eventually, the former members of the league dropped out and formed the Communist League, which advocated a multiracial communist party based on the writings of Lenin and Marx. It accepted whites and all people from the developing world and emphasized the role of industrial workers and professional revolutionaries.

The legacy of the League of Revolutionary Workers is extensive. Despite repression from the joined forces of Chrysler, Ford, General Motors, the UAW, and Detroit and suburban police departments, it distributed mass circulation newspapers and plant bulletins, organized pickets and rallies, formed community and student groups, ran opposition union candidates, and led wildcat strikes that successfully shut down production. In these ways the league is responsible for building the last sustained mass revolutionary union in the United States.

Jill E. Rowe-Adjibogoun

Further Reading

Boggs, James. *The American Revolution: Pages from a Negro Worker's Notebook*. New York: Monthly Review Press, 1963.

Boyd, Herb, and Robert Allen. *Brotherman: The Odyssey of Black Men in America*. New York: One World, 1995.

Georgakas, Dan, and Marvin Surkin. *Detroit: I Do Mind Dying*. New York: St. Martin's Press, 1975.

Geschwender, James A. *Class, Race and Worker Insurgency: The League of Revolutionary Black Workers*. New York: Cambridge University Press, 1977.

Gould, William. *Black Workers in White Unions*. Ithaca, NY: Cornell University Press, 1977.

Mast, Robert, ed. *Detroit Lives*. Philadelphia: Temple University Press, 1994.

Meier, August, and Elliot Rudwick. *Black Detroit and the Rise of the UAW.* New York: Oxford University Press, 1979.

Levison, Stanley

Although relatively unknown today, Stanley Levison played an important behind-the-scenes role in Dr. Martin Luther King Jr.'s campaign for civil rights. In 1956, Levison, a Jewish attorney from New York, began raising funds to support the Montgomery Bus Boycott and became acquainted with King. The two men developed a close relationship in which Levison not only advised King, but also aided him with the day-to-day administrative demands of the movement. In 1963, the Federal Bureau of Investigation (FBI) used King's relationship with Levison, who they believed to be a communist functionary, to justify surveillance of King.

Born in New York City on May 2, 1912, Stanley David Levison studied at the University of Michigan, Columbia University, and the New School for Social Research before earning two law degrees from St. John's University. As treasurer of the Manhattan branch of the American Jewish Congress, Levison became a champion of left-wing causes and supported the defense of Julius and Ethel Rosenberg and the campaign against the McCarran Internal Security Act. In the early 1950s, the FBI considered Levison to be a major financial coordinator for the Communist Party in the United States and began to monitor his activities.

In the mid-1950s, Levison turned his attention to the civil rights struggle. In 1956, Levison, Bayard Rustin, and Ella Baker created In Friendship, an organization that raised money for southern civil rights activists and organizations, including the Montgomery Improvement Association (MIA). Together they formulated the concept of a regional "congress of organizations" dedicated to mass action grounded in nonviolence, an idea that would later develop into the Southern Christian Leadership Conference (SCLC).

Throughout King's career, Levison drafted articles and speeches for him, prepared King's tax returns, and raised funds for SCLC. In 1958, Levison helped King edit *Stride toward Freedom* and secured a book contract with Harper & Brothers. In almost all instances, he performed these services without compensation. When King offered payment, Levison refused. "My skills," he wrote King, "were acquired not only in a cloistered academic environment, but also in the commercial jungle. . . . I looked forward to the time when I could use these skills not for myself but for socially constructive ends. The liberation struggle is the most positive and rewarding area of work anyone could experience."

The FBI's interest in Levison was suddenly rekindled in 1959, when the bureau learned of Levison's connection with King and the movement. FBI chief J. Edgar Hoover believed that Levison was a communist agent, and that through Levison, international communism influenced King's actions. He brought this concern to the attention of Attorney General Robert F. Kennedy, and Harris Wofford was enlisted by the John F. Kennedy administration to warn King to end his relationship with Levison. Unwilling to lose a trusted adviser because of vague allegations, King refused to act on the administration's request for over a year. In March 1962, Robert Kennedy authorized the FBI to begin electronic surveillance of Levison, including his contact with King.

Just before a June 22, 1963, White House meeting with civil rights leaders, Burke Marshall and Robert Kennedy separately repeated the warning to King, and this time included a recommendation to also fire Jack O'Dell. King demurred and requested proof of Levison's threat to national security. After the meeting, President Kennedy took King aside and repeated the request that he ban Levison and O'Dell directly. Over the next months, King debated how to handle the requests to cease contact with Levison. Levison, however, valued the administration's support for the movement and took the initiative to cut off all visible ties with King. He continued to advise King on important matters indirectly, often using Clarence Jones as an intermediary. In October 1963, evidence of the ongoing relationship helped convince Robert Kennedy to approve wiretaps in King's home and office.

Throughout the 1960s, Levison continued to lend King practical and moral support. Following the Selma-to-Montgomery march in 1965, Levison wrote King: "For the first time, whites and Negroes from all over the nation physically joined the struggle in a pilgrimage to the deep south." For Levison, Selma was a turning point in King's status as a leader: "It made you one of the most powerful figures in the country—a leader now not merely of Negroes, but of millions of whites."

In early 1967, when King became determined to participate in a public denunciation of the Vietnam War organized by Clergy and Laymen Concerned about Vietnam, Levison counseled him to refrain. Levison felt that King's planned "Beyond Vietnam" speech was unbalanced and would have disastrous consequences to SCLC's fund-raising campaign and King's personal prestige.

A year after publicly speaking out against the Vietnam War, King was assassinated in Memphis, Tennessee. Andrew Young, another of King's trusted advisers, called Levison a few hours afterward to tell him the news. Young wrote in his autobiography that "Martin had confided in Stan his worries and doubts and hopes ever since Montgomery and had defied the FBI and the president of the United States for their friendship. I knew he . . . would want to hear from one of us personally."

After a long battle with diabetes and cancer, Levison died at his home in New York City in 1979. Upon hearing of his death, Coretta Scott King called him "one of my husband's loyal and supportive friends" whose "contributions to the labor, civil rights, and peace movements" are relatively unknown.

Clayborne Carson

Further Reading

Garrow, David J. *The FBI and Martin Luther King, Jr.* New Haven, CT: Yale University Press, 1981.

Theoharis, Athan, ed. *From the Secret Files of J. Edgar Hoover.* New York: Ivan R. Dee, 1991.

Lewis, John

John Lewis, a longtime U.S. Congress member from Georgia, was one of the most prominent student leaders of the civil rights movement, serving as chair of the Student Nonviolent Coordinating Committee (SNCC) from 1963 to 1966. As a young man, he displayed extreme courage confronting southern segregationists as he took part in virtually every important event of the civil rights era.

John Robert Lewis was born on February 21, 1940, in rural Troy, Alabama, one of 10 children. His parents were poor sharecroppers who managed to buy their own small farm when Lewis was four years old. As a boy, he made his playmates listen to impromptu sermons he gave, and he imagined becoming a pastor. As he grew older, he heard Martin Luther King Jr.'s radio preaching, and at age 16, Lewis's pastor allowed him to give his first sermon. He was in high school when the Montgomery Bus Boycott started.

In 1957, he went to American Baptist Theology (ABT) Seminary in Nashville, Tennessee, a school that allowed students to work in exchange for tuition. He met James Bevel at ABT, another man who would emerge as a civil rights leader. The next year, Lewis met James Lawson and began studying the principles of nonviolence with him. Nashville students began having regular workshops in preparation for nonviolent actions protesting segregation in the future, which included role-playing sessions in which some students would pretend to be segregationists while others acted as protesters.

On February 1, 1960, four African American students sat at a whites-only lunch counter at a Woolworth's in Greensboro, North Carolina. Lewis and his peers had been preparing for a moment like this, and the Nashville sit-ins began February 13. Within a couple of weeks, protesters were being attacked and arrested. This movement was eventually successful, and Nashville's lunch counters were integrated. Following the spread of the sit-in movement throughout the South, students formed SNCC in April, and Lewis was a major organizer. In the wake of the sit-ins, northern universities began inviting Lewis and other leaders to speak about the movement.

In 1961, Lewis took part in the Freedom Rides, designed to test a Supreme Court ruling banning segregation on interstate buses and in bus terminals. The interracial group of Freedom Riders planned to board buses in Washington, D.C., and ride them to New Orleans. Lewis had to leave the original group early because of an obligation, but he returned to Nashville to organize additional riders to keep the rides going in light of the violence the original riders endured. Lewis left on a bus with a group from Nashville and faced a violent mob at Birmingham's bus terminal. When Lewis disembarked in Montgomery, he faced a worse situation, and mobs beat Lewis and other riders severely. Police arrested Freedom Riders in Jackson, Mississippi; they were eventually sent to Parchman Prison. Hundreds of other students, witnessing these events, began following Lewis's path on buses throughout the South.

Lewis and his peers next turned their efforts to discrimination against African Americans in employment. The Nashville Student Movement (NSM) picketed and boycotted Nashville stores that took African Americans' money but would not employ them. In the fall, Lewis enrolled at Fisk University and became chair of the NSM.

In June 1963, Lewis was elected as SNCC's chair, and he moved to Atlanta to fulfill his duties. He thus was one of the "Big Six" civil rights leaders at the August 1963 March on Washington. Lewis also gave one of the speeches at the march, although other leaders pressured him to revise his speech because they thought it too inflammatory. He and his SNCC colleagues did so moments before the speech was to begin.

Lewis continued working on a variety of civil rights projects. Major projects included the Mississippi Freedom Democratic Party (MFDP), which would run a slate of African American candidates in that state; and Freedom Summer in 1964, which would bring hundreds of white volunteers from the North into Mississippi, well known as the most dangerous southern state for civil rights workers. In fact, on June 21, the day the first wave of volunteers began their journey South, three civil rights workers were murdered—one African American and two whites. The results of Lewis's and his colleagues' efforts in Mississippi were mixed: many African Americans registered to vote, but the Democratic Party refused to seat the MFDP's delegation at its August convention.

After Freedom Summer, SNCC faced increasing organizational problems. Because of its growth, it was becoming difficult for committee members to continue making decisions by consensus. In addition, more and more SNCC workers were becoming less attached to nonviolence as a tactic, whereas others, like Lewis, remained deeply committed to it as a philosophy. SNCC had projects in operation all over the South, and although Lewis tried to keep abreast of all of them, in January 1965, he turned his attention to voter registration in Selma, Alabama. This action involved potential voters marching to the courthouse and attempting to register, where they were refused entrance and often arrested or beaten.

In the wake of protester Jimmie Lee Jackson's death—police shot him in the stomach as he tried to protect his mother from a beating—Lewis and others organized a march from Selma to Montgomery. The day the march was to begin, March 7, is now known as "Bloody Sunday" because mounted police severely beat, stomped, and teargassed protesters as they attempted to cross the Edmund Pettus Bridge. Lewis led the marchers and was among the first to be beaten; he had to be hospitalized with a fractured skull.

After passage of the Civil Rights Act of 1964 and Voting Rights Act of 1965, the already simmering issues of African American separation and the rejection of non-violence came to the fore within SNCC. In May 1966, at the end of SNCC's annual meeting—in this case a long, contentious, emotion-filled one—SNCC elected the fiery Stokely Carmichael as chair, replacing Lewis. He remained with SNCC for a short time, leaving in the wake of controversy over the June Meredith March in Mississippi and the emergence of the Black Power slogan.

After leaving SNCC, Lewis began serving as the U.S. Representative from Georgia's 5th District in 1986, representing Atlanta. Before becoming a member of Congress, he worked on the Voter Education Project in the South and then in the Jimmy Carter administration as associate director of ACTION, which oversaw volunteer programs. Lewis also served on Atlanta's City Council, taking office in 1982.

Erin Boade

Further Reading

Arsenault, Raymond. *Freedom Riders: 1961 and the Struggle for Racial Justice.* New York: Oxford University Press, 2006.

Branch, Taylor. *Parting the Waters: America in the King Years, 1954–63.* New York: Simon & Schuster, 1988.

Carson, Clayborne. *In Struggle: SNCC and the Black Awakening of the 1960s.* Cambridge, MA: Harvard University Press, 1995.

Hogan, Wesley. *Many Minds, One Heart: SNCC's Dream for a New America.* Chapel Hill: University of North Carolina Press, 2007.

Lewis, John, and Michael D'Orso. *Walking with the Wind: A Memoir of the Movement.* New York: Simon & Schuster, 1998.

Lewis, Rufus

African American Rufus Lewis was best known as an ardent black voting rights activist and politician and a major participant in the Montgomery Improvement Association (MIA), which headed the Montgomery Bus Boycott of 1955. Rufus Andrew Lewis was born in Montgomery, Alabama, on November 30, 1906, to parents Lula and Jerry Lewis. He graduated from Fisk University in 1931 with a degree in business administration. He worked as an assistant librarian and athletic coach at Alabama State College from the mid-1930s to 1941, becoming head coach of the track-and-field team in 1934. Due to the team's success under his leadership, he gained the longtime nickname "Coach Lewis." In 1943, Lewis was drafted by the military but was ultimately rejected due to previous injuries sustained. Instead, he served for two years as a civilian in the National Defense Project. He later taught night school for World War II veterans. In 1958, after his wife's death, he began operating her family's funeral business.

After years of witnessing the oppression of African American suffrage, Lewis became a staunch advocate of black voting rights. A member of Alpha Phi Alpha fraternity and the National Association for the Advancement of Colored People (NAACP), Lewis established the Citizens Club in 1952, a social club that provided voter registration assistance. He also organized the Citizen Coordinating Committee in 1954 with Jo Ann Robinson and E. D. Nixon "to develop united efforts in voting, to get more people registered and to create civic consciousness." Lewis also traveled throughout the South training voter registration workers. According to author Donnie Williams and journalist Wayne Greenhaw, Lewis would personally provide transportation to the courthouse's registrar office for people who had not yet registered to vote. He frequently declared his favorite motto, "A voteless people is a hopeless people."

On December 5, 1955, Lewis nominated his pastor, Martin Luther King Jr., as president of the MIA at its founding meeting even though King was only 26 years old at the time. Once described by King as having "an inextinguishable passion for social justice," Lewis headed the MIA's transportation committee and cochaired its committee on registration and voting. He offered his Citizens Club as the MIA headquarters when they had trouble securing space, only to rescind his offer when he was warned that his license could be suspended. As the Montgomery boycott came to a close, Lewis attributed its success to the unity of the black community: "The mass meetings help to keep the spirit up in the minds of the common man. Negroes know what they want, although it's expressed by someone else." Lewis continued chairing the registration and voting committee after the end of the boycott and sent King a letter asking him to support a get-out-the-vote drive in 1958.

Lewis was active in the Democratic Party in Alabama; he helped establish the Alabama Democratic Conference in 1960 and served as the first president of the Montgomery County Democratic Conference. Additionally, he cofounded the East Montgomery NAACP branch. These and other efforts led to his election to the Montgomery Parks and Recreation Board and the Montgomery Community Action Committee. In 1976, he was elected to the Alabama House of Representatives, resigning in 1977 when President Jimmy Carter appointed him a U.S. Marshall and he became the first African American from the Middle District of Alabama to hold the position.

Lewis died on August 19, 1999, at 92 years of age. The Lewis Collection archives, containing over 40,000 documents and artifacts, are located at H. Councill Trenholm State Technical College in Montgomery, Alabama.

Clayborne Carson

Further Reading

Fields, Uriah J. "Minutes of Montgomery Improvement Association Founding Meeting." December 5, 1955, in *Papers* 3: 68–70. Available at: http://mlk-kpp01.stanford.edu/primarydocuments/Vol3/5-Dec-1955_MIAMinutes.pdf

King, Martin Luther, Jr. *Stride toward Freedom: The Montgomery Story.* Boston: Beacon Press, 1957.

King, Martin Luther, Jr. Draft, chap. 4 of *Stride toward Freedom.* May 1958.

Lewis, Rufus A. Interview by Donald Ferron. January 20, 1956. Preston Valien Collection, Amistad Research Center Collections, Tulane University, New Orleans, Louisiana.

Williams, Donnie, and Wayne Greenhow. *The Thunder of Angels: The Montgomery Bus Boycott and the People Who Broke the Back of Jim Crow.* Chicago: Lawrence Hill Books, 2006.

Little Rock Nine

In the battle for school integration, nine black students became heroes to civil rights supporters when they enrolled at Central High School in Little Rock, Arkansas, for the 1957 school year. The "Little Rock Nine," as the students were known, participated in one of the more famous integration conflicts, as white students and parents actively opposed their attempt to integrate the Little Rock school district. After the 1954 *Brown v. Board of Education* decision, in which the Supreme Court ruled segregation illegal in public schools, members of the Little Rock School Board began working on a plan for integration. After three years of deliberations and controversy, the board settled on a plan that would gradually integrate the district, beginning with high schools in the 1957–1958 school year. Initially, the board selected 17 black students to attend Central High, but by August, the number had dwindled to nine. A group of anti-integration Central High parents, called the Mother's League, sought a federal injunction to stop the school from integrating, but a judge refused their request. The students planned to enter the school for the first time on September 3, 1957.

Orval Faubus, the governor of Arkansas, had not been as militant in his opposition to integration as some of his southern counterparts, but he ultimately decided to oppose the integration of Central High. The night before the students were scheduled to attend school there, he addressed the state via television. Claiming to have received word that white supremacists were traveling to Little Rock to prevent the integration of Central High, he ordered troops from the Arkansas National Guard to prevent any black students from entering the school. The students did not attend class the first day of school, but Daisy Bates, an official with the National Association for the Advancement of Colored People (NAACP), decided that the students should attempt to enter Central on September 4. The group planned to arrive at school together with Bates. Eight of the students did meet before school, but one student, Elizabeth Eckford, did not have a phone and was not aware of the plan. When the eight students arrived, they were shouted at and threatened by an angry mob of white segregationists, and National Guard troops denied the students entrance into the school. Because of the violence, NAACP leaders decided to postpone integration until they could expect better conditions for the students.

Determined to enforce the orders of the federal courts, President Dwight D. Eisenhower arranged a meeting with Faubus. At the meeting, Faubus agreed to order National Guard troops to protect the students, but he later reneged on that promise. On September 20, a federal judge ruled that Governor Faubus could not legally use the Arkansas National Guard to deny the students entrance into Central High. Although he expressed disappointment with the decision, Faubus accepted it and agreed not to send troops to the school. On September 23, the students planned to attend school. Before they arrived, another angry mob of white parents and segregationists gathered outside the school. They harassed and physically harmed several black reporters who were in Little Rock to cover the event. When the students arrived, the mob attacked them, shouting insults and threats. Although the students made it safely inside the building, by late morning, the city police who were patrolling the school felt the mob was uncontrollable. Worried about the physical safety of the children if the mob overcame police barricades, school officials sent the students home out the back entrance of the school.

To ensure that the children could attend the school without threat of physical injury, President Eisenhower ordered the U.S. Army's 101st Airborne Division into Little Rock to protect the students. With the troops' assistance, the students were able to attend school safely. To make sure that the students were safe once inside the building, members of the 101st served as escorts for them. After several months, the 101st troops left, and the students had to fend for themselves. They faced constant persecution from their fellow students, including threatening letters, harassing phone calls, and physical abuse. Despite the harassment, the black students continued to attend school. Eight of the nine students completed the school year. Minnijean Brown was suspended in December for responding to harassment by pouring her soup on two white boys. She was expelled during the spring semester for insulting white students. Ernest Green was the only senior of the group; in May, he became the first black graduate of Central High School. The following school year, Governor Faubus closed down Little Rock schools in an effort to avoid further integration. When courts ruled his act unconstitutional, the school district was forced to integrate for the 1959 school year. Jefferson Thomas and Carlotta Walls, two of the original Little Rock Nine, were the only two black students assigned to Central High. The students' ordeal was another example of tenacious white resistance to integration. The actions of the Little Rock Nine ensured that, despite white resistance, Little Rock schools would eventually integrate.

Blake A. Ellis

Further Reading

Bates, Daisy. *The Long Shadow of Little Rock: A Memoir.* Fayetteville: University of Arkansas Press, 1986.

Beals, Melba Pattillo. *Warriors Don't Cry: A Searing Memoir of the Battle to Integrate Little Rock's Central High.* New York: Washington Square Press, 1994.

Huckaby, Elizabeth. *Crisis at Central High, Little Rock, 1957–1958.* Baton Rouge: Louisiana State University Press, 1980.

Jacoway, Elizabeth, and C. Fred Williams, eds. *Understanding the Little Rock Crisis: An Exercise in Remembrance and Reconciliation.* Fayetteville: University of Arkansas Press, 1999.

Record, Wilson, and Jane Cassels Record, eds. *Little Rock, U.S.A.: Materials for Analysis.* San Francisco: Chandler, 1960.

Long Hot Summer Riots, 1965–1967

The term "Long Hot Summer" is often applied to the riots occurring in the United States during the spring and summer months of 1965, 1966, and 1967. These violent disturbances often began in hot weather, often required the assistance of the National Guard, and caused much financial damage, many arrests, and many deaths. They helped to point out to the nation the discrimination still prevalent at the time as well the reforms needed to heal a nation divided by race.

Part of understanding the Long Hot Summer Riots is understanding the effect of the Great Migration. From about 1890 until 1965, black Americans from the South migrated to northern cities. They were looking for opportunity and a better life. In the South, there was violence against blacks, lynchings, and Jim Crow laws (laws that limited the voting rights of black Americans). And, the primarily agricultural-based economy of the South was in trouble: there was an attack of the boll weevil as well as a drought. The North offered opportunity, especially during World War I when European immigration declined and there was a growing need for laborers in northern factories and businesses.

Typical of other immigrants, these black Americans who migrated to the North congregated in neighborhoods—most often in the older, less desirable parts of inner cities. But unlike other immigrants, blacks were excluded from moving into better neighborhoods because of discriminatory practices. In fact, segregation by neighborhoods continued into the latter part of the twentieth century. (The Fair Housing Act of 1968 legally put an end to these practices.) Continued discrimination, overcrowding, high unemployment, and inadequate schools made these neighborhood potential powder kegs, especially if their populations were aware of news being reported by the media.

Although the media did report on continuing civil rights gains before to the period of 1965 through 1967, they also presented images of racism and violence.

In 1955, 14-year-old Emmett Till was lynched in Money, Mississippi, and pictures of his battered body appeared in *Jet* magazine. This was also the year of the highly publicized stance by Rosa Parks in Alabama. In 1957, media images showed federal troops in Little Rock as they enforced the desegregation of Central High School. In 1963, there were violent outbreaks in Savannah, Cambridge, Maryland, Philadelphia, Chicago, and especially in Birmingham, Alabama, where racists bombed a church, killing four little girls. In 1964, there were a number of disturbances and racially motivated murders: three civil rights leaders were lynched in Mississippi, and law enforcement was implicated; blacks started using Molotov cocktails; a number of cities, including the New York neighborhoods of Harlem and Bedford-Stuyvesant, had violent altercations. All of these events were reported in the media. Things were heating up.

Then, on August 11, 1965, in the Watts neighborhood of Los Angeles in the middle of a summer heat wave, a simple incident ignited a major riot. A highway patrolman stopped a speeding black driver and arrested him for driving under the influence. A mob started to congregate and events escalated. Passing white motorists were dragged out of their cars and beaten; automobiles were overturned and set on fire. Eventually, the National Guard had to be called in to restore order. In all, 34 people were killed, nearly 4,000 people were arrested, and damages totaled $35 million.

In the spring of 1966, emotions again flared in Watts, although not to the extent they had the previous year. But in July, Chicago exploded with rock-throwing and fire-bombing. Again it required the National Guard to quell the violence. Three people were killed by stray bullets, and there were 533 arrests. Within weeks, violence requiring the National Guard also broke out in the Hough neighborhood of Cleveland. Later the same month, the courts had to ban demonstrations by white extremists in Baltimore, Maryland. In all, 43 different cities had racially violent events in 1966.

In 1967, nearly 150 cities had racial disturbances. Those in Detroit and Newark were major. But it seemed that just as a violent situation in one city began to calm, violence broke out in another, from Nashville (April 7), to Jackson, Mississippi (May 10), to Houston (May 16), to Tampa (June 11), to Cincinnati (June 12), and to Atlanta (June 17).

Then in July 1967, the two worst riots of the summer broke out, the first in Newark, New Jersey. Lasting from July 14 to July 17, the riots in Newark began in the Central Ward and spread into the downtown area. In the end, there was $10 million dollars in damage, 725 people injured, 1,500 arrested, and 23 people killed. The unemployment rate for black males between 16 and 19 was 37.8 percent, and there was a long history of perceived police brutality. The Detroit riots began on July 23 and lasted for five days. The flash point for the violence was the arrests of 82 people who were at an after-hours bar celebrating the return of two Vietnam War veterans near the home of Danny Thomas, a Vietnam veteran who had been killed by a gang of white youths. The neighborhood became inflamed and the violence escalated. In the end, there was more than $35 million in damage, more than 900 people seriously injured, and 34 people killed—the youngest was 4 years old, and the oldest, 68—and 4,000 people arrested.

As a result of all the violence, President Lyndon Johnson appointed a National Advisory Commission on Civil Disorders on July 28, 1967, to be chaired by Governor Otto Kerner of Illinois. The commission's famous conclusion stated, "Our nation is moving toward two societies, one black, one white—separate and unequal" (National Advisory Commission on Civil Disorders 1968, 1).

William P. Toth

Further Reading

Allen, Rodney F., and Charles H. Adair, eds. *Violence and Riots in Urban America*. Worthington, OH: Charles A. Jones Publishing, 1969.

Fuguitt, Glenn V., John A. Fulton, and Calvin L. Beale. *The Shifting Patterns of Black Migration from and into the Nonmetropolitan South, 1965–95*. Washington, DC: U.S. Department of Agriculture, Rural Development Research Report No. 93, 2001.

National Advisory Commission on Civil Disorders. *The Kerner Report*. New York: Pantheon, 1968.

Upton, James N. *A Social History of 20th Century Urban Riots*. Bristol, IN: Wyndham Hall Press, 1984.

Lorraine Motel

The Lorraine Motel in Memphis, Tennessee, is equally an iconic place and an iconic moment. In April 1968, the world awoke to a photograph, now indelibly etched in the collective American consciousness, of three men on a motel balcony pointing urgently upward across the street while another crouches down with a dying Martin Luther King Jr. Just outside Room 306 of the Lorraine Motel about 6:00 p.m. on the evening of April 4, 1968, an assassin's bullet had struck down the prominent leader of the civil rights movement. The nondescript motel exterior, with the metal railings of its narrow second-story balcony and the large drapery-covered windows, instantly became in that moment the place of martyrdom for one of America's most controversial civil rights leaders.

The motel still looks today as it did on the fateful day in 1968, serving as a poignant façade to the National Civil Rights Museum. A place of collective memory; a pilgrimage destination that honors the life and martyrdom of Martin Luther King Jr.; an educational center focusing on the history of the civil rights movement; a site for carrying on the work of King through social activism; a tourist attraction that bolsters the local economy—the Lorraine Motel encompasses all of these and more.

The motel became the Lorraine in 1942 when Walter and Loree (short for Lorraine) Bailey bought the business and changed its name. Under their ownership, it became a favorite lodging house for prominent African Americans visiting Memphis in the segregated South. Over the years, such luminaries as Nat "King" Cole, B. B. King, Aretha Franklin, and Jackie Robinson all stayed at the Lorraine. But their most special guest was Martin Luther King Jr.; they always reserved for him number 306, a double room that he preferred, and never charged him for it.

Just hours after King's assassination, Loree Bailey suffered a stroke and fell into a coma; she died five days later, the same day as King's funeral. Her husband was at a loss as to what to do with the motel. Bailey continued operating it on his own, but he knew right away that with thousands of people driving by every week to see the place of the notorious event, the Lorraine Motel had already become a hallowed shrine. He glassed in the portion of the balcony where King fell, and inside Room 306 he collected photographs, newspaper clippings, and plaques documenting the life and death of King. But the goldmine Bailey envisioned never materialized. As he sank further into debt, he looked for a buyer who would respect the hallowed ground where King had given his life.

The deteriorating condition of the Lorraine Motel caught the attention of local attorney and civil rights activist D'Army Bailey (no relation to the motel's owner). He organized the Lorraine Civil Rights Museum Foundation that first acquired the motel property at a bankruptcy auction, and then sought government funding to establish the National Civil Rights Museum at the site. In 1987, the foundation transferred ownership of the property to the state of Tennessee but agreed to take continuing responsibility for operating the education center and museum there.

With allocations of $8.8 million from state and local governments, the Lorraine Civil Rights Museum Foundation was able to build a full-scale, professional museum. The museum preserves the façade of the Lorraine Motel that includes the balcony where King was shot. But the rest of the motel building and complex were removed to make room for the new museum building. Inside, visitors can view temporary exhibitions on display in a special gallery just inside the main entrance. Next is a small auditorium where a short introductory film begins the tour of the museum. The galleries follow a chronological walk through African American history and the civil rights movement. The museum tour culminates with a solemn viewing of the shrine to Martin Luther King Jr. in the reconstructed Room 306 of the Lorraine Motel. Visitors can also peer out a window onto the balcony at the very spot where the slain civil rights leader fell, and look across the street to the small window at the back of the rooming house where the assassin fired from.

Leaving the somber experience of gazing into King's disheveled room as it was at the moment he died (reconstructed for the benefit of visitors), the path leads down a flight of stairs and into the museum gift shop. Visitors can continue their visit across the street where they pass through a ground-level tunnel that enters the former rooming house from where the assassin fired his deadly shots. The expansion of the museum includes the reconstructed room where convicted shooter James Earl Ray stayed and the bathroom from where the fatal shot was fired. The multimedia displays include conspiracy theories about the assassination as well as exhibits about the progress of the civil rights movement since 1968. The tour ends with a film about nonviolent protests around the world and the international progress of civil rights.

Thomas S. Bremer

Further Reading

Benderly, Beryl Lieff. "Heartbreak Motel." *Preservation* 55 (2003): 30–35.

Hall, Dennis R., and Susan Grove Hall, eds. *American Icons: An Encyclopedia of the People, Places, and Things That Have Shaped Our Culture.* Westport, CT: Greenwood Press, 2006.

Shearer, Lloyd. "The Lorraine Motel . . . Moneymaker, Memorial to Martin Luther King, Jr. or Both?" *Parade*, June 30, 1968, 4.

Los Angeles Riot of 1965

The Los Angeles Riot of 1965, also known as the Watts Riot or Watts Rebellion, was one of the most explosive, racially charged civil disturbances of the 1960s. The Watts Riot, associated with the urban African American neighborhoods of South Central Los Angeles, was indicative of long-standing socioeconomic conditions and institutionalized racism that plagued American cities.

The riot began on August 11 when a white police officer, Lee W. Minikus, stopped Marquette Frye, a 21-year-old African American man, and Ronald Frye, his 22-year-old brother, for reckless driving. After Marquette, the driver, failed the standard California Highway Patrol (CHP) sobriety test, Minikus informed him that he was under arrest for drunk driving. Having arrived on a motorcycle with no way to take Marquette to jail, Minikus radioed for a police vehicle and a tow truck to remove the car from its location at 116th Street and Avalon Boulevard, a predominantly African American neighborhood two blocks away from the Frye home in the Watts community.

After learning that Minikus would not release the car to him, Ronald went home to find his mother, hoping she could claim the vehicle and prevent impoundment. Mrs. Frye, Ronald, the tow truck, the patrol vehicle, and Minikus's motorcycle partner arrived simultaneously, as a growing number of residents and passersby watched Marquette's arrest unfold. By this time, Minikus called in for more reinforcements as the number of onlookers quickly swelled from dozens to hundreds, intensifying tensions between the Frye family and the officers. These tensions erupted into violence within minutes when Mrs. Frye became enraged over the forcible arrest of Marquette. Witnesses grew increasingly more hostile, as Marquette, Ronald, and their mother fought with the arresting officers, leading to the subsequent arrest of the entire Frye family. As the scene cleared, the crowd became irate, throwing bottles and rocks—even spitting—at officers, resulting in the arrests of two other African Americans who police allegedly incited the crowd to violence.

Within hours of the arrests, rumors spread throughout the Watts community about police treatment of the Frye family and those arrested from the crowd; chaos and rebellion ensued. A number of Watts community members engaged in violence and vandalism throughout the night and into the early hours of the morning. By the next day, police still failed to gain complete control over the pockets of disturbances erupting throughout Watts. Over the course of the next two days, local community activists, religious leaders, teachers, business owners, and the Los Angeles County Human Relations Committee worked to prevent further outbreaks of violence and destruction, but their efforts were largely unsuccessful. Violence, looting, and destruction permeated the Watts community and some adjacent areas for the next few days.

In an attempt to restore peace, Governor Pat Brown sent the California National Guard to quell the unrest. The arrival of the National Guard, however, only served to heighten tensions and spread the destruction into southeast Los Angeles. Guardsmen found it difficult to control each incidence of rebellion; they also found it difficult to distinguish African American victims of the riot from African American participants, prolonging the riot. Lasting six days, the riot left 34 people dead, more than 900 seriously injured, and 4,000 arrested, as well as more than $35 million in property damage and destruction.

To many white Americans, the rioting and destruction in Watts appeared to be a violent reaction to an isolated event. To others, the rioting was simply inexplicable, an unlawful and terrifying response to things of which they had no complete knowledge. Furthermore, media images and descriptions of African American rioters served to intensify already demonized perceptions of African Americans held by whites, who had little to no real contact with them. The Frye arrest symbolized much more for many of the residents of Watts, and rioting represented a dramatic solution to deeply rooted problems within the African American community that both the local and federal government ignored for decades.

When the rioting ended, Brown enlisted the help of a government panel, the McCone Commission, to find reasons why the Watts community exploded as it had, and to provide details on what exactly occurred during the days of unrest. The commission, led by former Central Intelligence Agency (CIA) director John McCone, released a comprehensive report—*Violence in the City: An End or a Beginning?*—in December 1965, detailing their findings on the revolt and pointing to several of its underlying determinants. The commission concluded that unemployment, underemployment, inadequate schooling, and a tense relationship between the Los Angeles Police Department (LAPD) and African American residents all contributed to the unfolding of the Watts riot. They also maintained that the presence and illegal activities of African American gangs and petty criminals were other important mitigating factors in the six-day rebellion.

Although the McCone Commission arrived at many accurate conclusions, in a sense, those conclusions were obvious, particularly to those living in African American communities in and around Los Angeles. Moreover, implicit and explicit prejudices about poor African Americans and Latinos informed the commission's conclusions. They overlooked and underestimated the persistence of conflicts within poor African American families caused by outside factors of unemployment, insufficient educational resources, and a lack of proper housing in Watts and other African American communities in Los Angeles. Furthermore, the report downplayed the ongoing problem of police brutality against African Americans by the LAPD, an issue that, by the 1960s, became more salient as its occurrences rose. Therefore, the assertion that the LAPD struggled to control African American criminal activity in Watts, without acknowledgment of its tendency to brutalize and terrorize African Americans—specifically young African American men—was a major failure in the McCone Commission report. This, however, was merely one of several instances within the report in which the McCone Commission overlooked or minimized the social and historical factors that led to the riot.

In the two decades before the Los Angeles riot, African Americans experienced extreme prejudice in the job and housing markets, and the same sources of discrimination largely excluded them from full participation in the American economy. Also, despite the gains of civil rights activists such as Thurgood Marshall and organizations such as the National Association for the Advancement of Colored People (NAACP), forcing integration in the educational system through legislation, many schools throughout the United States remained segregated. White Americans fled into suburban communities (white flight) to avoid sending their children to school with African American youths, allowing middle-class African Americans to move into formerly white-occupied areas and increasing the number of poor African American neighborhoods throughout the country. Despite the diligent efforts of civil rights activists to create greater African American inclusion in American society, African American communities continued to endure restrictive housing provisions limited to overcrowded urban areas or underdeveloped suburban and rural areas. Likewise, employment opportunities for African Americans were often limited to positions of service to white Americans. In short, where African Americans did not create political, economic, educational, and social spaces in which they could participate fully, few, if any, existed. The McCone Commission's failure, or inability, to recognize these overwhelming problems in the daily lives of many African Americans in Los Angeles reflects perhaps their greatest source of discontent, for it was an outgrowth of yet another point of frustration in African American life—invisibility.

High levels of segregation, poverty, and discrimination made African Americans, poor African Americans especially, in Los Angeles figuratively invisible to white and middle-class Americans. At the very least, they were domestic, and public, servants of varying sorts, those who lived on the other side of town. At most, they were agitators of racial integration and racial equality, or sources of racial conflict. Invisibility, therefore, played a significant role in the actions of many African Americans during the Watts riots. For some, it was an attempt at gaining national attention, a drastic move to expose the great inconsistencies within the professed American ideals of freedom and equality, and the praxis of those ideals. Indeed, a significant number of studies revealed that African American rioters did not randomly destroy property in Los Angeles, but that much of the property burned or looted belonged to business owners who discriminated against African American community members. Conversely, a significant number of rioters had no underlying political motives; the civil unrest provided an opportunity to commit crimes or provided access to things they would not have ordinarily afforded. Still others in the African American community did not participate in the riots; the extent of their involvement was through the media, or through voluntary aid to those seriously injured during the riots. Consequently, the commission's failure to address or acknowledge the issues vital to preventing further outbreaks of civil rebellion left many in the African American community disillusioned.

Watts and other African American communities in Los Angeles remained largely poor communities segregated from upper- and middle-class Los Angeles residents. The plight of poor African Americans in Los Angeles gained greater media coverage, and increased white Americans' awareness of their plight, but white American attitudes about African Americans shifted very little, if at all. White Americans now understood what happened in African American communities, but because of the riot, they were less inclined to sympathize, thus maintaining a strenuous relationship between white Americans and African Americans. Conversely, African American rioting in Los Angeles and other African American communities forced all Americans to rethink the nature and impact of race on all groups within the United States. For those who did riot with underlying political agendas, at least some part of their grievances was recognized. Still, gaining heightened recognition for the multitude of problems plaguing urban African American communities did not necessarily generate useful solutions. Yet another impact of the riot was the shift in African American leadership, from the older generation of African Americans who used legal strategies and nonviolent means of civil disobedience to address discrimination, to the younger generation who had lost faith in the previous strategies of political agitation and were not opposed to violent means of civil disobedience if necessary. This new leadership represented a shift in the civil rights movement that brought with it messages of cultural pride, nationalism, and empowerment, and gave rise to organizations such as the Black Panther Party (BPP) and the Black Arts Movement.

Lacey P. Hunter

Further Reading

Bullock, Paul. "Violence in the City: An End or a Beginning?" The McCone Commission Report on Watts, and *Watts: The Aftermath*." In *"Takin' It to the Streets": A Sixties Reader*, edited by Alexander Bloom and Wini Breines, 142–52. New York: Oxford University Press, 1995.

Harding, Vincent, Robin D. G. Kelley, and Earl Lewis. "We Changed the World: 1945–1970." In *To Make Our World Anew: A History of African Americans*, edited by Robin D. G. Kelley and Earl Lewis, 445–542. New York: Oxford University Press, 2000.

Horne, Gerald. *The Fire This Time: The Watts Uprising and the 1960s*. Charlottesville: University Press of Virginia, 1995.

Johnson, Paula B., John B. McConahay, and David O. Sears. "Black Invisibility, the Press, and the Los Angeles Riot." *American Journal of Sociology* 76, no. 4 (1971): 698–721.

Lowndes County Freedom Organization

The Lowndes County Freedom Organization (LCFO) was an effort initiated by the Student Nonviolent Coordinating Committee (SNCC) in 1966 to organize an independent political party in Lowndes County, Alabama. Black residents of rural Lowndes County were impoverished, and few if any blacks actually owned land. Although blacks made up the majority of the population in the county, they held no elected offices and were virtually excluded from participating in local politics. Lowndes County was often referred to as "Bloody Lowndes" because of its history of racial violence.

Before the passage of the Voting Rights Act of 1965, African Americans in Alabama who were registered to vote constituted less than 20 percent of those eligible to vote. Civil rights organizations like the Southern Christian Leadership Conference (SCLC), SNCC, and Congress of Racial Equality (CORE), along with the Alabama Democratic Conference (ADC)—a political action group—worked to increase the number of black registered voters in the state. The famous voter registration activity in neighboring Selma in 1965 spurred some action in dormant Lowndes County.

Unlike the Mississippi Freedom Democratic Party (MFDP), an interracial political party created to empower rural southern blacks, LCFO was not an alternative to the Alabama Democratic Party, but rather, a third party. The goal of LCFO was not initially to form an all-black political party; the lack of participation by whites facilitated such circumstances. The goal of the organization, however, was to circumvent the existing political structures that prevented blacks from participating in the local political process. The LCFO, also known as the Black Panther Party, adopted the image of a black panther as the symbol for the party. The panther symbol, when juxtaposed against the Alabama Democratic Party's symbol of a white rooster, was meant as a representation of strength. If the LCFO were successful, SNCC planned to organize political parties similar to the LCFO in other areas of Alabama.

Despite the dangers that African Americans faced when they attempted voter registration activity, local blacks met with members of SCLC on March 19, 1965, and formed the Lowndes County Christian Movement for Human Rights (LCCMHR). The LCCMHR was created to facilitate black voter registration as well as to act as an intermediary between the black community and the local government. John Hulett, a Lowndes County native and one of only two African Americans registered to vote in the county, was elected the first chairman. Although SCLC had initially helped to establish the LCCMHR, it failed to continue to support the organization. When no support staff was sent to Lowndes County to begin political organizing, Hulett reached out to SNCC for help.

The passing of the Voting Rights Act of 1965 outlawed disenfranchisement tactics such as literacy tests, and as a result, Lowndes County saw an increase in black voter registration. However, the rise in black political activity strengthened white opposition. On August 20, 1965, civil rights worker Jonathan Daniels was killed when a deputy sheriff fired a shotgun at a group of protesters. SNCC cited the deaths of white civil rights sympathizers Daniels and Viola Liuzzo as pivotal events that strengthened the resolve of the organization to raise black political consciousness in Lowndes County. SNCC took the lead in helping to form the Lowndes County Freedom Organization. John Hulett was also elected to head LCFO.

A specification in Alabama state law permitted the establishment of a political party at the county level. After the failed seating of the MFDP at the Democratic National Convention in Atlantic City in 1964, members of SNCC decided that an independent political party would better serve the black residents of Lowndes County. The independent party could gain recognition when that party's nominated candidates received 20 percent of the votes in the county election. The 1966 elections proved to be crucial for LCFO. Despite the defeat of LCFO candidates in the general election, scholars believe that the creation of LCFO proved to be an important step in the emergence of Black Power politics.

The LCFO represented a change from previous SNCC projects. Stokely Carmichael served as project director and brought a brash new militancy that counterbalanced the rural grassroots movement in Lowndes County. The Lowndes County project was the first project since the 1964 Mississippi Freedom Summer project that was not an interracial movement. In 1966, Huey P. Newton and Bobby Seale founded the Black Panther Party for Self-Defense in Oakland, California. Inspired so much by Carmichael and the LCFO, Newton and Seale adopted the black panther symbol to represent their organization. In 1969, the LCFO merged with the National Democratic Party of Alabama.

Shirletta J. Kinchen

Further Reading

Branch, Taylor. *At Canaan's Edge: America in the King Years, 1965–1968*. New York: Simon & Schuster, 2006.

Carmichael, Stokely, and Michael Thelwell. *Ready for the Revolution: The Life and Struggle of Stokely Carmichael (Kwame Ture)*. New York: Scribner Publishing, 2003.

Carson, Clayborne. *In Struggle: SNCC and the Black Awakening of the 1960s*. Cambridge, MA: Harvard University Press, 1981.

Eagles, Charles W. *Outside Agitator: Jon Daniels and the Civil Rights Movement in Alabama*. Chapel Hill: University of North Carolina Press, 1993.

Jeffries, Hasan Kwame. *Bloody Lowndes: Civil Rights and Black Power in Alabama's Black Belt*. New York: New York University Press, 2009.

Walton, Hanes. *Black Political Parties: An Historical and Political Analysis*. New York: Free Press, 1972.

M

Malcolm X

Malcolm X (1925–1965) was an author, activist, and minister of the Nation of Islam who has become the most enduring contemporary symbol of African American militant protest. Given the name Malcolm Little at birth, he became Malcolm X after entering the Nation of Islam and finally changed his name to el-Hajj Malik el-Shabazz while on pilgrimage to Mecca in 1964. Malcolm X's public career lasted only six years and ended abruptly with his assassination. Nonetheless, his influence on recent African American history is enormous. He left behind no lasting organization or movement, no record of changed legislation, no institutional legacy, no accomplishment of improved conditions for black people in America, and no developed political philosophy. His achievements were cultural. His most important and long-lasting contribution was *The Autobiography of Malcolm X*, written with Alex Haley. Beyond that, as a media figure between 1959 and 1964, he introduced the black community to a new model of black leadership, an unprecedented public display of black rage, and a new mode of aggressive black masculinity that continues to have a profound effect on popular culture today.

Born May 19, 1925, in Omaha, Nebraska, Malcolm was his father's seventh child. Reverend Earl (Early) Little, a freelance Baptist minister and a part-time organizer for Marcus Garvey's Universal Negro Improvement Association (UNIA), already had three children from a previous marriage and three children with his second wife, Louise (Louisa), Malcolm's mother. According to Malcolm, Louise was so fair that she looked white, while his father was very dark-skinned. Malcolm begins his autobiography with an account of his mother, pregnant with him, confronting armed Ku Klux Klan riders who surrounded the family house in Omaha while his father was away; however, Louise Little denied that this incident ever occurred.

Malcolm was more light-skinned than any of his brothers and sisters, with reddish-brown hair. He was apparently his father's favorite child. His relationship with his mother was more troubled. There was considerable violence within the home. Earl beat Louise and also beat his children almost savagely, except for Malcolm. All of Malcolm's beatings came from his mother. In 1931, when Malcolm was six years old, his father was killed. Malcolm would later insist that he was murdered by white supremacists, but all contemporary evidence indicates that he died in a streetcar accident. With seven children to care for and overwhelmed by poverty during the Depression, Louise Little tried to maintain her

Malcolm X, late-20th-century Black Power activist and leader of the Nation of Islam. (Library of Congress)

family intact, but without success. Malcolm was placed in the care of a white family by the welfare authorities. He admitted to being glad when it happened. In 1939, after giving birth to an eighth child and being abandoned by the new baby's father, Louise was judged insane and was formally committed to a state mental hospital. She remained there for 25 years. Malcolm visited her occasionally, but she did not recognize him. In his autobiography, he blames social workers for driving his mother insane.

In 1941, at the age of 15, Malcolm moved to Boston to live with his half-sister, a daughter of his father's first marriage, Ella Collins. Despite her efforts to introduce him to her respectable friends and to keep him in school, Malcolm was almost immediately attracted to the criminal underworld of the city. His first part-time job as a shoeshine boy in the Roseland State Ballroom men's room was a thin disguise for a number of illegal activities, such as selling marijuana or putting his customers in touch with prostitutes. He also began a long-term relationship, over Ella's furious objections, with an older white woman he called "Sophia" in his autobiography (Beatrice Caragulian, later Beatrice Bazarian). Drafted into the army during World War II, he managed to avoid service by feigning insanity. He pursued a career of petty criminality that included a short stay in Harlem before he returned to Boston. There he was arrested for burglaries he had carried out with the help of his white girlfriend, her sister, and his male cohorts. In February 1946, at the age of 20, he was sentenced to three concurrent 8- to 10-year sentences at hard labor. Malcolm attributed the harsh punishment to the judge's anger over his sexual relationship with a white woman.

During his early days in prison, Malcolm earned the nickname "Satan" because of his outspoken atheism and his hostility toward religion. As he relates in his autobiography, his efforts to educate himself in prison began long before his conversion to the Nation of Islam. He enrolled in correspondence courses, studied the dictionary, and voraciously read books from the prison library. While serving time in prison, Malcolm was introduced to the teachings of the Nation of Islam by his brother Reginald, who had joined the group. Initially showing no interest, Malcolm was a deeply committed convert by the time he was released from prison in August 1952.

Ella had arranged for Malcolm to move to Detroit, where his brothers Wilfred, Philbert, and Wesley and his sister Hilda lived, after his release from prison. All of his siblings were now active members of the Nation of Islam there. Malcolm soon visited the leader of the movement, Elijah Muhammad, in Chicago, where he was given special recognition. Like most members of the Nation of Islam, he changed his last name to X, to symbolize his rejection of white oppression. He explained in his book: "The Muslim's 'X' symbolized the true African family name that he never could know. For me, my 'X' replaced the white slavemaster name of 'Little' which some blue-eyed devil named Little had imposed upon my paternal forebears. . . . Mr. Muhammad taught that we would keep this 'X' until God Himself returned and gave us a Holy Name from His own mouth" (*The Autobiography of Malcolm X*, 199).

He actively recruited new converts for the Nation of Islam and was an effective proselytizer. The Federal Bureau of Investigation opened a file on Malcolm in 1953, after learning that he had referred to himself as a communist. He remained under FBI surveillance for the rest of his life. He expanded the Nation of Islam in Detroit, established the Nation's first temple in Boston, and found new recruits in Philadelphia. In 1954, he was chosen to head Temple No. 7 in Harlem, and he rapidly expanded its membership there also.

In 1958, after receiving permission from Elijah Muhammad, Malcolm married Betty X (née Sanders, later Betty Shabazz) in Lansing, Michigan. The couple eventually had six daughters: Attallah (b. 1958), Qubilah (b. 1960), Ilyasah (b. 1962), Gamilah Lumumba (b. 1964); and twin girls, Malaak and Malikah, born in 1965 after their father's death. During the marriage, Malcolm was often away from the home traveling, speaking, or attending to the business of the Nation of Islam. Malcolm X first became a public media figure in 1959, when he appeared in a television documentary broadcast in New York City, entitled *The Hate That Hate Produced*. On that program he explained that, according to the teaching of the Nation of Islam, black people were a divine race; he frankly denounced the white race as evil, incapable of good. The audience saw footage of the University of Islam, where Muslim children were taught that whites were devils. This message appeared in such sharp contrast to the theme of brotherhood being put forward by the civil rights movement that the Nation of Islam, and Malcolm in particular, immediately became the objects of national media attention. Although Malcolm would later complain about the negative publicity, it was his almost demonic media image that brought the National of Islam into the fore. He did everything he could to cultivate that image in media interviews.

At this time, Malcolm's public statements adhered strictly to the teachings of the Nation of Islam as given by Elijah Muhammad. Malcolm unabashedly spoke of a self-righteous hatred of whites. In his autobiography, begun in 1963, Malcolm repeated the Nation of Islam's official teaching that white people were an artificial race of mutant people who had been created in prehistory, through genetic experimentation, by an evil black scientist named Yacub.

Elijah Muhammad imposed a strict rule against political activity and protest on the Nation of Islam, including banning social involvement that might improve conditions for blacks. His teaching was that God would soon liberate his people without effort on their part, and that the followers of the Nation of Islam should simply wait for this inevitable divine event. All of these teachings would eventually become a problem for Malcolm X and lead to his break with the movement.

Malcolm X became the national representative and chief spokesman for the Nation of Islam. He was in much demand as a public speaker on college campuses and other venues and was sought after for television appearances. He was also interviewed as a spokesman for black Americans by journalists from other countries. He established the Nation of Islam's first national newspaper, *Muhammad Speaks*. From these platforms, he sharply criticized the leaders of the civil rights movement for advocating that blacks should integrate into white society, rather than build separate black institutions. He rejected their stance that black people should respond with nonviolence when faced with attacks from the white community.

Malcolm's popularity with the media and his obvious position as the second-most important leader of the Nation of Islam, after Elijah Muhammad himself, caused tensions to develop within the movement. A book about the Nation of Islam, *When the Word Is Given*, published in 1963, featured Malcolm X on its cover and included transcripts of five of his speeches, but only one of Elijah Muhammad's, much to the chagrin of the latter. Publishers asked for the rights to Malcolm's autobiography, not for Elijah Muhammad's. Members of Elijah Muhammad's family and other high-ranking Muslim leaders in Chicago began to maneuver against Malcolm's position within the Nation.

Tensions developed between Malcolm and his leader, Elijah Muhammad, over the Nation of Islam's general noninvolvement policy, with Malcolm moving toward more action and engagement in the black social struggle taking place around them in the early 1960s. For example, when Ronald Stokes, member of the Nation, was killed and six other Muslims were wounded in a police raid on the Muslim Temple in Los Angeles in April 1962, a furious Malcolm X sought to organize the black community around the issue and bring a legal case against the police for brutality. Elijah Muhammad, however, eventually ordered him to discontinue his efforts in Los Angeles and return to New York. In the summer of 1963, Malcolm (without authorization from Elijah Muhammad) announced that Temple No. 7 in Harlem would begin a voter registration drive. Against standing policy, he publicly advocated that the Nation of Islam should form a "united black front" with civil rights organizations. Malcolm was also deeply shaken by his knowledge of financial corruption at the Nation's headquarters in Chicago and the increasing confirmation he received of Elijah Muhammad's adulterous affairs and illegitimate children with former secretaries. He began discussing these issues with a few other Muslims.

These conflicts came to a head with the assassination of President John F. Kennedy. In keeping with his policy of caution and noninvolvement, Elijah Muhammad had strictly instructed all Muslim ministers to make no comment on the assassination. Malcolm complied for a few days, but then after one of his talks in New York, someone asked about Kennedy. Comparing the assassination to that of Patrice Lumumba and other deaths that he said the president had been responsible for, Malcolm remarked: "Chickens coming home to roost never did make me sad; they've always made me glad" (*The Autobiography of Malcolm X*, 300–301). This statement was widely reported and criticized in the press.

The next day, Elijah Muhammad suspended Malcolm from making any public statements for 90 days in order to distance the Nation of Islam from his remarks. A few weeks later, Malcolm was relieved of his positions as the national representative of the Nation and as the minister of Temple No. 7. Loyal Muslims were quietly told to shun him and perhaps even to kill him. The ban on his public speaking was extended indefinitely. Realizing that his disputes with the Nation of Islam were now irreconcilable, Malcolm announced his break with the movement on March 8, 1964. He formed the Muslim Mosque, Inc., in Harlem, to continue his work to liberate and uplift African American people. He would later also found the Organization of Afro-American Unity (OAAU), a secular organization devoted to the same ends. Both organizations were a direct challenge to the Nation of Islam.

Almost immediately after leaving the Nation of Islam, Malcolm decided to make a pilgrimage to Mecca. The trip was financed by his sister, Ella. He was received with hospitality by the Saudi royal family, who made him a guest of the state. The deputy chief of protocol for Prince Faisal accompanied him on his pilgrimage. Malcolm claimed that his pilgrimage amounted to a conversion experience that allowed him to reject the idea that white men were devils and embrace the racial brotherhood taught by orthodox Islam. While in Mecca, he changed his name to el-Hajj Malik el-Shabazz. In any case, the pilgrimage provided Malcolm with an opportunity to reformulate his message to his followers and to the public.

From Saudi Arabia, he conducted a campaign of writing letters, postcards, and public statements to proclaim his conversion to orthodox Islam and his newfound belief in the unity of the human race.

After his return from pilgrimage, Malcolm X remained a popular media figure. He spoke regularly at the Muslim Mosque, Inc., and at meetings of the Organization of Afro-American Unity. Tensions with the Nation of Islam escalated, and there were a number of threats and attempts on his life. On February 21, 1965, while addressing a meeting of the OAAU at the Audubon Ballroom in New York, and before an audience of 400 supporters, who included his wife and children, Malcolm was shot 16 times, with a shotgun and with pistols, by at least three assassins. He died at the podium. The gunmen were seized by the crowd and by Malcolm's bodyguards. Three men, all affiliated with the Nation of Islam, were eventually convicted of the murder and served prison sentences. They were later released.

Malcolm X certainly had a greater impact on the African American community after his death than he did while he was alive. His autobiography was published posthumously and became a best seller. His militant stance was echoed by subsequent black activists such as the Black Power movement and the Black Panthers, for which his book was a standard inspiration. During the late 1980s and early 1990s, Malcolm's face and the symbol "X" were marketed on T-shirts, baseball caps, and other casual attire. The clutter of "X" products and paraphernalia eventually lost touch with any political message. In 1992, Spike Lee released a major motion picture based on Malcolm's life that was successful at the box office. While this commercial popularity has since waned, Malcolm X remains an iconic figure for an entire generation of African American youth.

Anthony A. Lee

Further Reading

Carson, Clayborne. *Malcolm X: The FBI File*. New York: Carroll & Graf, 1991.

Clegg, Claude Andrew, III. *An Original Man: The Life and Times of Elijah Muhammad*. New York: St. Martin's Press, 1997.

Collins, Rodney P., and A. Peter Bailey. *The Seventh Child: A Family Memoir of Malcolm X*. London: Turnaround, 2002.

Dyson, Michael Eric. *Making Malcolm: The Myth and Meaning of Malcolm X*. New York: Oxford University Press, 1996.

Jenkins, Robert L., ed. *The Malcolm X Encyclopedia*. Westport, CT: Greenwood Press, 2002.

Malcolm X, with the assistance of Alex Haley. *The Autobiography of Malcolm X*. New York: Ballantine Books, 1965.

Perry, Bruce. *Malcolm: The Life of a Man Who Changed Black America*. Barrytown, NY: Station Hill Press, 1991.

Shabazz, Ilyasah, with Kim McLarin. *Growing Up X*. New York: One World, 2002.

March on Washington

On August 28, 1963, between 200,000 and 250,000 demonstrators from all across the country descended on the nation's capital to participate in the March on Washington (officially called the March on Washington for Jobs and Freedom). Not only was this march the largest demonstration for human rights in U.S. history, but it also showcased, for the first time, unity among the various civil rights organizations. The event began with a rally at the Washington Monument featuring several celebrities and musicians. Participants then marched across the mile-long National Mall to the Lincoln Memorial. The three-hour-long program at the Lincoln Memorial included speeches from prominent civil rights and religious leaders. The day ended with a meeting at the White House between leaders and organizers of the march and President John F. Kennedy.

The idea for the 1963 March on Washington was conceived by A. Philip Randolph, international president of the Brotherhood of Sleeping Car Porters, president of the Negro American Labor Council, and vice president of the AFL-CIO. Randolph, a longtime civil rights activist, was committed to improving the economic condition of black Americans.

In 1941, Randolph threatened to assemble 100,000 African Americans in the capital to help convince President Franklin D. Roosevelt to sign an executive order banning discrimination in the armed services and creating the Fair Employment

Civil rights advocates lead hundreds of thousands of people in the March on Washington on Washington, D.C. in August 1963. The march was held to peacefully demand civil rights and equal opportunity for African Americans. (Lyndon B. Johnson Library)

Practices Committee. As a result of this meeting with Roosevelt, Randolph post-poned his idea for more than two decades. In 1962, however, the 73-year-old elder statesman of the civil rights movement reprised his idea with renewed motivation. With black unemployment at double the rate of white unemployment, and with civil rights for black Americans still unrealized, Randolph proposed a new march for jobs and freedom. When he first proposed the march in late 1962, he received little response from other civil rights leaders. However, he knew that cooperation would be difficult because each of the civil rights groups had their own agenda, and the leaders competed for funding and press coverage. Nonetheless, the success of the March on Washington would depend on the participation of the "Big Six" civil rights organizations. These organizations and their leaders were: Roy Wilkins, of the National Association for the Advancement of Colored People (NAACP); Whitney Young Jr., of the National Urban League (NUL); Dr. Martin Luther King Jr., of the Southern Christian Leadership Conference (SCLC); James Farmer, of the Congress of Racial Equality (CORE); and John Lewis, of the Student Nonviolent Coordinating Committee (SNCC).

By June 1963, King had agreed to cooperate with Randolph on the march. The older, more conservative NAACP and NUL were still ambivalent. But after winning Randolph's promise that the march would be a nonviolent, nonconfronta-tional event, Wilkins of the NAACP pledged his organization's support. The prom-ise of a nonviolent and nonconfrontational demonstration disappointed the more militant CORE and SNCC leaders who had already joined with Randolph. In addition, white supporters such as labor leader Walter Reuther, as well as Jewish, Catholic, and Presbyterian leaders, offered their participation and help.

The organization and details of the march were handled by Bayard Rustin, a close associate of Randolph. Rustin, an antiwar and civil rights activist, had exten-sive experience in organizing mass protests. Before the March on Washington, his most notable mass protest was organizing the earliest Freedom Ride in 1947. He had also participated in Randolph's plans for the 1941 march. With only two months to plan, Rustin established his headquarters in Harlem, with a smaller office in Washington. He and his core staff, consisting of 200 volunteers, quickly organized the largest peaceful demonstration in U.S. history. While Randolph and the NUL focused on jobs, the other civil rights groups centered on freedom. To finance the march, money was raised from the sale of buttons promoting the march at 25 cents each. Thousands of people also sent in cash contributions.

A flyer produced by the National Office of the March on Washington for Jobs and Freedom articulated the six major goals of the march: meaningful civil rights laws, a massive federal works program, full and fair employment, decent housing, the right to vote, and adequate integrated education. More specifically, what was demanded in the March on Washington was passage of "meaningful" civil rights legislation at this session of Congress—no filibustering; immediate elimination of all racial segregation in public schools throughout the nation; a major program of public works to provide jobs for of all the nation's unemployed, including job training and a placement program; a federal law prohibiting racial discrimination in hiring workers, either public or private; a minimum wage of two dollars an hour across the board nationwide; withholding of federal funds from programs that discriminate; enforcement of the Fourteenth Amendment; reducing congressional representation of states where citizens are disenfranchised; a broadened Fair Labor Standards Act to include currently excluded employment areas; and authority for the attorney general to institute injunctive suits when any constitutional right is violated.

As plans progressed, however, the primary goal of the march turned toward passing federal civil rights legislation put forward by President Kennedy in the wake of the demonstrations led by King in Birmingham, Alabama. The proposed march initially caused great concern within the Kennedy administration. From the administration's point of view, they had major cause for concern. In May, massive black demonstrations in Birmingham had culminated with a night of rioting. Other parts of the country were ready to explode as well. Robert Moses, field secretary for SNCC—testifying before a House subcommittee on the president's civil rights bill to end discrimination in public places, education, and employment—warned congressional members that they were facing a situation in Mississippi that had the potential to be far worse than Birmingham. With this information in hand, Kennedy believed that a mass gathering in Washington had the potential to undermine efforts being made to secure civil rights legislation and would damage the image of the United States globally. The president was also concerned that the event might intensify already heightened racial tensions across the country, and that it might erode public support for the civil rights movement at large. Kennedy called King and other civil rights leaders to the White House in late June 1962 to try to convince them to cancel the march, but he was unable to persuade them.

Various influential organizations and individuals also opposed the march. Beside the expected groups, such as southern segregationists and members of the Ku Klux Klan, the black Muslim separatist group, the Nation of Islam, and its outspoken representative, Malcolm X, also opposed the march. Malcolm X referred to it as the "farce on Washington," and any member of the Nation of Islam who attended the march was subjected to a 90-day suspension from the organization. The National Council of the AFL-CIO also chose not to support the march, adopting a position of neutrality. A number of international unions, however, independently declared their support and attended the march in substantial numbers. Hundreds of local unions also fully supported the march.

On August 28, the marchers arrived in chartered buses, trains, planes, and private cars. More than 200,000 people had assembled at the Washington Monument on the National Mall, where the march was to begin. It was a very diverse crowd consisting of black and white, rich and poor, young and old, white collar, blue collar, unemployed, celebrities, and everyday people. The diversity of those in attendance was also reflected by the event's presenters and performers. Some of these included Marian Anderson, Daisy Lee Bates, Joan Baez, Bob Dylan, John Lewis, Odetta, Rabbi Joachim Prinz, A. Philip Randolph, Walter Reuther, Bayard Rustin, Josh White, Roy Wilkins, Whitney Young Jr., and Peter, Paul, and Mary.

Televised live to an audience of millions, the march provided many legendary rhetorical moments in the form of speeches, songs, prayers, and actions (i.e., black and white people holding hands). Although the march's official goals included an endorsement of Kennedy's civil rights bill—in part because the Kennedy administration had officially cooperated with the march—some of the most passionate speeches criticized the bill as incomplete. John Lewis, the 23-year-old president of SNCC, promised that without meaningful legislation, blacks would "march throughout the South." His speech (prepared with other members of SNCC) had originally suggested in the speech that they could not support the Kennedy legislation because it did not guarantee the right of black people to vote. In another part of the speech, SNCC had suggested that there was very little difference between the major political parties. They suggested that, as a movement, blacks could not wait on the president or members of the Congress; they had to take matters into their own hands. Some people thought that this portion of the speech was too inflammatory and that it might motivate people to riot. As a result, Lewis was forced to rewrite his original speech, which generally called the Kennedy legislative agenda for civil rights "too little, too late." Randolph and Wilkins also gave speeches. The most memorable speech of the day, however, came from Dr. King. The speech, reportedly delivered extemporaneously, would forever be known as the "I Have a Dream" speech. King's speech began with a powerful indictment of the nation's injustices against black Americans, then focused on a message of hope and determination, and a proclamation of what America could become, epitomizing the day's message of racial harmony and love, and a belief that blacks and whites could live together in peace. "I Have a Dream" is considered one of the greatest and most influential speeches in American history.

The march was an American landmark event for the civil rights movement, and an overwhelming success owing to the organizers, leaders, participants, and extensive coverage by the media. The march is partly credited with winning passage of the federal Civil Rights Act of 1964. Although there was a presigned executive order authorizing military intervention (with more than 1,000 troops) in case of rioting, there were no major disturbances. The behavior of the participants and onlookers proved that the presence of the military was unnecessary. Many Americans witnessed, for the first time, black and white people united, marching, and celebrating together.

After the march, King and other civil rights leaders met with President Kennedy and Vice President Lyndon B. Johnson at the White House. Feeling the pressure of more than 200,000 Americans, Kennedy told them that he intended to throw his whole weight behind civil rights legislation. The march had not only achieved tangible goals, but it had also brought widespread attention to the struggle for civil rights.

Janice D. Hamlet

Further Reading

Carson, Clayborne, David J. Garrow, Gerald Gill, Vincent Harding, and Darlene Clark Hine, eds. *The Eyes on the Prize: Civil Rights Reader: Documents, Speeches, and Firsthand Accounts from the Black Freedom Struggle, 1954–1990.* New York: Penguin Books, 1991.

Hampton, Henry, and Steve Fager, eds. *Voices of Freedom: An Oral History of the Civil Rights Movement from the 1950s through the 1980s.* New York: Bantam Books, 1990

King, Martin Luther, Jr. *The Autobiography of Martin Luther King, Jr.* Edited by Clayborne Carson. New York: Warner Books, 1988.

Williams, Juan. *Eyes on the Prize: America's Civil Rights Years, 1954–1965.* New York: Penguin Books, 1982.

Marshall, Thurgood

Thurgood Marshall (1908–1993) was born Thoroughgood Marshall (a name he later shortened legally) to Norma and William Marshall in the age of Jim Crow. Although Thurgood Marshall is perhaps best remembered for his historic position as the first black Supreme Court Justice, and other men such as Martin Luther King Jr. have garnered more fame for their leadership in the civil rights movement, Marshall's most direct and lasting contributions to the advancement of the race came in the years before the movement. Marshall, as an activist, laid the groundwork for the movement. As a direct result of Marshall's and other civil rights leaders' efforts to uplift the race by overturning their subordinate legal status, blacks have earned political influence and arguably a stronger sense of community.

Throughout his life, Marshall was intimately and passionately involved with issues pertaining to equal rights for all men and women, regardless of race, ethnicity, or creed. Marshall's activism extended from his time at the NAACP (1932–1961) through his time as U.S. solicitor general (1965–1967). This can also be seen in the opinions and dissentions he wrote on the country's highest court (1967–1991). His NAACP tenure was a pivotal time for the organization when overturning racial segregation was one of its primary mandates. It was at the beginning of his career that Marshall began his work on his first segregation case, *Murray v. Pearson*, to open admission at the University of Maryland Law School to blacks—the same institution that denied him admittance only a few years earlier. By the time Marshall joined the bench of the Supreme Court, he had argued 32 cases before that body and won 29 of them, mostly in the name of racial desegregation and other civil rights causes.

The gains made by the *Murray* decision were small, for it only opened the law school; other graduate programs would be sued in the coming decade. Nevertheless, *Murray* was a significant step toward the larger educational accomplishments of Marshall and the NAACP. During the next two decades leading up to *Brown v. Board of Education* (1954), which overturned *Plessy v. Ferguson* (1896), Marshall's cases challenged the foundation of American law itself. His goal was not merely to remind the nation to adhere to the Fourteenth Amendment—equal protection—but to demonstrate that the rules that he fought to overturn were wrong.

Marshall challenged segregation in case after case. Although most of his cases dealt with educational equality, the future justice also fought for blacks' right to vote in Texas primaries (*Smith v. Allwright*, 1944), the right to rent or buy any place of residence, and for equality of pay. In 1954, Marshall argued *Brown v. Board* in front of the U.S. Supreme Court. The *Brown* case encompassed five school segregation cases in Virginia, South Carolina, Delaware, Kansas, and Washington, D.C. After 17 years of success in opening postsecondary and graduate education through a series of court cases, Marshall, the Legal Defense Fund, and the NAACP were ready to take on educational segregation on a primary school level. Separate was clearly unequal. This inequality was apparent in Clarendo County, South Carolina, for example; per capita spending for white students was $179 compared to spending for black students of $43, and the student-to-teacher ratio in the white schools was 28:1, but in the black school system it was nearly double, 47:1.

Topeka, Kansas, was different. The facilities were equal. Marshall's argument in *Brown* had to go further than the need for equal facilities; otherwise, the Supreme Court could uphold *Plessy* and again rule that school segregation was permissible as long as facilities were equal. Marshall wanted educational integration. He focused on testimony presented by experts about the terrible effects of state-sponsored segregation on black children. Marshall argued "that segregated schools, perhaps more than any other single factor, are of major concern to the individual of public school age and contribute greatly to the unwholesomeness and unhappy development of the personality of Negroes which the color caste system in the United States has produced" (Smith 2003, 52). The case was not easily won; it was almost a year and a half after the court began hearing the case that Chief Justice Warren finally read the court's unanimous decision "Separate educational facilities are inherently unequal" (*Brown v. Board of Education*, 347 U.S. 483). The Supreme Court extended the *Brown* decision beyond education by expanding the principle to desegregate other public facilities. Through a series of signed and *per curiam* opinions, the court ordered equal access to public parking lots, restaurants, cemeteries, hospitals, parks, golf courses, buses, beaches, and amphitheaters.

Marshall realized the impact of the *Brown* decision. He believed that *Brown* "probably did more than anything else to awaken the Negro from his apathy to demanding his right to equality" (Ball 2001, 147). Therefore, the 1954 decision can be seen as the foundation for the civil rights movement; however, Marshall did not think *Brown* alone made the movement. When reflecting on the importance of his victories in *Smith* and *Brown*, Marshall once said, "I don't know whether the voting case or the school desegregation case was more important. Without the ballot, you've got no goddamned citizenship, no status, no power, in this country. But without the chance to get an education, you have no capacity to use the ballot effectively. Hell, I don't know which case I'm proudest of" (Smith 2003, 75).

Noah D. Drezner

Further Reading

Ball, Howard. *A Defiant Life: Thurgood Marshall and the Persistence of Racism in America*. New York: Three Rivers Press, 2001.

Drezner, Noah D. "Thurgood Marshall: A Study of Philanthropy through Racial Uplift." In *Uplifting a People: Essays on African American Philanthropy in Education*, edited by Marybeth Gasman and Katherine V. Sedwick, 98–100. New York: Peter Lang, 2005.

Smith, J. Clay, ed. *Supreme Justices: Speeches and Writings*. Philadelphia: University of Pennsylvania Press, 2003.

Memphis Sanitation Workers' Strike

The night before his assassination in April 1968, Martin Luther King Jr. told a group of striking sanitation workers in Memphis, Tennessee: "We've got to give ourselves to this struggle until the end. Nothing would be more tragic than to stop at this point in Memphis. We've got to see it through." King believed the struggle in Memphis exposed the need for economic equality and social justice that he hoped his Poor People's Campaign would highlight nationally.

On February 1, 1968, two Memphis garbage collectors, Echol Cole and Robert Walker, were crushed to death by a malfunctioning truck. Twelve days later, frustrated by the city's response to the latest event in a long pattern of neglect and abuse of its black employees, 1,300 black men from the Memphis Department of Public Works went on strike. Sanitation workers, led by garbage collector turned union organizer T. O. Jones, and supported by the president of the American Federation of State, County, and Municipal Employees (AFSCME), Jerry Wurf, demanded recognition of their union, better safety standards, and a decent wage.

The union, which had been granted a charter by AFSCME in 1964, had attempted a strike in 1966, but failed in large part because workers were unable to arouse the support of Memphis's religious community or middle class. Conditions for black sanitation workers worsened when Henry Loeb became mayor in January 1968. Loeb refused to take dilapidated trucks out of service or pay overtime when men were forced to work late-night shifts. Sanitation workers earned wages so low that many were on welfare and hundreds relied on food stamps to feed their families.

On February 11, more than 700 sanitation workers attended a union meeting and unanimously decided to strike. Within a week, the local branch of the National Association for the Advancement of Colored People (NAACP) passed a resolution supporting the strike. The strike might have ended on February 22, when the City Council, pressured by a sit-in of sanitation workers and their supporters, voted to recognize the union and recommended a wage increase. Mayor Loeb rejected the City Council vote, however, insisting that only he had the authority to recognize the union, and he refused to do so.

The following day, after police used mace and tear gas against nonviolent demonstrators marching to city hall, Memphis's black community was galvanized. Meeting in a church basement on February 24, 150 local ministers formed Community on the Move for Equality (COME), under the leadership of King's longtime ally, local minister James Lawson. COME committed to the use of nonviolent civil disobedience to fill Memphis's jails and bring attention to the plight of the sanitation workers. By the beginning of March, local high school and college students, nearly a quarter of them white, were participating alongside garbage workers in daily marches; and over 100 people, including several ministers, had been arrested.

While Lawson kept King updated by phone, other national civil rights leaders, including Roy Wilkins and Bayard Rustin, came to rally the sanitation workers. King himself arrived on March 18 to address a crowd of about 25,000—the largest indoor gathering the civil rights movement had ever seen. Speaking to a group of labor and civil rights activists and members of the powerful black church, King praised the group's unity, saying: "You are demonstrating that we can stick together. You are demonstrating that we are all tied in a single garment of destiny, and that if one black person suffers, if one black person is down, we are all down." King encouraged the group to support the sanitation strike by going on a citywide work stoppage, and he pledged to return that Friday, March 22, to lead a protest through the city.

King left Memphis the following day, but the Southern Christian Leadership Conference's (SCLC) James Bevel and Ralph Abernathy remained to help organize the protest and work stoppage. When the day arrived, however, a massive snowstorm blanketed the region, preventing King from reaching Memphis and causing the organizers to reschedule the march for March 28. Memphis city officials estimated that 22,000 students skipped school that day to participate in the demonstration.

King arrived late and found a massive crowd on the brink of chaos. Lawson and King led the march together but quickly called off the demonstration as violence began to erupt. King was whisked away to a nearby hotel, and Lawson told the mass of people to turn around and go back to the church. In the turmoil that followed, downtown Memphis shops were looted, and a 16-year-old was shot and killed by a police officer. Police followed demonstrators back to the Clayborn Temple, entered the church, released tear gas inside the sanctuary, and clubbed people as they lay on the floor to get fresh air.

Loeb called for martial law and brought in 4,000 National Guard troops. The following day, over 200 striking workers continued their daily march, carrying signs that read, "I *Am* a Man." At a news conference held before he returned to Atlanta, King said that he had been unaware of the divisions within the community, particularly of the presence of a black youth group committed to "Black Power" called the Invaders, who were accused of starting the violence.

King considered not returning to Memphis, but decided that if the nonviolent struggle for economic justice was going to succeed, it would be necessary to follow through with the movement there. After a divisive meeting on March 30, SCLC staff agreed to support King's return to Memphis. He arrived on April 3 and was persuaded to speak by a crowd of dedicated sanitation workers who had braved another storm to hear him. A weary King preached about his own mortality, telling the group, "Like anybody, I would like to live a long life—longevity has its place. But I'm not concerned about that now ... I've seen the Promised Land. I may not get there with you. But I want you to know tonight that we, as a people, will get to the Promised Land."

The following evening, as King was getting ready for dinner, he was shot and killed on the balcony of the Lorraine Motel. While Lawson recorded a radio announcement urging calm in Memphis, Loeb called in the state police and the National Guard and ordered a 7:00 p.m. curfew. Black and white ministers pleaded with Loeb to concede to the union's demands, but the mayor held firm. President Lyndon B. Johnson then charged Undersecretary of Labor James Reynolds with negotiating a solution and ending the strike.

On April 8, an estimated 42,000 people led by Coretta Scott King, SCLC, and union leaders silently marched through Memphis in honor of King, demanding that Loeb give in to the union's requests. In front of city hall, AFSCME pledged to support the workers until "we have justice." Negotiators finally reached a deal on April 16, allowing the City Council to recognize the union and guaranteeing a better wage. Although the deal brought the strike to an end, several months later, the union had to threaten another strike to press the city to follow through with its commitment.

Clayborne Carson et al.

Further Reading

Honey, Michael K. *Going Down Jericho Road*. New York: W. W. Norton, 2008.

King, Martin Luther, Jr. "Address at Mass Meeting at the Bishop Charles Mason Temple." March 18, 1968. Mississippi Valley Collection, Memphis State University, Memphis, Tennessee.

King, Martin Luther, Jr. "I've Been to the Mountaintop." In *A Call to Conscience: The Landmark Speeches of Martin Luther King, Jr.*, edited by Clayborne Carson and Kris Shepard. New York: Warner Books, 2001.

Meredith, James

James Meredith, a civil rights activist, is best known for becoming the first African American student to attend the University of Mississippi, in October 1962. Meredith's entry into the school served as a major turning point for the civil rights movement.

James Howard Meredith was born on June 25, 1933, in Kosciusko, Mississippi, to two farmers, Moses and Roxie Meredith. Moses Meredith was one of the few African Americans in Mississippi who not only owned his own farm, but was also registered to vote, and he made a strong effort to make sure that James and his nine brothers and sisters were sheltered from the racism of the surrounding community. After graduating from high school, Meredith immediately joined the U.S. Air Force, in which he served from 1951 to 1960. In 1956, he married Mary June Wiggins, and they had three sons. After his discharge from the military, Meredith enrolled at Jackson State College for two years before applying for a transfer to the University of Mississippi at Oxford. Despite his excellent grades, he was denied admission twice before finally gaining acceptance in 1962. Then governor Ross Barnett adamantly opposed Meredith's admission to Ole Miss, and personally traveled there to prevent Meredith from registering for classes. On October 1, 1962, Meredith finally gained entrance to the university, where his presence sparked riots all over the campus. In all, 5,000 federal troops and 500 U.S. marshals were needed to quell the violence, which left two people dead and hundreds injured.

Many students treated Meredith poorly during his two semesters at the university. Although some apparently accepted his presence and he made friends, some students living in his dorm would bounce basketballs on the floor directly above Meredith's room at all hours of the night to disturb him. When Meredith would go to the cafeteria, people turned their backs to him, and if he sat at a table with other students, those students, who were all white, would immediately get up and move to another table. Despite this poor treatment, Meredith graduated with a degree in political science on August 18, 1963.

Following his time at the University of Mississippi, Meredith continued his education at the University of Ibadan in Nigeria before receiving a law degree from Columbia University in 1968. In addition to continuing his studies, Meredith remained a pivotal figure in the civil rights movement throughout the 1960s. Most notably, he led a civil rights march from Memphis, Tennessee, to Jackson, Mississippi, in the summer of 1966. Calling his march the "Walk against Fear," he hoped that his example would encourage the nearly half-million disenfranchised blacks in Mississippi to overcome their fear of white retaliation and register to vote. Meredith did not invite any national civil rights groups to join him, instead choosing to march alone. On June 6, the day after the march started, Meredith was shot by sniper Aubrey James Norvell after walking only 28 miles. Although wounded,

Meredith healed enough to finish the march two weeks later, this time joined by Dr. Martin Luther King Jr. and other nationally recognized civil rights activists. A photograph of Meredith after he was wounded won a Pulitzer Prize in photography in 1967.

Meredith ceased his civil rights activism in the late 1960s and authored a memoir about his time at the University of Mississippi entitled *Three Years in Mississippi*, published in 1966. He then settled into a career as a stockbroker before running unsuccessfully for a congressional seat in 1972, and then serving as a domestic adviser on the staff of U.S. Senator Jesse Helms, a one-time segregationist, beginning in 1989. Although he received a barrage of criticism from the civil rights community, Meredith, a staunch Republican, defended his decision to work for Helms, stating that he had written letters to every member of the House of Representatives and Senate offering his services, and only Helms had replied. Meredith's historical work, *Mississippi: A Volume of Eleven Books*, was published in 1995. He presented his papers to his alma mater, the University of Mississippi, on March 21, 1997. In 2002, Meredith's son Joseph graduated from the University of Mississippi with a doctorate in business administration. Joseph Meredith also received honors for being the most outstanding student in the School of Business Administration.

In later years, Meredith distanced himself from the civil rights movement of which he was such an instrumental part, referring to himself instead as a citizen who fought to protect the rights extended to all Americans. At the time of this writing, he lived in Jackson, Mississippi, with his second wife, journalist Judy Alsobrooks, and ran a small used-car dealership.

Sara K. Eskridge

Further Reading

Barrett, Russell H. *Integration at Ole Miss*. Chicago: Quadrangle Books, 1965.

Doyle, William. *An American Insurrection: The Battle of Oxford, Mississippi, 1962*. New York: Doubleday, 2001.

Lord, Walter. *The Past That Would Not Die*. New York: Harper and Row, 1965.

Meredith, James. *Three Years in Mississippi*. Bloomington: Indiana University Press, 1966.

Mississippi Freedom Democratic Party

The Mississippi Freedom Democratic Party (MFDP) was a short-lived political party during the civil rights movement designed to highlight and challenge the segregated Democratic Party in the South. It staged a public stand at the 1964

Democratic National Convention. MFDP's failure pushed many African American activists into an increasingly militant stance.

In 1964, civil rights workers descended on Mississippi to register African Americans to vote. Freedom Summer became a violent showdown between racist white Mississippians and African Americans trying to exercise their constitutionally guaranteed right to vote. One of the leading organizations involved in the civil rights action in Mississippi was the Council of Federated Organizations (COFO). COFO registered African Americans to vote and registered 60,000 Mississippians for a new political party that did not discriminate based on race, the Mississippi Freedom Democratic Party. This new party may have been the greatest achievement of Freedom Summer.

The MFDP denied the legitimacy of the Mississippi Democratic Party since the regular party did not allow African Americans to participate. In August, the MFDP convened in Jackson, Mississippi, and selected 68 delegates to attend the Democratic National Convention in Atlantic City, New Jersey; all but four delegates were African American. The MFDP hoped to challenge the state Democratic Party's right to represent the state at the national convention. Although the delegation left for Atlantic City with little more than moral outrage, it came to mount a serious challenge to the party's rules.

Lyndon B. Johnson, who was set to be nominated as the Democratic presidential candidate, did not want internal strife in the party at the convention. Despite the MFDP's support of Johnson, the president feared that if the maverick party were recognized, Democratic Party delegates from Mississippi and other southern states would walk out of the convention. Such a defection among southern Democrats would have severe electoral repercussions, and Johnson did not wish to be known as the one who drove southerners out of the Democratic Party. Consequently, Johnson maneuvered his supporters to thwart the MFDP. Johnson allies offered the MFDP two voting delegates—one black, one white—with "at large" status, rather than representing Mississippi. The rest of the MFDP delegation would be admitted to the convention with nonvoting, honorary status. In the future, Johnson promised, rules would be changed to prevent racial discrimination in the selection of delegates.

Meanwhile, the MFDP went before the credentials committee, the group in charge of determining legitimate delegates, and made a national spectacle. Fannie Lou Hamer eloquently spoke about being jailed and abused—physically and verbally—just for trying to register to vote. Her testimony riveted the nation in a nationally televised broadcast. Many of the MFDP's allies within the northern liberal ranks of the Democratic Party hoped to put to a vote whether the MFDP should be allowed to represent Mississippi to the entire convention. The Credentials Committee, however, stuck to the compromise offered by Johnson through Senator Hubert H. Humphrey, who was promised the vice presidential nomination. The compromise substantiated the Mississippi Democratic Party's legitimacy and thus undermined the entire purpose of the MFDP. Some African American leaders such as Martin Luther King Jr., Bayard Rustin, Roy Wilkins, and James Farmer urged the MFDP to concede and accept the compromise proffered because they believed the two voting positions represented a practical political victory. Hamer and others who journeyed to Atlantic City felt betrayed. Hamer said, "It's a token of rights on the back row that we get in Mississippi. We didn't come all this way for that mess again."

Many militants in the civil rights movement and the MFDP were outraged at the way the delegates were treated by white liberals like Johnson and Humphrey. In the aftermath of the 1964 Democratic convention, the MFDP disbanded. However, after 1964, the MFDP experience led to more militant stances by other civil rights organizations, particularly the Student Nonviolent Coordinating Committee.

Adam Sowards

Further Reading

Dittmer, John. *Local People: The Struggle for Civil Rights in Mississippi*. Urbana: University of Illinois Press, 1994.

Sitkoff, Harvard. *The Struggle for Black Equality, 1954–1992*. Rev. ed. New York: Hill and Wang, 1993.

Walter, Mildred Pitts. *Mississippi Challenge*. New York: Bradbury Press, 1992.

Mississippi Freedom Summer

During the summer of 1964, hundreds of black and white students volunteered to enter the Deep South to work on a program called Freedom Summer. The impetus behind Freedom Summer was to work on African American voter registration, establish Freedom Schools, and get the black community involved in local politics. Most of the volunteers were members of the Student Nonviolent Coordinating Committee (SNCC), the Congress of Racial Equality (CORE), and the National Association for the Advancement of Colored People (NAACP). These groups combined to form the Mississippi Council of Federated Organizations for the sole purpose of politically organizing black communities in Mississippi.

Mississippi was an important place for civil rights work for several reasons. First, perhaps out of the entire South, blacks in Mississippi had horrible political and economic conditions, especially in the Mississippi delta. In 1962, Mississippi had only 6.7 percent of the black population registered to vote. Despite the constitutional right of all citizens to be able to vote, black Mississippians were constantly in fear of losing their homes, jobs, and lives from white retaliation. Furthermore, the white political machine continually disenfranchised the black community through enforcement of poll taxes and literacy tests.

Volunteer worker urges African Americans in the South to register to vote, 1964. (National Archives)

The second reason Mississippi was important was the continued economic oppression facing the black community. The Mississippi delta was severely impoverished. Mechanization had caused many workers to lose their jobs, and those who still had jobs were in fear of losing them because they had fought for the right to vote. Black Mississippians and SNCC organizers believed the key to a brighter economic future rested in the hands of those who ran the government. Many communities in Mississippi had a black majority, so they should not only be able to vote, but also to hold political office.

One of the local individuals who helped organize and galvanize a nation for political and economic improvement in Mississippi was Fannie Lou Hamer. Born in Montgomery County, Mississippi, Hamer was raised by sharecroppers and continued working as a sharecropper in the Mississippi delta. Once SNCC became active in Mississippi during the summer of 1962, Hamer worked with them to educate and register to vote thousands of poor blacks living in the area. Hamer was also not intimidated by the white community. When the owner of the plantation she worked for asked her not to register to vote, she did so anyway, despite the threats of being removed from the land on which she had worked so hard.

Still, Hamer continued to work for voting rights in Mississippi. One of the events that put her into the national spotlight was her arrest in Winona, Mississippi, after returning from a citizenship class in Charleston, South Carolina. She was arrested on trumped-up charges and severely beaten while in jail. There was a highly publicized court case, in which the defendants were found not guilty. After all the publicity from Hamer's beating and subsequent trial, however, her name began garnering national attention both for her personally and for the state of Mississippi.

Hamer was also a founder and organizer of the Mississippi Freedom Democratic Party (MFDP) in the spring of 1964. The creation and sustaining of the MFDP became one of the primary goals of Freedom Summer. Volunteers traveled from house to house in the black community urging individuals to vote and become active in the political process. The creation of the MFDP was especially important because of the upcoming presidential election. They wanted to make President Lyndon B. Johnson realize that the needs of the black community had to be met and that the Democratic Party, as it was currently configured, did not represent black America. The main goal of the MFDP was to unseat the all-white Mississippi Democratic regulars at the Democratic Convention in Atlantic City, New Jersey, and be recognized as the true representatives of Mississippi.

On August 20, 1964, MFDP delegates arrived, including Hamer. Upon their arrival, the convention had to decide who would represent Mississippi on the convention floor. The Credential Committee held a hearing that was broadcast live across the nation. Hamer spoke on the injustices going on in Mississippi and the political climate of the South. Just as her speech was starting to become impassioned, President Johnson interrupted the broadcast with an impromptu press conference.

Despite Johnson's attempt to cut Hamer off, the nation had already seen enough to give national support to the MFDP. Johnson was afraid that if he issued his support for the MFDP, he would lose the southern Democratic vote and ultimately the presidency. A compromise had to be reached. The convention decided to offer the MFDP two seats at large and bar any delegation guilty of discrimination. All but four of the regular Democratic delegates from Mississippi walked off the floor, and the MFDP tried to obtain those seats but were not allowed on the floor. Ultimately, the MFDP turned down the two seats. The MFDP did not get seated at the convention, but the creation and support of the party helped to achieve a major goal of Freedom Summer—getting the local community interested and active in local politics and moving the nation's attention toward black voting rights in the South.

Beyond the local community, hundreds of white volunteers from the North helped spread the word and educate Mississippi's black community about their voting rights. Community centers were created where children could have not only "traditional" educational classes, but also organize for political change in their communities. Before these northern volunteers went to Mississippi, they received training in Oxford, Ohio, led by James Forman and other SNCC members, including Hamer. The purpose of the training was to introduce them to nonviolent tactics and give them an understanding of what mob violence might be like. If past events, like the Freedom Rides, were any indication of how white mobs might react to both black and white volunteers, the volunteers knew that violence, if not death, was likely.

Nothing illustrated that threat better than the 1964 disappearance of a black volunteer, James Chaney, and two white volunteers, Andrew Goodman and Michael Schwerner. These three men set out on June 21 for Philadelphia, Mississippi, to investigate the bombing of a black church. However, the men were arrested and then released that same evening, never to be seen again. Press conferences were held, and the families of all three men begged the public for any information about their whereabouts. President Johnson even launched an FBI investigation into their disappearance. The wife of Michael Schwerner, Rita, publicly addressed the fact that if all the men had been black, there would be no national attention over their disappearance and that it was a shame that white men had to die before the violence in Mississippi, and the South in general, would be noticed by the American public. Eventually, the scorched remains of their car were found, leading everyone to fear that they were dead. These suspicions were confirmed on April 4 when their bodies were found buried together in an earthen dam. The FBI had offered $30,000 to a Ku Klux Klan member for the information on where they were buried. All three were killed by gunshots to the head, and Chaney was also severely beaten. The families of the three men wanted them all to be buried together, but because of continued segregation in southern cemeteries, their wish could not be fulfilled.

Despite the tragedy, the disappearance of Chaney, Goodman, and Schwerner did have a positive impact on the events of that summer. It placed more media attention on the volunteers and perhaps resulted in less violence than normal toward the workers. Despite the media attention, approximately 80 volunteers were beaten and 1,000 were jailed over the course of the summer. In addition, houses, Freedom Schools, churches, and other centers of volunteer activity were burned or firebombed. Despite the fear of violence, students were eager to work in Mississippi. Although cooperation between black and white workers showed the nation how all people could work together to effect change in Mississippi, however, people began to question whether the presence of whites was actually a positive move for accomplishing the goals of Freedom Summer.

For instance, local blacks could expect more harassment from local whites for just talking with the volunteers. Immediately, white youths started driving through the black communities where white volunteers were staying and would break windows, start fires, or make other threats against blacks. The black community was inviting violence by talking to the volunteers, and this was obviously a very dangerous situation. Some white volunteers would become frustrated because any black person who was outspoken or supported the efforts of the volunteers would lose their jobs or worse. It was not uncommon for the local police or local whites to follow the volunteers into the black community and report their findings back to their employers or other members of the community.

Another issue was the role of white women. Southern attitudes about what "white womanhood" meant and how it was threatened by going into the black community did not go over very well with southern white men. In an effort to protect volunteers and black citizens, a majority of white women were given jobs that involved Freedom Schools instead of canvassing the black communities. As a result, volunteers were able to open up more schools than they had originally planned, and many more students wanted to attend the schools than previously thought. Some students were so eager to learn, they showed up for school as early as 6:00 a.m.

The Freedom Schools went beyond the scope of a regular classroom. The children learned not only American and world history, but also about their culture and American politics. Children were taught why it was important to be active in their community politics and how to be an activist throughout their life. This lesson was an essential goal of Freedom Summer, as the organizers wanted the black community to learn to be a social force not only in Mississippi, but throughout the country.

In all, Freedom Summer left behind a strong legacy. First, black disenfranchisement was brought to the forefront with the passage of the Voting Rights Act of 1965. The passage of the Voting Rights Act would allow federal examiners to take over voting registration in places where there was a history of discrimination, and those examiners could ban literacy tests as a requirement for registering to vote. The impact on voter registration in Mississippi was tremendous. The percentage of blacks registered to vote rose from 6.7 percent to nearly 60 percent. There was also a substantial increase in voter registration across the country. Second, the MFDP had opened up the world of politics to black Mississippians. Thus, all black Americans realized that they could and should have a place in American politics.

Lastly, Freedom Summer opened up Mississippi to the rest of the country. As a result, more Americans were aware of the various civil rights issues plaguing Mississippi, and not just black Americans were saying that change had to occur. White Americans were becoming just as vocal as black Americans, and this made the rest of the country stand up and take notice.

Cristy Casado Tondeur

Further Reading

Carmichael, Stokely. *Ready for Revolution: The Life and Struggles of Stokely Carmichael.* New York: Scribner, 2003.

Carson, Clayborne, David J. Garrow, Gerald Gill, Vincent Harding, and Darlene Clark Hine, eds. *The Eyes on the Prize: Civil Rights Reader: Documents, Speeches, and First-hand Accounts from the Black Freedom Struggle, 1954–1990.* New York: Penguin Books, 1991.

Mills, Hay. *This Little Light of Mine: The Life of Fannie Lou Hamer.* New York: Penguin Group, 1993.

Payne, Charles. *I've Got the Light of Freedom: The Organizing Tradition and the Mississippi Freedom Struggle*. Berkeley: University of California Press, 1995.

Montgomery Bus Boycott

The Montgomery Bus Boycott is often heralded as the beginning of the modern civil rights movement. Sparked by Rosa Parks's refusal to give up her seat for a white passenger, the bus boycott engaged all of Montgomery's African American community in a nonviolent, mass protest of Jim Crow segregation that spanned 381 days, financially crippling the Montgomery City Lines. After the U.S. Supreme Court affirmed a lower-court ruling that Alabama's segregated bus law was unconstitutional, the community boycott and segregated buses in Montgomery ended. Yet the Montgomery Bus Boycott by the city's black community ushered in an era of direct action by African Americans across the South against the inequities of Jim Crow laws.

The social, political, and economic structure of the South rested on a bifurcated racial hierarchy and institutionalized racial segregation that permeated virtually every aspect of southern life. This Jim Crow system consistently deprived African Americans of equal opportunity, access to public spaces and facilities, and their constitutional rights. Southern white society controlled African Americans with

Rosa Parks, whose refusal to give up her bus seat to a white passenger sparked the Montgomery Bus Boycott and fueled the civil rights movement, sits in the front of a bus on December 21, 1956. After the court ruling, the Interstate Commerce Commission banned segregation in public transit. (Library of Congress)

time-worn customs and inequitable Jim Crow laws, as well as the use of intimidation and terror. Overt threats and merely the intimation of lynching kept many African Americans from challenging the status quo.

In Montgomery, Alabama, as in many cities throughout the segregated South, African Americans rode in the rear of the bus. The front was reserved for white passengers. Blacks paid at the front, just as white passengers did, but they then had to exit the bus and walk to the rear to board through the back door. As part of the degradation inherent in Jim Crow, bus drivers—this often depended on the capriciousness or the viciousness of the individual bus driver—sometimes drove away before they could board at the rear, leaving them stranded, their bus fare lost. Although the black section was always in the rear, the color line was not static. When whites were not on the bus, blacks could sit nearer to the front. As more whites boarded, and the seats filled, the color line moved farther back. Black passengers, at that point, were expected to give their seats to white passengers, gender notwithstanding.

The Women's Political Council (WPC), headed by Jo Ann Robinson, an English professor at Alabama State College, had been entertaining for some years the idea of a boycott of the bus system and looking for a test case to challenge Montgomery's segregation ordinances. The case of Claudette Colvin initially seemed to be the most promising. On March 2, 1955, the 15-year-old Colvin had been arrested for not giving up her seat after the bus driver ordered her to move. Colvin had been seated in a row not normally reserved for whites, which Montgomery's segregation ordinance did not specifically cover. Robinson and others in the WPC consulted with E. D. Nixon, president of the Montgomery NAACP, and Clifford Durr, a former Franklin D. Roosevelt New Dealer and local white attorney. In the end, they decided against using Colvin's arrest as either a test case or to rally support for a boycott. Colvin's standing in the community—she was young, unwed, and pregnant—did not bode well for its success. In all, they rejected three possible test cases before Rosa Parks's arrest.

As Parks rode home from work on the evening of December 1, 1955, she sat in the first row of seats reserved for African Americans. When more passengers boarded bus No. 2857, and the white rows filled, the bus driver, James F. Blake, ordered Parks and three others to give their seats to the white passengers. Although the other three complied, Parks refused. Dispelling the myth that she refused to move because her feet hurt, Parks later said, "the only tired I was, was tired of giving in." Blake called the police, and police officers Fletcher B. Day and Dempsey W. Mixon arrested Parks in front of the Empire Theater for violating the city's segregation ordinance. Parks had problems with Blake previously, in 1943, when he forced her off the bus for not exiting the front door after paying her fare and entering the bus from the rear. After that incident, Parks avoided Blake's bus for more than 12 years.

Nixon and Durr arranged for Parks's release on bond, and she agreed to allow her arrest to be used as a test case. Parks had a sterling reputation in the community: she was married, articulate, a local officer with the NAACP, and held a stable job at the Montgomery Fair, a popular department store. When contacted by black attorney Fred Gray (who had been contacted by Nixon) about Parks's arrest, Robinson and the WPC began circulating thousands of leaflets calling for a boycott of the city's buses. Nixon organized a meeting of black leaders for the night of December 2 at Dexter Avenue Baptist Church, where he challenged them to lead such an effort.

The first day of the boycott, December 5, was highly successful. More than 90 percent of the black community boycotted the buses. That same day, a Montgomery court convicted Parks and fined her $10, plus $4 in court costs. In an afternoon meeting at the Mount Zion African Methodist Episcopal (AME) church, community leaders created an organization to run the boycott, the Montgomery Improvement Association (MIA), the name suggested by Reverend Ralph D. Abernathy of the black First Baptist Church of Montgomery. At this meeting, the MIA's first president, 26-year-old Martin Luther King Jr., the pastor of Dexter Avenue Baptist Church, had been unanimously elected, not because of his "potential of leadership" but because of the rivalries between other black leaders in Montgomery. Also, King had been in the city only a short time and had not yet made enemies in the community. Mount Zion AME hosted a mass meeting that night, but the boycott's initial success and Parks's conviction clearly meant that the boycott would continue until the bus line changed their policies. The African American churches played a major role in disseminating information and providing a source of strength and support for the black community during the boycott.

The MIA demanded three things from the Montgomery City Lines: courtesy from bus drivers; the hiring of four black bus drivers; and more equitable seating on the buses, although they did not demand integrated seating. The MIA's plan called for blacks to be seated from the rear to the front and whites from the front to the rear, without any seats being reserved for a specific race. According to Jo Ann Robinson, the reason that they did not demand integration openly was that "no one was brazen enough to announce publicly that black people might boycott city buses for the specific purpose of integrating those buses. Just to say that minorities wanted 'better seating arrangements' was bad enough. . . . To admit that black Americans were seeking to integrate would have been too much; there probably would have been much bloodshed and arrests of those who dared to disclose such an idea!" The bus company refused to meet any demands.

For the next 381 days, African Americans refused to ride the buses in Montgomery. They walked and they organized carpools. Those who owned their own automobiles volunteered their vehicles or drove people themselves. Black cab drivers charged only a fraction of their fares to black riders. The MIA purchased station wagons to transport people back and forth from work or the store. Donations poured in from outside the state as churches, both black and white, raised money and sent gifts such as shoes.

The bus boycott also had white support, but it was extremely limited in scope. White liberals such as Clifford and Virginia Durr and Reverend Robert Graetz, the white minister of Trinity Lutheran Church, openly supported the boycott. Others, such as Juliette Hampton Morgan, wrote letters to the newspaper praising the effort. In many cases, white employers picked up and dropped off their maids and housekeepers or paid their cab fare. In response, Montgomery police ticketed white women for transporting their maids and newly organized White Citizens' Councils used pressure and threats to stop the practice. The Montgomery City Lines, which depended heavily on black riders, suffered tremendous financial hardship without them.

During the course of the boycott, King and other black leaders became the targets of white discontent. The Montgomery police arrested King for speeding, and both his and Nixon's homes were bombed. Such harassment created greater solidarity among the black community at large and reinforced their commitment to resist injustice and maltreatment. Other supporters of the boycott faced white violence as well. Even after the boycott ended, white extremists bombed Abernathy's and Graetz's homes as well as Bell Street Baptist Church, Hutchinson Street Baptist Church, Abernathy's First Baptist Church, and Mount Olive Baptist Church.

Montgomery's city government also tried to stop the boycott, but without such overt violence. The Alabama legislature had passed an antiboycott law in 1921 that Montgomery city officials used in an attempt to end the boycott. A Montgomery grand jury indicted 89 black leaders, 24 of them ministers, for conspiring to boycott the Montgomery City Lines. King, of all of the 89 conspirators, was the only one tried. He was found guilty and levied a $500 fine. King's trial, far from quashing the boycott, attracted national attention and helped establish him as a national figure. In the aftermath of the trial, *Jet* magazine described King as "Alabama's Modern Moses."

Although the MIA initially wanted to use Parks's case to challenge bus segregation, it also decided to challenge segregation directly in federal court. On February 1, 1956, attorneys Fred Gray and Charles D. Langford filed suit on behalf of four African American women—Aurelia S. Browder, Susie McDonald, Mary Louise Smith, and Claudette Colvin—who had been mistreated on Montgomery city buses. As Gray made clear, "I wanted the court to have only one issue to decide—the constitutionality of the laws requiring segregation on the buses in the city of Montgomery." Gray feared that having Parks's prosecution associated with the petition might distract from that issue.

Browder v. Gayle (Montgomery mayor William A. Gayle) came before the three-judge U.S. Court of Appeals for the Fifth Circuit. On June 5, 1956, the panel, in a two-to-one decision, ruled Alabama's segregation bus laws unconstitutional. Judges Frank M. Johnson Jr. and Richard T. Rives, both white Montgomerians, courageously found for the plaintiffs at great personal cost, citing *Brown v. Board of Education* as a precedent for their decision. On November 13, 1956, the U.S. Supreme Court affirmed the judgment of the Fifth Circuit, upholding the lower court's decision. The high court rejected the city and state's appeals on December 17. The Supreme Court order to desegregate the buses arrived in Montgomery on December 20, 1956, prompting the MIA to end the bus boycott.

The Montgomery Bus Boycott demonstrated the power and influence of a committed African American community. Unlike subsequent civil rights campaigns, the press played a relatively minor role in the boycott's success, the credit for which should be attributed largely to Montgomery's black leadership. As historian J. Mills Thornton notes, "the participants in the demonstrations by and large derived their enthusiasm and dedication from the prospect of effecting specific changes in their own municipalities" rather than a devotion to larger, national civil rights strategies. In this way, the Montgomery Bus Boycott foreshadowed future civil rights campaigns.

Dan J. Puckett

Further Reading

Branch, Taylor. *Parting the Waters: America in the King Years, 1954–63*. New York: Simon & Schuster, 1988.

Garrow, David J., ed. *The Walking City: The Montgomery Bus Boycott, 1955–1956*. Brooklyn, NY: Carlson Publishing, 1989.

Gray, Fred D. *Bus Ride to Justice: Changing the System by the System: The Life and Works of Fred Gray*. Montgomery, AL: Black Belt Press, 1995

King, Martin Luther, Jr. *Stride toward Freedom: The Montgomery Story*. New York: Harper and Brothers, 1958.

Robinson, Jo Ann. *The Montgomery Bus Boycott and the Women Who Started It: The Memoir of Jo Ann Gibson Robinson*. Edited by David J. Garrow. Knoxville: University of Tennessee Press, 1987.

Thornton, J. Mills. *Dividing Lines: Municipal Politics and the Struggle for Civil Rights in Montgomery, Birmingham, and Selma*. Tuscaloosa: University of Alabama Press, 2002.

Moses, Robert

Robert Moses was an African American civil rights activist, known for his involvement with the Student Nonviolent Coordinating Committee (SNCC) in the civil rights movement of the 1960s and his advocacy of mathematics education for African American students.

Robert Parris Moses was born on January 23, 1935, in Harlem, New York. Moses's family was not well off, and he grew up in a Harlem housing project. His intellectual prowess was evident early on and, after passing a citywide exam, he gained entrance to an elite public school, Stuyvesant High School.

After graduating from high school in 1952, Moses earned a scholarship to Hamilton College in New York and later earned a master's degree from Harvard University in 1957. Although Moses specialized in mathematical logic, he studied philosophy and was greatly influenced by the work of French philosopher Albert Camus. Through reading Camus and in his travel abroad during college, Moses was exposed to the ideals of pacifism, ideals that would remain at the core of his value system for the rest of his life. In 1959, while teaching high school math at Horace Mann in Manhattan, Moses helped civil rights activist Bayard Rustin organize the second Youth March for Integrated Schools. The next spring, Moses took part in a demonstration in Newport News while visiting his uncle in Virginia. From that point forward, Moses would dedicate himself to the civil rights movement.

Moses placed a great deal of emphasis on developing local African American leadership in Mississippi because these local residents not only had a vital stake in the successful outcome of civil rights projects, but they could also identify with each other and help each other along. Local African Americans thought about their work with SNCC in terms of making some sense out of living in Mississippi. In addition, Moses encouraged young people to enter the civil rights struggle because he felt that young African Americans would not be limited as much by the economic responsibilities that faced their elders and would be free to act more assertively. Moses was also keenly aware of the necessity to face and minimize African American fears while conducting the Voter Registration Project in Mississippi. Moses led the way by example, quelling the fear of anxious Mississippi residents by putting himself squarely in front of danger.

In 1960, after seeing the resolute southern African Americans taking part in the sit-in movement, Moses went to work in the Atlanta office of the Southern Christian Leadership Conference (SCLC). There was little there for him to do but stuff SCLC fund-raising packages, however, and when Jane Stembridge, a member of SNCC who worked in the same office, suggested that he assist that organization by recruiting African American leaders in the South, Moses readily agreed. From Atlanta, Moses traveled through Mississippi in the summer of 1960, during which he met Amzie Moore, the head of the National Association for the Advancement of Colored People (NAACP) in Cleveland, Mississippi. In the summer of 1961, Moses headed a voting registration project in McComb, Mississippi, where he, Reginald Robinson, and John Hardy opened a school to train African American residents to take Mississippi's literacy test for voters. Moses experienced his first confrontation with the state's authorities on August 15 of that year when, after escorting three African American residents to the courthouse in Liberty, Mississippi to register to vote, he was arrested and charged with interfering with the discharge of the arresting officers' duties. The arresting officer, who knew exactly who Moses was and how important the voter registration project was in changing the balance of power in the state, asked, "You the nigger that came down from New York to stir up a lot of trouble?" Following his own code of ethics that mandated the struggle begin with the individual, Moses stood up to the officer and subsequently spent two days in jail before allowing the NAACP to post his bond.

Almost two weeks later, Moses experienced a more violent encounter after attempting to register more local African Americans. Billy Jack Caston, cousin of the local sheriff, and two other white residents beat Moses nearly unconscious, a crime for which Caston was acquitted. On September 25, 1961, an event occurred that would bring the voting rights project to a standstill for the remainder of that year. On that day, E. H. Hurst, a white state legislator, shot and killed Herbert Lee, a founding member of the Amite County NAACP. Hurst, who claimed Lee attacked him with a tire iron, was never charged with Lee's murder. Although Moses and practically all of the local African Americans who had worked closely with him had been jailed and the McComb experience acted as a temporary setback for SNCC, Moses remained determined to make progress.

In the summer of 1962, Moses went to work expanding his young SNCC staff, and by the spring of 1963, six SNCC offices and 20 African American field secretaries were operating in Mississippi. In an effort to minimize conflict between the various civil rights organizations, SNCC field secretaries worked under the auspices of the Council of Federated Organizations (COFO), where Moses was named director of voter registration. Moses continued his efforts to the western part of the state, this time edging away from his earlier policy of relying on entirely local African American leadership. SNCC organized a food drive for residents of Leflore County that involved a number of the organization's northern branches and thus made the problems of poor rural Mississippians visible to a wider range of people. Moses and SNCC linked receiving assistance to taking personal responsibility for achieving freedom by registering to vote.

In an April 1963 meeting before the SNCC general conference, Moses argued that Mississippi's African Americans were unlikely to gain the franchise quickly enough to win electoral victories before they lost their jobs to industrial automation and lack of education. He insisted that because illiterate whites were allowed to vote, and because African Americans in the state were denied equal educational opportunities, African Americans were owed either the right to vote irrespective of being literate or the opportunity to immediately learn to read and write. As such, Moses's position initiated the "one man, one vote" campaign, a movement that would encourage all African Americans in the state to participate in the political process.

The 1964 Mississippi Freedom Summer project, designed specifically to expose the intolerance of racist white communities to a national audience while creating the environment for a confrontation between state and federal authorities whereby federal agents would be forced to protect civil rights activists, was another turning point in the evolution of SNCC. By this time, although local African Americans had worked to achieve voting rights, Moses was convinced that only outside intervention and greater national publicity about the deplorable conditions in rural Mississippi would bring about the kind of large-scale change he was trying to create. This would require bringing in hundreds of whites from around the country to help with the voter registration project, a marked departure from the almost exclusive use of local African Americans thus far in the voting rights campaign. The first step was for Moses and Allard Lowenstein, a white activist and friend of Moses, to organize a "Freedom Vote." This campaign would allow local African Americans to vote for their own set of candidates in their own communities, as many African Americans were barred from voting in the 1963 November general election. In what was deemed as an encouraging sign, more than 80,000 local African Americans voted in this symbolic election, setting the stage for the next challenge.

Building on the success of the Freedom Vote, Moses and COFO set about creating a nonracist political organization that would lay legitimate claim to the Democratic Party delegation at the Democratic National Convention in 1964. To that end, on April 26, 1964, the Mississippi Freedom Democratic Party was formed at a rally in Jackson, Mississippi. In addition to creating a political party, COFO members established Freedom Schools to teach traditional academic subjects as well as contemporary issues, leadership development, and political skills. Although the MFDP was unable to unseat the regular Democratic delegation at the Democratic National Convention in Atlantic City, New Jersey, it brought the issues of white supremacy and voting rights for the state's African Americans front and center on a national stage and forced long-term changes in the Democratic Party. The MFDP's challenge served notice to the nation that being African American and poor was no longer going to act as a barrier in the way of the residents of Mississippi as they laid claim to their rights as U.S. citizens.

Shortly after the Summer Project concluded, SNCC arrived at a crossroads, as an ideological split between James Forman and Moses pointed in two different directions. Forman, who viewed SNCC as a permanent organization, believed that it also needed a more centralized leadership to carry out its mission. Moses, on the other hand, was committed to SNCC's emphasis on informal leadership and consensus building, where a broad range of voices had equal opportunities to be heard. As a result of his unwillingness to push his own agenda and his sense that large segments of SNCC and COFO had grown dependent on his leadership, Moses grew ever reluctant to express his views, and his influence on policy decisions waned through the mid-1960s. Moses resigned as director of COFO in late 1964. He was discouraged with the hard-line approach SNCC had taken under the leadership of militant African American civil rights activist Stokely Carmichael, an approach that attempted to centralize control of the organization under a small group of people who wanted to dictate what local branches should be doing. In 1965, Moses took a leave of absence from SNCC to focus on antiwar activities.

He challenged the argument made by many African American leaders that civil rights activists should devote their energy to African American community organizing and not risk previous gains by involving themselves in the antiwar or other movements. Moses quit SNCC in 1966 and moved to Canada to avoid the draft.

After living in Canada and then teaching in Tanzania from 1969 to 1975, Moses returned to the United States, where he completed a doctorate at Harvard University and taught high school math. In 1982, he received a MacArthur Foundation Genius Grant and started the Algebra Project, a program that teaches math literacy. According to Moses, algebra is a gatekeeper subject that students must master or they are effectively shut out of higher-level math-based subjects such as physics, calculus, and engineering. As he saw it, math literacy is a contemporary civil rights issue much the way the right to vote was in the 1960s, because proficiency in these subjects is critical for being successful in the technology-driven twenty-first century. The Algebra Project runs in more than 25 cities and serves more than 40,000 students.

Paul T. Miller

Further Reading

Branch, Taylor. *At Canaan's Edge: America in the King Years, 1965–68*. New York: Simon & Schuster, 2006.

Carson, Clayborne. *In Struggle: SNCC and the Black Awakening of the 1960s*. Cambridge, MA: Harvard University Press, 1981.

Hogan, Wesley C. *Many Minds, One Heart: SNCC's Dream for a New America*. Chapel Hill: University of North Carolina Press, 2007.

Moses, Robert. *Radical Equations: Math Literacy and Civil Rights*. Boston: Beacon Press, 2001.

Motley, Constance Baker

Civil rights lawyer Constance Baker Motley was the first African American woman appointed a federal judge. As a lawyer for the National Association for the Advancement of Colored People (NAACP) Legal Defense and Education Fund, she argued and won dozens of cases from the 1940s through the mid-1960s. She once said: "You can have twenty-seven degrees from twenty-seven different universities, but if your skin is different, you're still forced to use the door marked 'colored.' We want an end to that—and everything like it."

Born in New Haven, Connecticut, Motley worked in the National Youth Administration after graduating from high school in 1939. Despite childhood dreams of being a lawyer, her family's poverty did not make a college education a realistic goal. She was president of the New Haven Negro Youth Council and involved in Dixwell Community House, a gathering place for African Americans. At a meeting about the center's programs and facilities with the center's governing board, Motley pointed out that no African Americans served on the board and explained that African Americans did not have a sense of ownership in the center. In the audience was a philanthropist who provided financial support to Dixwell. Impressed by Motley's comments, he later contacted her and asked her the reasons why she was not in college. When she explained that she could not afford it but that she wanted to be a lawyer, he told her that he would pay for her education. Motley earned her bachelor's degree in economics from New York University in 1943 and her law degree from Columbia School of Law in 1946.

While she was a law student, Motley volunteered at the NAACP Legal Defense and Education Fund beginning in 1945 and joined the staff after graduating. The NAACP had turned its attention to racial segregation in education, the area in which Motley was first involved. Much of Motley's work was in the South, where racism reigned, danger stalked civil rights workers, and neither whites nor African Americans were accustomed to black professionals. For example, when Motley and a colleague served as counsel in a Mississippi case to equalize black teachers' salaries in 1949, they were the first African Americans to try a case in the state in the twentieth century.

From 1950 to 1954, she participated in the landmark *Brown v. Board of Education* school desegregation case. In that case, the U.S. Supreme Court decided that the equal protection clause of the Fourteenth Amendment prohibits states from maintaining racially segregated public schools. According to Motley, the decision began a period of the greatest social upheaval since the Civil War: "The Brown decision was the catalyst which changed our society from a closed society to an open society and created the momentum for other minority groups to establish public interest law firms to secure their rights." Over the next years, Motley played a significant role in almost every major school integration case, including cases in Alabama, Florida, Georgia, Ohio, and other states.

Motley became associate counsel for the NAACP Legal Defense and Education Fund in 1961, the first woman to hold the position, the second highest in the organization. That year, she argued a case before the U.S. Supreme Court, probably the first African American woman to do so. In 1961 and 1962, she successfully represented James Meredith in his effort to gain admission to the then all-white University of Mississippi. Motley persisted despite the opposition displayed by the state's judicial, executive, and university officials, including their defiance of appeals courts' decisions. Motley was a member of the team who represented Martin Luther King Jr. throughout his Birmingham, Alabama, campaign and successfully fought the suspension of over 1,000 African American students from Birmingham who participated in the demonstrations that accompanied King's campaign. In 1963, she defended four civil rights workers convicted of breaking a Georgia insurrection law, which was punishable with the death penalty. She won the case in federal court, which declared the law unconstitutional.

A summary of the U.S. Supreme Court cases in which Motley participated includes three related to the exclusion of blacks from juries, 14 involving lunch-counter sit-ins, 20 school desegregation cases, and 18 other discrimination cases. Of the 10 Supreme Court cases in which she was the lead counsel, Motley successfully argued 9 of them, with the 10th decided without argument. In addition, she participated in 73 cases that went to the U.S. Court of Appeals.

In 1964, Motley became the first African American woman elected to the New York Senate. From 1965 to 1966, she served as borough president of Manhattan, the first woman to hold the position. She also became the first woman to sit on the New York City Board of Estimates. In 1966, President Lyndon Johnson appointed Motley federal judge of the Southern District of New York State, making her the first African American woman named a federal judge. In 1982, Motley was appointed federal district court judge. She was named a senior federal judge in 1986.

Suzanne O'Dea Schenken

Further Reading

Current Biography Yearbook, 1964. New York: H. W. Wilson, 1964.

Motley, Constance Baker. *Equal Justice under Law: An Autobiography.* New York: Farrar, Straus, and Giroux, 1998.

MOVE Bombing

The MOVE bombing of May 13, 1985, was one of the most controversial episodes in Philadelphia's history and perceived as an example of excessive force by police against militant organizations. MOVE emerged around 1972 in Philadelphia as a small but radical group of African Americans led by John Africa. His commune first settled at North 33rd Street near Pearl Street in the Powelton Village area of Philadelphia. There they lived according to the self-styled teachings of Africa, who promoted a communal "back to nature" lifestyle, vegetarianism, reverence for all animal life, and scorn for "The Establishment." From their house, MOVE members often gave public speeches denouncing Philadelphia's mayor and police department. In addition, the presence of open garbage, insects, rats, and other animals on the MOVE premises posed public health hazards for Osage Avenue residents.

Neighborhood complaints about MOVE brought the radical organization into conflict with the city of Philadelphia throughout the 1970s. On March 28, 1976, Philadelphia police confronted several MOVE members at the 33rd Street house. MOVE later claimed that Janine Africa and her baby were thrown to the floor by police and that the baby later died. Angry MOVE members stepped up criticism of Philadelphia mayor Frank Rizzo; Rizzo reacted with a court order to demolish the MOVE compound. On August 6, 1978, a gun battle between police and MOVE erupted during which MOVE member Delbert Africa was beaten by Philadelphia police officers and one police officer was killed. Delbert Africa and eight other MOVE members were arrested and brought to trial; nine MOVE members were sentenced. In 1981, however, the three police officers accused of beating Delbert Africa were acquitted.

After the 1978 incident, MOVE went underground. It reemerged in 1982, settling in the house of John Africa's sister, Louise James, in a Philadelphia neighborhood known as Cobbs Creek. During this time, MOVE members who were frustrated about not winning the release of their jailed members stepped up their public harangues against the neighborhood and the police. On Memorial Day 1984, W. Wilson Goode, Philadelphia's first African American mayor, met with Osage Avenue residents who asserted that MOVE was infringing on their rights. Goode was advised by the Federal Bureau of Investigation (FBI) and other law enforcement officials that there were no grounds for action against MOVE. The neighbors of MOVE, however, formally organized themselves in February 1985 into a group called "United Residents of the 6200 Block of Osage Avenue." On May 1, 1985, the United Residents said in a press conference that the MOVE house had become a military bunker. The next day, the United Residents informed Mayor Goode that a five-gallon gasoline can was hoisted to the roof of 6221 Osage Avenue. It was then that the mayor and Philadelphia police knew that a violent confrontation between the city and MOVE was imminent. Arrest warrants for four MOVE members were approved by a city judge.

On May 13, 1985, Mayor Goode authorized Philadelphia police to surround the house at 6221 Osage Avenue, which now had a bunker constructed on its roof as well as a gasoline can. Using a bullhorn, police asked that the four MOVE members for whom they had arrest warrants come out and surrender. None did. Then the mayor gave permission for a pilot in a police helicopter to drop a bomb in order to dislodge the bunker. The bomb missed its target and instead hit the gasoline can, igniting the entire house. City officials decided not to put out the fire immediately but to "let the bunker burn." Eleven MOVE members burned to death, including five children. Among the dead was MOVE founder John Africa. A woman, Ramona Africa, and a boy, Birdie Africa, escaped from the house alive. Ramona Africa was arrested and taken into custody by police. In 1986, Ramona Africa was put on trial and was found guilty of riot and conspiracy charges and was given a seven-year sentence. She was released from prison in 1992.

The MOVE bombing made international headlines. Some applauded the city of Philadelphia's handling of the crisis, but others, such as MOVE supporters, condemned it. Philadelphia African Americans in particular were critical of Mayor Goode, who in response formed an investigatory commission. The Philadelphia Special Investigation Commission issued its report in 1986. The commission found the city of Philadelphia negligent in the death of the 11 people and careless in its handling of conflict resolution. It found that Mayor Goode did not negotiate with MOVE earlier and that he allowed the confrontation to spin out of control.

More than 60 houses on Osage Avenue and Pine Street also burned down in the aftermath of the incident, leaving 250 people homeless. Between 1985 and 1996, the city of Philadelphia rebuilt the Osage Avenue homes, but many residents were unhappy, citing various defects. Milton Street, elected mayor of Philadelphia in 1999, sympathized with their plight and offered each family $150,000 for a new house and moving expenses. In all, 37 families on Osage Avenue and part of Pine Street took the buyout offer, but 24 families refused. So in 2003, they went back to court. In April 2005, a U.S. District Court jury awarded each homeowner a sum of $530,000 for punitive damages against city officials, breach of contract, and damages for emotional distress. At the time of this writing, MOVE was still active in Philadelphia but members kept a low profile.

Eric Ledell Smith

Further Reading

Anderson, John, and Hilary Hevenor. *Burning Down the House: MOVE and the Tragedy of Philadelphia*. New York: W. W. Norton, 1987.

Bracey, LaVon Wright. *Making Them Whole: A Philadelphia Neighborhood and the City's Recovery from the MOVE Tragedy*. Philadelphia: Affie Enterprises, 1990.

Goode, W. Wilson, and Joann Stevens. *In Goode Faith*. Valley Forge, PA: Judson Press, 1992.

Philadelphia Special Investigation Commission. *The Findings, Conclusions, and Recommendations of the Philadelphia Special Investigation Commission, March 6, 1986*. Philadelphia: The Commission, 1986.

N

NAACP Legal Defense and Educational Fund

The NAACP Legal Defense and Educational Fund, later known as the Legal Defense Fund (LDF), was the legal arm of the National Association for the Advancement of Colored People (NAACP) that led the civil rights movement in the federal courts and was victorious in the landmark case *Brown v. Board of Education* (1954). While it pursued a policy to end de jure Jim Crow legislation in the South, it also struggled to end de facto segregation in the rest of the country, thereby protecting the legal equality of African Americans in U.S. society.

The roots of the LDF were in the early history of the NAACP. After Nathan Margold outlined a strategy for the NAACP in the Margold Report to systematically challenge segregation, the NAACP hired Charles Houston, then dean of the Howard University Law School, to be its first full-time legal staff member. Houston filed lawsuits to force southern universities to open their graduate and professional schools to African Americans. In 1938, the NAACP had its first victory with *Missouri ex rel. Gaines v. Canada*. In 1939, the NAACP Legal Defense and Educational Fund was incorporated as a separate group so that the LDF could receive tax-exempt charitable donations while the NAACP continued its lobbying activities, which made it ineligible for such tax-exempt deductions. One board of directors directed both organizations.

Houston hired Thurgood Marshall to help, and by the end of the year, Marshall was named the director of the LDF. Marshall led the court battles, building on the success of the Gaines case with a victory in *Sweatt v. Painter* (1950), in which the U.S. Supreme Court decided that segregated professional school facilities for blacks had to be equal to those available for whites, which meant that they were likely to be prohibitively expensive. After *Sweatt*, the LDF began its battle directly against segregated elementary and secondary schools. This resulted in the victories in 1954 in *Brown v. Board of Education* and *Bolling v. Sharpe*. In the following decade, the LDF had to defend itself against southern state legislatures, which were passing legislation to attempt to keep the LDF and NAACP from working in their states. In 1963, the U.S. Supreme Court concluded that the LDF and NAACP's actions were protected by the First Amendment in *NAACP v. Button*.

By the early 1950s, the LDF was developing a separate identity as an organization, and in 1952, it moved to a separate facility three blocks from the NAACP home at Freedom House in New York City. The LDF became a separate tax-exempt organization with a distinct board of directors in 1956 after an Internal Revenue Service challenge over the NAACP's tax exemption. The two organizations had been having personality and policy differences. The NAACP added its own legal staff to pursue desegregation in the North, while the LDF concentrated its efforts on the South. In 1957, both boards passed a resolution ensuring that the boards would be entirely separate and that no member could serve on the two boards simultaneously. In 1961, Marshall became a federal judge and was replaced at the LDF by Jack Greenberg.

The LDF was victorious in several key school desegregation implementation decisions, including the *Swann* (1971) and *Keyes* (1973) cases. By the end of 1972, the NAACP LDF was working on about 1,200 cases. It concentrated on southern cases since victory in northern cases was so questionable. The LDF employed 24 lawyers in offices in New York, Washington, and Los Angeles. In 1994, the LDF considered dropping the NAACP initials from its name because of the problems at its parent organization, quite ironically given its battle to keep these initials in 1966 and again in the late 1970s. In 1996, the LDF had a staff of 68 and a budget of just under $9 million to support litigation for defending legal and constitutional rights of minorities not only in education but also in housing, employment, voting, land use, and health care.

The LDF was an early practitioner of public interest law, forging a general strategy to overcome racial segregation and moving beyond the interests of particular clients. The LDF defeated the white primary election, enforcement of restrictive housing covenants, and segregation in interstate travel, but it is best known for its legal work in school desegregation cases. The LDF primarily focused on the strategy of ending segregation. For example, the LDF had a continual discussion over whether to attack segregation per se or attack the unequal situation of African Americans under *Plessy v. Ferguson*.

As of 2010, the LDF continued to work against disenfranchisement, institutionalized racism, and the disproportionate number of people of color on death row, among other major social justice issues confronting African Americans and other people of color.

Jeffrey Raffel

Further Reading

Kluger, Richard. *Simple Justice: The History of* Brown v. Board of Education *and Black America's Struggle for Equality.* New York: Vintage Books, 1977.

Orfield, Gary. *Must We Bus: Segregated Schools and National Policy.* Washington, DC: Brookings Institution, 1978.

Ware, Gilbert. "The NAACP-Inc. Fund Alliance: Its Strategy, Power, and Destruction." *Journal of Negro Education* 63 (Summer 1994): 323–35.

Nash, Diane

Diane Nash is a pacifist and outspoken advocate of civil rights for African Americans, women, veterans, and young people. She became the leader of the Nashville, Tennessee, sit-in movement in 1960 at the age of 22. Nash continued to exercise nonviolent protest for civil rights in the South during the 1960s and is one of the most iconic and well-known female leaders to emerge from the era commonly known as the civil rights movement.

Diane Judith Nash was born on Chicago's South Side on May 15, 1938. Nash's father, Leon Nash, migrated north from Mississippi and held a clerical job in the military during World War II. Dorothy Bolton Nash, Diane's mother, also migrated north from her Tennessee birthplace. Raised by her grandmother, Carrie Bolton, until she was seven, Nash was taught to turn a blind eye toward racial injustice and strive to be a polite and accepting girl. Growing up, she attended the Sisters of the Blessed Sacrament parochial school, which was operated by nuns who taught only minority students. Later she would attend public high school and go on to Washington, D.C., to begin her college career at Howard University. Soon after, in 1959, Nash decided to transfer to Fisk University in Nashville.

Although the racial climate in Chicago was by no means harmonious, Nash was still shocked by the severity of segregation in Nashville and throughout the South. Years later, in an interview she gave for the renowned civil rights documentary *Eyes on the Prize*, Nash stated that she understood the facts and stories surrounding segregation but had no emotional relationship with the policy. It was only after she moved to the South and saw the signs that said "white" and "colored" and actually could not drink out of certain water fountains or was banned from certain ladies' rooms that Nash said she had a real emotional reaction.

After a degrading encounter at the Tennessee State Fair, Nash vowed to seek out people and organizations intent on putting an end to segregation. Nash soon found that a man attending Vanderbilt Divinity School named Reverend James M. Lawson Jr. was organizing a series of workshops that added the methods of nonviolent protest to the arsenal of tactics used by young persons in their quest for equal rights.

At first, Nash was skeptical of the nonviolent approach, and she later confessed that it was years before she was convinced. After taking part in the workshops held under the auspices of the Nashville Christian Leadership Conference (NCLC), Nash was elected chair of the Student Central Committee. Although the workshops involved role-playing that often got rough, it was not until she and the other Nashville students staged sit-ins at the lunch counters of two of the city's department stores during November and December 1959 that she was given a chance to test the effectiveness of nonviolent protest. Nash, along with John Lewis, James Bevel, Marion Barry, and several others repeatedly bought items and attempted to sit at lunch counters. Unfortunately, the actions did not achieve the goal of desegregation. However, Nash and her fellow protesters did not give in easily.

It was not until the sit-in staged in Greensboro, North Carolina—by four students from North Carolina Agricultural and Technical College on February 1, 1960—that the sit-in movement was launched into the national spotlight. The Nashville student group attempted to desegregate Nashville's lunch counters once again, and this time they were successful. From February 13 to May 10, 1960, the Nashville sit-in movement directed protest at Kress, Woolworth's, McClellan's, Walgreens, and city bus terminals. At first, there was little resistance, but after two weeks, the 81 protesters were jailed for disorderly conduct. Although the NCLC and its allies raised enough bail money to release them, the students chose to stay in jail on principle.

After escalation of white violence, the students marched to city hall, and upon reaching the steps of the building, Nash confronted Mayor Ben West, asking: "Do you feel it is wrong to discriminate against a person solely on the basis of their race or color?" Mayor West confessed that he did. Nash and the student group she led had initiated desegregation of public places in Nashville, which became the first southern city to begin departing from Jim Crow laws.

It was also during this time that Diane Nash had the opportunity to become active with the Student Nonviolent Coordinating Committee (SNCC) as it was beginning to take shape. From April 1960, Nash, along with James Bevel and Marion Barry, traveled to Raleigh, North Carolina, to attend a conference at Shaw University that would serve to solidify goals and unite all participants of the movement. It was here that Nash, who was one of the few young women leading the student movement, met the legendary Ella Baker, who became a much-needed female role model and source of confidence for Nash.

Instead of returning to Fisk to resume her traditional education, Nash devoted her time and energy to keeping the momentum of nonviolent protest going. Taking the helm of the Direct Action Committee of SNCC, Nash, along with Charles Sherrod, J. Charles Jones, and Ruby Doris Smith, traveled to Rock Hill, South Carolina, in early February 1961. While rallying support for nine students from Friendship College who had been convicted of trespassing and sentenced to 30 days of hard labor after participating in lunch counter sit-ins, Nash along with her companions were immediately arrested as well. She was sent to the York County Jail, where she penned a poignant letter to the editor of the *Rock Hill Herald* stating that the protesters were only trying to help focus attention on a moral problem.

Nash also became involved with another sort of protest in the form of Freedom Rides. The first of the Freedom Rides began in Washington, D.C., in May 1961, with the purpose of testing enforcement of a Supreme Court ban on segregation in interstate bus travel and terminals. Discouraged by the levels of violence from southern white mobs, some Freedom Riders wanted to abandon the endeavor, but Nash stepped in, arguing that if they let them stop protesters with violence, then the movement would die. After this, Nash coordinated Freedom Rides from

Birmingham, Alabama, to Jackson, Mississippi. In the end, Attorney General Robert F. Kennedy successfully urged the Interstate Commerce Commission to enforce total desegregation of all interstate terminals.

After a second victory, Nash moved on from fighting for desegregation to advocating for voting rights for blacks in the South. In 1962, Nash was sentenced to serve two years in prison for teaching lessons of nonviolent protest to children in Jackson, Mississippi, where she and her husband, James Bevel, were living. This time, Nash was four months pregnant. She was released on appeal and did not serve the full term.

For her work with the Voting Rights Committee of SNCC, President John F. Kennedy asked Nash to serve on the committee that led to the passing of the Civil Rights Act of 1964. She also joined the staff of the Southern Christian Leadership Conference and worked closely with Dr. Martin Luther King Jr. as an organizer, strategist, field-staff person, race-relations staff person, and workshop instructor. In 1965, she and Bevel were awarded the Southern Christian Leadership Council's Rosa Parks Award for planning and carrying out the tumultuous campaign for voter registration in Selma, Alabama.

Nash's lifework was to empower young people to feel that they can bring awareness to any injustice they may be experiencing in their lives through nonviolent means. She spoke at countless college and universities, youth organizations, and human rights conferences, and worked for several decades in Chicago, engaged in tenant organizing, housing advocacy, and real estate.

In 2003, Nash received the "Distinguished American Award" presented by the John F. Kennedy Library Foundation. A year later, the LBJ Award for Leadership in Civil Rights was bestowed on Nash by the Lyndon Baines Johnson Library and Museum. She was also honored with the bestowal of the National Civil Rights Museum's Freedom Award in 2008.

Mary Jo Fairchild

Further Reading

Halberstam, David. *The Children*. New York: Random House, 1998.

Mullins, Lisa. *Diane Nash: The Fire of the Civil Rights Movement*. Miami, FL: Barnhardt & Ashe Publishing, 2007.

Williams, Juan. *Eyes on the Prize: America's Civil Rights Years, 1954–1965*. New York: Penguin, 1988.

Wynne, Linda T. "The Dawning of a New Day: The Nashville Sit-Ins, February 13–May 10, 1960." *Tennessee Historical Quarterly* 50 (1991): 42–54.

Nation of Islam

The Nation of Islam (NOI) is an African American Muslim organization, which, while controversial for its theology and its stances on race relations, has also been significant given its prominent advocacy of African Americans in the civil rights movement and in fostering self-help within various urban African American communities. Moreover, it is best known for prominent African American civil rights leaders Malcolm X and Louis Farrakhan, who were both integral in its leadership.

NOI had its beginnings in Detroit during the 1930s. In the context of both the Great Migration and the Great Depression emerged Wallace Dean (W. D.) Fard Muhammad. Influenced by Noble Drew Ali's Moorish Science Temple of America, Black Nationalist Marcus Garvey, and the African American church, Fard Muhammad spread his unique interpretation of Islam among African Americans in Detroit. Based on police and Federal Bureau of Investigation (FBI) records, he was born in either New Zealand or Portland, Oregon, on February 25, 1891, to Hawaiian or British and Polynesian parents. Using a variety of aliases, Fard Muhammad had married and fathered a son before abandoning his family to move to Los Angeles by the 1920s. Between 1918 and 1929, he was in and out of prison until leaving Los Angeles permanently in June 1929.

Fard Muhammad relocated to Detroit, with a brief stop in Chicago, where he became a retail salesman and, in the lore of the NOI, he was a "silk peddler." While displaying and selling his wares, Fard Muhammad would discuss African American history, racial oppression, and Islam with his potential customers. By 1931, he rented public halls in order to deliver lengthy speeches, and these

Elijah Muhammad, as spiritual leader of the Nation of Islam in the United States, established a religious organization that gave poor urban African Americans a sense of racial pride and economic and political self-sufficiency. (Library of Congress)

meetings became the actual genesis of the Lost-Found Nation of Islam in the Wilderness of North America.

According to Fard Muhammad—who would famously claim to be Allah in the flesh—he was sent on a mission to wake the "dead" and lost nation in North America, to teach them the truth about white people, and to prepare them for the coming Battle of Armageddon. In his unique rendition of Armageddon, when the forces of good and evil would prepare for battle at the mountain of Megiddo in the Great Plain of Esdraelon in Asia Minor, the combatants would really be black "Asiatics" and white "Devils," and the location of the battle would be North America. For the next three years, Fard Muhammad spread his teachings, until his mysterious disappearance in 1934. In the meantime, he encountered a very impressionable Elijah Poole (later Elijah Karriem and, eventually, Elijah Muhammad). During their first encounter, Fard Muhammad revealed to Poole that he was the returned redeemer—Jesus—although he would later claim to all of his followers that he was, in reality, Allah himself.

After Fard Muhammad's disappearance in 1934, Elijah Muhammad became the "messenger" and leader of the NOI. The movement grew steadily until World War II, when Muhammad and his followers refused to bear arms for the United States. In 1943, Muhammad was convicted of encouraging resistance to the draft and served 3.5 years of a 5-year sentence in a federal prison. When he was released in 1946, the NOI's membership dropped from a high of 8,000 in the last year of Fard Muhammad's leadership to just under 1,000 by the end of World War II. In the two decades between 1946 and 1966, however, Elijah Muhammad was to turn this situation around and make the NOI one of the strongest black organizations in North America.

Upon his release from prison in 1946, Muhammad relocated to Chicago in order to establish a foothold in the city. In 1954, Temple No. 2 on Chicago's South Side was established and became the headquarters of the NOI. Between 1946 and 1955, a total of 12 new Muslim temples were constructed in various parts of the country. By 1959, NOI had 50 temples in 22 states and the District of Columbia and an estimated 3,000 registered and paying Muslim members, 15,000 believers, and about 50,000 sympathizes (or people who did not attend services at a temple and who were likely Christians, but who supported NOI). Through their newspaper, *Muhammad Speaks*, founded by Malcolm X in 1957, hundreds of thousands of African Americans read and were inspired by the words of Elijah Muhammad. In July 1959, a TV documentary entitled *The Hate That Hate Produced* was aired, which introduced the NOI to white America and put Malcolm X on a national stage as the most articulate and passionate spokesman of African American frustrations. Liberal whites and moderate civil rights leaders joined in their condemnation of what they considered a black hate group that advocated black supremacy.

With charismatic and transcendent leaders and members like Malcolm X, Muhammad Ali, Khalid Muhammad, and Louis Farrakhan, NOI perfected a formula for remaining relevant to African American urban communities across the United States. However, NOI is a politically conservative organization, influenced heavily by both African American leaders Booker T. Washington and Garvey. Beginning with Elijah Muhammad, leaders of the organization lectured about self-reliance, hard work, and moral uplift. Members of NOI have strictly regimented lives. Members cannot drink alcohol, engage in public cursing, use drugs, fornicate, carry concealed weapons, buy on credit, or purchase pornography.

Theologically, the brand of Islam embraced by members of NOI differs radically with what can be considered more orthodox variations of the religion. With a blend of Black Nationalism, a strong antipathy for white people, and some basic tenants of Islam, the "true knowledge," as members refer to it, has both intriguing and problematic aspects. According to NOI doctrine, 66 trillion years ago, there were 13 black tribes of humanity (the original man) until one was destroyed in an incident that led to the creation of the moon. From that time and until 6,000 years ago, NOI claimed that 12 black tribes ruled the planet uncontested until a "big-headed" scientist named Yacub sought to create his own tribe. A master of genetics and the principles of magnetism, Yacub realized that "like" repels, but "unlike" attracts. Thus, if he could create a race so different from others, they would attract—and therefore dominate—all others. On the island of Patmos, Yacub grafted germs (genes) from the original black Asiatics to make brown people, then red people, yellow people, and finally whites. With each successive generation of lighter peoples, the races of Yacub became more and more susceptible to wickedness and evil. Thus, whites were "grafted Devils" and, with the use of "tricknology," they conquered the world and continued to control it.

The concept of Black Nationalism within NOI is wrapped around the unique theology of the organization. According to their teachings, Allah would allow the grafted white Devils to rule the world for 6,000 years before destroying them. The time of the grafted Devils was to end in 1914 (the onset of World War I), but Allah issued a reprieve, for destroying the Devils in North America would also lead to the destruction of his chosen people—the lost-found Nation. Fard Muhammad was sent to awaken the lost-found Nation—the black Asiatic people—and convince them to separate from white America. Their teachings claim that the Book of Revelations includes the prediction that 1970 would be the year that Allah was to destroy the grafted Devils once and for all. If African Americans had not managed to separate from whites by then, they too would be destroyed by Allah's wrath. In the last iteration of this story, Allah had issued another reprieve—this time until the year 2000. At that time, Allah would send a mothership to transport his chosen people away from North America before destroying whites. After 2000, NOI moved away from making predictions about Armageddon and the end of the reign of white people.

NOI has been key in reforming and transforming ex-convicts, with Malcolm X serving as the epitome of this phenomenon. In 1985, it began the "Dopebusters" antidrug program in Washington, D.C.'s Mayfair Mansions. In the course of a handful of months, NOI task forces cleaned drugs and drug dealers out of an African American government project. Likewise, Louis Farrakhan and NOI provided the organizational apparatus for the 1995 Million Man March, the 1997 Million Woman March, and the 2000 Million Family March. Finally, NOI temples and mosques engage in community outreach and employment programs.

Walter C. Rucker

Further Reading

Curtis, Edward E. *Black Muslim Religion in the Nation of Islam, 1960–1975.* Chapel Hill: University of North Carolina Press, 2006.

Gardell, Mattias. *In the Name of Elijah Muhammad: Louis Farrakhan and the Nation of Islam.* Durham, NC: Duke University Press, 1996.

Muhammad, Elijah. *Message to the Blackman in America.* Phoenix, AZ: Secretarius MEMPS Ministries, 1973.

Ogbar, Jeffrey Ogbonna Green. *Black Power: Radical Politics and African American Identity.* Baltimore: Johns Hopkins University Press, 2004.

White, Vibert L. *Inside the Nation of Islam: A Historical and Personal Testimony by a Black Muslim.* Gainesville: University Press of Florida, 2001.

National Association for the Advancement of Colored People

Currently headquartered in Baltimore, Maryland, the National Association for the Advancement of Colored People (NAACP) is an advocacy and civil rights organization that has fought to ensure equality, justice, and inclusion for African Americans throughout its long and distinguished history. With approximately 400,000 members as of 2007, the NAACP is the largest civil rights organization in the United States, with regional offices in California, New York, Michigan, Missouri, Georgia, and Texas, as well as local, youth, and college chapters in practically every state in the United States.

The origins of the NAACP can be found within two separate historical trajectories, both linked directly or indirectly to lynching and racial violence. First, the savage 1899 lynching of Sam Hose, in Newnan, Georgia, set into motion a series of events that would lead to the founding of the Niagara Movement. On April 23, 1899, Hose—an African American migrant farm worker who had previously killed his white employer—was tortured, dismembered, and burned alive in front of 2,000 whites. W. E. B. Du Bois, having heard about the arrest of Hose and fearing the potential of his lynching, prepared a letter to be delivered to Joel Chandler Harris, editor of the *Atlanta Constitution*, which sought to provide a reasoned description of the evident facts. Before Du Bois arrived at the editorial office, news had reached him that Hose had already been lynched and that his knuckles were on display at a grocery store in downtown Atlanta. As Du Bois would later recount in his autobiography, the Hose lynching served as a "red ray," which disrupted his goal of becoming a "scientist" who would seek to resolve issues regarding equality and justice through scholarship and his work as a professor at Atlanta University. In many ways, the Hose lynching was the genesis of Du Bois's transformation into a scholar-activist.

In the decade leading up to Hose's lynching, 115 black Georgians had been murdered by white mobs. Du Bois and others demanded that Governor Allen Candler actively protect the state's black population from these frequent acts of murderous violence. This appeal fell on deaf ears, and the Hose incident was linked to the tumult that surrounded the issue of black suffrage by white supremacist politicians. This was the height of the black nadir, and the white South was seemingly determined to ignore the Fourteenth and Fifteenth Amendments, using any justification available. The myth of the black murderer and rapist represented a sufficient rationalization for the continued subjugation of African Americans throughout the South. The emotion of the Hose case and the continued frustrations created by white opposition to the human rights of African Americans coalesced in the form of a political statement by Du Bois—*The Souls of Black Folk* (1903).

In attacking the problematic leadership of Booker T. Washington, Du Bois created a platform for future black activism in *The Souls of Black Folk*. He called for suffrage rights, civil rights, and the education of black youth. Although he had earlier been a strong supporter of Washington's economic program, Du Bois grew to realize that Washington's accommodationist doctrine had shifted the burden of resolving the racial divide squarely on the shoulders of African Americans—the victims of suffocating levels of oppression. As a direct result of Washington's efforts to accommodate white supremacy, white southerners not only placed the blame on the victims of their deleterious policies, but also began to steadily erode the few remaining rights of African Americans. In Du Bois's diatribe against Washington in *The Souls of Black Folk*, he rightly points out that during the years of Washington's leadership, the movement to disenfranchise black men in the South had widened, the Supreme Court had moved to officially sanction racial segregation, and monetary aid was being steadily withdrawn from black liberal arts colleges. The specter of Sam Hose denied any attempt to blame the victims of white supremacy and, in Du Bois's evolving worldview, made necessary resistance, constant pressure, and activism.

The Souls of Black Folk produced a significant amount of political momentum and led to the founding of the Niagara Movement in Fort Erie, Ontario, in July 1905. A total of 32 prominent African Americans, including Du Bois, William Monroe Trotter, and John Hope, met to discuss the means by which civil rights and an end to racial discrimination could be achieved. Expanding on the platform Du Bois outlined in *The Souls of Black Folk*, this organization listed a number of major objectives: voting rights, an end to discrimination in public accommodations, social integration, judicial equality, and the education of black youth.

Despite Du Bois's attempt to credit William Monroe Trotter with creating the organization's political platform, the Niagara Movement's goals were largely based on concepts articulated by Du Bois two years earlier. At the next meeting, scheduled for August 15, 1906, in Harpers Ferry, West Virginia, the estimable Ida B. Wells-Barnett joined the Niagara Movement and the group incorporated her anti-lynching campaign into its platform. By the end of 1906, the Niagara Movement had established 30 branches and, although underfunded and understaffed, the organization had managed a handful of victories for civil rights at the local level.

The second historical trajectory that led to the founding of the NAACP was the 1908 Springfield, Illinois, race riot. In a city preparing to celebrate the centennial of its most famous son in 1909, Abraham Lincoln, a race riot began on August 14, 1908, which led to seven deaths—including one lynching—and the destruction of dozens of homes and businesses. White progressives in Springfield and across the country were appalled by the details of the riot and the fact that it occurred in, of all places, the birth city of Lincoln. In response to the race riot, socialist William English Walling wrote an article entitled "Race War in the North" for the *Independent* that described, in graphic detail, the Springfield riot and called on progressive whites to come to the aid of their fellow black citizens. Among those influenced by the article was Mary White Ovington, a New York socialist and social worker.

Ovington sought out Walling and, along with Jewish social worker Dr. Henry Moskowitz, the three white progressives launched a call for a national conference on the plight of African Americans during the commemoration of Lincoln's centennial birthday on February 12, 1909. Among the 60 people attending the conference were a number of notable African American activists and intellectuals: Du Bois, Wells-Barnett, Mary Church Terrell, Mary McLeod Bethune, and Arthur Spingarn, among others.

During the February 12, 1909, conference, the National Negro Committee was formed to serve as the organizational apparatus that would articulate a platform for African American civil rights. In May 1910, the National Negro Committee organized a permanent body to be known as the National Association for the Advancement of Colored People, and Ovington was appointed as the executive secretary. Other members of the NAACP's executive committee included Moorfield Stoery (national president), William English Walling (chair of the executive committee), John Milholland (treasurer), and Du Bois (director of publicity and research); Du Bois was the only African American in the NAACP's early leadership core. The platform and goals set forth by the NAACP were adopted from the Niagara Movement. In this way, the two historical trajectories—the Niagara Movement and progressive/radical whites—merged together to create one of the most powerful and effective civil rights organizations in U.S. history.

Notable early activities of the NAACP include the 1913 protest against segregation in the federal government sanctioned by Woodrow Wilson, the boycott of the 1915 film *The Birth of a Nation*, and the 1917 Silent March against lynching and racial violence in New York City. As a result of its early emphasis on local organizing and rigorous recruitment, the NAACP's membership grew dramatically. In addition, the number of branches increased from just 50 offices and 6,000 members in 1914 to more than 300 branch offices and 90,000 members reported by 1919. With the publication of *Thirty Years of Lynching in the United States: 1889–1918*, the NAACP launched a more concerted effort to record and investigate lynchings, with the goal of encouraging legislative action to bring an end to this evil practice.

Although the NAACP never successfully forced antilynching legislation at the federal or state level, the organization's commitment and efforts in this regard led to the gradual decline in the annual number of lynchings in the United States. One effective mechanism used by the NAACP to highlight lynchings was the distribution of flags to all branches that denote each time "A Black Man Was Lynched Today."

In the midst of its ever-expanding fight against lynching and racial violence, the NAACP began to address other areas of African American life that needed dire attention. By the 1930s, the NAACP began to look at education, housing, health care, public transportation, employment, and other issues that limited the life chances of African Americans. It was also during this era that the organization's hesitance to engage in mass direct action became apparent. Instead of staging mass marches, pickets, or boycotts, the organization engaged in courtroom battles and political lobbying as means to fight for enforcement of the Fourteenth and Fifteenth Amendments. In the three decades after 1936, the NAACP won or significantly contributed to a number of courtroom and legislative battles, including *Murray v. Maryland* (1936), *Gaines v. Canada* (1938), *Smith v. Allwright* (1944), *Morgan v. Virginia* (1946), *Shelley v. Kraemer* (1948), *Sipuel v. University of Oklahoma* (1948), *Sweatt v. Painter* (1950), *McLaurin v. Oklahoma State Regents* (1950), *Brown v. Board of Education* (1954), the Civil Rights Act of 1957, the Civil Rights Act of 1964, and the Voting Rights Act of 1965. The work of Charles Hamilton Houston, Thurgood Marshall, Walter White, and Roy Wilkins were significant in these victories.

By the 1960s, the NAACP began to expand its activism beyond the court room and state and federal law-making bodies and began to engage in direct action. In 1960, the NAACP's Youth Council began a series of lunch-counter sit-ins around the South, resulting in the desegregation of more than 60 department store lunch counters. In addition to sit-ins, NAACP organizers engaged in other forms of nonviolent social protest, including marches and civil rights rallies. As a result of the successes of direct action as a tactic, the NAACP named its first field director to oversee the legal and safety concerns of nonviolent protesters. Ironically, field director and highly successful organizer Medgar Evers was fatally shot outside his home in 1963.

In keeping with the constant changes occurring with the Civil Rights movement, the NAACP went through various transformations as well. By the 1970s and 1980s, the organization became a strong advocate for black political participation and actively engaged in voter registration drives, the creation of voting sites in high schools, and extension of the Voting Rights Act. In addition to emphasizing political engagement and participation in the African American community, the NAACP helped increase the mounting global pressure against apartheid in South Africa by encouraging a boycott of the nation. By 1993, the antiapartheid movement was successful, owing in part to the concerted activities of the NAACP and allied organizations.

Walter C. Rucker

Further Reading

Berg, Manfred. *The Ticket to Freedom: The NAACP and the Struggle for Black Political Integration*. Gainesville: University Press of Florida, 2005.

Bernstein, Patricia. *The First Waco Horror: The Lynching of Jesse Washington and the Rise of the NAACP*. College Station: Texas A&M University Press, 2005.

Hughes, Langston. *Fight for Freedom: The Story of the NAACP*. New York: Norton, 1962.

Jonas, Gilbert. *Freedom's Sword: The NAACP and the Struggle against Racism in America, 1909–1969*. New York: Routledge, 2005.

Kellogg, Charles Flint, ed. *NAACP: A History of the National Association for the Advancement of Colored People, Volume I, 1909–1920*. Baltimore: Johns Hopkins University Press, 1973.

Sullivan, Patricia. *Lift Every Voice: The NAACP and the Making of the Civil Rights Movement*. New York: New Press, 2009.

Tushnet, Mark V. *The NAACP's Legal Strategy against Segregated Education, 1925–1950*. Chapel Hill: University of North Carolina Press, 1987.

Wedin, Carolyn. *Inheritors of the Spirit: Mary White Ovington and the Founding of the NAACP*. New York: Wiley, 1998.

Zangrando, Robert L. *The NAACP Crusade against Lynching, 1909–1950*. Philadelphia: Temple University Press, 1980.

Newton, Huey P.

Huey P. Newton was a leader and cofounder of the Black Panther Party for Self-Defense (BPP). Through his activism in the BPP as well as his myriad written works, Newton was part of the more militant elements of the civil rights movement, advocating self-defense and Black Nationalism, rather than nonviolence and integration.

Huey P. Newton poses in Black Panther poster. (Library of Congress)

Named after Louisiana senator Huey Long, Huey Pierce Newton was the seventh child of Armelia and Walter Newton, born on February 17, 1942, in Monroe, Louisiana. At age three, Newton migrated to Oakland, California, with his family, searching for economic opportunity and a better quality of life. During the years following World War II, Oakland boasted a burgeoning African American population and a busy port. However, Oakland was characterized by myriad problems for the African American community: schools were substandard, living accommodations were meager at best, and jobs were ephemeral.

Melvin Newton and Walter "Sonny Man" Newton Jr., Newton's two older brothers, and Walter Newton Sr., Newton's father, were most influential in Newton's childhood development. Melvin attended San Jose State College (renamed San Jose State University in 1974) and taught his brother Newton the value of learning. Sonny Man, leaving home as a teenager, thrived in the illegal economy and showed Newton the allure of street life. Walter provided Newton with lessons to negotiate life on Oakland's streets. To Newton Jr., Newton Sr. was the glue that held their family together. Holding multiple jobs and performing the duties of a Christian minister, Newton Sr. combined spirituality with pragmatism and taught his sons the necessity of opposing white racism.

Never feeling at home in structured classrooms, Newton received his education during his formative years on the streets of Oakland. There he and his friends experimented with, acted out, and constantly engaged the politics of masculinity and found the hustler's life appealing. In the 10th grade at Oakland Technical High School, Newton was expelled for his behavior and he transferred to Berkeley High School in nearby Berkeley. It was at Berkeley High School that Newton's trouble with the law began, forcing him to go to juvenile hall. Unable to attend Berkeley High School upon leaving juvenile hall, Newton returned to Oakland Technical High School and graduated in 1959.

Social promotion and the politics of bureaucratic public high schools allowed Newton to graduate without possessing requisite scholastic aptitude. After a period of self-directed study under the tutelage of his brother Melvin, however, Newton entered Oakland City College in the autumn of 1959. It was at Oakland City College from 1959 to 1966 that Newton began actively seeking answers to the problems plaguing African American communities nationwide. Reading radical social and political theorists like Ernesto "Che" Guevara, Malcolm X, Frantz Fanon, Karl Marx, and Mao Zedong, and participating in African American cultural and political organizations, Newton began to develop his own theoretical framework. The first organizations he joined were the Afro-American Association and the Soul Students Advisory Council, student groups devoted to studying African American history, political thought, and cultural production, and creating a black studies curriculum on campus. Disappointed with the presence of political consciousness but lack of political activity in the two organizations, especially the two groups' dismissal of black working poor men, Newton and Bobby Seale, a friend and student at Oakland City College, created the BPP.

The Black Panthers were initially organized in 1966 as an armed police patrol to protect African American community residents from police violence. By 1969, with Bobby Seale as its chairman and Newton as its minister of self-defense, the organization expanded nationwide, with more than 40 chapters devoted to the daily concerns of urban African American communities. In 1966, when the party was initially organized, Newton was a Black Nationalist and posited that only black people's control of capitalists' institutions in their community could bring about African American empowerment. In 1969, Newton's understanding of Marxism led him to embrace revolutionary socialism as an ideology necessary to seize economic and political power from the elite ruling class and end the exploitation of the poor and working classes.

By 1970, Newton hypothesized that only an internationalist struggle linking radical and progressive forces in different countries could bring about fundamental change. In 1971, Newton's intercommunalism combined ideas of empire and imperialism to articulate an understanding of social movements that transcended the confines of national boundaries. Newton was the BPP's chief theoretician. In 1966, after six years of study, Newton received his associate's degree, was awarded a bachelor's degree in education and politics from the University of California at Santa Cruz (UCSC) in 1974, and won his doctorate from the History of Consciousness Program at UCSC in 1980 by successfully defending his dissertation "War against the Panthers: A Study of Repression in America." Newton was a prolific writer who (co)authored five books and scores of articles, essays, and position papers.

After Newton was pulled over for unknown circumstances in the early morning hours of October 28, 1967, an altercation with the police left officer John Frey dead, officer Herbert Heanes wounded, and Newton near death with a bullet in his stomach. Treated for his bullet wounds at Kaiser Hospital, Newton was interrogated, brutalized, and chained to a gurney by police. Newton retained the services of Charles Garry, a prominent lawyer known for working with leftist causes. Accused of murder, felonious assault, and kidnapping, Newton awaited trial in San Quentin Prison and the Oakland County Jail. After months on trial, on September 8, 1968, Newton was found guilty of manslaughter and sentenced to a 2-to-15-year sentence at the California Men's Colony, East Facility, in San Luis Obispo, California. Most of Newton's 22 months at the penal colony were spent in isolation. While Newton was imprisoned, Charles Garry feverishly worked to obtain an appeal. On May 29, 1970, the California Appellate Court reversed Newton's conviction and determined that, because the jury had been denied critical information in determining Newton's fate, a new trial was needed. In August 1970, Newton was released on bail. In the early 1970s, Newton's defense team participated in two more trials to save him from imprisonment. Both ended in mistrials. Cleared of all charges, Newton set out to rebuild the BPP.

The Federal Bureau of Investigation's Counter-Intelligence Program (COINTELPRO) from 1970 to 1974, however, made bolstering the BPP difficult, as did Newton's move to possess absolute authority in the party, going by names such as the supreme commander, the servant of the people, and the supreme servant of the people. Furthermore, Newton's stardom among the country's celebrities, who provided him with luxury items, drugs, and alcohol, compromised his position among those individuals the party purported to serve. Newton's drug abuse and alcoholism further estranged the BPP from African American communities and may have contributed to his fleeing the country in 1974.

In late 1973, Newton allegedly shot a prostitute, Kathleen Smith, and brutalized a tailor, Preston Callins, for calling him "baby." Shortly after being arrested and posting bail for assaulting Callins, Newton fled the United States and obtained asylum in Cuba, where he remained until 1977, relinquishing control of the declining BPP to Elaine Brown. Upon his return to the United States, Newton was imprisoned, released on bail, and eventually acquitted for the murder of Smith. Callins's case was dropped after he declared that he could not remember his assaulter. Newton also resumed control of the party after Elaine Brown resigned her post, citing irreconcilable differences with Newton.

After the BPP officially disbanded in 1982, Newton's wife, Fredericka, left him, and his drug and alcohol abuse, as well his problems with law enforcement, continued. In 1985, he was suspected but never indicted for burglary. In 1986, he was cleared of possessing illegal firearms. In 1988, Newton served time in prison for a parole violation. On August 22, 1989, Newton was fatally wounded after being shot three times in what seems to have been a drug deal gone awry.

Jamie J. Wilson

Further Reading

Foner, Philip S. *The Black Panthers Speak*. New York: Da Capo Press, 1995.

Jeffries, Judson. *Huey P. Newton: The Radical Theorist*. Jackson: University Press of Mississippi, 2002.

Lockwood, Lee. *Conversations with Eldridge Cleaver, Algiers*. New York: Dell Publishing, 1970.

Newton, Huey P. *Revolutionary Suicide*. New York: Harcourt Brace Jovanovich, 1973.

Newton, Huey P. *To Die for the People: The Writings of Huey P. Newton*. New York: Vintage Books, 1972.

Newton, Huey P. *War against the Panthers: A Study of Repression in America*. New York: Harlem River Press, 1996.

Pearson, Hugh. *The Shadow of the Panthers: Huey Newton and the Price of Black Power in America*. Reading, MA: Addison Wesley Publishing, 1994.

Seale, Bobby, *Seize the Time: The Story of the Black Panther Party and Huey P. Newton*. New York: Random House, 1970.

Nixon, E. D.

Union leader and civil rights advocate E. D. Nixon helped launch the Montgomery Bus Boycott, the event that propelled Martin Luther King Jr. into the national spotlight. Described by King as "one of the chief voices of the Negro community in the area of civil rights," and "a symbol of the hopes and aspirations of the long oppressed people of the State of Alabama," Nixon worked behind the scenes to launch the Montgomery Improvement Association (MIA) and to then organize and sustain the boycott.

The son of a Baptist minister and a maid-cook, Edgar Daniel Nixon was born on July 12, 1899, in Lowndes County, Alabama. Nixon received only 16 months of formal education, but after working his way up from a job in the train station baggage room, he became a Pullman car porter, a job he held until 1964. In 1928, he joined A. Philip Randolph's Brotherhood of Sleeping Car Porters Union and later helped form its Montgomery branch, acting as its president for many years. Nixon later said of Randolph's impact on him: "Nobody in all my years influenced me or made me feel like A. Philip Randolph did."

On December 1, 1955, Rosa Parks was arrested for refusing to give up her bus seat to a white man. Nixon, former head of the Montgomery National Association for the Advancement of Colored People (NAACP), felt her arrest was the perfect case to challenge Montgomery's segregated bus system. Nixon recalled in an interview with African American studies scholar Steven M. Millner: "When Rosa Parks was arrested, I thought 'this is it!' 'Cause she's morally clean, she's reliable, nobody had nothing on her, she had the courage of her convictions." Nixon then worked with the Women's Political Council to convince black residents to support the boycott.

Together with Clifford Durr, a white attorney, Nixon bailed Parks out of jail and quickly began to mobilize Montgomery's black community. Impressed by King's address to the local NAACP chapter several months earlier, Nixon asked him to host a bus-boycott planning meeting at his church on December 2. After the successful one-day boycott on December 5, Montgomery's black leaders met again. King was elected to lead the boycott as president of the newly created MIA, and Nixon was elected treasurer.

Nixon supplied the MIA with contacts for various labor and civil rights organizations, which provided both financial and political support for the boycott. In 1957, tensions between King and Nixon developed over leadership and decision making in the MIA. Nixon resigned his post as MIA treasurer in 1957, citing resentment at "being treated as a newcomer." However, Nixon maintained respect for King. Referring to King's handling of his arrest in Montgomery on September 3, 1958, Nixon applauded King, "Because of your courage in face of known danger I want to commend you for your stand for the people of color all over the world, and [especially] the people in Montgomery. Your action took the fear out of the Negroes and made the white man see himself as he is."

Until his death at the age of 87, Nixon continued to work for civil rights, focusing his later years on improving conditions at housing projects and organizing programs for African American children. Nixon received the Walter White Award from the NAACP in 1985, and in 1986, a year before his death, Nixon's home in Montgomery was placed on the Alabama Register of Landmarks and Heritage. He died on February 25, 1987.

Clayborne Carson

Further Reading

Carson, Clayborne, et al., eds. *The Papers of Martin Luther King, Jr.* Berkeley: University of California Press, 2007.

King, Martin Luther, Jr. *Stride toward Freedom: The Montgomery Story.* Boston: Beacon Press, 1957.

Millner, Steven M. "Interview; E. D. Nixon." In *The Walking City*, edited by David J. Garrow. Brooklyn, NY: Carlson Publishing, 1989.

Operation Breadbasket

In 1962, the Southern Christian Leadership Conference (SCLC) launched Operation Breadbasket in Atlanta. According to Martin Luther King Jr., "The fundamental premise of Breadbasket is a simple one. Negroes need not patronize a business which denies them jobs, or advancement [or] plain courtesy." "Many retail businesses and consumer-goods industries," King explained, "deplete the ghetto by selling to Negroes without returning to the community any of the profits through fair hiring practices."

Operation Breadbasket was modeled after a selective patronage program developed by Leon Sullivan in Philadelphia, Pennsylvania. King brought Sullivan to Atlanta in October 1962 to meet with local ministers about replicating the program. Breadbasket used the persuasive power of black ministers and the organizing strength of the churches to create economic opportunities in black communities. The group obtained employment statistics for industries selling their products in black communities and, if these statistics demonstrated that blacks were underemployed or restricted to menial positions, ministers from Operation Breadbasket asked the company to "negotiate a more equitable employment practice." If the company refused, clergy encouraged their parishioners to boycott selected products and picket businesses selling those products. By 1967, Atlanta's Breadbasket had negotiated jobs bringing a total of $25 million a year in new income to the black community.

Operation Breadbasket expanded to Chicago in 1966 as part of SCLC's Chicago Campaign. King called it SCLC's "most spectacularly successful program" in Chicago. Under the leadership of Chicago Theological Seminary student Jesse Jackson, Breadbasket targeted five businesses in the dairy industry. While three companies negotiated to add black jobs immediately, two complied only after boycotts. Chicago Breadbasket went on to target Pepsi and Coca-Cola bottlers, and then supermarket chains, winning 2,000 new jobs worth $15 million a year in new income to the black community in the first 15 months of its operation. Going beyond jobs and patronage for black-owned businesses, Chicago-based Operation Breadbasket became a cultural event, focused around weekly Saturday workshops, which drew thousands to hear Jackson preach in person and on the radio.

Jackson became the national director of Operation Breadbasket's programs in 1967. After King's assassination in 1968, Jackson continued to lead the program; however, tensions emerged between Jackson and SCLC's new leader, Ralph

Abernathy, over fund-raising and the location of Breadbasket's national head-quarters. Abernathy wanted Jackson to move Breadbasket from Chicago to Atlanta in early 1971, but Jackson refused and resigned from SCLC in December. A week later, he launched his own economic empowerment organization called Operation PUSH (People United to Save Humanity). Breadbasket continued through the next year, experiencing several leadership changes before its eventual demise.

Clayborne Carson

Further Reading

Garrow, David. *Chicago 1966: Open Housing Marches, Summit Negotiations, and Operation Breadbasket*. New York: Carlson Publishing, 1989.

King, Martin Luther, Jr. "One Year Later in Chicago." January 1967. Southern Christian Leadership Conference Records, Martin Luther King, Jr. Center for Nonviolent Social Change, Atlanta, Georgia.

Orangeburg Massacre of 1968

The Orangeburg Massacre, an incident in which three African American students were killed and 27 others were wounded in a confrontation with police, occurred in February 1968 on the adjoining campuses of South Carolina State College (now South Carolina State University) and Claflin College (now Claflin University), two historically black colleges in Orangeburg, South Carolina.

Although a great deal of violence occurred during antiwar and civil rights movement demonstrations of the 1960s, the Orangeburg Massacre was unprecedented because it was the first time in U.S. history that students were killed on an American college campus. Another aspect of the Orangeburg Massacre that makes it an unparalleled event in the annals of American history is that even though the deaths of the students at South Carolina State and Claflin Colleges occurred two years before the Kent State University shootings in which four students were killed and nine others were wounded on May 4, 1970, the Orangeburg Massacre received negligible media coverage. In fact, compared to the national and international media coverage that the tragedy at Kent State received, it was almost as if the Orangeburg Massacre did not happen at all, or, at the very least, was not important enough to report. Perhaps the only event of its kind that received even less media attention was the deaths of two students during an incident at Jackson State University in Mississippi on May 14, 1970. Ironically, the 150 African American students at Jackson State were protesting the incident at Kent State when the National Guard fired into the crowd, leaving two students dead.

There are many possible reasons why the Orangeburg Massacre was neglected by the press. Even in death and injury, it seemed that the students of South Carolina State and Claflin Colleges had fallen prey to the racial discrimination they spent their lives trying to overcome. However, an equally plausible reason is that less than two months after the Orangeburg Massacre, while the incident was still under investigation, the nation, particularly the individuals in the civil rights movement who had committed their lives to ending discrimination in this country, were shocked and angered by the assassination of Martin Luther King Jr. on April 8, 1968.

Whatever the reason for the neglect of the topic, the fact is that on Thursday night, February 8, 1968, members of the South Carolina Sheriff's Office, the South Carolina Police Department, and the South Carolina Army National Guard shot 30 African American college students who had organized what was intended to be a peaceful protest. Approximately 200 students gathered on the adjoining campuses of South Carolina State and Claflin Colleges to protest the continued segregation of the All Star Bowling Lane, a bowling alley on Russell Street, within walking distance of the two colleges. The bowling alley was owned by Harry Floyd, a local businessman. Students were frustrated after a week's attempt to persuade the owner of the bowling alley to comply with the Civil Rights Act of 1964, which, in part, authorized the national government to abolish segregation and discrimination based on race, color, religion, national origin, and, in the case of employment, sex. The act was signed into law on July 2, 1964, by President Lyndon B. Johnson and, even though the law stressed voluntary compliance, it also included a stipulation that encouraged resolution of problems by local and state authorities.

During the days leading up to February 8, several representatives from South Carolina State and Claflin Colleges met with the mayor of Orangeburg, the chief of police, and the city manager. The students requested but were denied a permit to march through the streets of Orangeburg or to demonstrate in front of the All Star Bowling Lane.

On Monday, February 5, 1968, a group of students from Claflin and South Carolina State Colleges attempted to desegregate the only bowling alley in town, but they were denied entrance and the police were summoned by the proprietor. After a brief standoff, the majority of the students returned to their respective campuses.

This effort to abolish segregation was not something new for students of Claflin and South Carolina State Colleges. They, along with black and white citizens in South Carolina, played an active role in the civil rights movement. In July 1955, 57 African Americans petitioned the school board to desegregate the public schools in Orangeburg. A year later, students from South Carolina State and Claflin Colleges organized a nonviolent protest march through the streets of Orangeburg. During February and March, students from Claflin, Morris, and Friendship Colleges conducted sit-ins to desegregate the lunch counter at S. H. Kress, a novelty store. On March 15, 1960, demonstrators were drenched with fire hoses and teargassed as they marched to protest the segregated lunch counter. In September 1963, over 1,000 protesters were arrested for picketing local merchants. A review of this brief history suggests that the events that took place in

Orangeburg during February 1968 were not an aberration but part of the long struggle to abolish segregation and racial discrimination, which was a fundamental goal of the civil rights movement.

On Tuesday night, February 6, the local police were waiting when students arrived. The door of the bowling alley was locked, but the students refused to move. Chief of Police Roger Poston was called. When he arrived, the door was unlocked to allow him entrance. Several students rushed the door. They were asked to leave. When they refused, 15 were arrested for trespassing.

When rumors of the arrests reached the campuses, over 300 students gathered outside the bowling alley. They were met by the Orangeburg Police Department, state police, state highway patrol, deputies from the sheriff's office, and the state law enforcement division (SLED). A city fire truck arrived. The students chose that moment to rush the bowling alley. Someone smashed a plate glass window. The police beat back the crowd with nightsticks. Eight students and one officer were injured.

On Wednesday morning, student representatives from both colleges attended a meeting with city officials to discuss the events of the past couple of days and prevent any potential escalation. The students were again denied a permit to hold a demonstration but were able to submit a list of grievances; their list included: (a) closing of the All Star Bowling Lane until it changed its policy toward segregation; (b) establishment of a biracial Human Relations Committee; (c) service from the Orangeburg Medical Association for all persons, regardless of race, color, creed, religion, or national origin; and (d) compliance of local and state officials with the Civil Rights Act of 1964.

On Thursday, February 8, 1968, another meeting was convened on campus and was organized by the Black Awareness Coordinating Committee (BACC), a student organization that included members of the Student Nonviolent Coordinating Committee (SNCC), the National Association for the Advancement of Colored People (NAACP), and the Southern Christian Leadership Conference (SCLC). Some members of BACC felt that they had been defeated by compromise when the group was denied another permit. The meetings lasted until evening without reaching a solution. The students were denied their permit to demonstrate, and the bowling alley remained segregated. Exhausted, frustrated, and disappointed about their lack of progress, dozens of students conversed in small groups. Others wandered aimlessly around the campuses.

Because it was a cold winter night, someone suggested a bonfire. It was not long before the blaze became a beacon for other students. It also attracted the attention of the police. A fire truck arrived followed by an ambulance, which elicited an angry response from the students. As the firemen extinguished the already dying embers of the bonfire someone out of the darkness yelled, "I'm hit." The police immediately opened fire. Students, stunned by the sudden assault, ran, screamed, fell to their knees, or dove for shelter. From start to finish, the terror lasted only seconds, but in that interval, 27 students were wounded and three young men—Samuel Ephesians Hammond, Jr., Henry Ezekial Smith, and Delano Herman Middleton—were killed.

Hammond, a freshman from Fort Lauderdale, Florida, was shot in the upper back. Smith, a sophomore from Marion, South Carolina, was shot in the right and left sides and in the neck. Middleton, a 17-year-old high school student from Orangeburg, was shot in the spine, thigh, wrist, and forearm.

Even after an investigation, it was difficult to state exactly what triggered the confrontation. The police claimed that they fired in self-defense. Students claimed that the only shots fired were by the police—that they fired without warning into a defenseless crowd with no means of protecting themselves. The controversy over what actually ignited the Orangeburg Massacre has never been resolved. However, during the 112th Session of the South Carolina General Assembly in 1997–1998, the following resolution was passed (Bill 4576):

> To express profound gratitude for the supreme sacrifice made on February 8, 1968, by three young students, Samuel Hammond, Jr., Delano Herman Middleton, and Henry Ezekial Smith, and to recognize their courageous effort by declaring February 8, as Smith-Hammond-Middleton Memorial Day.
>
> Be it further resolved that we pray the governor of our great state immediately issue posthumously to those three brave young men The Order of the Palmetto, and pray also that these awards be presented to South Carolina State University on February 8, 1998, and that South Carolina State University display them in positions of honor and prominence in its Smith-Hammond-Middleton Memorial Center.

Every year, friends, family, and survivors gather on the campuses of Claflin and South Carolina State Universities to commemorate the Orangeburg Massacre.

John G. Hall

Further Reading

Bass, Jack, and Jack Nelson. *The Orangeburg Massacre.* Macon, GA: Mercer University Press, 1996.

Brown, Linda Meggett. "Remembering the Orangeburg Massacre (South Carolina State University)." *Black Issues in Higher Education*, March 1, 2001.

Watters, Pat, and Weldon Rougeau. *Events at Orangeburg: A Report Based on Study and Interviews in Orangeburg, South Carolina, in the Aftermath of Tragedy.* Southern Regional Council, South Carolina, February 25, 1968.

Williams, Cecil J. "Selected Movement Photographs of Cecil J. Williams." http://www.crmvet.org.

Organization of Afro-American Unity

The Organization of Afro-American Unity (OAAU) was founded by African American civil rights activist Malcolm X on June 28, 1964, in Harlem, New York. It was a Black Nationalist organization that hoped to unite African Americans to defend their civil and human rights. The OAAU advocated self-determination, self-defense, and a number of political, economic, and educational initiatives aimed at empowering African Americans. Inspired by the Organization of African Unity (OAU), which sought unity among recently decolonized African nation-states, the OAAU promoted Pan-African unity and framed the African American struggle for civil rights in a global context.

In March 1964, Malcolm X officially broke with the Nation of Islam (NOI). Personal tensions with the NOI contributed to the split, but Malcolm X also wanted to take bolder action on civil rights issues. Although he started his own separate religious organization, the Muslim Mosque Inc., the formation of the OAAU represented his decisive shift toward secular political organizing. Malcolm X's 1964 travels in Africa and the Middle East also shaped the OAAU. He was exposed firsthand to the anticolonial struggle and to nationalist ideology and practice. He came to view recently decolonized nations and their leaders as potential allies, and he began perceiving the African American struggle in an international framework.

The OAAU was a "nonsectarian" and "nonreligious" organization that sought unity among all African Americans fighting for civil rights. It supported the self-determination and cultural uplift of African American urban communities and advocated self-defense, education, and the mobilization of African Americans' internal resources. It sponsored or planned to sponsor a wide range of activities. These included the formation of "defense units" and "rifle clubs" and political initiatives such as voter registration and the formation of political clubs. Malcolm X advocated such tactics as rent strikes and called for community control of African American schools. The OAAU stressed the need for education and established a Liberation School that offered classes on history and politics, as well as consumer education, child care, and other spheres of private life. Malcolm X proposed a number of OAAU activities, including a drug rehabilitation program, a "Guardian system" for youth, and community anticrime initiatives.

The OAAU viewed the African American struggle in global terms. It saw black people in the United States as part of a global majority rather than a domestic minority, and it viewed newly decolonized African governments and the African diaspora as allies. This "internationalizing" of the civil rights movement presented new strategic openings for the OAAU. Malcolm X began referring to "human rights" instead of "civil rights" as a goal, and he announced plans to bring the United States before the United Nations on charges of racism. He also became more critical of capitalism and began calling for a new political, economic, and social system.

During its brief existence, the OAAU held rallies in Harlem, with attendance typically between 250 and 800 when Malcolm X was present. It had its headquarters in Harlem and started a short-run newsletter, the *Blacklash*, with an average circulation of between 200 and 300. Its membership was never more than several hundred, with a few dozen dedicated people at its core. Dues were $1, with a $2 initiation fee to join. The OAAU also established international branches in Britain, France, Ghana, Kenya, and Egypt, and it founded an Information Bureau in Ghana to exchange news regarding African and African American activism.

Malcolm X was the leader of the OAAU, but he had a circle of intellectuals and professionals around him who played secondary leadership roles. Malcolm X was not able to fully devote himself to the OAAU while he was alive, and his assassination undercut his plan to spend more time building the group. The OAAU was an all-black organization, although Malcolm X's views on white alliances had shifted since the exclusionist views of his NOI days. Although still skeptical of whites and still insistent on an all-black organization that could achieve independent Black Power, he was more open to forming alliances with anyone who shared the OAAU's goals.

Throughout its existence, the OAAU faced obstacles. It was under constant surveillance by the Federal Bureau of Investigation (FBI) and other intelligence organizations, and a leading member turned out to be a police infiltrator. Malcolm X wanted the group to be a collectively run organization, but this desire clashed with the OAAU's dependence on Malcolm X's prestige, charisma, and leadership. Furthermore, traditional black Muslims were skeptical of the OAAU's secular orientation, whereas some members thought Malcolm X was becoming "soft" on white racism with his increased openness to working with whites. Malcolm X consciously included women in leadership roles, but they still struggled with sexism within the OAAU.

Malcolm X's sister, Ella Collins, assumed control of the OAAU shortly after his assassination on February 21, 1965. Without Malcolm X's leadership, however, the organization quickly withered away.

Derek Wolf Seidman

Further Reading

Breitman, George. *The Last Year of Malcolm X*. New York: Merit Publishers, 1967.

Sales, William W. *From Civil Rights to Black Liberation: Malcolm X and the Organization of Afro-American Unity*. Boston: South End Press, 1994.

P

Parks, Rosa

On December 1, 1955, Rosa Louise Parks (1913–2005) refused to give up her seat on a Montgomery, Alabama, bus for a white passenger. This act of defiance against Jim Crow segregation sparked the Montgomery Bus Boycott—often heralded as the beginning of the modern civil rights movement—a nonviolent economic boycott of Montgomery's bus system by the black community that successfully ended racial segregation on the city's public transit. For her courage and actions, Parks is widely considered the mother of the civil rights movement.

Rosa Louise McCauley was born on February 4, 1913, in Tuskegee, Alabama, to James and Leona McCauley. After James and Leona separated, Leona moved with her children, Rosa and Sylvester, to Pine Level, Alabama, a town on the outskirts of Montgomery, where they lived with Leona's parents. By the age of 11, Rosa attended the Montgomery Industrial School for Girls, and a few years later, she attended the laboratory school at Alabama State Teacher's College for Negroes in Montgomery. Family illnesses forced Rosa to abandon her education to support her family.

While living in Montgomery, 18-year-old Rosa met Raymond Parks, a barber. The self-educated Parks had been one of the charter members of Montgomery's NAACP and had been actively involved in supporting the Scottsboro Boys' defense in the early 1930s. Raymond's courage, at a time when black activism was extremely dangerous, deeply impressed Rosa. They were married on December 18, 1932, in Pine Level. Historian and Parks's biographer Douglas Brinkley has noted that her husband was a significant factor in her radicalization during the Great Depression, as he would discuss the NAACP and its strategies for encouraging African American suffrage and integration with Parks. Encouraged by her husband, Rosa Parks returned to school and earned her high school diploma in 1933.

Until World War II, Parks had not been involved in the black civil rights struggle. This changed after she took a job at Maxwell Field in Montgomery in 1941. By 1943, all military bases, Maxwell Field included, had been desegregated. Unlike Montgomery's city buses, she rode integrated trolleys on base, and her experience at desegregated Maxwell prompted her to join the Montgomery NAACP. At her first meeting, Parks was elected secretary of the organization. In this capacity, she helped lead a voter registration drive, although white registrars worked diligently to keep African Americans off the voter rolls. It took until April 1945 for Parks to finally be registered to vote.

After the war, Parks continued as secretary of the Montgomery NAACP, but she also worked as a housekeeper and seamstress, most notably for the liberal white activists Clifford and Virginia Durr. In July 1955, Virginia Durr arranged for Parks to attend a two-week session on racial desegregation at the Highlander Folk School in Monteagle, Tennessee. The experience at Highlander, and her exposure to individuals such as civil rights pioneer Septima Clark, strengthened her desire to work for civil rights.

Just months after her return from Highlander, on the evening of December 1, 1955, Parks violated segregation laws by refusing to give her seat to a white passenger on a city bus. Parks initially had been seated in the first row of the black section, but as more whites boarded the bus, the color line moved farther back. When this occurred, African Americans were expected to relinquish their seats to make room for the white passengers. Parks refused. The bus driver, James F. Blake, called the police and had Parks arrested. As she recounted in her autobiography, she was not physically tired. A few days later, Parks was found guilty of disorderly conduct and violating a Montgomery ordinance and fined $10, plus $4 in court costs.

In response to Parks's arrest, E. D. Nixon, NAACP chapter president, and Jo Ann Robinson, a professor at Alabama State College, met to discuss a boycott of the bus system by Montgomery's African Americans. At a subsequent mass meeting, Martin Luther King Jr., the pastor of Dexter Avenue Baptist Church, was chosen to lead the effort. The entire African American community supported the Montgomery Bus Boycott, refusing to ride the city's buses for 381 days, placing a tremendous financial strain on the bus company. On May 11, 1956, a federal court decision in *Browder v. Gayle* ruled Alabama's bus segregation laws unconstitutional, upheld by the U.S. Supreme Court on November 13, 1956. The boycott came to an end on December 20, 1956, after the city passed a desegregation ordinance for the city's buses. Whereas the boycott propelled King into national prominence as the leader of the civil rights movement, Parks's courageous refusal to give in to the inequities of the Jim Crow system made her a symbolic figure whose inspiration reached well beyond the borders of the United States.

Hounded by death threats and at odds with the local leaders of the civil rights movement, Rosa and Raymond Parks, along with Leona McCauley, moved to Detroit, Michigan, in July 1957, to live with family members. In Detroit, Parks worked as a seamstress but continued to be involved in the civil rights movement, lecturing widely to diverse groups. Her interest in politics led in 1965 to a job with U.S. representative John Conyers, for whom she work until she retired in 1988. In honor of her husband Raymond, who died in 1977, she founded the Rosa and Raymond Parks Institute for Self-Development in February 1987, to mentor youths to achieve their full potential.

Although Parks was a symbol of the civil rights movement and an inspiration to millions because of her courage and quiet dignity, official recognition of her contributions to American history came late in her life. On September 9, 1996, President William J. Clinton presented her with the Presidential Medal of Freedom, the highest award given to a civilian. A few years later, on May 3, 1999, she received a Congressional Gold Medal. *Time* magazine also recognized her as one of the 100 most influential people of the twentieth century. Rosa Parks died on October 24, 2005, in Detroit at the age of 92. In striking contrast to her notoriety as one of the most detested figures in the United States after the boycott, Rosa Parks became the first woman in American history to lie in state in the U.S. Capitol. It is estimated that 50,000 people paid their respects to the "Mother of the Civil Rights Movement."

Dan J. Puckett

Further Reading

Branch, Taylor. *Parting the Waters: America in the King Years, 1954–63*. New York: Simon & Schuster, 1988.

Brinkley, Douglas. *Rosa Parks*. New York: Viking Penguin, 2000.

Parks, Rosa, with Gregory J. Reed. *Quiet Strength: The Faith, the Hope, and the Heart of a Woman Who Changed the Nation*. Grand Rapids, MI: Zondervan Publishing House, 1994.

Parks, Rosa, with Jim Haskins. *Rosa Parks: My Story*. New York: Dial Books, 1992.

Peck, James

A radical pacifist, trade union proponent, and white civil rights activist, James Peck was actively involved in the civil rights movement, particularly in the Freedom Rides of 1961. Peck also wrote the introduction to a Congress of Racial Equality (CORE) reprint of Martin Luther King Jr.'s article, "Our Struggle: The Story of Montgomery," which originally appeared in *Liberation*. "By encouraging and supporting actions such as that in Montgomery," Peck informed readers, "we who adhere to the principles of nonviolence hope to hasten complete abolition of segregation within our social system."

The son of a wealthy clothier, Peck was born in New York City on December 19, 1914. He briefly attended Harvard University before becoming a full-time activist. Peck was interned for 28 months during World War II as a conscientious objector, and in 1947, he participated in CORE's Journey of Reconciliation. Thereafter, he worked with the War Resisters League and CORE, editing the newsletter *CORElator* for 17 years.

During the Montgomery Bus Boycott, Peck helped the Montgomery Improvement Association raise funds by sending the group matchbooks bearing slogans.

In 1960, King wrote the introduction to Peck's pamphlet, "Cracking the Color Line: Non-Violent Direct Action Methods of Eliminating Racial Discrimination." In the introduction, King praised CORE for using "brains and imagination as well as good-will, self-discipline, and persistence."

Peck was the only participant in the original Journey of Reconciliation to join the Freedom Rides in 1961. When the bus he was riding arrived in Birmingham, Alabama, he was knocked unconscious and suffered a gash that required 53 stitches to close. In February 1962, Peck sent King a copy of his memoir *Freedom Ride*, informing King that the book's chapter on Montgomery quoted "at length" from King's *Liberation* article.

Although he was ousted from CORE in 1966 when that group adopted Black Power policies and abandoned its previous policy of interracial cooperation, Peck continued to be active in the movement to end the Vietnam War. He expressed his continuing admiration for King in a June 1966 letter to the Southern Christian Leadership Conference leader: "Despite the increasing clamor for 'black power' and 'self-defense,' you adhere to the principles of equality and nonviolence."

By the early 1980s, Peck was actively involved with Amnesty International. However, after suffering a stroke, which paralyzed his side, he moved into a nursing home in 1985. Peck died in Minneapolis, Minnesota, on July 12, 1993.

Clayborne Carson et al.

Further Reading

Arsenault, Raymond. *Freedom Riders: 1961 and the Struggle for Racial Justice.* New York: Oxford University Press, 2006.

Poor People's Campaign

The Poor People's Campaign was a movement organized and led by the Southern Christian Leadership Conference (SCLC) and its director, Dr. Martin Luther King Jr. It was intended to dramatize the plight of the nation's poor and address economic injustice. The plan was to bring thousands of poor people of all races to Washington, D.C., where they would engage in radical nonviolent direct action in order to convince Congress and President Lyndon B. Johnson to make eliminating poverty the number-one goal of the nation.

The masses of African Americans appeared to be untouched by the most sweeping legislation guaranteeing civil rights since Reconstruction. In 1965, almost one-third of African Americans lived below the poverty line, and half of all black households lived in substandard dwellings. Indeed, the percentage of poor blacks had actually increased between 1959 and 1965. The unemployment rate for blacks was almost double that of whites; for black teenagers, it was more than

Poor People's March in Washington, D.C., on June 18, 1968. The Poor People's Campaign was a movement organized and led by the Southern Christian Leadership Conference (SCLC) and its director, Dr. Martin Luther King Jr. to draw attention to the plight of the nation's poor and address economic injustice. (Library of Congress)

twice that for white teens. The crumbling infrastructure of inner-city neighborhoods was further eroded by so-called urban renewal; the employment situation was exacerbated by the movement of jobs to the suburbs. The high school dropout rate soared, drug abuse became rampant, and fragile families were further strained.

Northern urban communities with thousands of poor, black residents were also fertile ground for the nascent Black Power movement. The nonviolent direct action that had been so successful in the past held no appeal for the hundreds of thousands of blacks who were trapped there with little to no opportunity for improvement. Nor had the War on Poverty, developed by the administration of President Lyndon B. Johnson to eradicate poverty in America, provided much help. Although noble, its efforts were too little, and it was opposed by powerful politicians at the local level and whites who felt Johnson was giving handouts to the undeserving poor. The poor, their hopes raised by community action programs and maximum feasible participation, again found their hopes unanswered. As such, the cities became simmering cauldrons of frustration, alienation, and hopelessness that exploded in 1965.

Every summer from 1965 through 1969, northern cities were visited by urban rebellions, sometimes referred to as race riots. The Los Angeles neighborhood of Watts was the first of these, on August 11, 1965. Six days of rioting reduced Watts to rubble, claimed 34 lives, and recorded property damage of $35 million. Urban rebellions also occurred in 1966, but arguably the worst year of the phenomenon was 1967. A total of 59 riots occurred, the deadliest being in Newark, New Jersey, and Detroit, Michigan. The Newark rebellion left 27 dead, including children, a police officer, and a firefighter, and caused millions of dollars in damage. Conditions in Detroit were so bad that 43 blacks were killed. Not even 800 state and city police and the National Guard could restore order. President Lyndon Johnson was forced to send in the 82nd and 101st Airborne Divisions to restore order.

After the Newark and Detroit riots, Johnson established the National Advisory Commission on Civil Disorders, commonly known as the Kerner Commission after its leader, Governor Otto Kerner of Illinois. Johnson recognized that the only way to end the despair of the masses of blacks was a sustained government program designed to end joblessness, substandard housing, poverty, and disease. The Kerner Commission report surprisingly blamed white racism as the chief cause of the riots and warned that America was once again becoming a dual society, one black and one white. King and the SCLC were keenly aware that the times called for bold measures. He recognized that the campaign would be different from those implemented during the civil rights movement; it was demanding nothing less than a wholesale transformation of American capitalism. Moreover, King intended to force the nation to choose between eliminating poverty, which he saw as a moral issue, and continuing an increasingly unpopular war in Vietnam, against which he had become a vocal critic. To him, the two were inextricably linked.

The Poor People's Campaign had three stages. First, it would crisscross the nation putting together a group of several thousand black, Latino, Native American, and white Appalachian poor people who would travel to Washington to live in a shantytown much like that erected by the Bonus Army of the early 20th century. They would participate in daily demonstrations in the capital and be joined by parallel demonstrations in cities across the country. These would be crowned by a mass march echoing the 1963 March on Washington. Second, the demonstrations would engender mass arrests as they had in the South, further dramatizing the plight of the poor. Finally, there would be an economic boycott of the most powerful businesses in the United States. The Poor People's Campaign would show that all the gains of the civil rights movement were hollow without economic parity and opportunity. It would either be a brilliant success or a humiliating failure.

King and the SCLC were instantly attacked by the media, the political left, and white Americans who were weary of the struggle for equality. Leaders of the other civil rights organizations also criticized King, not only for the campaign, but for his stinging and public rebuke of the Vietnam War. Most of organized labor refused to support the effort. Finally, President Lyndon Johnson turned against King, too, and he lost the warm working relationship they had developed. But King pressed on.

His empathy for and support of the poor took him to Memphis, Tennessee, where he marched in solidarity with city garbage collectors who were seeking a living wage and better working conditions. On April 4, he was assassinated. Coretta Scott King, his widow, and the SCLC decided to continue the Poor People's Campaign under the leadership of the Reverend Ralph Abernathy, King's close friend and confidant. From May 14 to June 24, more than 2,500 poor people lived in a shantytown they had erected and named Resurrection City. The camp boasted a city hall, a cultural capital, a medical facility, a dining hall, a psychiatrist, a university, and a zip code. It fanned out across the Reflecting Pool to the base of the Lincoln Memorial. Residents policed themselves and provided a model for interracial cooperation. Thousands of them fanned out daily across locations in the capital to shame the U.S. government into significant action against poverty.

Unfortunately, conditions in the camp quickly turned miserable. Washington was unusually cool that year in May and June, and it rained 28 of the 42 days of the operation. Residents were soon knee-deep in mud, trash, and rotting food. On June 4, Senator Robert F. Kennedy, who had become a champion of the poor and was running for the Democratic nomination for president, was assassinated. Finally, it was clear that the leadership of Dr. King was sorely missed; Reverend Ralph Abernathy lacked the charisma and contacts of Dr. King, and he spent little time at the camp, appearing to prefer the comfort of the black-owned Pitts Hotel to the muddy squalor of Resurrection City. By the middle of June, fewer than 300 people remained in the camp.

Fighting and near-riots broke out in the camp on June 22. Police were called in, but police dogs and more than a thousand tear gas grenades failed to stem the trouble. On June 24, about 1,000 police closed Resurrection City, arresting Reverend Abernathy and 175 people. Charges of assault against police officers, disorderly conduct, curfew violations, and public drunkenness were levied against those arrested. The Poor People's Campaign failed to persuade public officials to pour more resources into eliminating poverty, and it was deemed a failure and the end of the civil rights movement.

Recent scholarship, however, has reevaluated the campaign and somewhat redeemed its reputation. The Poor People's Campaign ignited the third wave of the civil rights movement: economic empowerment. The interracial structure of the effort showed that a strong alliance based on class was not only important, but necessary. Indeed, the Reverend Jesse Jackson would bring this alliance to fruition with his emphasis on a Rainbow Coalition during his 1988 presidential campaign. The Poor People's Campaign highlighted the weaknesses of runaway capitalism and consumerism in a manner not seen since the Great Depression.

Marilyn K. Howard

Further Reading

Freeman, Roland L. *Mule Train: A Journey of Hope Remembered*. Nashville, TN: Thomas Nelson. 1998.

Honey, Michael. *Going Down Jericho Road: The Memphis Strike, Martin Luther King's Last Campaign.* New York: W. W. Norton, 2007.

McKnight, Gerald. *The Last Crusade: Martin Luther King, Jr., the FBI and the Poor People's Campaign.* New York: Westview Press. 1998.

Powell, Adam Clayton, Jr.

Adam Clayton Powell Jr. was one of Harlem's most charismatic and controversial political leaders. He was also a community religious leader as well as one of New York City's most prominent civil rights activists.

Powell was born in New Haven, Connecticut, on November 29, 1908. During Powell's youth, his family moved to New York City, where his father, Adam Clayton Powell Sr., served as the 17th pastor of Abyssinian Baptist Church in Harlem. As a child, the younger Powell attended New York City public schools. He earned a BA in 1930 from Colgate University, and in 1932, he received an MA in religious education from Columbia University Teachers College. The next year, Powell married Isabel Washington, a line dancer at Harlem's Cotton Club.

Shortly after graduating from Columbia, Powell served as an associate pastor at his father's church, where he developed a charismatic preaching style. He assisted his father in alleviating the economic strain of the Great Depression on the black community in Harlem by organizing soup kitchens, distributing clothing to the poor, and finding jobs for the unemployed. On November 1, 1937, Powell succeeded his father as pastor of Abyssinian. During his early tenure as pastor, Powell substantially increased the size of the congregation through community outreach and inspired preaching.

During President Franklin D. Roosevelt's New Deal, Powell used his status to improve the employment situation of African Americans in New York City. In the late 1930s, he cofounded the Greater New York Coordinating Committee for Fair Employment, an organization that consisted of various professional groups, including black fraternities and sororities, Black Nationalists, and communists. Powell's organization protested throughout the city against antiblack hiring practices in public utilities, such as the electric and telephone companies.

In the 1930s, Powell also helped organize rent strikes and public boycotts, which led to the hiring and promotion of African American employees in restaurants and department stores in Harlem, New York City public transit, public utilities, Harlem Hospital, and the 1939 New York World's Fair. Along with his community activism, from 1936 to 1944, Powell cofounded and published the radical weekly newspaper the *People's Voice*. The paper served as a platform for Powell to inform the African American community about his advocacy for better housing, schools, and employment opportunities.

In the early 1940s, Powell became a professional politician and began representing Harlem in 1941 by winning a seat on the New York City Council. While serving on the council, Powell continued his campaign against racial discrimination, bringing attention to employment discrimination at the telephone company and city colleges. Between 1942 and 1944, he also served as a member of the New York State Consumer Division, Office of Price Administration. From 1942 to 1945, he was a member of the Manhattan Civilian Defense. Powell used his growing political clout to speak at rallies in support of World War II—and used those speaking opportunities to denounce racial segregation in the military.

In 1945, Powell was elected on the Democratic ticket to serve in the U.S. House of Representatives, representing Harlem's 22nd Congressional District. Thus, Powell became the first black member of Congress from New York. In the same year, he divorced Isabel and married popular pianist and actress Hazel Scott, who gave birth to his first child, Adam Clayton Powell III, in 1946.

On his arrival in Washington, Powell continued his civil rights campaign. Although Powell was only one of two African American members of Congress, he successfully challenged de facto segregation on Capitol Hill. At that time, black representatives were prohibited from using Capitol dining areas, which were reserved only for white congressional leaders. Powell, however, would bring Harlem residents to eat with him in these restaurants. Powell also confronted the racial bigotry of staunch segregationists like John E. Rankin of Mississippi on the floor of the House.

In the House, Powell would attach an antidiscrimination clause to significant pieces of legislation. His clause eventually became referred to as the Powell Amendment. In 1955, he attended the historic Bandung Conference of Asian and African nations in Bandung, Indonesia. These formerly colonized countries met to discuss ways in which to promote cultural and economic cooperation and to oppose U.S. and European colonialism. On Powell's return to the United States, he urged President Dwight D. Eisenhower to support these emerging but less developed countries. During the same decade, Powell began to experience legal problems, and in the mid-1950s, he stood trial for tax evasion and fraud. After a hung jury, the Department of Justice decided not to retry the case.

In 1960, Powell divorced and married for the final time. This time he wed Yvette Diago, and she bore him a second son, Adam Clayton Diago Powell. In addition to a new marriage, Powell became chairman of the powerful Labor and Education Committee in 1961. During that decade, as a supporter of President Lyndon B. Johnson's Great Society program, Powell's committee passed dozens of measures that authorized federal programs to improve education and training for the deaf, provide college student loans and public school lunches, and increase the minimum wage, thus expanding opportunities for all U.S. citizens, including African Americans.

Powell's legal and professional troubles continued into the 1960s. Colleagues accused him of misappropriating his committee's budget, taking trips overseas at taxpayers' expense, and missing congressional sessions and committee meetings. He was also criticized for refusing to pay a slander judgment to a Harlem constituent, Ester James. In 1967, the House Democratic Caucus removed Powell as committee chair and refused to return him to his seat until the federal government investigated the allegations against him.

In June 1969, the Supreme Court ruled that the House had unconstitutionally excluded Powell from Congress, and he returned to his seat in the 90th Congress, but without any seniority or back pay. In the summer of 1970, Charles Rangel defeated Powell in the Democratic primary in Powell's district in New York City. Powell then tried and failed to make the November ballot as an independent candidate. In 1971, he resigned as pastor of Abyssinian Baptist and permanently retired to the Bahamian island of Bimini. On April 4, 1972, he died at the age of 63 of complications from prostate cancer at Jackson Memorial Hospital in Miami, Florida.

Dwayne A. Mack

Further Reading

Hamilton, Charles V. *Adam Clayton Powell, Jr.: The Political Biography of an American Dilemma*. New York: Atheneum, 1991.

Haygood, Will. *King of the Cats: The Life and Times of Adam Clayton Powell, Jr.* New York: Houghton Mifflin, 1993.

Powell, Adam Clayton, Jr. *Adam by Adam: The Autobiography of Adam Clayton Powell, Jr.* New York: Dial Press, 1971.

Powell, Adam Clayton, Jr. *Marching Blacks: An Interpretive History of the Rise of the Black Common Man*. New York: Dial Press, 1945.

R

Radio Free Dixie (1962)

Radio Free Dixie was a radio program broadcast from Havana, Cuba, on Friday evenings at 11:00 p.m. from 1962 to 1965. Robert F. Williams, helped by his wife, Mabel, was its conductor. The program's strong signal made it heard almost everywhere in the United States, although it was primarily aimed at African Americans living in the South because, as Williams put it, they did not have any voice. *Radio Free Dixie* called on African Americans to rise and free themselves. As Williams said, *Radio Free Dixie* was the first radio program on which black people could say whatever they wanted and did not have to worry about sponsors.

Although the program had its roots in African American cultural traditions, it was also highly innovative, for Williams was close to the black arts movement and the Black Panther Party (BPP). His choice of music included such African American artists as Leadbelly, Joe Turner, Abbey Lincoln and Max Roach, Otis Redding, Nina Simone, the Impressions, and Josh White. Selections heard on *Radio Free Dixie* included not only jazz (dubbed "freedom jazz"), but also blues and soul music. Among the well-known listeners were Amiri Baraka, Richard Gibson, Conrad Lynn, and William Worthy. Listeners sent Williams hundreds of records to be played. The show highlighted the anthems of the southern movement. Williams' use of jazz was intended as a new type of political propaganda. He saw *Radio Free Dixie* as much more than a radio program; for Williams, it was a political act meant to reassure African Americans and help them free themselves from an overly racist American society. Williams mixed music with news about racial violence or voter registration campaigns in the South. Music was intended to motivate people in their struggle.

Dixie was a familiar song composed in 1859 by Dan Emmett, a member of the Bryant's Minstrels troupe in New York. During the Civil War, the song reinforced and strengthened white identity in the South, which it pictured as a happy land. For a large number of Americans, the song retained its wartime and racial connotations in the twentieth century. During the civil rights movement, *Dixie* served as an anthem for white southerners and a reminder of racism and slavery for African Americans. Williams rejected the white southerner vision of the South as a happy land and used the word *Dixie* in an attempt to free the South from cultural, as well as political, racism. In a press conference after a trial in which a white man was acquitted for the attempted rape of a black woman, Williams said in

1959: "If the United States Constitution cannot be enforced in this social jungle called Dixie, it is time that Negroes must defend themselves."

Williams was at odds with the civil rights movement. He called for black self-defense and published *Negroes with Guns*, although he also called for the continued pressure of nonviolent direct action. Williams believed in flexibility in the freedom struggle. For some time, he was leader of the local chapter of the National Association for the Advancement of Colored People and helped increase the membership from 6 to 200. He also formed the Black Guard, an armed group committed to the protection of the local black population, since calls of African Americans to law enforcement often went unanswered. He brought to the attention of national and international media the reality of Jim Crow.

Although Williams eventually went into exile, living in Cuba, the Soviet Union, and Red China, he was neither a communist nor a Black Nationalist, but called himself an internationalist. He realized that lack of freedom tainted communist regimes, and their view of the United States as imperialist distorted a political reality that was much more complex. Moreover, communist regimes did not understand the racism faced by African Americans, either because there were no important ethnic communities in their countries, or because such communities had already been marginalized and removed from the public consciousness.

Radio Free Dixie provided African Americans with a new way of grappling with racial stereotypes and lack of confidence. Williams was an influential figure in the struggle for civil rights, and his call for flexibility was followed by young black activists across the South who rejected the tactics of nonviolence. By broadcasting for the South, Williams intended to raise the level of confidence in African Americans. He gave new arguments to the Black Power movement and, although far from the United States for a number of years, he was an inspiration to, and a strong supporter of, the African American struggle for civil rights.

Eventually, CIA jamming and Cuban censorship ended *Radio Free Dixie*, but WBAI in New York and KPFA in Berkeley, California, often rebroadcast tapes of the shows. Bootleg tapes were also circulated in Watts and Harlem. The program ended in 1965, but Williams's influence has continued ever since.

Santiago Rodríguez Guerrero-Strachan

Further Reading

Carmichael, Stokely, and Charles V. Hamilton. *Black Power: The Politics of Liberation in America*. London: Jonathan Cape, 1967.

Carson, Clayborne. *In Struggle: SNCC and the Black Awakening of the 1960s*. Cambridge, MA: Harvard University Press, 1981.

Tyson, Timothy B. *Radio Free Dixie: Robert F. Williams and the Roots of Black Power*. Chapel Hill: University of North Carolina Press, 1999.

Williams, Robert F. Press conference, Monroe, NC, 1959. www.youtube.com/wathc?v=koLtBqe0Bby

Randolph, A. Philip

A. Philip Randolph was an African American trade union and civil rights leader who advocated the use of labor movements as a tool in the African American struggle for civil rights. He founded the Brotherhood of Sleeping Car Porters and organized mass protests to end segregation and discrimination in industry and the U.S. Army.

Asa Philip Randolph was born on April 15, 1889, to an African Methodist Episcopal minister and a seamstress in Crescent, Florida. Although Randolph grew up in a very religious environment, he later became an atheist but always maintained his strong belief in nonviolence. In 1891, his family moved to Jacksonville, Florida, a city with a thriving African American community. His parents wanted to provide a good education to Randolph and his brother and sent them to Cookman Institute. Randolph was an excellent student and was the valedictorian of his class. After high school, he experienced employment discrimination and segregation firsthand, in that he could find only low-paying manual labor jobs. During this time, he gained his first experience in organizing African American workers to protest against their situation.

Part of the first wave of the Great Migration from the Deep South to northern cities in search for better economic opportunities, Randolph moved to New York

Leader of the Sleeping Car Porters Union, A. Philip Randolph was a civil rights leader who advocated for civil rights and racial justice in the mid-20th century. (Library of Congress)

City and settled down in Harlem with plans to become an actor. Working again in menial jobs during the day, he took classes at the City College of New York and New York University at night. He soon realized that the employment opportunities and conditions of African Americans in the North were not as different from the Deep South as he had hoped. After his parents forbade him from pursuing an acting career, he switched majors from drama to politics and economics, but he never graduated.

In 1914, he married Lucille Green, a widow six years his senior, who operated a beauty shop and was able to finance them both. Through his wife, Randolph met Chandler Owen, a Columbia University student, who shared his ideas and socialist convictions. They both joined the American Socialist Party and dispersed their ideas as soapbox orators in Harlem. Both men considered socialism the remedy for the social and political problems of the United States and the route to promote social justice and political equality for African Americans. As the majority of African Americans were part of the national labor force, Randolph believed organizing and mobilizing African American workers in labor movements was the way to eventually achieve civil rights. He fused labor rights with civil rights. Although never opposing racial integration, Randolph oscillated between all-black activism and interracial cooperation. Randolph was convinced that change had to come from within the African American community. Randolph believed that only the pressure of African American mass movement and nonviolent civil disobedience could change politics and public opinion and improve the position of African Americans.

In November 1917, Randolph and Owen began publishing the *Messenger*, a socialist monthly magazine that gained an excellent reputation in the African American community. The *Messenger* advocated socialism and unionism among African Americans. Through the magazine, Randolph opposed World War I and African American participation in the war and protested racism and racial violence in the United States. Randolph rejected racial separatism and became one of Black Nationalist Marcus Garvey's most fervent opponents. For Randolph, racial pride and racial integration were compatible. With the help of African American socialist journalist George Schuyler, the two managed to continue publishing the financially variable magazine.

Between 1917 and 1923, Randolph and Owen independently founded numerous labor unions to include African Americans in the labor movement. Randolph continuously fought unions and the American Federation of Labor (AFL) and the Congress of Industrial Organizations (CIO) for their racism and exclusion of African American workers. Although Randolph was initially a staunch advocate of socialism, he was to remain a fervent anticommunist throughout his life.

In 1925, knowing Randolph's support of African American workers' rights, the Pullman porters, an all-black service staff of the Pullman sleeping cars, asked him to help them found and lead a trade union to fight for their rights. Underpaid and exploited, they wanted better employment and working conditions. Randolph met with the porters, and on August 25, 1925, they founded the Brotherhood of Sleeping Car Porters (BSCP). For the next 10 years, under Randolph's leadership and using the *Messenger* and later his magazine *Black Worker* as a medium, the union struggled to reach their goals. The Pullman Company defamed Randolph and continuously refused to negotiate with the union. In 1935, the union finally forced the company to negotiate. After two years of bargaining, the company agreed to a contract that included wage increases and work-hour reduction. With the signing of the contract, the BSCP became the officially accepted representative of the Pullman porters. It was the first victory of an all-black union over an American company. Randolph remained the president of the BSCP until 1968. In 1978, the union dissolved, and its remaining members merged with the Brotherhood of Railway and Airline Clerks.

Through his efforts for economic improvement combined with civil rights, Randolph gained a respected status in the African American community. In 1936, during his struggle for the BSCP, Randolph became president of the newly founded National Negro Congress (NNC). The NNC was a loose association of African American groups and white supporters. It was especially committed to the labor movement and cooperated closely with trade unions to create an African American mass movement. Randolph left the NNC when he thought it to be increasingly influenced by communists and white labor movements.

With the rising number of job opportunities in the defense industry in the late 1930s and early 1940s as a result of World War II, the second wave of the Great Migration took place. However, African Americans encountered racial discrimination when searching for work in the defense industry. Despite serious efforts and pleas, President Franklin D. Roosevelt did not help improve the situation of African Americans who became increasingly frustrated and angry. Basing his activism on this anger, Randolph called for a march of 100,000 African Americans on Washington to protest discrimination in the defense industry and the armed forces. He launched the March on Washington Movement (MOWM), demanding an executive order to abolish discrimination in the defense industry and the military.

With his plan for mass mobilization, Randolph became the advocate of a new approach in the civil rights movement. The date for the all-black march was set for July 1, 1941. Initially hesitant to submit to the pressure, Roosevelt gave in due to the mere threat of a protest march of tens of thousands of African American in Washington. On June 25, 1941, President Roosevelt issued Executive Order 8802 that forbade government contractors to practice employment discrimination based on race, creed, color, or national origin and included the creation of a Fair Employment Practices Committee (FEPC) to enforce the order. Randolph canceled the march. After the political success of the planned march, he continued the MOWM. The all-black mass movement that stood for nonviolent civil disobedience acted locally and organized rallies against discrimination.

After the war, Randolph turned his attention to an issue that he had failed to attain with his March on Washington in 1941—the integration of the armed forces. In 1947, the Congress and the American public discussed a Selective Service Act and Universal Military Training without considering the abolishment of segregation. To fight military segregation, Randolph and U.S. Army chaplain Grant Reynolds founded the Committee against Jim Crow in the Military Service and later the League of Nonviolent Civil Disobedience against Military Service.

Initially, the committee used traditional means of communication and publishing, but soon it stepped up pressure by threatening that African Americans would no longer bear arms for the United States if the armed forces did not integrate and ban discrimination. It urged black youth to resist induction and military service. In a meeting with President Harry S. Truman and a speech before the Senate Armed Service Committee, Randolph laid out his position and could not be dissuaded from his militant plans to launch a mass movement boycotting the military. Needing the African American vote in the upcoming presidential election and fearing Randolph's civil unrest, President Truman issued Executive Order 9981 on July 26, 1948. It ordered the equal treatment and opportunity for all and the formation of an advisory committee. Randolph called off the civil disobedience campaign in August 1948.

After the end of the League of Nonviolent Civil Disobedience against Military Service in 1948 and of the Committee against Jim Crow in the Military Service with the beginning of the Korean War, Randolph worked again more powerfully for an end to labor discrimination and trade union segregation. In 1955, he was elected vice president of the newly merged AFL-CIO's Executive Council. To pressure trade unions and the AFL-CIO to improve the position of African Americans in unions, Randolph founded the Negro American Labor Council (NALC), over which he presided from 1960 to 1966.

Randolph cooperated more closely with the National Association for the Advancement of Colored People (NAACP) and other civil rights groups and gave up his idea of establishing his own civil rights movement. With his trade union activism, he also organized protest marches for the integration of schools. He continued to organize marches, pressuring the administration for change. In cooperation with the NAACP and Martin Luther King Jr., for example, he organized the Prayer Pilgrimage on May 17, 1957, where about 50,000 people protested and prayed for freedom in front of the Lincoln Memorial.

In March 1962, Randolph conceived a plan for a new march on Washington protesting slow economic progress, especially of black youth. Randolph worked with King, and his planned Jobs Rights March and Mobilization became the March on Washington for Jobs and Freedom. The movement was an interracial project that, in contrast to Randolph's initial plans, was a protest for new civil rights acts rather than only economic improvement. Randolph became the director of the march and cooperated closely with Bayard Rustin, whom he considered the best organizer and logistician. On August 28, 1963, a march on Washington conceived by Randolph finally materialized. Though broadened in its aims and modernized, it was based on his earlier MOWM and the fulfillment of his long-held goals. After the 1963 March on Washington, African American protest movements radicalized and often rebutted nonviolent civil disobedience. Randolph rejected these developments and stood for more traditional and less militant methods of activism. The new movements often criticized him for his opinion.

In 1964, Randolph received the Presidential Medal of Freedom from President Lyndon B. Johnson. In 1968, he retired as the president of the BSCP and became president of the A. Philip Randolph Institute, a national organization of African American trade unionists, founded by Randolph and Bayard Rustin in 1965. Supported by the AFL-CIO, the institute pledged to bridge the gap between the African American community and the trade unions. In May 16, 1979, Randolph died at the age of 90.

Christine Knauer

Further Reading

Anderson, Jervis. *A. Philip Randolph: A Biographical Portrait*. New York: Harcourt Brace Jovanovich, 1973.

Barber, Lucy G. *Marching on Washington: The Forging of an American Political Tradition*. Berkeley: University of California Press, 2002.

Bates, Beth Tompkins. *Pullman Porters and the Rise of Protest Politics in Black America, 1925–1945*. Chapel Hill: University of North Carolina Press, 2001.

Davis, Daniel S. *Mr. Black Labor: The Story of A. Philip Randolph, Father of the Civil Rights Movement*. New York: E. P. Dutton, 1972.

Garfinkel, Herbert. *When Negroes March: The March on Washington Movement in the Organizational Politics for FEPC*. Glencoe, IL: Free Press, 1959.

Harris, William H. *Keeping the Faith: A. Philip Randolph, Milton P. Webster, and the Brotherhood of Sleeping Car Porters 1925–37*. Urbana: University of Illinois Press, 1977.

Pfeffer, Paula F. *A Philip Randolph, Pioneer of the Civil Rights Movement*. Baton Rouge: Louisiana State University Press, 1990.

Wright, Sarah E. *A. Philip Randolph. Integration in the Workplace*. Englewood Cliffs, NJ: Silver Burdett Press, 1990.

Ray, James Earl

James Earl Ray (1928–1998) was a career criminal who confessed to the slaying of Dr. Martin Luther King Jr. in Memphis, Tennessee, on April 4, 1968. Despite his admission of guilt in open court the next year, Ray's ambiguous statements before, during, and after his trial raised serious questions about what had motivated him and whether or not he had acted alone. The entire truth about the assassination may never be known.

Born in Alton, Illinois, on March 10, 1928, Ray was the oldest of the nine children of George (Speedy) and Lucille Maher Ray. Raised in extreme poverty in the country town of Ewing, Missouri, Ray dropped out of school and left home at the age of 16. After enlisting in the U.S. Army just before his 18th birthday, he served in Germany for almost three years until December 1948, when he was given a general discharge for ineptness and lack of adaptability for military service.

Within a year of his dismissal from the army, Ray began a life of crime and punishment. He committed a number of armed robberies, and from October 1949 until his escape from the Missouri State Penitentiary in April 1967, Ray spent more than 14 years behind bars. While a fugitive, he traveled extensively using money most likely accumulated from dealing contraband in prison. After visiting New Orleans in December 1967, he apparently began to stalk King for the purpose of killing him. Ray's racism had been obvious to many people who came in contact with him, and his intolerance of African Americans had festered for years.

Ray purchased a high-powered rifle, scope, and ammunition in Alabama at the end of March and drove to Memphis a few days later. He checked into a rooming house across the street from the Lorraine Motel where King and other members of the Southern Christian Leadership Conference were staying. They had come to support black sanitation workers in their strike against the city and planned to lead a march downtown on the following day. As the group prepared to leave the motel for dinner at about 6:00 p.m., a single gunshot rang out, fatally wounding King.

Ray left the scene immediately, narrowly avoiding a police dragnet. Investigators recovered a rifle with Ray's fingerprints on it almost immediately. The assassin drove to Atlanta, got on a northbound bus, and slipped across the border to Canada less than 40 hours after the murder. Two months later, immigration officers at Heathrow Airport in London apprehended Ray when he attempted to board a plane for Brussels. The British government quickly extradited him to the United States.

After Ray fired his first lawyer, Judge Preston Battle reset the legal proceedings for April 7, 1969. Instead of standing trial, Ray took his attorney's advice and pled guilty to murder in exchange for a 99-year sentence. Within days, he changed his mind, dismissed his counsel, and petitioned the judge for a reversal of his sentence. From that time until his death from liver disease in 1998, Ray proclaimed his innocence and insisted that an elaborate conspiracy lay behind the assassination of King. Despite his constant agitation, the state of Tennessee never granted him a new trial.

Michael Thomas Gavin

Further Reading

McMillan, George. *The Making of an Assassin: The Life of James Earl Ray.* Boston: Little, Brown, 1976.

Posner, Gerald. *Killing the Dream: James Earl Ray and the Assassination of Martin Luther King, Jr.* New York: Random House, 1998.

Seigenthaler, John. *A Search for Justice.* Nashville, TN: Aurora Publishers, 1971.

Reeb, James

James Reeb, a white Unitarian minister, became nationally known as a martyr to the civil rights cause when he died on March 11, 1965, in Selma, Alabama, after being attacked by a group of white supremacists. Reeb had traveled to Selma to answer Dr. Martin Luther King Jr.'s call for clergy to support the nonviolent protest movement for voting rights there. Delivering Reeb's eulogy, King called him "a shining example of manhood at its best."

Reeb was born on New Year's Day 1927, in Wichita, Kansas. He was raised in Kansas and Casper, Wyoming. After a tour of duty in the U.S. Army at the end of World War II, Reeb became a minister, graduating first from a Lutheran college in Minnesota and then from Princeton Theological Seminary in June 1953. Although ordained a Presbyterian minister, Reeb transferred to the Unitarian Church and became assistant minister at All Souls Church in Washington, D.C., in the summer of 1959. In September 1963, Reeb moved to Boston to work for the American Friends Service Committee. He bought a home in a slum neighborhood and enrolled his children in the local public schools, where many of the children were black.

On March 7, 1965, Reeb and his wife watched television news coverage of police attacking demonstrators in Selma as they attempted to march across the Edmund Pettus Bridge on what became known as "Bloody Sunday." The following day, King sent out a call to clergy around the country to join him in Selma in a second attempt at a Selma to Montgomery March that Tuesday, March 9. Reeb heard about King's request from the regional office of the Unitarian Universalist Association on the morning of March 8, and was on a plane heading south that evening.

As Reeb was flying toward Selma, King was considering whether to disobey a pending court order against the Tuesday march to Montgomery. In the end, he decided to march, telling the hundreds of clergy who had gathered at Brown's Chapel, "I would rather die on the highways of Alabama, than make a butchery of my conscience." King led the group of marchers to the far side of the bridge, then stopped and asked them to kneel and pray. After prayers, they rose and retreated back across the bridge to Brown's Chapel, avoiding a violent confrontation with state troopers and skirting the issue of whether or not to obey the court order.

Several clergy decided to return home after this symbolic demonstration. Reeb, however, decided to stay in Selma until court permission could be obtained for a full-scale march, planned for the coming Thursday. That evening, Reeb and two other white Unitarians dined at an integrated restaurant. Afterward, they were attacked by several white men, and Reeb was clubbed on the head. Several hours elapsed before Reeb was admitted to a Birmingham hospital, where doctors performed brain surgery. While Reeb was on his way to the hospital in Birmingham, King addressed a press conference lamenting the "cowardly" attack and asking all to pray for his protection. Reeb died two days later.

Reeb's death provoked mourning throughout the country, and tens of thousands held vigils in his honor. President Lyndon B. Johnson called Reeb's widow and father to express his condolences, and on March 15, he invoked Reeb's memory when he delivered a draft of the Voting Rights Act to Congress. That same day, King eulogized Reeb at a ceremony at Brown's Chapel in Selma. "James Reeb," King told the audience, "symbolizes the forces of good will in our nation. He demonstrated the conscience of the nation. He was an attorney for the defense of the innocent in the court of world opinion. He was a witness to the truth that men of different races and classes might live, eat, and work together as brothers."

In April 1965, three white men were indicted for Reeb's murder; they were acquitted that December. The Voting Rights Act was passed on August 6, 1965.

Clayborne Carson

Further Reading

Johnson, Lyndon B. "Special Message to Congress: The American Promise, March 15, 1965." In *Public Papers of the Presidents: Lyndon B. Johnson, 1965*, bk. 1. Washington, DC: GPO, 1966.

King, Martin Luther, Jr. "Eulogy for James Reeb." CBC, March 15, 1965.

Revolutionary Action Movement

The Revolutionary Action Movement (RAM), founded in 1962, was one of the first revolutionary Black Nationalist formations of the 1960s created in response to the oppression of people of African descent living in the United States. Although there were many perspectives on how to attain liberation from oppression, there were two major ideological camps involved in the Black Power movement. There were those who advocated for integration and demanded that the U.S. government live up to the promises of citizenship and equality and those who believed chances were slim that America would recognize black citizens as equal and therefore advocated for black separatism. RAM's ideology favored the latter and consisted of ideals around black people constituting a separate nation within the United States, although not all of their members agreed with this. Their ideals of black separatism influenced many of the other Black Power groups in the 1960s.

This organization existed primarily underground, resulting in details about its being more limited than other black revolutionary nationalist groups. Those included in the ranks of this group were college students, working-class members, and some intellectuals who identified themselves as New Afrikan nationalists. New Afrikan nationalists adhere to the idea that people of African descent are a distinct nation within the United States and should have sovereignty. Students played a large role in the formation of RAM. During the 1960s, many groups fighting race-based oppression were either started or comprised mainly of students on college campuses throughout the United States, and RAM was no exception.

This organization was composed of individuals commonly defined as black revolutionary nationalists, and they used a motto of "One Purpose, One Aim, One Destiny," with theoretical underpinnings much like that of Marcus Garvey's Universal Negro Improvement Association (UNIA). The organization produced two publications, the bimonthly *Black America* and the weekly *RAM Speaks*. In addition to educating black communities using this literature, this grassroots organization had "street meetings" consisting of informal gatherings targeting urban youth to inform them about the ideals RAM espoused and as a means of recruitment.

Max Stanford, popularly known as Akbar Muhammad Ahmad, the first field chair, proposed a number of objectives for the organization, including giving black people a sense of racial pride, solidarity, dignity, unity, and commitment to the struggle for independence. Another of RAM's objectives was for people of African descent everywhere to be free of colonial and imperialist rule. Also, those of African descent in America should demand sovereign nationhood and reparations and take the U.S. government to the World Court and the United Nations for human rights violations and genocidal treatment of this group. To reach these objectives, members of RAM believed they should engage in guerrilla warfare. Because of their decision to operate underground, members of this group often conducted their work through other established groups such as Malcolm X's Organization of Afro-American Unity (OAAU), the Afro-American Association, the Student Nonviolent Coordinating Committee (SNCC), the Conference of Racial Equality (CORE), the National Association for the Advancement of Colored People (NAACP), the Dodge Revolutionary Union Movement (DRUM), and the League of Revolutionary Black Workers (LRBW) in Detroit. Their primary objective was to make these groups more militant, often resulting in a revolutionary faction within the respective groups. RAM was also successful at organizing black youth into a paramilitary force called the Black Guards in 1967.

RAM's ideals of separatism did not stop with black communities in the United States but encompassed a Pan-African stance, with some members identifying as black internationalists. RAM's internationalist ideals aligned with beliefs that non-European people throughout the world should seek to free themselves from imperialist domination through revolution.

The organization's existence was relatively short, ending in 1968 as a result of the Federal Bureau of Investigation (FBI) counterinsurgency program COINTELPRO, as well as internal issues. RAM, among other Black Nationalist groups, was identified and targeted as a threat to the United States by then FBI director J. Edgar Hoover and consequently came under attack. Although the individuals who made up the various Black Nationalist groups were under constant assault and scrutiny, as one group disbanded, another was in its formative stages. For instance, former RAM members created the Black Liberation Party, the Black Panther Party for Self-Defense, and the Provisional Government of the Republic of New Afrika.

Efua S. Akoma

Further Reading

Kelley, Robin. "Stormy Weather: Reconstructing Black (Inter)Nationalism in the Cold War Era." In *Is It Nation Time? Contemporary Essays on Black Power and Black Nationalism*, edited by Eddie S. Glaude Jr., 67–90. Chicago: University of Chicago Press, 2002.

Robinson, Dean. *Black Nationalism in American Politics and Thought*. Cambridge: Cambridge University Press, 2001.

Umoja, Akinyele O. "Repression Breeds Resistance: The Black Liberation Army and the Radical Legacy of the Black Panther Party." *New Political Science* 21, no. 2 (1999): 131–55.

Van Deburg, William, ed. *Modern Black Nationalism: From Marcus Garvey to Louis Farrakhan*. New York: New York University Press, 1997.

Richardson, Gloria

An outspoken grassroots leader who counseled direct action and socioeconomic improvement over civil rights, Gloria Richardson led the fight to integrate the town of Cambridge, Maryland, in 1963. Richardson was born to an elite family in Baltimore, Maryland, on May 6, 1922. She was the only child of John and Madel (St. Clair) Hayes. When Richardson was six, the family moved to Cambridge, Maryland. Following graduation from Frederick Douglass High School, Richardson attended Howard University. Scholars like E. Franklin Frazier and Rayford Logan inspired her to understand the dynamics of social interaction before her graduation in 1942.

Although African Americans had voted in Cambridge since 1869, the rest of their lives were deeply segregated. Richardson recalled, "I experienced the same kinds of things that all other blacks did in Cambridge. My father died because he could not go to the hospital ... I was not able to get a job of any kind since I didn't want to teach. I could not go into the restaurants if I wanted to." Gerrymandering effectively nullified the ability of African Americans to elect African

American leaders. As a result, black unemployment hovered near 50 percent, and affordable housing remained difficult to find.

When Richardson became cochair of the Cambridge Nonviolent Action Committee (CNAC) in June 1962, she was the most outspoken and visible African American leader in the city. Although she came from a rich family, she quickly recognized the problems faced by poor and middle-class blacks. The CNAC issued 15 demands to the local white government to improve health care, housing, and employment for African Americans. Richardson's criticism of black treatment in Maryland went beyond mere violations of civil rights; she broadened her critique to include economic issues as well.

Richardson made her concerns public in early 1963. The CNAC met with the Cambridge City Council to demand integration and socioeconomic equality. Dissatisfied by the slow pace of change, Richardson and 80 others were arrested in late March for picketing and sit-ins at city hall, the county courthouse, and the jail. A mass trial ensued (dubbed the "Penny Trials"), after which each defendant was fined a penny and given a suspended sentence. Although more demonstrations followed, peace was established in mid-May by authorities who agreed to listen to the CNAC's demands.

Following the arrest of 12 minors for disturbing the peace during a picket of the Board of Education office, the open dialogue between the CNAC and local white leaders ended. The picketing escalated, matched by an increase in economic boycotts by African Americans. Richardson contacted Attorney General Robert F. Kennedy on May 31, 1963, and asked him to investigate violations of the constitutional rights of African Americans in Cambridge. After two juveniles were sentenced to open-ended terms in a Maryland correction school on June 10, violence erupted, fires blazed, and incendiary bombs were discovered throughout the city.

State authorities responded immediately. Meeting with Richardson and other African American leaders in Annapolis, Governor J. Millard Tawes informed them he was declaring martial law and sending the National Guard into Cambridge. On June 15, 500 troops and 235 state troopers patrolled the city. The National Guard left on July 8, but violence erupted once again, forcing the troops to return on July 11. Meanwhile, Richardson met with Maceo Hubbard, a civil rights lawyer sent by the Justice Department to stem the violence. The violence ended finally after a moratorium was declared to allow a biracial commission to investigate conditions.

Richardson's determination made a deep impression on leaders in Washington, D.C. At the request of Assistant Attorney General Burke Marshall, a conference was held in Washington that included Kennedy and Robert Weaver, head of the Housing and Home Finance Agency. On June 23, 1963, African Americans and Cambridge city officials signed the five-point Treaty of Cambridge. The agreement called for the immediate desegregation of schools, integrated busing and hospitals, the construction of 200 low-rent houses for African Americans, and increased employment for African Americans in the postal service and police department.

The fight for racial justice in Cambridge was unique compared to previous civil rights protests. The Cambridge movement was the first grassroots effort outside of the Deep South; the first campaign to address economic conditions in addition to civil rights; the first time that nonviolence was questioned as a strategy; the first occasion that President John F. Kennedy's administration intervened in a strong way; and the first civil rights fight led by a woman, the unstoppable Richardson.

During the Cambridge agitation, Richardson affiliated more with the rising leaders of black militancy, such as Malcolm X, Stokely Carmichael, and John Lewis, rather than such traditional nonviolent church leaders as Martin Luther King Jr., who at one point criticized her for the violence in Cambridge. Her belief in direct action and continual agitation despite promises of political reform from white and black leaders further alienated her from the National Association for the Advancement of Colored People and President Kennedy's administration, which counseled a gradualist approach to improving race relations.

Following her work in Cambridge, Richardson moved to New York and married her second husband, Frank Dandridge. She had a daughter, Donna, by a previous marriage.

ABC-CLIO

Further Reading

Bradley, David, and Shelley Fisher Fishkin, eds. *The Encyclopedia of Civil Rights in America.* Vol. 3. Ann Arbor: University of Michigan Press, 1998.

Cashman, Sean Dennis. *African-Americans and the Quest for Civil Rights, 1900–1990.* New York: New York University Press, 1991.

Robeson, Paul

Paul LeRoy Bustill Robeson (1898–1976), a truly multitalented genius, was a singer, actor, linguist, amateur and professional athlete, and ardent advocate of African American civil rights and anti-imperialism. He was born on April 9, 1898, in Princeton, New Jersey, to Reverend William Drew Robeson and Maria Louisa Bustill Robeson. In 1860, Paul's father—likely a descendant of Igbo-speaking people from the Niger River delta—had escaped from a North Carolina plantation at age 15, graduated from Lincoln University in Pennsylvania, and eventually became a pastor of Witherspoon Street Presbyterian Church. Robeson's mother was a schoolteacher who came from an abolitionist Quaker family. Although his mother died in a fire by the time Robeson turned six, both his parents instilled in him the importance of education and sharpening his considerable mental abilities.

During his senior year at Somerville High School, Robeson won a statewide scholarship competition and entered Rutgers College in 1915. He was only the

Paul Robeson, world famous stage and film performer, leads workers in singing the "Star-Spangled Banner" at the Moore Shipyard in Oakland, California in September 1942. Robeson entertained Allied forces during World War II. (National Archives)

third African American to be admitted to Rutgers and was the only student of color on campus during his four years there. During freshmen tryouts for the Rutgers football team, Robeson was savagely beaten by several white players, leaving him with a broken nose and a dislocated shoulder. After recovering from his injuries, Robeson made a second attempt at tryouts in which a future teammate stepped on his hand with a cleated foot, ripping away several of Robeson's fingernails. After Robeson literally lifted the player over his head, in an attempt to injure him, the coaches of the football team informed him that he had made the varsity squad. An imposing 6'2", 210-pound player at defensive end, Robeson's athletic prowess was certainly a factor in Rutgers's average margin of victory of 41 points during the 1915 season. His freshman campaign was followed by two consecutive seasons as a first-team football All-American. In addition to football, Robeson also played varsity basketball and baseball and ran track. In total, he accumulated 15 varsity letters before his graduation.

Robeson's athletic prowess was matched, or surpassed, by his abilities in the classroom. After maintaining a 3.8 GPA during his freshman year, Robeson was one of only three students at Rutgers accepted into Phi Beta Kappa and one of four students selected in 1919 to Cap and Skull, the honors society at Rutgers. That same year, he delivered the valedictory speech, in which he predicted that he would be governor of New Jersey by 1940 and a prominent African

American leader. After graduation, Robeson entered Columbia Law School in 1920 and moved to Harlem. While a full-time law student, he began playing professional football for the Akron Pros and the Milwaukee Badgers in the American Professional Football Association, which later became the National Football League. In addition to his professional football career, Robeson also began performing as a singer and stage actor to pay his way through Columbia.

While maintaining a busy career, Robeson married Eslanda Cardozo Goode, head of the pathology laboratory at Columbia Presbyterian Medical Center and daughter of a prominent mixed-race family in New York, in August 1921. Despite Paul's extramarital affairs, the two stayed married until Eslanda's death in 1965. In 1923, Robeson graduated from Columbia Law School and accepted a job at Stotesbury and Miner in New York City while singing part-time at Harlem's world-famous Cotton Club. His interest in law soon faded after a white secretary refused to dictate from him. Robeson soon quit the firm and became a full-time performer and part-time student at the School of Oriental Languages at the University of London. In 1924, he played two leading roles in *All God's Chillun Got Wings* and Eugene O'Neill's *The Emperor Jones*. By 1925, Robeson's professional singing career reached a new height as he began to sing Negro spirituals at concert halls throughout the United States and Europe.

At the age of 29, Robeson was already considered one of the most famous and recognizable Americans in the world. He was voted into the "All Time All-American College Eleven," the first college football hall of fame, in 1927. His deep bass voice, chiseled face, and imposing physique were iconic hallmarks. In 1928, he sang "Ol' Man River" for the first time while playing Joe in the London production of *Show Boat*. In many ways, this song became his personal signature. Not only is his rendition of "Ol' Man River" considered definitive, but Robeson would consciously change the lyrics over time, rendering the once southern lament into a song of social change and revolution. If "Ol' Man River" was the song that became his signature, then his 1930 role as *Othello* in England held a similar stature. Although no U.S. production company would employ Robeson to play Othello, given his close physical interactions, on stage, with a white Desdemona, he reprised the role in New York in 1943 and toured the United States until 1945. Robeson was a 1945 winner of the NAACP's Spingarn for his role as Othello, and his Broadway run of the play was the longest of any Shakespeare play in history.

In 1933, Robeson starred in the movie version of *The Emperor Jones* and began intensive language training at the School of Oriental Languages. Over the course of several years of formal and self-study, he learned to read and sing in Spanish, Russian, Chinese, Arabic, French, German, Swahili, and several other African languages. In sum, Robeson mastered as many as 20 languages. In the 1930s alone, Robeson starred in four movies, three plays, and sang internationally, all while taking language courses in London.

Although Robeson was one of the most famous Americans in the 1930s and early 1940s, from the late 1940s until his death in 1976, he almost completely disappeared from public view, and specific efforts were made to erase him from history and public record. Robeson was retroactively removed from the 1918 All-American first team. Likewise, Rutgers University systematically removed his name from sports records, a move that was not reversed until 1995. As a result of his political affiliations and public pronouncements, the U.S. government moved to undercut his influence abroad and his ability to earn income at home. Robeson was essentially blacklisted. Prevented from movie and stage roles, singing in concert halls, or appearing on radio or TV, his income went from more than $100,000 per year in the 1930s to less than $6,000 year in the late 1940s and throughout the 1950s.

With his facility for the languages of the world community and his fame as a performer, Robeson used his stage to combat Jim Crow in the United States, fascism and Nazism in Europe, and imperialism in Africa and Asia. Moreover, at the height of the Cold War, McCarthyism, and red baiting in the United States, Robeson embraced communism and the Soviet Union. This culminated in the 1949 Peekskill, New York, riot in which anticommunist (and largely antiblack and anti-Semitic) protesters violently disrupted a Robeson concert in the weeks after a controversial statement he made at the World Peace Conference in Paris about African Americans not wanting war against the Soviets. In 1950, the State Department revoked his passport, and during an appeals hearing in February 1952, the State Department issued a brief citing Robeson's political activity on behalf of the colonial peoples of Africa as a reason why he should be denied the right to travel beyond the borders of the United States.

Investigated by the House Un-American Activities Committee (HUAC) and publicly criticized by Eleanor Roosevelt, Jackie Robinson, Roy Wilkins of the NAACP, and just about every other African American leader with the exception of W. E. B. Du Bois, Robeson was increasingly isolated as a result of his unwavering political stances. In 1958, he published his only book entitled *Here I Stand*, which was a detailed articulation of his political ideology. Later that same year, his passport was restored, and Robeson returned to the international stage as a performer and political activist. His last two decades were fraught with poor health, exhaustion, and rumors of CIA and MI5 surveillance. After retiring from the public eye to live a relatively quiet life in Philadelphia, Robeson died on January 23, 1976. Since 1995, Robeson has been the posthumous recipient of a number of awards and honors in an attempt to rewrite his important legacy back into history and public memory.

Walter C. Rucker

Further Reading

Boyle, Sheila Tully, and Andrew Bunie. *Paul Robeson: The Years of Promise and Achievement*. Amherst: University of Massachusetts Press, 2001.

Brown, Lloyd L. *The Young Paul Robeson: On My Journey Now.* Boulder, CO: Westview Press, 1997.

Foner, Philip Sheldon, ed. *Paul Robeson Speaks: Writings, Speeches, Interviews, 1918–1974.* New York: Brunner/Mazel, 1978.

Ford, Carin T. *Paul Robeson: "I Want to Make Freedom Ring."* Berkeley Heights, NJ: Enslow, 2008.

Robeson, Paul. *Here I Stand.* Boston: Beacon Press, 1988.

Robinson, Jackie

The Negro Leagues showcased some of the greatest players in the history of baseball. Although perhaps not the greatest player in Negro League baseball history, Jackie Robinson (1919–1972) is certainly the most famous. Robinson is well known for breaking the color barrier in white professional baseball. Born January 31, 1919, in Cairo, Georgia, to sharecroppers Millie and Jerry Robinson, Jackie Roosevelt Robinson grew up in Pasadena, California. Of the five Robinson children, Jackie was the youngest. His mother taught him at a young age to combat racism by using his talents. Jackie's means of showcasing his talents became sports.

After a stint at Pasadena Community College, Robinson attended the University of California at Los Angeles (UCLA) in 1939. While there, he excelled in the classroom and in football, track, and baseball. He earned varsity letters in all four sports, the first to do so at UCLA. After college, Robinson played semiprofessional football in Hawaii. He also worked for a few months as an athletic director in the National Youth Administration. He was drafted by the U.S. Army in 1942 to fight in World War II. He was sent to Fort Riley, Kansas, where he became an officer and was part of a segregated unit there.

In 1943 in Fort Hood, Texas, Robinson was involved in a racial incident when a bus driver tried to make him go to the back of a bus. His refusal to give up his seat led to his being charged with conduct unbecoming an officer and willful disobedience. This experience sharpened his sense of racial injustice, so he spoke assertively about the unjust conditions to which African Americans were subjected. With the help of the black press, fellow servicemen, and the NAACP, the court-martial was dropped, and he was later acquitted and honorably discharged in 1944. Thus, his spirit of activism became evident before he embarked on the famous "experiment."

Before the Dodgers came calling, Robinson coached a basketball team in Austin, Texas. By 1945, he had signed to play second base with the famous Kansas City Monarchs in 1945, where he performed admirably on a team of talented veterans like Satchel Paige. In 1946, Branch Rickey signed Robinson to play with the Brooklyn Dodgers. Robinson became the player to end segregation in Major

League Baseball. A primary reason Rickey chose Robinson instead of one of the more talented, established Negro League stars was Robinson's stamina and tolerance, extreme patience, and forbearance.

In 1947, while stoically enduring incredible racial abuse such as name calling and foul play during games from players on both sides, fans, and umpires, Robinson led his team to the National League title, won Major League Rookie of the Year, and finished with a.297 batting average and a league-leading 29 stolen bases. After three years of silence, Robinson began to speak up when pitchers narrowly missed his head, fans shouted epithets, or obscene mail came to his home. He fought the denial of equal service in eating and sleeping quarters, or wherever he faced discrimination. Finally, the curative effects of time and recognition of Robinson's value to the team caused the majority of players to settle into the spirit of cooperation.

Jackie Robinson's performance made the world recognize that black people, and especially Negro League players, could perform exceptionally well. In fact, with Robinson on the roster, the Dodgers won National League pennants in 1947, 1949, 1952, 1953, 1955, and 1956. In 1955, they defeated the New York Yankees in the World Series. Robinson is remembered not just for his enormous talents on the field, but for his inner resolve and human character that allowed him to restrain himself from retaliating against severe racist abuses with so much at stake. Throughout Robinson's career, he was able to persevere and achieve at high levels despite the overt racism in American sports and society. In his later years, Robinson was attacked for being conservative, particularly as a result of his well-publicized criticisms of Paul Robeson and other African American leaders. During the McCarthy era, Robinson was called before the House Un-American Affairs Committee (HUAC) to denounce Robeson as a communist sympathizer. Despite the criticism regarding Robinson's political stances, none can deny the radical statement his integration of Major League Baseball made in 1947.

Thabiti Lewis

Further Reading

Lewis, Thabiti. *Ballers of the New School Race and Sports in America*. Chicago: Third World Press, 2009.

Rampersad, Arnold. *Jackie Robinson: A Biography*. New York: Knopf, 1997.

Robinson, Jo Ann

Jo Ann Gibson Robinson was a crucial figure in the Montgomery Bus Boycott of 1955–1956. She is credited with leading efforts to convince African Americans in Alabama's capital to stop using public transportation in a protest that launched the modern civil rights movement.

Jo Ann Gibson was born on April 17, 1912, near Culloden in rural Georgia, the youngest of 12 children. She went to high school in Macon, graduated from Georgia's Fort Valley State College in 1936, and earned an MA in English from Atlanta University in 1948. She married Wilbur Robinson in 1943. An educator throughout her life, her master's degree from Atlanta University led her to accept a professorship at Alabama State College in 1949. There she joined the Women's Political Council (WPC). After Robinson experienced a humiliating experience on a bus at the hands of a racist driver who objected to her sitting in the fifth row on a nearly empty bus, she decided to convince the other WPC women to focus on segregation in public transportation.

Segregation on the Montgomery City Lines was similar to that in public transportation in most southern cities and towns. The first five rows of seats were reserved for white patrons, and African Americans were required to use the back four rows, which meant that African Americans had to stand beside empty whites-only seats if the rest of the seats were full. In addition, if the first five rows were full and a white rider boarded, and all other seats were occupied, four African American riders would be forced to give up their seats so the white rider could sit, as African Americans were barred from sitting in the same row as a white. These rules resulted in situations such as what Robinson experienced, when she was asked to vacate a seat regardless of the lack of other passengers; and what Rosa Parks experienced, when she refused to give up her seat on a full bus.

For the next six years, the WPC, along with other groups, complained to Montgomery's city commissioners about how badly bus drivers and white riders treated African American bus patrons, and they prepared for a boycott. Contrary to the narrative many learn about the Montgomery movement, it did not spontaneously erupt in the wake of Rosa Parks's arrest. In fact, Robinson wrote a letter to Montgomery's mayor in which she spoke of a potential bus boycott by African Americans, making it clear that they comprised the majority of the bus system's patrons and thus could take away its profits. She wrote this letter shortly after the *Brown v. Board of Education* (1954) decision declared school segregation unconstitutional.

Following Rosa Parks's arrest on December 1, 1955, Robinson and other African American leaders decided that the perfect time had come to execute their one-day boycott plans. Others had been arrested that year as well, but Robinson and others felt that their cases would not be as sympathetic; one of those arrested was a teenage girl who was a few months pregnant. Parks, on the other hand, was well respected, and she was a local officer of the National Association for the Advancement of Colored People (NAACP). Robinson, two fellow faculty members, and two students stayed up all that night copying and bundling notices announcing the boycott, set to begin December 5, the day of Parks's trial. Members of the WPC distributed tens of thousands of flyers the next day, and by the end of that Friday, almost all Montgomery African Americans knew of the plans.

The boycott proved so successful that boycotters decided to continue it. Robinson and others organized the Montgomery Improvement Association (MIA), and Robinson served on its executive board and edited its newsletter, which eventually expanded to four pages. The MIA handled donations, organized car pools and taxis to transport boycotters to work, and served as a liaison between the mass movement and white bus and city officials. Robinson was selected to be a member of this latter delegation.

The MIA delegation's initial proposals included the following: bus drivers should be courteous to African American passengers; African Americans would take seats from the back to the front of the bus and whites from front to back, and once the bus was full, no one would have to give up a seat; and African American drivers should be hired on predominantly African American routes. In a series of meetings, white officials continued to reject these proposals, so the boycott continued. In late January, white officials announced they would no longer meet with the African American contingent to discuss options, and police harassed boycotters; Robinson herself received 17 unjustified traffic tickets. By February, pro-boycott attorneys filed suit against the city, and this suit eventually made its way to the Supreme Court, which struck down segregation. Meanwhile, a grand jury in Montgomery declared the boycott illegal and ordered the arrest of its leaders, including Robinson. On December 20, 1956, however, the marshals served the Supreme Court order on Montgomery's city officials; the next day, African Americans again rode the buses, this time integrated ones.

Several years after the boycott was over, Robinson and other teachers left Alabama State in the wake of investigations by a state committee into those faculty members it suspected of organizing the boycotts. These investigations intensified because of a 1960 sit-in that some of the college's students had organized. Robinson resigned after the spring semester in 1960. She took a position at Grambling College in Louisiana but left the next year, leaving the South to teach high school in Los Angeles until retiring in 1976. Her memoir about her Montgomery years was published in 1987, and the Southern Association for Women Historians gave it a publication award. Robinson died in 1992.

Erin Boade

Further Reading

Branch, Taylor. *Parting the Waters: America in the King Years 1954–63*. New York: Simon & Schuster, 1998.

Crawford, Vicki L., Jacqueline Anne Rouse, and Barbara Woods, eds. *Women in the Civil Rights Movement: Trailblazers and Torchbearers, 1941–1965*. New York: Carlson Publishing, 1990.

Garrow, David J. *Bearing the Cross: Martin Luther King, Jr., and the Southern Christian Leadership Conference*. New York: William Morris, 1986.

Robinson, Jo Ann Gibson. *The Montgomery Bus Boycott and the Women Who Started It.* Knoxville: University of Tennessee Press, 1987.

Robnett, Belinda. *How Long? How Long? African-American Women in the Struggle for Civil Rights.* New York: Oxford University Press, 1997.

Rustin, Bayard

Bayard Rustin was a significant civil rights leader and strategist involved in the Fellowship of Reconciliation (FOR) and the Congress of Racial Equality (CORE). He was a key organizer of the 1963 March on Washington despite his exclusion from the event.

Bayard Rustin was born on March 17, 1912, in West Chester, Pennsylvania, the illegitimate son of Florence Rustin. Florence's parents, Janifer and Julia, raised Bayard in West Chester. After his high school graduation in 1932, Rustin studied at Wilberforce University and Cheyney State University but did not graduate. Rustin went to New York City to live with a relative in 1937. He found temporary employment in New York through the Works Progress Administration (WPA). In 1938, he enrolled at the City College of New York but again did not graduate because he was performing with the folk group Josh White Singers and folk singer Huddie Ledbetter. Furthermore, Rustin had become a youth organizer for the Young Communist League (YCL). In June 1941, however, after the YCL declared that the fight against fascism was more important than fighting racism, Rustin resigned. He had met the socialist labor union leader A. Philip Randolph while with the YCL, and when he left the YCL, Rustin went to work for him.

In the late summer of 1941, Rustin was hired as race relations secretary of FOR, a religious pacifist organization. In 1942, Rustin and others cofounded CORE. While still at FOR, Rustin took an additional job as a CORE field secretary. On a bus trip to Nashville, Tennessee, in 1942, Rustin defied the law by sitting in the "whites-only" section. He was arrested but later released. In 1944, Rustin registered as a conscientious objector but refused to report for a physical examination for assignment to a camp for conscientious objectors. As a result, Rustin served 28 months in a federal penitentiary for draft evasion.

In 1947, Rustin was part of a group of 16 CORE and FOR activists participating in what may be the earliest known "freedom ride" in the South, officially known as the Journey of Reconciliation. The purpose of the journey was to test enforcement of the 1946 U.S. Supreme Court decision *Morgan v. Virginia*, outlawing discrimination in interstate travel. CORE and FOR riders deliberately sat in segregated sections of buses and trains while traveling through the South. In Chapel Hill, North Carolina, Rustin and three others were arrested and charged with violation of the state's segregation laws. Rustin was sentenced to 30 days of hard labor on a chain gang, but he was released because of good behavior after 22 days.

Rustin's work with FOR took on an international dimension in 1951 when he helped organize the Committee to Support South African Resistance, which later became the American Committee on Africa. In 1952, FOR sent Rustin to Africa to meet with two of the leaders of the African independence movement: Kwame Nkrumah of Ghana and Nnamdi Azikiwe of Nigeria. Back in the United States, Rustin was touring to raise money for another African trip when disaster struck. Openly gay, Rustin was arrested on a "moral charge" in Pasadena, California, in 1953 and was sentenced to 60 days in jail. His arrest made national news. In disgrace, Rustin resigned from FOR. He soon found a job with a secular pacifist group, the War Resisters League (WRL). During Rustin's 12 years at WRL, he served as executive director, coeditor of the magazine *Liberation*, and spokesperson for the WRL at international pacifist meetings.

Randolph helped Rustin obtain a leave of absence from WRL to assist Martin Luther King Jr. during the Montgomery Bus Boycott in 1956. King knew of Gandhi's writings but was unclear about how a nonviolent protest should be carried out. Rustin's involvement in the bus boycott ended when other boycott leaders asked him to leave town for fear that publicity about his past would harm the campaign. Yet King continued to call on Rustin. In 1957, he asked Rustin to help organize the Southern Christian Leadership Conference (SCLC)'s Prayer Pilgrimage to the Lincoln Memorial in Washington, D.C. Rustin also organized the National Youth Marches of 1958 and 1959. He was set to organize a SCLC demonstration at the 1960 Democratic Convention until Representative Adam Clayton Powell Jr. (D-NY) threatened to expose him as gay unless he quit the project.

When a March on Washington was proposed in 1963, Rustin and Randolph saw an opportunity to carry out what they dreamed of doing. Because he originated the idea of a march back in 1942, Randolph was selected to be executive director of the march. Randolph, in turn, selected Rustin as his deputy director, and it was Rustin who actually coordinated the planning of the event. Planning was going smoothly until South Carolina senator Strom Thurmond took the floor of the U.S. Senate and denounced Rustin as a communist, a draft dodger, and gay. Although Thurmond's tirade triggered a call by some civil rights leaders for Rustin's resignation, Randolph and King continued to back Rustin as the march's strategist. Rustin's job was anticipating the marchers' needs for housing and transportation, reconciling differences between civil rights and labor groups, lining up speakers and performers, and working with law enforcement officials to ensure a peaceful march. More than 200,000 whites and blacks attended the historic event on August 28, 1963. At the end of the day, the major civil rights leaders met with President John F. Kennedy at the White House. But Rustin was not among them because the other leaders said his presence would embarrass them. Nevertheless,

Rustin's accomplishment as strategist of the 1963 March on Washington was the high point of his life.

Rustin and Randolph believed that the 1963 march owed its success to an alliance between organized labor and civil rights groups. Therefore, Rustin and Randolph cofounded the A. Philip Randolph Institute, an organization funded by the American Federation of Labor and the Congress of Industrial Organizations (AFL-CIO). Rustin was president of the institute from 1966 to 1979 and cochair from 1979 until his death. When he began working at the Randolph Institute, Rustin resigned from his job at the WRL and left the pacifist group the Committee for Nonviolent Action.

With no time available for the peace movement, Rustin refused to participate in antiwar demonstrations during the 1960s and 1970s. After the 1940s, Rustin wrote many essays, speeches, and editorials that were published in newspapers and magazines. In 1971, Rustin published a number of these writings in a book entitled *Down the Line*. A second book followed in 1976: *Strategies for Freedom: The Changing Patterns of Black Protest*.

During the final decades of his life, Rustin worked with the A. Philip Randolph Institute as well as two international organizations. He was active in the International Rescue Committee (IRC), a group devoted to dealing with refugee problems around the world. With IRC, Rustin traveled to places like Southeast Asia espousing refugee relief. Rustin was in Haiti assisting in setting up democratic elections in 1987 when he suddenly became ill and was rushed back to the United States. He died in New York City on August 24, 1987.

Eric Ledell Smith

Further Reading

Anderson, Jervis. *Bayard Rustin: Troubles I've Seen—A Biography*. New York: Harper-Collins, 1997.

Carbide, Devon W., and Donald Weise, eds. *Time on Two Crosses: The Collected Writings of Bayard Rustin*. San Francisco: Cleis Press, 2003.

D'Emilio, John. *Lost Prophet: The Life and Times of Bayard Rustin*. New York: Free Press, 2003.

Haughton, Buzz. "Bayard Rustin: An Annotated Bio-Bibliography." *Afro-Americans in New York Life and History* 24, no. 2 (2000): 7–56.

Levin, Daniel. *Bayard Rustin and the Civil Rights Movement*. New Brunswick, NJ: Rutgers University Press, 2000.

S

Seale, Bobby

Bobby Seale is a prominent civil rights advocate and cofounder of the Black Panther Party. Seale and the Black Panthers advocated a militant approach to civil rights. The organization in general and Seale in particular strongly opposed the nonviolent and integrationist stances of Martin Luther King Jr. and other moderate civil rights leaders. Seale and the Panthers, furthermore, advocated militancy when necessary in order to acquire black liberation.

Robert George Seale was born on October 22, 1936, in Dallas, Texas. Bobby and his family resided in Texas until World War II, and then moved to Oakland, California. Seale attended Berkeley High School until his senior year. Right before graduation, Seale was informed that he would not graduate owing to poor grades in the last term. In anger, he tried to enter both the army and the air force. Seale was turned down by both organizations because of an injury he received years earlier when a car ran over his foot. Angered by his failure, Seale returned to the air force recruitment center and tried to plead his case. After convincing doctors and recruiters that his foot injury would not inhibit his ability to perform, the air force inducted him into their program. After completing basic training, Seale went to Amarillo, Texas, to train as an aircraft sheet metal mechanic. After six months in Texas, Seale chose to go to Rapid City, South Dakota. Seale's specialties were needed at the Ellsworth Air Force Base in Rapid City. After almost four years in the air force, Seale was discharged for disorderly conduct.

Seale's discharge came after a battle between him and his commander. When the commander ordered Seale to hand in his drums, Seale refused, and was discharged. Seale's discharge was only one example of many when his temper and rage overcame him—characteristics that became attached to his reputation over the course of his lifetime. While in the air force, he had even beaten a fellow troop member with a bed-adaptor.

After his discharge, Seale returned to Oakland to work as a sheet metal mechanic at various plants. He simultaneously worked to earn his high school diploma while attending night school. He finally received his diploma and, in 1962, began school at Merritt College, the city college of Oakland. At Merritt, Seale took classes in engineering and drafting. To make money on the side, he was a bartender and stand-up comedian. While attending Merritt, Seale joined the Afro-American Association. Through this organization, Seale met Huey Newton. Within a few years, Newton and Seale became frustrated with the

Afro-American Association. To Newton and Seale, the association was not going far enough. Both men believed strongly in Malcolm X and the Black Power philosophy that he professed. In place of the Afro-American Association, Newton and Seale created the Soul Students Advisory Counsel.

Around this time, Seale married, and on July 9, 1965, he and his wife Artie had a son, Malik Nkrumah Stagolee Seale. While Seale had started a family, he continued his fight for black liberation. In October 1966, Seale and Newton organized the Black Panther Party for Self-Defense (BPP). Fellow classmate and friend Bobby Hutton was enlisted as the first member and became the treasurer of the party. The goal of the BPP was set forth in their famous 10-point program. The program advocated self-defense and militancy to bring black liberation. The Black Panthers, however, did not necessarily advocate separatism. The organization frequently worked with whites, if they too wished to advance the black race. The Panthers also set up a number of community programs, such as their infamous free breakfast program.

Although the BPP started out as an Oakland organization, it quickly gained national attention. The BPP adopted uniforms that contained black berets, black pants, black leather jackets, black shoes, and powder-blue shirts. By 1968, BPP offices were opening up nationwide. The militancy of the Black Panthers quickly gained the attention of the national government. The Black Panthers often carried guns, which furthered concerned and drew the attention of the government. In 1968, J. Edgar Hoover, head of the Federal Bureau of Investigation (FBI), ordered an investigation into the BPP.

Seale and many other Black Panthers gained additional national attention after protesting at the Democratic National Convention in Chicago in 1968. Seale's involvement in Chicago, however, landed him in significant trouble with the government. In September 1969, Seale and seven white radicals were indicted under the antiriot provision of the Civil Rights Act of 1968. The provision forbids anyone from crossing state lines to riot.

When Seale came to trial, the judge in the case declared him bound and gagged after numerous outbursts in court. Seale consequently was sentenced to four years in jail for contempt of court. While in jail, Seale was charged for ordering the execution of Alex Rackley, a former Black Panther who was suspected of being a government informer. In May 1971, Seale was cleared of all charges when a hung jury could not reach a decision. The following year, Seale was released from prison and the contempt charges were dropped.

When Seale returned to Oakland, he found a decimated Black Panther Party from the one he had left. The violence and militancy that the BPP advocated had left many members dead. Internal strife also had led to a decrease in popularity and membership. In 1973, Seale ran for mayor of Oakland but came in second out of nine candidates. He left the Black Panthers in 1974 but continued to fight against social and political injustices. At the time of this writing, Seale continued to support various organizations that fight injustices in the world. His own organization, REACH, is dedicated to youth education and advancement.

Mindy R. Weidman

Further Reading

Jones, Charles E., ed. *The Black Panther Party Reconsidered*. Baltimore: Black Classic Press, 1998.

Seale, Bobby. *A Lonely Rage: The Autobiography of Bobby Seale*. New York: New York Times Books, 1978.

Seale, Bobby. *Seize the Time: The Story of the Black Panther Party and Huey P. Newton*. Baltimore: Black Classic Press, 1991.

Selma March

The Selma march was a five-day event in 1965 during which an interracial group of protesters traveled more than 50 miles on foot from Selma, Alabama, to the state capital of Montgomery. It culminated in a mass rally on the steps of Alabama's capitol building, where a crowd of 25,000 people, including civil rights activists, religious leaders, and everyday people from across the United States, heard one of Martin Luther King Jr.'s most remembered speeches. The Selma march focused national attention on the exclusion of African Americans from the electoral process and galvanized public sentiment in support of the Voting Rights Act of 1965. The event was one of the last large-scale protest demonstrations of the civil rights movement's "classic" phase during which a series of public protests drew national attention to the impact of racial segregation and helped bring an end to the legal structures of the system of racial discrimination known as Jim Crow.

The march that eventually made it to Montgomery began on Sunday, March 21, 1965, when approximately 3,000 people left Brown Chapel AME Church in Selma, Alabama, and crossed the Edmund Pettus Bridge on the eastern edge of the city. The procession continued along both highways and rural county roads, enduring rain and cold weather, as well as threats of violence, along the way. By court order, only 300 of the marchers were permitted to walk the entire distance from Selma to Montgomery, but as the march made its official entry into Montgomery on Thursday, March 25, its ranks swelled once again.

The march that reached Montgomery actually represented the third attempt to do so. On Sunday, March 7, in an event known as "Bloody Sunday," a group of marchers made its way from Brown Chapel Church as far as the Pettus Bridge only to be set upon by state troopers and other law enforcement officers. With many of them attacking from atop horses, the officers pursued the marchers all the way back to Brown Chapel and continued their assault until no African Americans could be found on Selma's streets. John Lewis of the Student Nonviolent Coordinating Committee (SNCC) was among the most seriously injured, suffering a fractured skull, and numerous others were treated for cuts, broken bones, and exposure to tear gas. In a development that was unusually swift for the time, film footage of the attack aired that same evening on ABC, interrupting the network's broadcast of the film *Judgment at Nuremberg*.

Two days later, Martin Luther King Jr. fronted a second march, but once again it only went as far as the Pettus Bridge. Per an advance agreement designed to comply with a federal court's injunction against proceeding all the way to Montgomery, King did not attempt to lead the group across the bridge. Instead, the group knelt in prayer and returned to Brown Chapel. That evening, attacks by local whites resulted in the death of James Reeb, a white seminary student who had traveled to Selma from Boston to participate. Reeb's death and the violence of Bloody Sunday prompted an address by President Lyndon Johnson before a joint session of Congress in which he called for passage of the Voting Rights Act and invoked the civil rights anthem "We Shall Overcome." Six days after Johnson's speech, the court lifted its injunction, and the third and final march commenced.

The full story of the march, however, stretched back further even than Bloody Sunday. For several years before 1965, a cadre of SNCC fieldworkers had been working with local black leaders and organizations in an effort to challenge racial discrimination in Selma and develop indigenous black leaders. These activists built their efforts around the issue of voter registration and coordinated regular processions of would-be black registrants to Selma's downtown courthouse. Their efforts prompted sustained and often violent reactions from local whites including state, county, and city officials who jealously guarded the political hold they maintained across Alabama's Black Belt.

The ability to count on such stubborn resistance was one of the reasons why, in 1964, Martin Luther King Jr. and the Southern Christian Leadership Conference (SCLC) accepted an invitation to come to Selma and lend King's national recognition to the continuing demonstrations. Although his arrival amplified existing tensions between SNCC and the SCLC, King brought additional resources and exposure to the Selma campaign. Racial tensions increased after King's arrival as Dallas County sheriff Jim Clark met the protesters with violence and mass arrests. Clark jailed at least 4,000 demonstrators between January and March 1965. Events in Selma even prompted a visit from Malcolm X. In February, Jimmie Lee Jackson, a black resident of Marion, Alabama, was murdered during one of the numerous marches taking place simultaneously in the rural areas surrounding Selma. A proposal to carry Jackson's coffin to Alabama's state capital made his death the genesis of what became the Selma march.

In the years and decades that followed the Selma march, the city continued to be the site of civil rights activity as African Americans met resistance in their efforts to translate their newfound voting rights into tangible political power.

Although the persistence of racial tensions revealed the Selma march to have been less than a panacea for many local concerns related to race, its contributions to the national civil rights movement are undeniable.

Robert Warner Widell Jr.

Further Reading

Ashmore, Susan Youngblood. *Carry It On: The War on Poverty and the Civil Rights Movement in Alabama, 1964–1972*. Athens: University of Georgia Press, 2008.

Branch, Taylor. *At Canaan's Edge: America in the King Years, 1965–68*. New York: Simon & Schuster, 2006.

Chestnut, J. L. *Black in Selma: The Uncommon Life of J. L. Chestnut, Jr.* Tuscaloosa: University of Alabama Press, 2007.

Thornton, J. Mills. *Dividing Lines: Municipal Politics and the Struggle for Civil Rights in Montgomery, Birmingham, and Selma*. Tuscaloosa: University of Alabama Press, 2002.

Sharpton, Al

Alfred Charles Sharpton Jr. (b. 1954), a black Pentecostal minister and a civil rights activist known for his inflammatory speeches on racial injustice, led a series of protest marches and sit-ins during the 1970s and 1980s in New York City. This controversial public figure represented the extreme wing of black activism.

Sharpton was born in a middle-class neighborhood in Brooklyn, New York, until a domestic tragedy forced his move to a housing project in the Brownsville area of the borough. This firsthand experience of the living conditions in this poor neighborhood, along with his profound admiration of the developing new black conscious and protests in the decades after World War II, directed Sharpton to the civil rights movement. Dropping out of Brooklyn College, New York, he became the first youth director of Operation Breadbasket, an organization that boycotted and picketed corporations and supermarkets that conducted unfair business. In his biggest confrontation with the grocery chain store A&P, he was arrested along with Reverend Jesse Jackson.

In 1971, Sharpton became the youngest director of National Youth Movement (NYM), which aimed at combating police brutality and fighting drug abuse. Associating with James Brown, an American music legend, Sharpton organized Hit Brown, a black concert promotion strategy, and made concerted efforts to change the racial composition of the music business. But his endeavor in this direction did not bear fruit because he was suspected of having links with organized crime. This jeopardized his image and that of his movement in the community.

Sharpton protested against the New York City administration on several occasions. During the 1970 sit-in at New York city hall, he demanded more summer jobs for blacks and for fair hiring and proper treatment of African Americans. A few months later, he led a group of black leaders to the New York deputy mayor's office meeting to protest the death of a 14-year-old black youth. In both instances he was arrested for his role in instigating racial tensions.

During the series of killings in the 1980s, Sharpton was a vibrant voice in his community. He stood in the front line of protest marches and sit-ins. The first instance that ignited racial violence was during the shooting death of four black unarmed teens. Bernard Goetz, a white man, was charged for this crime but was later acquitted of murder charges. Sharpton and a group of his followers held a protest vigil at the steps of the New York City courthouse condemning the all-white grand jury for this decision. He led protest marches and sit-in strikes on transit rail tracks after a white mob assaulted three black men at Howard Beach in Brooklyn, New York.

In this atmosphere of racial polarity, Sharpton organized another strike at the Grand Central Station rail tracks during morning rush hour to protest the hiring policy of the Metropolitan Transit Authority (MTA). His public debate with New York governor George Pataki forced the highest official in the state to appoint the first black MTA board member, Laura Blackburn. This incident was a stepping stone for his rise to prominence in the national media as a civil rights leader.

In 1987, Tawana Brawley, an African American teen from Wappinger's Falls, New York, was found inside a garbage bag with racial epithets and dog feces smeared on her face. A gang of white men did the same to another black woman in Newton, New Jersey. In both these cases, justice was not served. Sharpton held rallies at the steps of the New York City courthouse and brought national media attention to these injustices in the judicial system. Two years later, a white mob killed a 16-year-old African American teen, Yusuf Hawkins, in Bensonhurst, New York. While Sharpton led a march to protest this crime, Michael Riccardi, a 27-year-old white man, stabbed the minister in the chest. After this incident, Sharpton changed his strategy in fighting racial injustice. Even though he adopted a conciliatory approach to race relations and tried to establish ground in the white community, he came under FBI investigation of his past income tax returns.

Sharpton twice attempted to run for the U.S. Senate, garnering only a small percentage of the vote in the election primaries. Despite this failure, he was one of the few African Americans who won a place as a power broker in the New York political scene, who led a campaign during the 2000 election in favor of Albert Gore Jr., the Democratic presidential candidate, and the only African American in the 2004 Democratic presidential primaries.

Sharpton stands as a committed advocate of the rights of the African Americans. He, along with Reverend Jesse Jackson and other civil rights leaders, has continued the fight against racism, urban poverty, and racial violence in the nation.

Sivananda Mantri

Further Reading

Sharpton, Al, and Karen Hunter. *Al on America*. New York: Dafina Books, 2002.

Sharpton, Al, and Anthony Watkins. *Go and Tell Pharaoh: The Autobiography of the Reverend Al Sharpton*. New York: Doubleday Dell Publishing Group, 1996.

Shuttlesworth, Fred

Reverend Fred Shuttlesworth, a minister and human rights activist, was one of the staunchest opponents of racial discrimination and segregation during the civil rights movement of the 1950s and 1960s. Shuttlesworth and the organization he led, the Alabama Christian Movement for Human Rights (ACMHR), were instrumental in desegregating Birmingham, Alabama, one of the most segregated cities in the South and the home of Eugene "Bull" Connor, the notorious segregationist who used violence to maintain racial discrimination. The civil rights demonstrations in Birmingham during the spring of 1963, where police dogs and fire hoses were used to assault peaceful civil rights activists, some of them children, were broadcast on television to the United States and the world, prompting widespread support for desegregation. More important, the violence compelled President John F. Kennedy to enact legislation that would eventually become the Civil Rights Act of 1964, which outlawed segregation in public accommodations. Although Dr. Martin Luther King Jr. and his organization, the Southern Christian Leadership Conference (SCLC), led the protests in conjunction with the ACMHR, King and the SCLC have received most of the credit for the success of the Birmingham demonstrations. Activists and scholars agree, however, that it was the work of Shuttlesworth and the ACMHR that ultimately made the demonstrations successful.

Fred Lee Shuttlesworth was born Freddie Lee Robinson on March 18, 1922, in Mount Meigs, Alabama, to Alberta Robinson and Vetta Green. The unmarried couple also produced a daughter, Cleola. It was from his mother that Shuttlesworth would get his combative personality, earthy spirituality, and indomitable will, traits that would prove invaluable when challenging the authority of Connor and the rigid code of race relations in Birmingham and the South as a whole. In 1925, Robinson and the children moved to Oxmoor, Alabama, where she would later marry William Nathan Shuttlesworth, a farmer and former miner. Both Fred and his sister would take his last name. Seven siblings would follow soon after. Although Shuttlesworth and his family grew up in poverty, they were able to maintain some stability. His childhood would cement identification with poor and working-class folk, and this segment of the African American population proved to be Shuttlesworth's staunchest supporters.

Birmingham was known as a rigidly segregated city that would not hesitate to violently keep African Americans in their "place." In fact, African Americans

Fred L. Shuttlesworth was an early civil rights leader active in the Southern Christian Leadership Conference (SCLC). (Library of Congress)

referred to the city as "Bombingham," and one black community was known as "Dynamite Hill," for the number of bombings that took place there. Any African American who protested against discriminatory treatment could be attacked or even killed. It was while attending high school in Birmingham that Shuttlesworth would come face to face with racial discrimination, growing resentful of the run-down conditions of buses used to transport black children to equally dilapidated schools while white children enjoyed newer facilities and more reliable transportation. He was also subjected to the discriminatory behavior of the Birmingham police force. Shuttlesworth would distinguish himself as a student and athlete at Rosedale High School, graduating as class valedictorian in May 1940. Within a year of graduating, Shuttlesworth would marry Ruby Keeler, a union that produced four children: Patricia, Ruby Fredericka (Ricky), Fred Jr., and Carolyn.

Now with a growing family, Shuttlesworth would gradually embark on a career as a minister, a vocation he began to think about after graduating high school. Moving the family to Mobile, Alabama, to work as a truck driver on an air base, Shuttlesworth would study the Bible. Initially an African Methodist, Shuttlesworth became a Baptist and began occasional preaching at the invitation of Pastor E. A. Palmer of Corinthian Baptist Church. Talented as a preacher, Shuttlesworth would receive invitations to preach before other congregations and would further his theological education at Cedar Grove Academy in Prichard, Alabama.

In September 1947, after completing studies at the academy, Shuttlesworth enrolled at Selma University. The next year, he was ordained as a Baptist minister on August 10, 1948, at Corinthian Baptist Church.

In 1949, the family moved to Montgomery, and Shuttlesworth enrolled at Alabama State College, later serving as pastor of First (African) Baptist Church in Selma in 1950. It was at First Baptist that Shuttlesworth would encounter some of the class conflicts within the black community that would later plague his relationship with some churches in Birmingham. Shuttlesworth's class orientation, folksy preaching style, and blunt, direct manner caused problems with the more middle-class sensibilities of the church congregation, and Shuttlesworth left after two years. The next year, Shuttlesworth accepted the pastorate of Bethel Baptist Church in an African American section of North Birmingham known as Collegeville. It was here that Shuttlesworth and his followers would begin a veritable crusade against the evils of Jim Crow segregation and other forms of racial discrimination in the city known unofficially as the "Johannesburg of the South."

Shuttlesworth began his crusade in earnest after the Supreme Court ruled in favor of the National Association for the Advancement of Colored People (NAACP) in the *Brown v. Board of Education* case in May 1954, which ruled school segregation unconstitutional. Determined to make the ruling a reality, Shuttlesworth joined the local branch of the NAACP. Headed by some members of the African American middle class, the leadership was slow to respond to Shuttlesworth's suggestions and demands, which included petitioning the city for more black police officers and complying with the *Brown* decision. The local leadership and the city both rejected the requests.

In reaction to increasing demands of African Americans to dismantle segregation and extend freedom and democracy to all American citizens in the aftermath of the *Brown* decision, white state authorities in Alabama in 1956 were successful in banning the Alabama NAACP, preventing the organization from operating within the state. Shuttlesworth and members of his congregation then formed the Alabama Christian Movement for Human Rights on June 5, 1956, to carry on the fight, basing the organization on Christian and patriotic principles while calling for desegregation and expanded employment opportunities. Its membership consisted of mostly working-class African Americans, with the majority being black women, and they used direct action protests such as marches and sit-ins to highlight grievances. The ACMHR also believed strongly that God supported their efforts, and their religious fervor spread rapidly to other African Americans. It would soon be the only organization in Birmingham to stand up to Connor and other segregationists.

Shuttlesworth's courage knew no bounds, and his actions suggested that he and his family were willing to make sacrifices to bring about equality. After bus segregation was declared unconstitutional on December 20, 1956, Shuttlesworth announced that African Americans would ride the buses on a nondiscriminatory basis, despite resistance from the city commission to a petition submitted by the ACMHR. On Christmas Day, Shuttlesworth's home next to the church was bombed when dynamite exploded under his bed. Although Bethel Baptist and the home were severely damaged, miraculously, Shuttlesworth received only scratches. Shuttlesworth and his followers took this as a sign that God was protecting him to lead the movement. Shuttlesworth would have other opportunities to put himself in harm's way. Demanding school desegregation, Shuttlesworth attempted to enroll his daughters at all-white Phillips High School; that same day, President Dwight D. Eisenhower signed the Civil Rights Act of 1957. A white mob beat Shuttlesworth severely with chains and baseball bats while his wife was stabbed and children suffered injuries. Again, Shuttlesworth survived. In 1958, the *Birmingham World* named Shuttlesworth "Newsmaker of the Year" for 1957.

Between 1958 and 1961, Connor increased his harassment of Shuttlesworth and the ACMHR as they continued to demand that the city commission hire black police officers and desegregate schools and parks. When black students began a sit-in at segregated stores and restaurants in 1960, Shuttlesworth encouraged them. Shuttlesworth was arrested several times during this period, and Bethel Baptist Church was also bombed for a second time. The activism would extend to Shuttlesworth's children, as Pat, Ricky, and Fred Jr. were arrested in Gadsden, Alabama, for allegedly causing a disturbance on a Greyhound bus on August 16, 1960. Shuttlesworth would experience personal problems, however, as he and Ruby disagreed over money, his civil rights activities, and church responsibilities. Shuttlesworth also experienced problems at Bethel Baptist, causing him to agree to the pastorate of Revelation Baptist Church in Cincinnati, Ohio, in 1961, although he continued to be heavily involved in Birmingham.

Shuttlesworth immersed himself in the civil rights movement in other parts of Alabama and throughout the South. He attended meetings of, and pledged financial support to, the Montgomery Improvement Association, the organization created after Rosa Parks refused to give up her seat on a segregated city bus on December 1, 1955, prompting the Montgomery Bus Boycott that brought King to national prominence. He was a founding member of the Southern Christian Leadership Conference in 1957, a major civil rights organization created for King to support local civil rights struggles throughout the South. And during the Freedom Rides of 1961, Shuttlesworth served as the point person for the Congress of Racial Equality (CORE), taking care of riders who were attacked in Birmingham.

In 1962, SCLC looked for a situation that would garner more national and international support for the civil rights movement. Shuttlesworth continuously urged King and the SCLC board to conduct demonstrations in Birmingham, feeling that if segregation could be broken there, it would cause desegregation in other parts of the South. At the same time, King and the SCLC needed something to push a reluctant federal government to end segregation. They hoped to do that by demonstrating to the public, through marches and sit-ins, how far segregationists would go to continue to deprive African Americans of their citizenship rights.

In spring 1963, King and the SCLC agreed to work with the ACMHR to carry out Project "C" (for confrontation) to advance the local and national movements, demanding total desegregation of schools and public facilities and the removal of obstacles to voter registration while forcing the Kennedy administration to act. Shuttlesworth led mass marches on city hall and helped organize other demonstrations and support. He later suffered injuries from a fire hose while demonstrating downtown. Although Shuttlesworth would disagree with some of King and the SCLC's decisions regarding negotiations with the city, it was he who declared the demonstrations ended in May 1963 when the SCLC and the city reached a limited agreement on gradual desegregation of public facilities and gradual upgrading of black employees. The demonstrations directly resulted in the Civil Rights Act of 1964, outlawing segregation in public accommodations among other provisions.

Shuttlesworth would continue his activism in the succeeding years, remaining involved in the local movement in Birmingham while also demonstrating against unfair conditions in and around Cincinnati. In March 1989, he established the Shuttlesworth Housing Foundation to provide low-cost housing to poor families. He experienced continued strained relationships in his personal life, divorcing his wife Ruby in 1970 after 29 years of marriage and resigning from Revelation Baptist Church in 1966 to form another congregation. Shuttlesworth received several accolades for his activism, the city of Birmingham renaming Huntsville Road in his honor in September 1978 and having a statue of his likeness erected in front of the Birmingham Civil Rights Institute and Museum in November 1992. In 2008, the Birmingham International Airport was renamed Birmingham-Shuttlesworth International Airport in his honor. He retired from the ministry in 2006. Shuttlesworth died on October 5, 2011, at Princeton Baptist Medical Center in Birmingham, at the age of 89.

Tony Gass

Further Reading

Branch, Taylor. *Pillar of Fire: America in the King Years, 1963–65*. New York: Simon & Schuster, 1998.

Eskew, Glenn T. *But for Birmingham: The Local and National Movements in the Civil Rights Struggle*. Chapel Hill: University of North Carolina Press, 1997.

Manis, Andrew. *A Fire You Can't Put Out: The Civil Rights of Birmingham's Reverend Fred Shuttlesworth*. Tuscaloosa: University of Alabama Press, 1999.

White, Marjorie, and Andrew Manis, eds. *Birmingham Revolutionaries: The Reverend Fred Shuttlesworth and the Alabama Christian Movement for Human Rights*. Macon, GA: Mercer University Press, 2000.

Sit-In Movement

The sit-in movement was just one of a number of techniques used by civil rights supporters in their campaign to end racial segregation. They appealed to the courts, the legislature, and sometimes the president of the United States for relief. From time to time, they depended on the actions of the federal government to sweep away discrimination in the military or in education. However, the sit-in movement, which was not mandated by a presidential executive order or driven by a Supreme Court decision, was just as important. It helped sweep away legal and cultural barriers that had blocked African Americans from equal access to food service, and it enabled the civil rights movement to take greater advantage of an untapped resource: young African Americans.

The idea of the sit-in as a way to end food service segregation was not new. It had been tried in Chicago and St. Louis in the 1940s and in Baltimore in 1953. However, little attention was paid to the attempts or the reasons for them. The idea gained new energy in the wake of the Montgomery Bus Boycott in 1955, where African Americans, using nonviolent methods, effectively ended the practice of segregated bus seating in Montgomery, the capital of Alabama. Montgomery's civic leaders expected African Americans to tolerate the humiliation of riding in the back of city buses to and from their downtown shopping trips. If the local economy could be crippled by a bus boycott, and whites required to treat African Americans with respect, could not the same be done by a sit-in?

In 1958, civil rights leaders began sponsoring a series of workshops throughout the South to train people in the ways of nonviolent protest. Many African American college students in and around the Nashville, Tennessee, area attended those workshops. Their ultimate goal was to desegregate the lunch counters in Nashville's department stores. It did not make sense to them that although the stores would sell them clothes and school supplies, they would refuse them service when they wanted something to eat. The students' training was designed to prepare themselves for the day when they would break the color barrier at Nashville's lunch counters.

But four African American students from North Carolina's College of Agriculture and Technology beat them to the punch. On February 1, 1960, Joseph McNeil, Franklin McCain, David Richmond, and Ezell Blair Jr. strolled into the Woolworth's department store in downtown Greensboro. They bought toothpaste and school supplies, and then settled into seats at the lunch counter and ordered coffee. First, they were ignored. Then they were told they would not be served. Finally, the store manager called the police to complain. The police did nothing because the protesters were doing nothing. Four well-dressed young African American college students were sitting quietly at the lunch counter, waiting for service and doing their homework while they waited. Exasperated, the manager closed early.

The four young men left, only to return. This time, however, there were six of them. By the end of the week, more than 300 African American students were seeking service at lunch counters at Woolworth's and at S. H. Kress and Company, another department store in Greensboro. They tried to order food. They were denied service, but remained at the counter, waiting quietly. Joining the sit-in were white students. Newspaper reporters and photographers were also on hand to record the events. When businesses considered the potential impact of the protest on their bottom line, many of them, including Woolworth's, rethought their policies and, by August 1960, desegregated their lunch counters.

However, the lunch counter sit-ins had repercussions that went far beyond Greensboro's city limits. Soon, black and white students were staging sit-ins at restaurants, play-ins at segregated parks, and read-ins at segregated libraries across the United States. A few weeks after the events in Greensboro, students in Nashville began sitting in at lunch counters in their city. There was violence, as white students attacked the demonstrators, and later arrests, as the police moved in to take them to jail. But every time an African American student was removed from a lunch counter, there was another student waiting to take his or her place. The nonviolent protests, and the sometimes violent reaction, continued until May, when Nashville changed its policies and began serving African Americans at department store lunch counters.

The sit-ins also caused the leadership of the civil rights movement to think about how best to capitalize on this infusion of youthful energy. The answer materialized in late 1960, when the Southern Christian Leadership Conference (SCLC) underwrote the creation of the Student Nonviolent Coordinating Committee (SNCC). "Snick," as it was called, was originally composed of black and white university students who would join the civil rights movement armed with energy and enthusiasm, determined to achieve equality wherever inequality might be found. In 1961, veterans of the sit-ins were participating in the Freedom Rides, venturing into the Deep South on commercial buses to test compliance with federal laws guaranteeing equal treatment in interstate bus terminals. Later those same students would be in Mississippi, helping to register voters for the 1964 presidential election. The lunch counter sit-ins energized the civil rights movement by adding youth to the campaign to end inequality and attracting national attention to the cause.

John Morello

Further Reading

Boyer, Paul. *Promises to Keep: The United States since World War II*. 2nd ed. Boston: Houghton Mifflin, 1999.

Garrow, David J. *Atlanta, Georgia, 1960–1961: Sit-Ins and Student Activism*. Brooklyn, NY: Carlson Publications, 1989.

Moss, George Donelson. *America in the Twentieth Century*. Upper Saddle River, NJ: Prentice Hall, 2004.

Oppenheimer, Martin. *The Sit-in Movement of 1960*. Brooklyn, NY: Carlson Publications, 1989.

Torres, Sasha. *Black, White, and in Color: Television and Black Civil Rights*. Princeton, NJ: Princeton University Press, 2003.

Williams, Juan. *Eyes on the Prize: America's Civil Rights Years, 1954–1965*. New York: Viking Press, 1987.

Sixteenth Street Baptist Church

Sixteenth Street Baptist Church in Birmingham, Alabama, is an important historic site of the civil rights movement. The home of Birmingham's first African American congregation, the church became a center of civil rights activity and the location of a tragic racially motivated bombing.

Birmingham's first African American church was established in 1873, less than two years after the city was incorporated. Founded by migrants from rural Alabama who had come to work in the new industrial city's mines and mills,

The Congress of Racial Equality conducts a march in memory of the four African American children killed in the bombing of the Sixteenth Street Baptist Church in Birmingham, Alabama on September 15, 1963. Marchers carry a sign reading "No More Birminghams" in the solemn demonstration held one week later in Washington, D.C. (Library of Congress)

The First Colored Baptist Church of Birmingham met in a tinner's shop. The growing congregation later moved into its own downtown building. In July 1882, the congregation purchased a lot on the corner of Sixth Avenue North and Sixteenth Street, where the church now stands, and took the name Sixteenth Street Baptist Church. By 1887, the congregation constructed an impressive gothic revival building on the site, with several members of the church mortgaging their homes to help complete the project. This building was demolished in 1909 and replaced in 1911 with the present structure, designed by African American architect Wallace A. Rayfield. Largely Romanesque in design, the brick church features a central entrance porch flanked by two towers and stained-glass windows.

By the early twentieth century, Sixteenth Street Baptist Church had grown to more than 1,000 members and was a major church of Birmingham's African American elite and middle class. Many members held professional positions, such as educators, and many were successful businesspeople and community leaders. Located in Birmingham's downtown black business district, and with a seating capacity of 1,600, the church hosted concerts and other cultural events and political meetings.

From the late nineteenth century to the 1960s, the city of Birmingham strictly enforced an extensive system of racial segregation. African Americans and whites were separated by law in many public facilities, including street cars and buses, theaters, hospitals, and restaurants. Separate schools, libraries, and parks were maintained for blacks and whites, and facilities for African Americans were always inferior to those provided for whites. Almost all African Americans in the city were prevented from voting, and before the late 1960s, Birmingham had no black elected officials, police officers, or firefighters.

African Americans protested segregation and racial discrimination through legal actions in the courts, boycotts, sit-ins, and street demonstrations. In the spring of 1963, the Southern Christian Leadership Conference, led by Martin Luther King Jr., worked with the Birmingham-based Alabama Christian Movement for Human Rights (ACMHR), led by Fred L. Shuttlesworth, to organize large-scale demonstrations. Sixteenth Street Baptist Church hosted some of the weekly mass meetings sponsored by ACMHR. Because of its size and central location, Sixteenth Street Baptist Church was used as a site to organize and launch daily demonstrations. These demonstrations generated worldwide publicity, as more than 3,000 demonstrators, including children, were jailed, and Birmingham authorities used police dogs and fire hoses against the demonstrators. Nationwide public reaction to the Birmingham protests encouraged the U.S. Congress to pass the Civil Rights Act of 1964.

Birmingham's public schools were desegregated during the second week of September 1963. Five African American students were placed in formerly all-white schools, and violent protests occurred around the schools. In retaliation for the school desegregation, members of the Ku Klux Klan placed a bomb outside Sixteenth Street Baptist Church sometime during the night of Saturday,

September 14. The bomb exploded the next morning at approximately 10:20 a.m., just as Sunday school classes were ending and before the start of the service. The explosion tore a large hole in the side of the church, blew out windows, and damaged the interior of the building. Four girls, 11-year-old Denise McNair and 14-year-olds Addie Mae Collins, Cynthia Wesley, and Carole Robertson, were killed inside the basement women's restroom; they were crushed by falling debris. Several other members of the congregation were injured.

White supremacists had committed dozens of racially motivated bombings in the Birmingham area since the late 1940s, but the Sixteenth Street Baptist Church bombing was the first in which people were killed. The bombing and the deaths of the four girls were reported worldwide, and the incident generated both sympathy and outrage. Birmingham mayor Albert Boutwell, a segregationist, wept when told of the deaths. The city of Birmingham established a reward fund to encourage witnesses to come forward with information.

Robertson's funeral was held Tuesday, September 17, at St. John African Methodist Episcopal Church, as Sixteenth Street Baptist Church was too badly damaged, and nearly 2,000 people attended. The next day, a mass funeral for the other three girls was held at Sixth Avenue Baptist Church. Martin Luther King Jr. preached the sermon at this service, and a crowd estimated at 7,000 people filled the church and the street outside.

The Birmingham Police Department, the Alabama Department of Public Safety, and dozens of agents from the Federal Bureau of Investigation investigated the bombing. On September 30, the state of Alabama arrested three known Klansmen—Robert Chambliss, John Wesley Hall, and Charles Cagle. But the suspects were charged only with illegal possession of dynamite and were fined.

The church received contributions from throughout the world totaling more than $200,000 to repair the damage done by the bombing. Sixteenth Street Baptist Church reopened in June 1964. In 1965, parishioners installed a large stained glass window over the front door of the sanctuary. Known as the Wales Window, it was donated by the people of Wales and depicts a black figure of Christ crucified and bears the inscription "You do it to me."

No other arrests were made until Alabama attorney general Bill Baxley reopened the investigation in 1971 and won a conviction of Robert Chambliss in 1977. Chambliss, whose nickname was "Dynamite Bob," was a long-time Klansmen suspected in other racial bombings. He was sentenced to life in prison and died in 1985.

Public and media attention to the bombing was sporadic for more than a decade after the Chambliss conviction. Neither state nor federal law enforcement agencies made any serious efforts to investigate the case further or indict more suspects. Nonetheless, the church became a symbol of civil rights activism and sacrifice and was added to the National Register of Historic Places in 1980. In 1992, the Birmingham Civil Rights Institute, a museum and research center, opened across the street from Sixteenth Street Baptist Church. Nearby Kelly Ingram Park was renovated, and several pieces of sculpture honoring Martin Luther King Jr. and the Birmingham civil rights demonstrators were placed in the park. More than 200,000 people visit the area, now designated the Civil Rights District, each year.

By 1995, a change of leadership in the Birmingham office of the Federal Bureau of Investigation (FBI) led to a reopening of the case. The FBI did not announce the reopening until 1997, and that same year, filmmaker Spike Lee released *Four Little Girls*, his documentary about the bombing. The film was nominated for an Academy Award and focused new international attention on the case. Also in 1997, President Bill Clinton appointed Doug Jones as U.S. attorney for the Northern District of Alabama. Jones worked closely with the FBI and, in 2000, secured murder indictments against the two suspects still alive, Tommy Blanton and Bobby Frank Cherry. The two were tried separately. Blanton was convicted in 2001 and Cherry in 2002. Both were sentenced to life in prison.

In the twenty-first century, the membership of Sixteenth Street Baptist Church has declined to about 200, but the church is a popular tourist and pilgrimage site. Because of the large number of visitors, weekly attendance at Sunday services averages 2,000. In 2007, the church completed the first phase of a major restoration, and fund-raising continued to complete the restoration of the structure.

James L. Baggett

Further Reading

Cobbs, Elizabeth H., and Petric J. Smith. *Long Time Coming: An Insider's Story of the Birmingham Church Bombing That Rocked the World*. Birmingham, AL: Crane Hill Publishing, 1994.

Fallin, Wilson, Jr. *The African American Church in Birmingham, Alabama, 1815–1963: A Shelter in the Storm*. New York: Garland Publishing, 1997.

Feldman, Lynne B. *A Sense of Place: Birmingham's Black Middle-Class Community, 1890–1930*. Tuscaloosa: University of Alabama Press, 1999.

Hamlin, Christopher M. *Behind the Stained Glass: A History of Sixteenth Street Baptist Church*. Birmingham, AL: Crane Hill Publishers, 1998.

Romano, Renee C., and Leigh Raiford, eds. *The Civil Rights Movement in American Memory*. Athens: University of Georgia Press, 2006.

Schnorrenberg, John M. *Aspiration: Birmingham's Historic Houses of Worship*. Birmingham, AL: Birmingham Historical Society, 2000.

Sikora, Frank. *Until Justice Rolls Down: The Birmingham Church Bombing Case*. Tuscaloosa: University of Alabama Press, 2005.

Southern Christian Leadership Conference

The Southern Christian Leadership Conference (SCLC) is a civil rights organization formed in January 1957 that played a key role in administering direct-action, nonviolent campaigns against legalized segregation in the United States. The chief founder and first president of SCLC, Dr. Martin Luther King Jr., successfully collected a partial payment on that "unpaid check" he had spoken of in his "I Have a Dream" speech in Washington, D.C. in August 1963, by overseeing the implementation of new laws and desegregating many aspects of public life in the South.

SCLC is located in the "Sweet Auburn" historic district, in the center of downtown Atlanta, Georgia. Originally housed at 208 Auburn Avenue, the SCLC offices were moved into the Prince Hall Masonic Temple building located at 334 Auburn. Today, the SCLC staff resides in their new headquarters on Edgewood Avenue, in the historic district of Atlanta. The significance of Auburn Avenue and the history of SCLC dates back to January 15, 1929, when King was born in the upstairs bedroom of a modest Victorian-style home located at 501 Auburn. From 1955 to 1960, the Reverend Martin Luther King Sr. was pastor of the Ebenezer Baptist Church located on the same avenue, just two blocks west of their home on Auburn. Young Martin would often deliver guest sermons at Ebenezer and eventually, in 1960, officially began serving as copastor.

It was at Ebenezer, within walls that reverberated with King's fiery speeches and sermons, that various African American leaders gathered in the first weeks of 1957 to discuss the formation of a southern organization grounded in Christian principles and committed to nonviolent social change. For civil rights leaders such as Bayard Rustin, Stanley Levison, Ella J. Baker, C. K. Steele, and many involved in the victorious Montgomery, Alabama, bus boycott from December 1, 1955, to November 13, 1956, King represented a distinctive approach to social reform.

In retrospect, it seems clear that King's move to Montgomery in May 1954 to become pastor of the Dexter Avenue Baptist Church began a new era in the African American liberation movement in the United States. Soon after his arrival, he joined the local NAACP and other advocacy organizations and encouraged participation by members of his church. King's personality played a decisive role in the bus boycott and the establishment of the first genuine grassroots movement directed pointedly against segregation in the South. King appeared as a vigorous and determined leader who bridged church and society as no one had in the long southern struggle for racial equality.

The founders of SCLC seized the grassroots momentum created in Montgomery and carried it into Atlanta. Ebenezer Church served as more than SCLC's founding location; in subsequent years, the church building provided accommodations for various meetings, rallies, and their 1967 annual convention. King, the church membership, and SCLC participants were molded into an inseparable, united movement.

The first SCLC convention was held in Montgomery in August 1957. During this meeting, members adopted their official name and selected King as their first president, with C. K. Steele as the first vice president. The key to understanding the effectiveness of SCLC lies in viewing the composition of the organization as a loose connection of church groups capable of uniting in a mobilized campaign under the auspices of their leadership.

Under the guidance of King and Steele, SCLC participants made the decade of the 1960s a pivotal period in the history of the American civil rights movement. In less than five years, successful SCLC campaigns prompted African Americans to find and enjoy a new freedom, as segregation, Jim Crow customs, and lynching became part of the South's past. Notably, the Albany, Georgia, campaign of 1961–1962 was pivotal in shaping the approach of SCLC to direct-action campaigns. In July 1962, while in an Albany jail, King became convinced that a "four-pronged approach" was the best means of unifying society. This approach consisted of legal action, direct action, selective buying, and voter registration.

During the Birmingham campaign of 1963, SCLC and King propelled the civil rights movement to national attention in an effort to gain leverage in negotiation and apply pressure to the U.S. government. In his "Letter from Birmingham Jail," King outlined four stages of a nonviolent campaign: investigation to determine whether injustice existed, negotiation with local officials, self-purification, and direct action. Subsequently, the St. Augustine, Florida, campaign of 1964 would test every stage of the nonviolence campaign. The following year brought the successful Selma, Alabama, campaign. The famous Selma-to-Montgomery march prompted Congress to pass the 1965 Voting Rights Act.

By 1965, King had led SCLC to three cardinal gains. First, it had psychologically raised the hopes of African Americans by giving them a sense of pride, dignity, and confidence in themselves as a people. Second, SCLC and its allies had gathered and consolidated a tremendous amount of political leverage in gaining desegregation of facilities and polling booths. Last, the SCLC campaigns had laid important groundwork and precedent for future generations who were now armed with the right to vote, eat, sit, study, and live as they wished.

SCLC Presidents

Martin Luther King Jr. (1957–1968)

Ralph D. Abernathy (1968–1977)

Joseph E. Lowery (1977–1997)

Martin Luther King III (1997–2004)

Fred Shuttlesworth (February 2004–November 2004)

Charles Steele Jr. (became president November 2004)

Bobby R. Holt

Further Reading

Abernathy, Ralph David. *And the Walls Came Tumbling Down: An Autobiography.* New York: HarperCollins, 1991.

Branch, Taylor. *Parting the Waters: America in the King Years, 1954–63.* New York: Simon & Schuster, 1989.

Branch, Taylor. *Pillar of Fire: America in the King Years, 1963–65*. New York: Simon & Schuster, 1989.

Fairclough, Adam. *To Redeem the Soul of America: The Southern Christian Leadership Conference and Martin Luther King, Jr.* Athens: University of Georgia Press, 2001.

Garrow, David J. *Bearing the Cross: Martin Luther King, Jr., and the Southern Christian Leadership Conference*. New York: William Morrow, 1986.

King, Martin Luther, Jr. *The Autobiography of Martin Luther King Jr.* Edited by Clayborne Carson. New York: Warner Books, 1998.

Peake, Thomas R. *Keeping the Dream Alive: A History of the Southern Christian Leadership Conference from King to the Nineteen-Eighties*. New York: Peter Lang, 1987.

Student Nonviolent Coordinating Committee

The Student Nonviolent Coordinating Committee (SNCC) was one of the most important organizations to participate in the 1960s civil rights movement. Often referred to as the "shock troops" of the movement, SNCC remained on the cutting edge of the southern black freedom struggle. The organization differed from other groups such as the Southern Christian Leadership Conference (SCLC) in its organizational style and leadership. In accordance with SNCC founder Ella Baker's famous stance that "strong people do not need strong leaders," SNCC based most of its actions on creating grassroots leadership in black communities.

SNCC's first major campaign began on the eve of the one-year anniversary of the Greensboro sit-ins. On January 31, 1961, 10 African Americans were arrested for sitting at a segregated lunch counter in Rock Hill, South Carolina. Upon their arrest, SNCC arrived in the city and began a campaign that would be known as "jail-ins." SNCC leaders knew that they would be arrested for sitting at the segregated lunch counters in Rock Hill, but did so anyway in order to fill the city's jails. This would apply pressure on city officials who would have to use a vast amount of resources to arrest and detain large numbers of protesters. The "jail-in" strategy that SNCC used in Rock Hill would become one of the most important tactics used during the civil rights movement.

Later that year, SNCC joined forces with the Congress of Racial Equality (CORE) to test a 1961 Supreme Court decision that banned segregation on interstate buses. In *Boynton v. Virginia*, the U.S. Supreme Court ruled that segregation on interstate buses and terminals was unconstitutional. Like every other victory for integration, however, the court decision would have to be tested to ensure that the U.S. government would back the rights of African Americans. Freedom Rides were designed to test *Boynton v. Virginia*. Members of CORE and SNCC planned to travel on buses through the South, desegregating bus terminals as they went. The original group included seven blacks and six whites who left Washington,

D.C., for New Orleans on May 4, 1961. The trip was relatively uneventful at first, but the Freedom Riders met violence upon reaching the Deep South. On May 9, two of the protesters were attacked at the bus terminal in Rock Hill.

A few days later, white segregationists slashed the bus tires outside of Anniston, Alabama, and the group had to switch buses to proceed even deeper into the Jim Crow South. The violence reached a pinnacle outside of Birmingham, Alabama, when white supremacists, aided by the absence of police officers, entered the bus and attacked all of the Freedom Riders and bombed their vehicle. Volunteer James Peck was beaten so badly that it took 53 stitches to close the wound he received from a blow to the head. The next day, pictures of the attack appeared on the front page of most of the nation's newspapers. This coverage of the violence that Freedom Riders faced forced the John F. Kennedy administration to provide protection for future Freedom Riders.

SNCC experienced its first major internal conflict during the months after the Freedom Rides. Two factions emerged within the organization. One faction encouraged direct action protests such as sit-ins and marches. Another favored voter registration. Baker suggested that both sides pursue their objectives by their chosen means, and SNCC grew into two separate entities that worked together but chose to conduct different forms of activism.

The first major voter registration project took place in McComb, Mississippi, and was led by Robert Moses, who had been stirred into action after learning of the nationwide sit-in movement that began in February 1960 at the Greensboro Woolworth's. Moses was a 26-year-old high school teacher in Harlem, New York, when he first heard of the sit-in movement. It immediately propelled him into action, and he joined SNCC in 1960. By 1961, Moses had become SNCC's field secretary in Mississippi after entering the nation's most segregated state with nothing more than a list of contacts gathered by Baker during her decades of prior activism. In Mississippi, Moses was able to connect into underground networks of activists who had been fighting for black freedom in the state for decades. These activists were able to connect Moses to local people. By 1961, Moses had created a beachhead in Mississippi.

True to SNCC's founding philosophy of grassroots organizing, most of the leaders in Mississippi were locals. Many outsiders entered the state to join Moses, but the majority of groundwork was done by local people who were mired in one of the nation's worst forms of poverty in 1961. The median income of local African Americans was less than half the poverty level for a four-person household. This poverty extended into the state's racist educational system as well. Mississippi African Americans were extremely undereducated. The state took aims to ensure that its black students did not achieve any form of academic freedom. Many local African Americans did not even know that they had a constitutional right to vote. If they did pursue this right, Mississippi's African Americans were subject to violence. Because of the incredibly dangerous characteristics of white supremacists in the state, SNCC was severely limited in its ability to recruit organizers and incorporated anyone willing to risk their lives into the organization. Women, older black men, black youths, and some whites played key parts in the state as SNCC's presence in Mississippi grew in 1961.

In August 1961, with the help of funds from the federal government's Voter Education Project (VEP), Moses began a voter registration project in McComb. SNCC workers traveled door to door in an attempt to convince potential black voters to register. Initially, the organization experienced some success as members began to venture out into other black communities to canvass potential voters and recruit new SNCC volunteers. Voter registration was often slow, however, owing to the prevalence of fear among black Mississippians. This fear was confirmed by the 1961 murder of Herbert Lee, a native Mississippian who had been transporting SNCC workers throughout black communities. Lee was shot in broad daylight by a member of the Mississippi state House of Representatives who was quickly acquitted. This confirmed to most black Mississippians that voter registration was impossible, and the murder greatly slowed SNCC's progress throughout the state.

The organization kept fighting, however, and continued to spread into other regions of Mississippi, including the rural Mississippi Delta where the majority of citizens were black. SNCC encountered the most impoverished and disenfranchised group in the state when it entered the delta, but it also incorporated an incredibly driven and able group of local black activists into the organization. Included among these local people was Fannie Lou Hamer of Ruleville, Mississippi, who did not know that she should be allowed to vote until she attended a SNCC-sponsored meeting that took place in her local church in 1962. She was 44 years old and became one of the most important local leaders in Mississippi and symbols of the potential of grassroots organizing.

The direct-action division of SNCC also experienced several setbacks in 1961. Led by former Freedom Riders Charles Sherrod and Cordell Reagon, SNCC entered Albany, Georgia, in October 1961 to lead protest activities in the city. The organization was effectively able to recruit local people to join movement activities, but it also encountered an obstacle that clashed with SNCC's basic philosophies. Initially, SNCC led marches and demonstrations in the city that were designed to protest segregation, discriminatory hiring practices, and the systematic disenfranchisement of black voters. Just weeks into their campaign, however, a local leader asked Martin Luther King Jr. to join black Albanians' fight for equality and freedom. King's leadership style was contradictory to the SNCC leadership tradition that promoted grassroots organizing.

Upon his arrival, King immediately assumed the leadership of peaceful marches through downtown Albany. He was arrested soon after, and building on SNCC's "jail-in" philosophy, King vowed to spend Christmas in prison if necessary. King arrived in Albany in December and brought the attention of the media with him.

SNCC always welcomed media attention that would expose the plight of African Americans, but the journalists focused almost exclusively on King. He became the face and symbol of the Albany, Georgia movement. This would have drastic repercussions for local people who were pushed from leadership positions.

Albany leaders, fearful of the media frenzy that the incarceration of the most famous black preacher in the United States could create, negotiated a deal with King without involving local leaders or SNCC. Upon King's release from prison, he declared victory and left the city. After King left Albany, local officials denied an accord had ever been reached. They reneged on their agreement with King, and Albany's racial caste system continued as usual. SNCC leaders then had a hard time remobilizing local people who had become so dependent on King's leadership and prestige. Over the next several months, SNCC struggled against white officials to achieve nothing more than a stalemate that hardly threatened the status quo before the organization's involvement in the city.

By July 1962, SNCC had begun to reestablish leadership in Albany. King and his SCLC followers returned to the city that same month to assume leadership of the local people that SNCC had spent months mobilizing. As he had the previous year, King began leading demonstrations in the city; however, King's absence over the previous seven months had left many local people wary of his leadership position, and he had trouble invoking large-scale protests. King was arrested twice more in Albany, but he could not fill the jails. SNCC was powerless to do so as well because King undermined the organization's leadership. Eventually, King left the city without any further concessions made by white officials.

Leadership had been split, and both King and SNCC had been rendered ineffective as a result of the changing characteristics of Albany leadership. The developments in Albany reinforced to SNCC that it had to remain largely autonomous from national movement figures, especially King, in order to be effective. It also motivated the student-led organization to recruit even more local people into leadership positions as it conducted localized campaigns throughout the South.

The year 1963 was a turbulent one in the civil rights movement and a definitive one for SNCC. In May, King-led protests in Birmingham captured the world's attention as police officers and firefighters used German shepherds and fire hoses to break up peaceful demonstrations on the Alabama city's streets. This protest inspired demonstrations across the country. In all, approximately 930 protests occurred in 115 U.S. cities. More than 20,000 people were arrested for demonstrating against Jim Crow and discrimination.

Later that year, the SCLC, the National Association for the Advancement of Colored People (NAACP), CORE, and SNCC led a massive March on Washington, during which more than 250,000 protesters gathered on the mall in D.C. to protest segregation. King gave his famous "I Have a Dream" speech during that protest and cemented the moral righteousness of the civil rights movement. SNCC conducted various direct-action campaigns across the South with the help of an influx of volunteers, including many whites. White individuals such as Bob Zellner, Sam Shirah, Jane Stembridge, and Sandra Hayden either joined the fight against Jim Crow or became more prevalent leaders in the organization. By the fall of 1963, 20 percent of SNCC members were white. Voter registration activities spread throughout the South's Black Belt, and SNCC began to experience breakthroughs in Mississippi.

In November 1963, SNCC conducted a mock election called the Freedom Vote in Mississippi. This campaign was designed to allow Mississippi's African Americans an opportunity to participate in their first election, as well as to show the federal government that black Mississippians truly desired a stake in national and state politics. To illustrate the political potential of African Americans in the state, SNCC conducted an independent election. Because African Americans had been systematically excluded from Mississippi's regular Democratic Party, SNCC created an alternative Democratic organization named the Mississippi Freedom Democratic Party (MFDP).

SNCC, which now included a large number of white volunteers, fanned the state. Black candidates ran on the MFDP ticket and were elected to mock offices, including the governorship. More than 80,000 black Mississippians participated in the Freedom Vote. This clearly showed that many more African Americans desired a vote in Mississippi than the average of approximately 5,000 African Americans who regularly voted in statewide elections. The Freedom Vote also helped lay the ground for a statewide voter registration campaign.

By the end of 1963, SNCC had come of age. The organization claimed large amounts of members from diverse racial and socioeconomic backgrounds. The civil rights movement was at its height, and the nation saw nearly 1,000 protests during the course of one year. SNCC leaders attempted to build on this momentum when planning for 1964. The organization knew that it could register black Mississippians if allowed. The Freedom Vote had showed that the disenfranchised African Americans in the state could and would be called into political action if SNCC took the proper measures. The other lesson that SNCC had learned over the previous years was that it could recruit a highly diverse and capable group of organizers from across the nation. Young people, including northern whites, cared about the SNCC cause and had shown in the years before 1964 that they were willing to risk injury and death in order to fight Jim Crow. These factors would all play a major influence on SNCC's planning for 1964.

In 1964, SNCC conducted the most ambitious and audacious civil rights campaign in the history of the United States when it launched an all-out campaign to crack Mississippi. Although the organization had achieved some previous successes in Mississippi, most of these, such as the Freedom Vote, were largely symbolic. The biggest deterrent in the state was the large-scale amount of unchecked violence that constantly threatened civil rights activists. SNCC could not get the federal government to help its cause even though Mississippi segregationists were blatantly violating the rights of black citizens. In 1964, SNCC decided that it needed a force large enough to effectively mobilize black Mississippians and prestigious enough to force the federal government to protect civil rights workers in the state.

Based on SNCC's recent influx of white volunteers and sympathetic groups throughout the nation, the organization believed that it could recruit a large force of white college students to join the black freedom struggle in Mississippi during the summer of 1964. SNCC also believed that such a large group of white volunteers would force the federal government to protect civil rights workers in Mississippi. In the winter of 1963, SNCC representatives began appearing on northern college campuses to recruit young white students to participate in its 1964 Freedom Summer campaign.

Perhaps the most important goal of Freedom Summer was drawing attention to Mississippi and forcing federal intervention. The volunteers who would arrive in the state during the summer of 1964 were well positioned to do so. During the winter of 1963–1964, SNCC had recruited the children of American privilege. The organization believed that the more affluent its summer workers were, the greater the chance of federal intervention. In all, 40 percent of the project's applicants came from Stanford, Harvard, Yale, and Princeton. Their parents included esteemed historian Arthur Schlesinger Jr., Representative Don Edwards, and UN ambassador Sidney Yates. As nearly 1,000 of these students poured into the state in late June, the nation took notice. However, SNCC's greatest success in drawing federal intervention came at the expense of three lives.

On June 21, SNCC workers Michael Schwerner, James Chaney, and Andrew Goodman were arrested in Philadelphia, Mississippi. Local police officers then held the three young men until dark before delivering them into the hands of members of the Ku Klux Klan from Meridian and Neshoba County. The Klansmen, who had been tracking SNCC veteran Schwerner's moves for months, then executed the three young men and buried them under an earthen dam just outside of Philadelphia. The disappearance of the three workers, two of whom were white, drew the nation's interest and forced the federal government to build a presence in the state. It took the deaths of three young men for the federal government to launch a campaign against the Ku Klux Klan in the state, but their deaths probably saved dozens of lives during Freedom Summer.

Another important aspect of Freedom Summer was a program designed to create an active leadership class among Mississippi's black youths. Freedom Schools were taught mainly by white volunteers and provided training in the basic remedial skills absent from regular black schools in the state. The schools were also explicitly designed to incorporate young African Americans into the freedom struggle. Freedom Schools educated young African Americans about the rich traditions of black protest. They also encouraged high levels of student participation and let the black youths dictate the subject matter. Finally, the schools included training in civil rights protest activities such as sit-ins, letter-writing campaigns, and various forms of organizing.

By the end of Freedom Summer, the students at Freedom Schools showed encouraging signs of leadership potential. The final, and perhaps most practical, goal of Freedom Summer was to register black voters. Hundreds of volunteers canvassed black communities to convince local people to attempt to register. The volunteers often met various forms of violent resistance and reluctance from the black community, but did successfully convince approximately 17,000 age-eligible voters to attempt to register. The canvassers solicited votes as part of the MFDP, which was planning its own ambitious civil rights demonstration to take place later that year.

Over the next several years, SNCC led protests across the southern Black Belt and did achieve meaningful successes. The level of activity after 1964, however, must be seen as disappointing in comparison to the massive campaigns before Freedom Summer.

William Mychael Sturkey

Further Reading

Carson, Clayborne. *In Struggle: SNCC and the Black Awakening of the 1960s.* Cambridge, MA: Harvard University Press, 1995.

Greenberg, Cheryl Lynn. *A Circle of Trust: Remembering SNCC.* New Brunswick, NJ: Rutgers University Press, 1997.

Hogan, Wesley C. *Many Minds, One Heart: SNCC's Dream for a New America.* Chapel Hill: University of North Carolina Press, 2007.

Murphree, Vanessa. *The Selling of Civil Rights: The Student Nonviolent Coordinating Committee and the Use of Public Relations.* New York: Routledge, 2006.

Zinn, Howard. *SNCC: The New Abolitionists.* Cambridge, MA: South End Press, 2002.

Students for a Democratic Society

Students for a Democratic Society (SDS) was a radical student group active in the 1960s. It evolved from the Student League for Industrial Democracy, which was the young people's branch of an organization developed in 1905 called the Intercollegiate Socialist Society. The group changed its name in the 1960s so as not to seem completely focused on labor issues, thereby appealing to a broader group of young people.

The organization held its first meeting in 1960 in Ann Arbor, Michigan. There, an SDS staffer named Tom Hayden introduced his political manifesto, the *Port Huron Statement*. Hayden criticized the political system in general and the U.S. government specifically for: its failure to realize world peace, the Cold War, the nuclear arms race, racial discrimination, economic inequality, and big business. He advocated reforming the two dominant political parties and developing a governmental system that would encourage, support, and sustain participatory democracy. Hayden also called for corporations to encourage more participation by their employees and an expansion of the welfare state to include a concerted effort to eliminate poverty. Finally, Hayden supported nonviolence as a tactic in the struggle for a more democratic, humane, and inclusive society.

The *Port Huron Statement* was unique among leftist political groups for several reasons. First was the recognition that every organization needed a clear vision about its reasons for being. Second, the statement recognized that the problems in society were linked to one another, meaning that a more holistic approach to their resolution was needed. Third, SDS made a commitment to work with any interested group regardless of its position in the political spectrum. Finally, unlike most left-leaning organizations, it rejected the militant anticommunism so prevalent in those organizations.

SDS grew slowly in part because of its policy of decentralization, a position it adopted from the Student Nonviolent Coordinating Committee (SNCC). The group had a national office with a president, vice president, and secretary, but it had few resources and was mostly a loose collection of campus-based chapters. During its early years, it mainly assisted SNCC in its civil rights work. Its 1964 summer convention revealed the fissures already developing between those who embraced traditional campus-based activism and those who wanted to branch out into other activities. Another outcome of the convention was the development of a more stable organization that included centralized administrative functions and increased attention to recruiting new chapters.

The year 1964 was a propitious one for SDS. On October 1 at the University of California, Berkeley, the free speech movement was established. Led by activist Mario Savio among others, students protested against the administration, demanded that it cancel the ban on political activities, and give students more academic freedom. Hundreds of students demonstrated, held meetings, and engaged in strikes, virtually shutting down the university.

The next year, the administration of President Lyndon B. Johnson escalated the Vietnam War by bombing the North Vietnamese and introducing ground troops into South Vietnam. The military draft was reactivated, and college students realized that there was more at stake than an esoteric exercise. SDS shifted its focus from civil rights to antiwar activities, and it held its first teach-in against the war at the University of Michigan. It also organized a march against the war, which was held in Washington, D.C., on April 17, 1965. Approximately 25,000 demonstrators converged on the city. Moreover, the organization expanded its antidraft activities to include protests against colleges and universities that had begun to supply the names and grade point averages of its male students, thereby assisting the military in deciding who would be drafted.

As the Black Power movement developed and white students became unwelcome in SNCC, SDS increasingly focused its attention on the development of campus-based activism through local chapters. It also stepped up its demonstrations against the Vietnam War and the draft, organizing several highly successful student strikes around the country. Like SNCC, it also became more militant. The organization demonstrated against businesses it deemed as profiting from the war, drawing the attention and increased criticism of the U.S. government. These activities drew the attention of the Federal Bureau of Investigation (FBI), who had for some time been working against SDS through a secret operation known as COINTELPRO.

In the autumn of 1967, SDS sponsored a well-attended demonstration at the University of Wisconsin–Madison. Madison police attacked the demonstrators and a number of students were injured and arrested. Their action signaled to SDS that the nonviolent tactics it had borrowed from the civil rights movement were no longer effective, and thereafter its demonstrations became more militant as they engaged in raids on draft offices.

Local SDS chapters organized a nationwide effort known as Ten Days of Resistance, which consisted of sit-ins, marches, and rallies against the war. In a show of interracial cooperation, SDS and Student Afro Society activists shut down Columbia University, and it was estimated that about one million students skipped class on April 26, 1968, the largest student strike ever reported. The organization experienced a huge increase in membership that year.

However, organizational solidarity was difficult to maintain for SDS. At the 1969 national convention, various factions of SDS faced off. A manifesto that said, in part, "You don't need a Weatherman to know which way the wind blows" was distributed to each conventioneer. Among the 11 members who contributed to the work, Bernardine Dohrn and Mark Rudd became the leaders of the so-called Revolutionary Youth Movement with SDS. Supporters of Dohrn and Rudd split off into yet another faction, which came to be known as the Weathermen or Weather Underground Organization. Its stated intention was the overthrow of the capitalist system, and its tactics were much more aggressive than any other campus-based organization.

SDS never held another national convention, and by 1970, the Weather Underground had issued a declaration of war, committing bombings, arson, robbery, and murder in support of its goals. Several of its members went underground, eluding authorities for decades; but by the 1980s, most had turned themselves in.

Marilyn K. Howard

Further Reading

Barber, David. *A Hard Rain Fell: SDS and Why It Failed.* Jackson: University Press of Mississippi, 2008.

Hayden, Tom. *The Port Huron Statement.* New York: Perseus Publishing, 2005.

Pekar, Harvey, Gary Dumm, and Paul Buhle. *Students for a Democratic Society: A Graphic History.* New York: Hill and Wang, 2008.

Rudd, Mark. *Underground: My Life with SDS and the Weathermen.* New York: William Morrow, 2009.

T

Till, Emmett

Emmett Louis Till (1941–1955) was a young Chicago native whose lynching in Mississippi helped galvanize the modern civil rights movement. He was born on July 25, 1941, to Mamie and Louis Till. The latter died serving in Europe during World War II, leaving only a ring with the initials L. T. At the age of five, Emmett was stricken with polio, which left him with a slight stutter.

In the summer of 1955, 14-year-old Till traveled to Money, Mississippi, to visit his great-uncle Moses Wright. Because of the Supreme Court's *Brown v. Board of Education* decision several months before, which mandated integrated schools, racial tensions in the area were volatile. Not long after his arrival, Till and some other teenagers visited Bryant's Grocery and Meat Market. Accounts of what happened have varied. Some say that Till whistled at store owner Carolyn Brant, which could have been misinterpreted because of Till's stutter. Others say Till said "bye baby" as he left the store. Four days later, Carolyn Bryant's husband Roy and his brother J. W. Milam threatened Moses Wright and kidnapped Till. Bryant and Milam were arrested for kidnapping Till, and three days later, Till's body was found in the Tallahatchie River tied to a cotton gin fan. The body could be identified only through the L. T. initial ring. Bryant and Milam were later charged with murder.

Emmett Till's body was brought back to Chicago, and newspaper photographers captured pictures of Mamie Till fainting. Till's mother decided to hold an open-casket funeral and invited the press so that everyone could see Till's body. Tens of thousands of people gathered at the funeral. *Jet* magazine and the *Chicago Defender* published pictures, and local television stations aired funeral footage. Although black communities throughout the South had experienced lynching before, this was one of the first times that the aftermath was widely publicized. In addition to mobilizing the black community around civil rights, Till's lynching also had an effect on white northern journalists: it cemented the fact that the South was "worthy" of national news coverage.

Roy Bryant and J. W. Milam's trial began in Sumner, Mississippi, on September 19. No black men or women of any ethnic background were allowed to serve on the jury. Although Moses Wright stood in open court and identified Bryant and Milam as the kidnappers, after 67 minutes of deliberation, the jury acquitted both men on the murder charges. A juror was later quoted as saying the deliberations would have taken less time if they had not taken a break. Outrage surrounding the verdict was published in newspapers all over the world, including

Belgium, France, and Germany. Moses Wright and Willie Reed, a black sharecropper who also testified against the men, fled to Chicago. Several months later, Wright and Reed returned to Mississippi to testify on the kidnapping charges; however, the grand jury refused to indict.

In January 1956, *Look* magazine offered Bryant and Milam $4,000 for an interview with journalist William Bradford Huie. Milam went on the record and admitted to kidnapping Till and stated that they only intended to beat him. Because Till remained defiant, however, Milam forced him to strip and shot him at close range in the head. Huie later wrote a follow-up article that stated Bryant and Milam were ostracized by both the black and white communities, which put their stores out of business.

J. W. Milam died in 1980 and Roy Bryant died in 1990, both of cancer. Mamie Till Mobley died in 2003 a few weeks before PBS aired a documentary chronicling Emmett's lynching. In 2004, Senator Charles Schumer and Representative Charles Rangel urged the Justice Department to reopen the investigation into Till's murder because of new evidence that suggested Bryant and Milam did not act alone. On May 10, 2004, the Justice Department and the Mississippi District Attorney's Office officially reopened the case.

Lisa Doris Alexander

Further Reading

Houck, Davis W., and Matthew A. Grindy. *Emmett Till and the Mississippi Press.* Jackson: University Press of Mississippi, 2008.

Metress, Christopher. *The Lynching of Emmett Till: A Documentary Narrative.* Charlottesville: University of Virginia Press, 2002.

Till-Mobley, Mamie, and Christopher Benson. *Death of Innocence: The Story of the Hate Crime That Changed America.* New York: One World, 2004.

Whitfield, Stephen J. *A Death in the Delta: The Story of Emmett Till.* New York: Free Press, 1988.

V

Voter Education Project

The Voter Education Project (VEP) was a collaborative effort by various groups that advocated for black voter education and registration from 1962 to 1968. In 1960 and 1961, as the sit-ins and activities of the Freedom Riders began to meet with success in desegregating lunch counters and interstate travel facilities, black civil rights leaders sought new goals for the civil rights movement. In September 1961, following months of debate and wrangling, the Congress of Racial Equality (CORE), the Student Nonviolent Coordinating Committee (SNCC), the National Urban League, and the National Association for the Advancement of Colored People (NAACP) joined together to launch VEP.

The project had the full support of the John F. Kennedy administration, which was willing to provide federal protection for civil rights workers engaged in registering voters, but not for protesters participating in direct action activities. Scheduled to last for two and one-half years and financed by $870,000 in grants from the Taconic Foundation and other northern foundations, VEP got underway in April 1962. The campaign targeted southern black populations in the rural Black Belt and Mississippi delta regions, where white election officials had manipulated literacy tests and complex registration forms to prevent even literate blacks from voting. At the beginning of the project, only about a quarter of voting-age southern blacks were registered; in Mississippi, the figure stood at about 5 percent.

Student activists working for CORE, SNCC, or one of the other organizations canvassed black voters throughout the rural South, conducted literacy and citizenship clinics, and encouraged black citizens to register and vote. In Mississippi, SNCC workers led by Robert Moses encountered determined opposition from local white racists. Student volunteers were threatened, jailed, beaten, bombed, and killed, but they persisted in their effort. U.S. attorney general Robert F. Kennedy assisted them by enlarging the Civil Rights Section of the Justice Department and directing it to begin wholesale prosecution of voting rights cases.

The results of VEP were mixed. The percentage of southern adult blacks who were registered to vote rose from 25 percent to 40 percent between 1962 and 1964, but the educational and political process was laborious, difficult, and dangerous. The frustrations and dangers involved in the voter registration campaign ultimately contributed to the passage of the Civil Rights Act of 1964 and the Voting Rights Act of 1965.

Charles D. Lowery

Further Reading

Nieman, Donald G. *Promises to Keep: African-Americans and the Constitutional Order, 1776 to the Present*. New York: Oxford University Press, 1991.

Sitkoff, Harvard. *The Struggle for Black Equality, 1954–1992*. 2nd ed. New York: Hill and Wang, 1992.

Voting Rights Act of 1965

In July 1964, President Lyndon B. Johnson signed the Civil Rights Act (1964), which contained some voting-related provisions. Title I condemned state discrimination in voter registration. The bill prompted outrage from conservative white southerners, who were only slightly mollified that it was signed by a Texan. Yet many in the African American community criticized the act as well, feeling that it had not gone far enough. Just as the Fourteenth Amendment of 1868 had failed to secure full legal rights for freed slaves, so the 1964 Civil Rights Act did not ensure the voting rights of African Americans. Recognizing this, Johnson followed the Civil Rights Act with a bill on voting rights, in an echo of Congress's actions in ratifying the Fifteenth Amendment in 1870 to prevent restriction of the ballot on the basis of race.

Existing federal antidiscrimination laws had not been sufficient to overcome state officials' resistance to the Fifteenth Amendment. Even after passage of the Enforcement Act of 1870 and the Force Act of 1871, black citizens encountered strong resistance to their enfranchisement. White supremacist groups practiced violent intimidation, and election districts were gerrymandered. In the 1890s, some states enacted disenfranchising laws—poll taxes, literacy tests, and disqualification for "crimes of moral turpitude." By 1910, nearly all black citizens in the former Confederate States of America were disenfranchised, and in 1965, only a third of eligible African Americans (compared to two-thirds of eligible whites) were registered in these states. Literacy tests and poll taxes kept black voting registration low, especially in Mississippi, Alabama, and Louisiana. Only 6 percent of eligible black citizens were registered in Mississippi.

Johnson began work on the new bill in the fall of 1964, right after "Freedom Summer," which saw three voter registration volunteers murdered in Mississippi. The Federal Bureau of Investigation declared that local law enforcement officials were involved in the murders. He announced the bill in his State of the Union address of January 1965, and on March 15, 1965, he gave a speech to Congress on voting rights. The speech, titled "The American Promise," pointed to the unkept promises of the Declaration of Independence and the Emancipation Proclamation (1863), then heralded the civil rights protest as the driving force behind the new legislation. There would have been no progress, Johnson said, were it not for the

President Lyndon B. Johnson moves to shake hands with Dr. Martin Luther King Jr. in the capitol rotunda following the signing of the Voting Rights Act on August 6, 1965. The law was the first national legislation to guarantee all Americans the right to vote. (Yoichi R. Okamoto/Lyndon B. Johnson Library)

faith and bravery of black campaigners. He quoted the anthem of the civil rights movement, a freedom song titled "We Shall Overcome."

On August 5, Congress passed Johnson's bill, which was the most comprehensive voting rights legislation to date. Section 2 followed the language of the Fifteenth Amendment: "No voting qualification or prerequisite to voting, or standard, practice, or procedure shall be imposed or applied by any State or political subdivision to deny or abridge the right of any citizen of the United States to vote on account of race or color." Section 4 ended the use of literacy requirements for voting in Alabama, Georgia, Louisiana, Mississippi, South Carolina, and Virginia, and in many North Carolina counties. The bill also provided for unprecedented federal intervention. It authorized the attorney general to appoint federal voting examiners and decreed that the Justice Department would take control of the registration process if any county failed to register 50 percent of eligible black voters. It did not prohibit the poll tax, instead directing the attorney general to challenge its use; but in 1966, the Supreme Court found Virginia's poll tax to be unconstitutional under the Fourteenth Amendment.

After his voting rights speech, Johnson went on to express support for equal outcomes policies. On June 4, 1965, he gave an address at Howard University titled

"To Fulfill These Rights." In language that would later be used by affirmative action advocates, he told the graduating students: "You do not take a person who, for years, has been hobbled by chains and liberate him, bring him up to the starting line of a race and then say, 'you are free to compete with all the others,' and still justly believe that you have been completely fair." It was not enough, Johnson explained, just to open the gates of opportunity. Citizens needed the ability to walk through.

Nonetheless, the act did have an impact. Most southern states opened voter registration lists to black citizens, and control passed to the Justice Department in the 62 counties that remained resistant. In Mississippi, black voting enrollment went from 6 percent to 44 percent by 1968. Johnson's bill was extended in 1970, again in 1975 (when it was amended to protect language minority citizens from voting discrimination), and again in 1982. On January 20, 2001, ahead of the Shadow Inauguration, some 2,000 people marched to the Supreme Court and took a vow to uphold Johnson's Voting Rights Act.

On June 25, 2013, the Supreme Court in *Shelby County v. Holder* struck down Section 4 of the Voting Rights Act, which includes the formula for determining which states must get changes to voting laws preapproved by the federal government. Without this section, the preapproval requirement, found in Section 5 of the act, would have no effect unless Congress sets up new criteria to determine which states will be covered. Shelby County originated in 2006 in Alabama, when that county government sought to overturn Sections 4 and 5 of the Voting Rights Act as applied to that county.

Zoe Trodd

Further Reading

Branch, Taylor. *Pillar of Fire: America in the King Years, 1963–65.* New York: Simon & Schuster, 1998.

Garrow, David J. *Protest at Selma: Martin Luther King, Jr. and the Voting Rights Act of 1965.* New Haven, CT: Yale University Press, 1978.

Kotz, Nick. *Judgment Days: Lyndon Baines Johnson, Martin Luther King Jr., and the Laws That Changed America.* New York: Houghton Mifflin, 2005.

Walters, Ronald W. *Freedom Is Not Enough: Black Voters, Black Candidates, and American Presidential Politics.* Lanham, MD: Rowman and Littlefield, 2007.

Walker, Wyatt

Civil rights leader Wyatt Walker served as executive director of the Southern Christian Leadership Conference (SCLC) from 1960 to 1964. Wyatt Tee Walker was born on August 16, 1929, in Brockton, Massachusetts, to John Wise and Maude Pinn Walker. Walker graduated in 1950 from Virginia Union University in Richmond, Virginia, with a BS in both chemistry and physics. He then entered Virginia Union's Graduate School of Religion, serving as student body president before receiving his BD in 1953. At a meeting of the Inter-Seminary Movement, Walker met King, then a student at Crozer Theological Seminary.

In 1953, Walker accepted a position as minister at Gillfield Baptist Church in Petersburg, Virginia. Walker also held a number of leadership roles with local civil rights organizations. He served as president of the local chapter of the National Association for the Advancement of Colored People (NAACP) and as state director of the Congress of Racial Equality (CORE). He was also a founder of the Virginia Council on Human Relations, a group working for desegregation, and led the Petersburg Improvement Association, which was modeled after the Montgomery Improvement Association.

In 1959, Walker organized and led the first local Prayer Pilgrimage for Public Schools, an event that protested Virginia state officials' attempts to block public school integration. The same year, Walker also joined the board of SCLC. In January 1960, King spoke at the second annual Prayer Pilgrimage, and in March of that year, Walker decided to remain in jail after being arrested while protesting segregation in the Petersburg Library. Meanwhile, King had mailed him an offer to become SCLC's new executive director. Walker replaced Ella Baker, who had served as interim director since John Lee Tilley's resignation in 1959. Walker subsequently moved to Atlanta with his family. He brought Dorothy Cotton and James R. Wood, two of his closest assistants from the Petersburg Improvement Association, with him to SCLC.

A firm administrator, Walker worked to bring order to the organization's fund-raising efforts and the wide-ranging activities of its staff. Walker was also a key tactician, authoring and evaluating protest strategies, including "Project C," the basis for SCLC's Birmingham Campaign in 1963. SCLC benefited from Walker's advice on organizational structure and strategy. Walker's leadership style also alienated some young activists affiliated with the Student Nonviolent Coordinating Committee (SNCC).

Such conflicts were the motivating forces behind Walker's eventual resignation from SCLC in 1964. When Walker was replaced by SCLC staff member Andrew Young, he went on to work as vice president of a new publishing venture, the Negro Heritage Library. In 1965, he became president of the organization, which sought to increase the attention paid to black history in school curricula. Walker and King maintained contact in the years following Walker's resignation, and King preached at his 1968 installation service at Canaan Baptist Church, praising Walker as someone who contributed significantly to SCLC.

Walker remained active in religion and social change activities after leaving SCLC. In 1975, he received his DMin from Colgate-Rochester Divinity School. Walker also served as New York governor Nelson Rockefeller's special assistant on urban affairs and held visiting professorships at Princeton Theological Seminary and New York University. An expert on gospel music, Walker published several books on the role music has played in the black religious tradition, including *Somebody's Calling My Name: Black Sacred Music and Social Change* (1979). In 2004, Walker retired as pastor of Canaan Baptist Church, a position he held since 1968.

Clayborne Carson

Further Reading

Eskew, Glenn T. *But for Birmingham: The Local and National Movements in the Civil Rights Struggle.* Chapel Hill: University of North Carolina Press, 1997.

Fendrich, James Max. *Ideal Citizens: The Legacy of the Civil Rights Movement.* Albany: State University of New York Press, 1993.

Morris, Aldon D. *The Origins of the Civil Rights Movement.* New York: Free Press, 1984.

War on Poverty

The War on Poverty was declared by Lyndon Johnson in his State of the Union address in 1964. It was a critical component of his larger vision of a Great Society and was intended to expand the reach of government to improve life for all Americans. At the time, approximately 35 million Americans lived in poverty. Moreover, the civil rights movement and events such as the *Brown v. Board of Education* decision, the Montgomery bus boycott, the decision to send federal troops to enforce desegregation at Central High School in Little Rock, and the Birmingham, Harlem, and Watts "riots" all highlighted previously unacknowledged links between race, poverty, and opportunity.

Ideologically, the War on Poverty was a progressive campaign drawn from the belief that the cause of poverty was a systemic lack of opportunity. Only government leadership directed toward changing the structures of opportunity that kept people impoverished could defeat the problem. In this way, Johnson's ideas aligned themselves with the liberal tradition of Franklin Delano Roosevelt and his New Deal.

For the War on Poverty to be fully implemented, all branches of government had to work together. For Johnson, this commitment was the only way to solve America's problems. Thus, the Economic Opportunity Act (EOA) required federal, state, and local participation and was designed to mobilize the resources of the country to address the numerous challenges it faced. The aim was not merely to expand old programs or improve what was already being done, but to chart a new course and address the cause of poverty, thereby eliminating it. The EOA was committed to lowering barriers to political participation, employment, housing, and education for African Americans. It also proposed economic development programs for American cities and towns.

Johnson subsequently established the Office of Economic Opportunity (OEO) as the legislative site with responsibility for administering War on Poverty programs. Some of the programs were Head Start, the Community Action Program, the Job Corps, food stamps, work study, Medicare/Medicaid, Volunteers in Service to America (VISTA), Upward Bound, comprehensive health services, family planning, emergency food and medical services, Senior Opportunity Services, and legal services. The OEO reported directly to the president. Between the time of its inception in 1964 and its demise in 1973, social welfare spending increased from $75 billion to $185 billion. In terms of percentage, spending increased about 4.6 percent between 1950 and 1965 and approximately 7.2 percent between 1965 and 1976.

OEO was officially disbanded in 1973 by President Richard Nixon. Responsibility for its many social welfare programs was transferred to the newly established Community Services Administration (CSA) in the Department of Health, Education and Welfare. CSA received little support from President Jimmy Carter and was finally dismantled by the Ronald Reagan administration in 1981. Between 1964 and 1973, however, the impact of the War on Poverty was such that it was impossible for government to embrace any new initiative without being asked, "How does it help the poor?"

Looking back, the results of the Great Society and its War on Poverty were less than hoped for. There are several explanations for its limited effectiveness. The first was funding. As military engagement in the Vietnam War escalated and thoughts of how to extricate U.S. troops occupied more of the nation's attention, the OEO received less of the funding it needed to carry out the programs it proposed. Local areas that had responsibility for many medical, emergency food, and legal services found themselves with little money to continue. Programs funded at the federal level (e.g., Head Start) remained intact but suffered under the weight of diminishing resources.

A second explanation was ideological. Four concerns have been cited. First, there was the split between those who viewed welfare as social insurance and those who saw it as public assistance. Second, there were those who claimed that the War on Poverty was unwilling to attribute the cause of poverty to the American economic system. Accordingly, the result was superficial, Band-Aid solutions. Although opportunities were created, structural inequalities were untouched. Third, many claim that the attention given to black America created a racial backlash. The white middle class felt that it was footing the bill for ever-increasing services to the poor, and as the economy declined during the 1970s, many whites lost sympathy for Great Society programs. Finally, women also felt they had been ignored. Despite the fact that the majority of positions (e.g., community aide, community worker, and parent aide) were filled by women, the OEO held the traditional view that women's work was voluntary, unpaid labor. Strategies for preventing poverty focused on expanding employment opportunities for poor men and neglected the actual contributions of women as staff members and administrators.

Today, of the many Great Society programs, most support remains for Medicare, which serves the elderly, and for Head Start, which serves the youngest of the poor. The basic assumption of the Great Society—that government must take the leadership in reducing poverty—has been replaced by the 1990s belief that government support for the poor leads to dependency and undermines the work ethic. Whereas the Great Society emphasized the institutional and structural roots of poverty, contemporary poverty policy focuses on the individual behaviors and choices of people who are poor.

Rickie Sanders

Further Reading

Clark, Robert. *The War on Poverty: History, Selected Programs, and On-going Impact.* Lanham, MD: University Press of America, 2002.

Harrington, Michael. *The Other America: Poverty in the United States.* New York: Touchstone, 1962.

Haveman, Robert. *A Decade of Federal Antipoverty Programs: Achievements, Failures, and Lessons.* New York: Academic Press, 1977.

Katz, Michael. *In the Shadow of the Poorhouse: A Social History of Welfare in America.* New York: Basic Books, 1996.

Wells-Barnett, Ida B.

Ida B. Wells-Barnett was an African American journalist, a civil rights activist, and an internationally prominent critic of lynching in the Jim Crow South, as well as a women's suffrage activist. On July 16, 1862, Wells was born a slave in Holly Spring, Mississippi, in the midst of the Civil War. Her parents, Jim and Elizabeth

Wells, were slaves, and she became the property of the respective plantation owner. With the conclusion of the Civil War in 1865, the life of the Wells family did not improve dramatically. Wells's father decided to continue working for the slave owner. In 1878, her parents died in a yellow fever epidemic that ravaged Holly Springs, leaving the 16-year-old Wells in charge of her seven brothers and sisters. She decided to get her certificate in teaching and gain employment at one of the local schools. In 1881, Wells took two of her younger siblings and went to Memphis, Tennessee, in search of better economic opportunities. While in Memphis, she continued to teach to support her siblings and attended Fisk University.

In the 1880s, Wells decided to challenge a particular aspect of the Jim Crow South. In 1884, she started a campaign against segregation on local railroads. In the summer of 1884, she was forcibly removed from a white-only carriage. She sued the Chesapeake, Ohio, and Southwestern Railroad. The lawsuit was instigated to try to weaken the Jim Crow laws in regard to segregation. The local courts judged in favor of Wells. However, the Court of Appeals repeatedly overturned the lower court decisions. Wells also became involved in journalism. In the summer of 1887, she was appointed as the secretary of the Afro-American Press Association.

In the late 1880s, lynching was a severe problem in the South. Local governments tolerated the practice, while the national government proved indifferent. In 1889, 728 African American men and women were lynched. On March 9, 1891, three African American proprietors who were also Wells's personal friends, Thomas Moss, Calving McDowell, and Wil Stewart of the People's Grocery Store, were lynched. Wells wrote a scathing editorial indictment of lynching called "Eight Men Lynched" in the *Free Speech and Headlight* (of which she had become part-owner in 1889) on May 21, 1892. This led to the destruction of the newspaper by Memphis citizens and her subsequent exile from the South. She then began writing for the *New York Age* and adjusted to her new life in the North. She immediately started a public campaign to publicize the atrocities of lynching. Wells, under the pseudonym of Iola, wrote editorial pieces and eyewitness accounts of lynchings in the South. Despite the repeated threats on her life, she continued to publicize lynching in the North as well as internationally.

On October 5, 1892, Wells gave a speech in New York City in front of 250 African American women about her difficult experiences dealing with the southern lynch codes. She subsequently published *Southern Horrors: Lynch Law in All its Phases*, a pamphlet describing the realities of African Americans in the South. In *Southern Horrors*, Wells traced a pervasive belief that African American men are natural "rapists." She concluded by noting that "lynching was an institutionalized practice supported and encouraged by established leaders of the community and the press they influenced."

In 1893, Wells moved to Chicago to continue her career in journalistic writing. The Chicago newspaper, the *Chicago Inter-Ocean*, hired Wells as editor to write exposé articles against lynching in the South. In a particular exposé, the paper proposed that Wells secretly pose as a widower to examine the lynching of C. J. Miller in the small town of Bardwell, Kentucky. By the time she arrived in Bardwell, the lynchers publicly acknowledged that they had killed the wrong man. After investigating the case, Wells concluded that the victim, Miller, was used as a scapegoat. Although thousands were involved in the lynching, no one was punished. Wells decided to depart for Chicago when she realized that there was no resolution to the problem. She received an invitation from the "Brotherhood of Man" to visit Britain for a lecture tour. She accepted the offer as a way to spread her opposition to lynching. At the same time, she sent articles to the *Chicago Inter-Ocean* newspaper. She also lectured at the British Anti-Lynching Commission as well as at other prominent antilynching societies in England.

In 1895, after her marriage to the prominent African American lawyer from Chicago, Ferdinand Barnett, Wells-Barnett continued to be a vocal and outspoken critic against lynching in the South. She published numerous articles and books, which offered statistical analysis of this chronic social problem. In her most important book, *The Red Record* (1895), she offered the first statistical report on lynching in the South. As a nationally prominent figure in the crusade against lynching, Wells-Barnett visited President William McKinley in 1898, demanding government action in the case against an African American postmaster who was lynched in South Carolina. A few years later, in 1901, she wrote *Lynching and the Excuse for It*. She offered a sociological examination of the reasons southerners engaged in this violent behavior. Wells-Barnett noted that white southerners engaged in lynching as a way to intimidate African Americans from getting involved in politics. The political system in the Jim Crow South was repressive to the extent that any challenge to that system would be viewed as a radical challenge. In 1896, Wells-Barnett formed a collective organization called the National Association of Colored Women.

Wells-Barnett also became involved in the Progressive movement in Chicago. Wells-Barnett, who was a friend of Progressive activist Jane Addams, decided that the settlement house concept devised by Addams would work in the African American community. Wells-Barnett opened a settlement house in Chicago, geared primarily for African Americans. She founded the Woman's Era Club, which was the first civic organization for African American women. The club aided African American women in occupations and culture. It was an efficient organization that in the long run proved to be successful in aiding the community. In addition to the settlement houses, Wells-Barnett and Addams also became involved in a campaign to block the continued segregation of public schools in Chicago. At this time, Wells-Barnett also served as secretary for the National African American Council and the Negro Fellowship League.

Wells-Barnett also became involved in national politics. She believed that Booker T. Washington's accommodationist stance was too lenient and did not offer African Americans any semblance of identity. Wells-Barnett was one of two African American women who supported the National Association for the Advancement of Colored People (NAACP). However, Wells-Barnett had a falling out with W. E. B. Du Bois over her alleged radicalism. Subsequently, Wells-Barnett turned her attention to other issues, specifically women's suffrage. Wells-Barnett became involved in the local suffrage movement in Chicago. In 1909, she became the first black woman suffrage associate at the Alpha Suffrage Club of Chicago, which had been a predominantly white organization. She was actively involved at the NAWSA march in Washington, D.C., in 1916.

In 1917, the United States became militarily involved in World War I. Many African Americans served in the U.S. armed forces in Europe; yet, within the United States, they were not given political and social rights, despite their sacrifices. In August 1917, African American soldiers, in reaction to continued segregation and abuse by the local police, attacked white citizens; 16 whites and four black soldiers died. The U.S. Army indicted 118 soldiers, 110 of whom were court-martialed. Nineteen African Americans were executed by hanging. Wells-Barnett publicized the event as another form of lynching through her writings, bringing it to national attention.

In the years after the war, Wells-Barnett focused on raising her four children. This new caretaker role did not diminish her continued involvement in social activism. During the 1920s, she worked with the federal government to legally end the practice of lynching. Her last work was the publication of her autobiography, *Crusade for Justice*.

Jaime Ramón Olivares

Further Reading

Barnett, Ida. *Crusade for Justice: The Autobiography of Ida Wells.* Chicago: University of Chicago Press, 1970.

Davis, Simone W. "The 'Weak Race' and the Winchester: Political Voices in the Pamphlets of Ida B. Wells-Barnett." *Legacy: A Journal of American Women Writers* 12, no. 2 (1995): 77–97.

Fradia, Dennis. *Ida B. Wells: Mother of the Civil Rights Movement.* New York: Clarion Books, 2000.

Logan, Shirley W. "Rhetorical Strategies in Ida B. Wells's '*Southern Horrors*': Lynch Law in All Its Phases." *SAGE: A Scholarly Journal on Black Women* 8, no. 1 (1991): 3–9.

McMurry, Linda O. *To Keep the Water Troubled: The Life of Ida B. Wells.* New York: Oxford University Press, 1998.

Ochiai, Akiko. "Ida B. Wells and Her Crusade for Justice: An African American Woman's Testimonial Autobiography." *Soundings* 75 (1992): 365–81.

Schecter, Patricia. *Ida B. Wells Barnett and American Reforms, 1880–1930*. Chapel Hill: University of North Carolina Press, 2001.

Thompson, Mildred I. *Ida B. Wells-Barnett: An Exploratory Study of an American Black Woman, 1893–1930*. Brooklyn, NY: Carlson, 1990.

White Citizens' Council

The White Citizens' Council was the southern white reaction to the Supreme Court's landmark 1954 *Brown v. Board of Education* decision, which mandated the end of racially segregated public schools. This reaction varied widely. Groups such as the Ku Klux Klan sought to resist integration through ritual violence and terror, and "high-minded" southern politicians hoped to forestall the demise of Jim Crow with a revival of archaic constitutional theories, such as nullification and interposition. The White Citizens' Council, a segregationist organization that would eventually draw in thousands of anxious members across the South, appealed to the more "respectable" elements of society in its quest to undermine *Brown* and sustain the racial caste. Eschewing the predatory tactics of the Klan, the Citizens' Council instead relied on political pressure, economic intimidation, and legal maneuvering to achieve its goals. Before petering out in the 1960s, the Citizens' Council became one of the most powerful and effective instruments in rallying white public opinion against desegregation.

Residents of Indianola, Mississippi, organized the first chapter of the White Citizens' Council in July 1954. Within a matter of months, the council movement had spilled over into Alabama, Georgia, Virginia, and eventually all the former states of the Confederacy. Events such as the Montgomery Bus Boycott and the integration of the University of Alabama by Autherine Lucy, along with efforts by the NAACP to desegregate local school districts in the wake of *Brown*, propelled thousands of whites into the group. By 1956, arguably the council's peak year, organizers claimed more than 250,000 dues-paying members, making it, in the vaunted words of one official, one of the greatest mass movements of public opinion in American history. To better facilitate action and policy between the scattered chapters, council officials created the Citizens' Councils of America (CCA) in April 1956 and established headquarters in the Delta town of Greenwood, Mississippi. Leadership of the national organization fell to Robert Patterson, cofounder of the original Citizens' Council in Indianola, and William J. Simmons, who became the editor of the group's widely distributed newsletter, the *Citizens' Council*.

The council movement found its most fertile ground in the Black Belt regions of the South, where African Americans composed a substantial portion of the population and, for the most part, continued to earn their livings as sharecroppers and tenant farmers. The ranks of the early councils were filled with the middle and upper classes of southern white society—planters, lawyers, bankers, doctors, business-men, and politicians—who foresaw an erosion of their political hegemony with the implementation of *Brown* and who shuddered at the thoughts of their children attending class alongside the offspring of their employees and clients. To counter such a threat, thousands of prominent lowland whites readily adopted the council philosophy, which demanded a rigorous defense of the social order, strict conformity to the ideals of white supremacy, and a veritable holy war against the evils of "miscegenation" and "mongrelization."

In its crusade to stamp out proponents of integration, the Citizens' Councils used numerous legal and economic tactics. Members were encouraged to fire black workers who supported desegregation or who attempted to register to vote. Tenants and sharecroppers were ordered to vacate farms if they were suspected of "radical" or otherwise questionable activity. And the council routinely published the names of NAACP members to discourage their continued activism.

African Americans were not the sole targets of the council's wrath. White racial moderates and others who appeared "soft" on integration also found themselves at the mercy of the expanding movement. Council leaders conducted scurrilous cam-paigns to destroy the political careers of such "neo-Populists" as Jim Folsom of Alabama and Earl Long of Louisiana, men who refused to trumpet the rhetoric of white supremacy and racism. As a result, both men lost sway with the elector-ate. In Arkansas, the Capital Citizens' Council led the opposition to the 1957 inte-gration of Central High School in Little Rock. Members flooded Governor Orval Faubus's office with letters, urging him to use emergency powers to prevent inte-gration; harangued local school board members for "betraying" the white race with plans for desegregation; and took out newspapers ads to expose the plot between the NAACP and school officials. Largely because of such efforts, the integration of Central High flared into a constitutional crisis. In Mississippi, council officials led by William J. Simmons enjoyed a veritable stranglehold on state government and routinely flexed their political muscle to ensure strict adherence to the organ-ization's racial orthodoxy. Councilors there pressured lawmakers into passing favorable segregationist legislation, scoured libraries and schools for pro-integration materials, and waged a brutal campaign to subvert the freedom of the press. As a result, the Magnolia State, according to one observer, became a "closed society" where moderation was tantamount to treason.

By the early 1960s, after enjoying years of unbridled political and social influ-ence, the Citizens' Council movement began to decline. Random acts of violence by council members, petty infighting, and, most important, its failure to uphold segregation destroyed the organization. After passage of the Civil Rights Act of 1964 and the Voting Rights Act of 1965, all that remained were the diehards and "bitter-enders" who refused to accept the inevitable tide of history.

Gary S. Sprayberry

Further Reading

Bartley, Numan V. *Rise of Massive Resistance: Race and Politics in the South during the 1950's*. Baton Rouge: Louisiana State University Press, 1969.

Cook, James Graham. *The Segregationists*. New York: Appleton-Century-Crofts, 1962.

Martin, John Bartlow. *The Deep South Says Never*. New York: Ballantine Books, 1957.

McMillen, Neil R. *The Citizens' Council: Organized Resistance to the Second Reconstruction, 1954–64*. Urbana and Chicago: University of Illinois Press, 1971.

Wilkins, Roy

Roy Wilkins (1901–1981) was a prominent member and leader of the National Association for the Advancement of Colored People (NAACP). During his tenure with the organization, Wilkins and the NAACP helped to usher in the popular civil rights movement of the 1960s and push for popular legislation such as the Civil Rights Act of 1964 and the Voting Rights Act of 1965.

Roy Ottoway Wilkins was born August 30, 1901, in St. Louis, Missouri. Wilkins remained in Missouri with his mother, father, sister Armeda, and brother Earl until the death of his mother. Then Armeda, Earl, and Roy moved to St. Paul, Minnesota, to live with their deceased mother's sister Elizabeth and her husband Sam. Although Roy's father was still alive, in many ways he respected and viewed his uncle Sam as his stand-in father.

Wilkins began school at the Whittier Grammar School at the age of six. He graduated salutatorian of his class in June 1919 and then went to the University of Minnesota. Wilkins grew up with a benign look at race. Although he was the only African American at Whittier, he was always treated fairly, and he never viewed race as an issue. When Wilkins began studying at the University of Minnesota, however, this view changed. In the summer of 1920, three African Americans in Duluth, Minnesota, were unfairly lynched for the rape of a white woman. While all the evidence supported the innocence of the African American boys, they nonetheless were found guilty. This incident in Duluth forever altered Wilkins's view of race.

In 1922, Wilkins became the editor of the St. Paul *Appeal*—the voice of African Americans at the University of Minnesota and in the St. Paul community at large. The next year, Wilkins graduated from the university with a degree in sociology and a minor in journalism. After graduation in October 1923, Wilkins moved to Kansas City to take a job with the *Kansas City Call*. Once in Kansas City, Wilkins became entrenched in the Jim Crow South. As he saw members of his race being treated unfairly and he himself treated unfairly, he became more and more active in the promotion of black equality. While at the *Call*, Wilkins fought southern racism in his articles and editorials.

In the late 1920s, Wilkins lost his aunt Elizabeth, his uncle Sam, and sister Armeda within one week's time. Roy's brother Earl moved to Kansas City to be with him. In September 1929, Wilkins then married Minnie Badeau. The two never had children but stayed together until Wilkins's death. Wilkins's outspoken editorials at the *Call* gained national attention from the NAACP. The organization offered Wilkins a position with their newspaper, the *Crisis*, but Wilkins turned it down. A few years later, in 1931, the NAACP again offered Wilkins a position as assistant secretary, which he accepted. The position at the *Crisis* was merely a business position to Wilkins. As assistant secretary, however, Wilkins would be able to work side by side with some of the most prominent civil rights advocates in the country. In August, he moved to New York and began work with the NAACP. In 1934, when W. E. B. Du Bois left the organization, Wilkins took over as editor of the *Crisis*.

In 1949, Executive Secretary Walter White requested a leave of absence from the NAACP. Wilkins temporarily took over the position. In 1951, White returned. Four years later, in 1955, White died, and Wilkins became the executive secretary of the NAACP. Although many African Americans in the 1950s were promoting a gradual or slow pace for civil rights, Wilkins pushed for greater progress. He felt blacks had been treated unfairly long enough. As executive secretary, Wilkins not only promoted, but participated in, civil rights events such as the March on Washington in 1963 and the Selma marches in 1966.

In the 1960s, the civil rights movement exploded. The NAACP had ushered in the civil rights movement, but many other organizations were on the scene by 1965. Many of these new groups supported Black Power and separation of the races. Wilkins fought hard for black equality, but he would never support separatism as advocated by Black Power supporters. To Wilkins, separatism was a reinstatement of *Plessy v. Ferguson* and the case's separate-but-equal doctrine.

Throughout Wilkins's time with the NAACP, he met with Presidents Roosevelt, Truman, Eisenhower, Kennedy, Johnson, Nixon, Ford, and Carter. Through these meetings, Wilkins helped to promote black equality. He encouraged Kennedy and Johnson to pass the famed Civil Rights Act of 1964 and the Voting Rights Act of 1965. Wilkins always advocated civil rights through legislative means. He protested to the legislative, executive, and judicial branches of the government. He felt it was through these organizations that African Americans would receive their long-awaited equality.

In July 1977, Wilkins retired from the NAACP. Although this was not the end of the relationship between Wilkins and the NAACP, it was the end of his active role in the organization's leadership. Until his death in 1981, Wilkins continued to advocate for the NAACP and civil rights.

Mindy R. Weidman

Further Reading

Wilkins, Roy, with Tom Mathews. *Standing Fast: The Autobiography of Roy Wilkins*. New York: Da Capo Press, 1982.

Williams, Hosea

Hosea Williams was a pastor and civil rights activist known for his boundless energy. He served as a participant and leader in numerous civil rights demonstrations and organizations, including the Southern Christian Leadership Conference (SCLC), the NAACP, the Poor People's Campaign, Bloody Sunday, and the Memphis Sanitation Workers' Strike.

Born January 5, 1926, in Attapulgus, Georgia, to blind parents, Hosea Lorenzo Williams was raised by his grandparents Turner and Lela Williams, after his mother died while giving birth to his younger sister Teresa. While growing up under his grandparents' guidance in Decatur County, a poor area in southwest Georgia, Williams's affection and concern for the poor and underprivileged began as he became aware that many whites limited the life chances of African Americans in order to prevent them from accumulating wealth and property.

In 1939, Williams had a more intense introduction to the racial tension of the segregated South. A group of racist whites from Decatur County accused him of having an "affair" with a white girl from the area and sought to lynch him for his alleged inappropriate behavior. This mob approached his grandparents' home seeking Williams, but as he described later, his grandfather held them at bay with a gun until a friendly white neighbor interceded to prevent further violence.

Williams later moved to Tallahassee, Florida, and then back to Decatur County, finding work on farms, cleaning homes, serving as a caretaker, and working at a bus station between Decatur County, Georgia, and Tallahassee. Williams enlisted in the U.S. Army in 1942, serving as a weapons carrier as well as, for a time, a staff sergeant under General George S. Patton. Williams fought in the Battle of the Bulge, one of the most significant battles in France during World War II.

After returning to the United States, Williams was awarded the Purple Heart for wounds received in service. Life after military service for Williams was not the happiest of times. At a segregated Greyhound bus station in Americus, Georgia, he drank from a "Whites Only" water fountain, and a mob of whites nearly beat him to death for his actions. Williams later enrolled at Morris Brown College in Atlanta, Georgia, receiving a BS in chemistry in 1951, and later earned an MA in chemistry from Atlanta University.

Williams moved to Savannah, Georgia, and was employed by the U.S. Department of Agriculture Bureau of Entomology, becoming one of the first African American research chemists in the South. In Savannah, he began working with W. W. Law, who was the Savannah NAACP president. Under Law's direction, Williams became vice president of the Savannah NAACP branch, and they would lead the first sit-ins and night marches in Savannah in the early 1960s. He would also help desegregate the DeSoto Hotel. Williams gained statewide attention with this local movement and later became vice president of the Georgia NAACP.

In 1962, Williams left Savannah for Atlanta to become part of the national civil rights movement as head of the national board of the NAACP. Faced with discrimination within the organization, in 1963, he was brought into the Southern Christian Leadership Conference (SCLC) by Martin Luther King Jr., who saw Williams as someone who could be beneficial to the movement. At this time, the SCLC began to implement marches as a tactic to combat the injustices adhered to through segregation.

Williams's role in the SCLC is first remembered as he and John Lewis, the national leader of the Student Nonviolent Coordinating Committee (SNCC), led a march from Selma, Alabama, to Montgomery, Alabama, on March 7, 1965. This march became known as "Bloody Sunday." The objective of the march was to give then Alabama governor George Wallace a petition demanding the voting rights of African Americans in Alabama as guaranteed by the Fifteenth Amendment to the U.S. Constitution. In the aftermath of Bloody Sunday, many marchers endured injuries; Williams suffered a concussion and a fractured skull. Within days, President Lyndon B. Johnson passed legislation guaranteeing voting rights for blacks in the United States. On August 6, 1965, this legislation was put into law, disposing of the literacy tests and other policies that were designed to disenfranchise blacks in the South from voting.

Despite the rifts within leadership, Williams was of great use to King and the SCLC. Many people did not agree with Williams's ideology but still had respect for him. Aside from his role in "Bloody Sunday," Williams served numerous roles after the civil rights movement. In 1968, he was director of King's Poor People's Campaign, a movement whose mission was to end poverty in the United States. Much of the aspirations for the Poor People's Campaign dwindled with the assassination of King at the Lorraine Motel in Memphis, Tennessee, on April 4, 1968. Williams was present with King at this unfortunate time.

Williams's numerous arrests demonstrated his dedication to African Americans gaining civil rights. Williams also founded the Hosea Williams Feed the Hungry and Homeless Foundation in 1970. In 1973, he led a boycott against the department store Rich's Incorporated, and later took Richard H. Rich, the founder of Rich's, to court on a civil action suit against the corporation's practices.

While serving in the Georgia General Assembly, to which he was elected in 1974, Williams, as head of the Atlanta chapter of the SCLC, led a demonstration outside of an Atlanta hotel where President Gerald Ford was in attendance. Williams and 50 other demonstrators demanded to see the president to ask for jobs for the poor. After refusing to listen to the pleas of one of the aides to President Ford, Williams and three others were arrested and charged with trespassing and disorderly conduct. In 1987, Williams led 20,000 people into Forsyth County, Georgia, just north of Atlanta, to protest the racial tensions in the area that were elevated by the Ku Klux Klan.

Throughout his life, Williams showed determination to accomplish what he had his heart set on—changing the social, political, and economic status of blacks in America. Williams died on November 16, 2000, after a three-year battle with cancer.

Robert A. Bennett III

Further Reading

Branch, Taylor. *Parting the Waters: America in the King Years, 1954–63.* New York: Simon & Schuster, 1989.

Fayer, Steve, with Sarah Flynn. *Voices of Freedom: An Oral History of the Civil Rights Movement from the 1950s through the 1980s.* New York: Bantam Books, 1990.

Garrow, David J. *Bearing the Cross: Martin Luther King, Jr., and the Southern Christian Leadership Conference.* New York: Vintage Books, 1988.

Hornsby, Alton, Jr. *Milestones in 20th-Century African American History*, 529. Detroit, MI: Visible Ink Press, 1993.

Marable, Manning. *Race, Reform, and Rebellion: The Second Reconstruction in Black America, 1945–1990*, 283. Jackson: University Press of Mississippi, 1991.

Raines, Howell. *My Soul Is Rested: Movement Days in the Deep South Remembered.* New York: G. P. Putnam's Sons, 1977.

Washington, James Melvin, ed. *A Testament of Hope: The Essential Writings of Martin Luther King, Jr.* San Francisco: Harper & Row, 1986.

Williams, Robert F.

Robert F. Williams (1925–1996) was born on February 26, 1925, in Monroe, North Carolina. In the 1950s, he became a militant civil rights activist whose radicalism would have a tremendous influence on the Black Power movement. As early as 1941, his resistance to racial discrimination during a federal job-training program prompted the Federal Bureau of Investigation (FBI) to launch an investigation into his ties with communists. Racial clashes in American cities during World War II, coupled with his 18-month military service, further politicized Williams, who was discharged in 1946. Between 1947, when he married Mabel Ola Robinson, and 1953, Williams worked in the auto industry in Detroit before returning to the South, where he honed his skills as a writer at several all-black colleges. In 1954, after working in Harlem and California, financial problems prompted Williams to join the U.S. Marines, but his defiance toward racist discrimination in the military led to an early discharge in 1955.

Back in Monroe, Williams revived the town's defunct chapter of the National Association for the Advancement of Colored People (NAACP). As the chapter's president, he attracted many working-class members and, in 1957, launched a nonviolent protest campaign against Monroe's segregated swimming pool. Faced with a wave of violent intimidation from the Ku Klux Klan, Williams organized a black self-defense organization that successfully protected the local movement against white aggression. A year later, Williams widely publicized the controversial case of two black boys who had been sentenced to reform school for kissing a white girl. Skillfully exploiting the ideological Cold War struggle between the United States and the Soviet Union, the NAACP activist eventually secured the release of the two children.

In 1959, Williams's public statement that blacks would have to meet violence with violence when confronted with racist terrorism cemented his radical reputation and prompted the national NAACP to dismiss him as president of the Monroe chapter. Undaunted, Williams continued his civil rights activism, publishing the newsletter *Crusader* to disseminate his militant ideas on self-defense, black pride, economic nationalism, and anticolonial internationalism. Williams counted among his friends white socialists, Black Nationalists such as Malcolm X, and revolutionaries such as Fidel Castro, but his uncompromising militancy prevented his acceptance into the mainstream of the civil rights movement.

In 1961, Williams and his family were forced into Cuban exile. That year, a nonviolent protest by student activists in Monroe escalated into racial violence. Williams fled to avert bloodshed and to elude the FBI, which sought to prosecute him for allegedly kidnapping a white couple during the race riot. In Havana, Williams produced his own radio program, *Radio Free Dixie*, and continued to publish the *Crusader* to spread his ideas, which became increasingly radical. Going beyond his original call for black self-defense to protect the struggle for racial integration, he now advocated revolutionary guerrilla warfare and favored black separatism. During the second half of the 1960s, Williams's militant program had a tremendous impact on Black Power groups such as the Black Panther Party, the Revolutionary Action Movement, and the Republic of New Africa.

By 1965, Williams's relations with the Cuban government had soured, prompting him to move to China. Residing in Beijing, he became an ardent opponent of the escalating Vietnam War and sought to influence its outcome by producing antiwar propaganda. In 1969, Williams finally returned to the United States, where he briefly worked at the University of Michigan's Center for Chinese Studies before withdrawing from the national limelight to settle for a secluded life in Baldwin, Michigan. In 1976, the state of North Carolina dropped the remaining criminal charges against him. Robert Williams died of Hodgkin's disease on October 15, 1996.

Simon Wendt

Further Reading

Cohen, Robert Carl. *Black Crusader: A Biography of Robert Franklin Williams*. Secaucus, NJ: Lyle Stuart, 1972.

Rucker, Walter. " 'Crusader in Exile': Robert F. Williams and the Internationalized Struggle for Black Freedom in America." *Black Scholar* 36 (2006): 19–34.

Tyson, Timothy B. *Radio Free Dixie: Robert F. Williams and the Roots of Black Power.* Chapel Hill: University of North Carolina Press, 1999.

Williams, Robert F. *Negroes with Guns.* New York: Marzani and Munsell, 1962.

Women's Political Council of Montgomery

The Women's Political Council (WPC) of Montgomery, Alabama, was established in 1946 by Mary Fair Burks to inspire African Americans to "live above mediocrity, to elevate their thinking . . . and in general to improve their status as a group." The WPC sought to increase the political leverage of the black community by promoting civic involvement, increasing voter registration, and lobbying city officials to address racist policies. The group's work expanded to include public protest in 1955, when it helped initiate the Montgomery Bus Boycott, the event that brought Dr. Martin Luther King Jr. and the civil rights struggle into the national spotlight.

The original WPC chapter was made up of middle-class professionals, most of whom were educators and taught at the all-black Alabama State College or in the city's public schools. Burks, who was head of Alabama State College's English Department, served as WPC president until 1950, when she was succeeded by Jo Ann Robinson. By 1955, the WPC counted over 200 members in three neighborhood chapters.

The WPC had been planning for a citywide boycott of buses long before the historic boycott of 1955. In 1953, the WPC approached Montgomery city commissioners about unfair practices, such as having African Americans enter through the back of the bus after paying their fare up front. On May 21, 1954, Robinson sent a letter suggesting a city law, much like the one already implemented in other cities, in which black passengers would be seated from back to front and white passengers seated from front to back, until all seats were filled. The WPC's concerns were consistently dismissed by city commissioners, even following Robinson's statement that "even now plans are being made to ride less, or not at all, on our buses." After the March 1955 arrest of Claudette Colvin for refusing to give up her seat, King, Rufus Lewis, E. D. Nixon, Robinson, Irene West, and Burks met with the city commissioners but made little headway.

On December 1, 1955, the arrest of Rosa Parks gave the WPC the opportunity it had been waiting for. After Nixon, with the help of Virginia and Clifford Durr, gained Parks's release from jail and secured her approval to use her arrest as a test case to challenge bus seating policies, Nixon called King and other black leaders to inform them of the effort, already under way, to boycott Montgomery's buses. By this time, Robinson and the WPC had already drafted, mimeographed, and begun circulating leaflets across the city, announcing the boycott. Throughout the boycott, the WPC engaged in the daily activities of driving in the carpools, organizing mass meetings, and communicating with protesters.

Burks later stated that "members of the Women's Political Council were trailblazers" and credited the WPC for its ability "to arouse black middle-class women to do something about the things they could change in segregated Montgomery." Their role in the boycott, however, was not without consequences. Many WPC members were also teachers at Alabama State College, where officials closely investigated everyone involved in the boycott and in other student demonstrations. Tensions on the campus, especially after the sit-ins of 1960, caused many of the women, including Robinson and Burks, to resign from the college and find employment elsewhere, an event that dispersed key members throughout the nation.

Clayborne Carson

Further Reading

Burks, Mary Fair. "Trailblazers: Women in the Montgomery Bus Boycott." In *Women in the Civil Rights Movement*, edited by Vicki L. Crawford et al. Bloomington: Indiana University Press, 1990.

Robinson, Jo Ann. *Montgomery Bus Boycott*. Knoxville: University of Tennessee Press, 1987.

Primary Documents

From President's Committee on Civil Rights, *To Secure These Rights* (1947)

In 1946, in the wake of several brutal lynchings, including the murder of a black World War II veteran, President Harry S. Truman established the President's Committee on Civil Rights to investigate race relations in the United States and to make recommendations based on its findings. Concerns over how racial incidents were affecting America's image abroad and its ability to contain communism prodded the commission to take an honest look at the subject. In 1947, the committee issued its report, entitled To Secure These Rights, *in which it delineated the basic rights and principles of a democratic society and detailed the many ways in which African Americans were denied them. The report was the first of its kind and contained the strongest official condemnation of racial inequality since at least Reconstruction. Shortly after the committee issued its report, the president desegregated the armed forces. However, most of the committee's other recommendations were not implemented until the mid-1960s.*

The Time Is Now

Twice before in American history the nation has found it necessary to review the state of its civil rights. The first time was during the 15 years between 1776 and 1791, from the drafting of the Declaration of Independence through the Articles of Confederation experiment to the writing of the Constitution and the Bill of Rights. It was then that the distinctively American heritage was finally distilled from earlier views of liberty. The second time was when the Union was temporarily sundered over the question of whether it could exist "half-slave" and "half-free."

It is our profound conviction that we have come to a time for a third reexamination of the situation, and a sustained drive ahead. Our reasons for believing this are those of conscience, of self-interest, and of survival in a threatening world. Or to put it another way, we have a moral reason, an economic reason, and an international reason for believing that the time for action is now.

The Moral Reason

We have considered the American heritage of freedom at some length. We need no further justification for a broad and immediate program than the need to reaffirm our faith in the traditional American morality. The pervasive gap between our aims and what we actually do is creating a kind of moral dry rot which eats away at the emotional and rational bases of democratic beliefs. There are times when the difference between what we preach about civil rights and what we practice is shockingly illustrated by individual outrages. There are times when the whole structure of our ideology is made ridiculous by individual instances. And there are certain continuing, quiet, omnipresent practices which do irreparable damage to our beliefs.

As examples of "moral erosion" there are the consequences of suffrage limitations in the South. The fact that Negroes and many whites have not been allowed to vote in some states has actually sapped the morality underlying universal suffrage. Many men in public and private life do not believe that those who have been kept from voting are capable of self rule. They finally convince themselves that disfranchised people do not really have the right to vote.

Wartime segregation in the armed forces is another instance of how a social pattern may wreak moral havoc. Practically all white officers and enlisted men in all branches of service saw Negro military personnel performing only the most menial functions. They saw Negroes recruited for the common defense treated as men apart and distinct from themselves. As a result, men who might otherwise have maintained the equalitarian morality of their forebears were given reason to look down on their fellow citizens. This has been sharply illustrated by the Army study discussed previously, in which white servicemen expressed great surprise at the excellent performance of Negroes who joined them in the firing line. Even now, very few people know of the successful experiment with integrated combat units. Yet it is important in explaining why some Negro troops did not do well; it is proof that equal treatment can produce equal performance.

It is impossible to decide who suffers the greatest moral damage from our civil rights transgressions, because all of us are hurt. That is certainly true of those who are victimized. Their belief in the basic truth of the American promise is undermined. But they do have the realization, galling as it sometimes is, of being morally in the right. The damage to those who are responsible for these violations of our moral standards may well be greater. They, too, have been reared to honor the command of "free and equal." And all of us must share in the shame at the growth of hypocrisies like the "automatic" marble champion. All of us must endure the cynicism about democratic values which our failures breed.

The United States can no longer countenance these burdens on its common con-science, these inroads on its moral fiber.

The Economic Reason

One of the principal economic problems facing us and the rest of the world is achieving maximum production and continued prosperity. The loss of a huge, potential market for goods is a direct result of the economic discrimination which is practiced against many of our minority groups. A sort of vicious circle is produced. Discrimination depresses the wages and income of minority groups. As a result, their purchasing power is curtailed and markets are reduced. Reduced markets result in reduced production. This cuts down employment, which of course means lower wages and still fewer job opportunities. Rising fear, prejudice, and insecurity aggravate the very discrimination in employment which sets the vicious circle in motion.

Minority groups are not the sole victims of this economic waste; its impact is inevitably felt by the entire population.

Discrimination imposes a direct cost upon our economy through the wasteful duplication and many facilities and services required by the "separate but equal" policy. That the resources of the South are sorely strained by the burden of a double system of schools and other public services has already been indicated. Segregation is also economically wasteful for private business. Public transportation companies must often provide duplicate facilities to serve majority and minority groups separately. Places of public accommodation and recreation reject business when it comes in the form of unwanted persons. Stores reduce their sales by turning away minority customers. Factories must provide separate locker rooms, pay windows, drinking fountains, and washrooms for the different groups.

Similarly, the rates of disease, crime, and fires are disproportionately great in areas which are economically depressed as compared with wealthier areas. Many of the prominent American minorities are confined—by economic discrimination, by law, by restrictive covenants, and by social pressure—to the most dilapidated, undesirable locations. Property in these locations yields a smaller return in taxes, which is seldom sufficient to meet the inordinately high cost of public services in depressed areas. The majority pays a high price in taxes for the low status of minorities.

... It is not at all surprising that a people relegated to second-class citizenship should behave as second-class citizens. This is true, in varying degrees, of all of our minorities. What we have lost in money, production, invention, citizenship, and leadership as the price for damaged, thwarted personalities—these are beyond estimate.

The United States can no longer afford this heavy drain upon its human wealth, its national competence.

The International Reason

Our position in the postwar world is so vital to the future that our smallest actions have far-reaching effects. We have come to know that our own security in a highly interdependent world is inextricably tied to the security and well-being of all people and all countries. Our foreign policy is designed to make the United States an enormous, positive influence for peace and progress throughout the world. We have tried to let nothing, not even extreme political differences between ourselves and foreign nations, stand in the way of this goal. But our domestic civil rights shortcomings are a serious obstacle.

We cannot escape the fact that our civil rights record has been an issue in world politics. The world's press and radio are full of it. This Committee has seen a multitude of samples. We and our friends have been, and are, stressing our achievements. Those with competing philosophies have stressed—and are shamelessly distorting—our shortcomings. They have not only tried to create hostility toward us among specific nations, races, and religious groups. They have tried to prove our democracy an empty fraud, and our nation a consistent oppressor of underprivileged people. This may seem ludicrous to Americans, but it is sufficiently important to worry our friends.

... Our achievements in building and maintaining a state dedicated to the fundamentals of freedom have already served as a guide for those seeking the best road from chaos to liberty and prosperity. But it is not indelibly written that democracy will encompass the world. We are convinced that our way of life—the free way of life—holds a promise of hope for all people. We have what is perhaps the greatest responsibility ever placed upon a people to keep this promise alive. Only still greater achievements will do it.

The United States is not so strong, the final triumph of the democratic ideal is not so inevitable that we can ignore what the world thinks of us or our record.

Source: To Secure These Rights: The Report of the President's Committee on Civil Rights (Washington, DC: GPO, 1947).

FBI Investigation of Malcolm X (1953–1964)

Under the leadership of J. Edgar Hoover, director of the U.S. Federal Bureau of Investigation (FBI), the Justice Department launched a series of sweeping, long-term probes of U.S. citizens. Begun in the early 1950s, these domestic intelligence and spying operations were carried out in secret and were part of the Counterintelligence Program or COINTELPRO.

According to FBI documents obtained under the Freedom of Information Act, these operations targeted a wide range of citizens, including prominent political figures such as John F. Kennedy, entertainers such as actor and singer Paul Robeson, notorious gangsters and ordinary citizens suspected to have affiliations with Communist groups, and other people involved in activity deemed to be suspicious by the FBI bureaus or Justice Department officials in Washington.

Some of the primary targets of the Counterintelligence Program were black civil rights leaders such as W. E. B. Du Bois, black union organizers such as A. Philip Randolph, and "the leadership of so-called Nationalist-Hate Groups," according to FBI documents. "We should emphasize those leaders and organizations that are nationwide in scope are most capable of disrupting this country. These targets [are] members, and followers of the: Student Nonviolent Coordinating Committee (SNCC), Southern Christian Leadership Conference (SCLC), Revolutionary Action Movement (RAM), and Nation of Islam (NOI). Offices handling these cases and those of Stokely Carmichael of SNCC, H. Rap Brown of SNCC, Martin Luther King of SCLC, Maxwell Stanford of RAM, and Elijah Muhammad of NOI, should be alert for counterintelligence suggestions," according to the documents.

While political and civil rights activists, community organizers, the U.S. Congress, the courts, and government agencies had begun to take steps to assimilate African Americans into mainstream culture through legislation, court rulings, and political accommodations, the FBI's secret campaign handicapped their efforts to ensure the legal and civil rights of black Americans.

One of the FBI's targets was Malcolm Little. The investigation of Little began in February 1953 when Malcolm used the name "Malcolm K. Little" and lived in Inkster, Michigan, according to official FBI memos. The FBI file said the agency began investigating him to verify communist influence. His FBI file totaled 4,065 pages at the time of his death in 1965.

During the 11-year investigation, Malcolm Little became Malcolm X. He also rose to second in command in the ranks of the Nation of Islam, a Black Nationalist organization. By March 1964, however, following a dispute with the NOI leader-ship in Chicago, he had left the Nation of Islam and formed the Muslim Mosque, Inc. and the Organization of Afro-American Unity. He had also became known as the minister of the Nation of Islam.

Malcolm X was assassinated in 1965 while delivering a speech in New York City. Norman Butler, Thomas Johnson, and Talmage Hayer were convicted of Malcolm X's murder, and all three were sentenced to life in prison. The following is an excerpt from the Malcolm X file compiled by the FBI.

MALCOLM K. LITTLE currently resides at 23–11 97th Street, East Elmhurst, Queens, New York, a one family dwelling. . . .

LITTLE is a key figure of the NYO [New York Nation of Islam Organization] and until December, 1963, he was the Minister of NOI Mosque #7, NYC, and the offi-cial national representative of ELIJAH MUHAMMAD the head of the NOI. He was considered to be the number two man in the NOI.

In December, 1963, he was suspended from the NOI for 90 days. Because of an alleged power struggle within the NOI in which members of ELIJAH's family fear that Malcolm will succeed to the leadership of the NOI, the suspension of subject was made indefinite in March, 1964.

On March 8, 1964, LITTLE announced that he was breaking with the NOI, although still a believer, and would speak out on his own forming his own "black nationalist" group. Although LITTLE indicated he would not form a rival organi-zation to the NOI, it cannot yet be definitely determined whether he will or will not form his own defacto organization.

Mar. 19, 1964
NY 105–8999, CONFIDENTIAL

It is felt that a tesur on his telephone would provide invaluable information relative to his proposed activities in his new role, his supporters if any, and whether or not he will in fact establish his own organization.

Because of his split with the NOI, Bureau sources therein are of no value relative to LITTLE. Further, by this split he has deprived himself of working space and it is felt that most of his business will be conducted at his home and over his telephone.

The NYO requests authority to conduct a survey to determine the feasibility of placing a tesur on the telephone of LITTLE.

ROUTE IN ENVELOPE

To: SAC, New York (105–8999)
From: Director, FBI (100–399321)–86
MALCOLM K. LITTLE
INTERNAL SECURITY—NOI, CONFIDENTIAL
REWRAIRTEL 3/11/64

Provided full security is assured, you are authorized to conduct a survey looking toward the instillation of a technical surveillance on telephone [number] OL1–6320 at the home of Malcolm K. Little, 23–11 97th Street, East Elmhurst, Queens, New York.

Promptly advise results of same together with our recommendation regarding the installation of the technical surveillance.

Note:

Subject is former minister of Muslin Mosque Number 7, New York City, of the National of Islam (NOI) who was indefinitely suspended by Muhammad, national NOI leader, for his remarks concerning the assassination of President Kennedy. Little has now announced he will form a politically oriented organization more militant than the NOI which will participate in civil rights activities. The New York Office believes technical surveillance on Little's residence would provide valuable information concerning his activities in this connection which would not otherwise be available

CONFIDENTIAL
Mar 23, 1964
UNITED STATES GOVERNMENT

Memorandum

To: Director, FBI, DATE 3/30/64
FROM: SAC, NEW YORK (105–8999)
Subject: RECOMMENDATION FOR INSTALLATION OF
TECHNICAL OR MICROPHONE SURVEILLANCE
RE; Title, Malcolm K. Little aka

1. Name and address of subject: MALCOLM K. LITTLE 23–11 97th Street, East Elmhurst, Queens, NY

2. Location of technical operation: C

3. Other technical surveillance on same subject. NONE

4. Cost and manpower involved: Cost not known until installed.

5. Adequacy or security: Believed to be secured.

6. Type of case involved: Internal security case on Muslim Mosque, Inc., the newly formed black nationalist organization.

7. Connection or status of subject in the case: Leader and founder of the Muslim Mosque, Inc.

8. Specific information being sought: Information concerning contacts and activity of LITTLE and activity and growth of the Muslim Mosque, Inc.

9. Reasons for believing the specific information will be obtained by technical surveillance: LITTLE conducts business from his residence.

10. Importance of case and subject: Organization has philosophy of black nationalism, and has entered racial field where it suggests formation of rifle clubs by negroes to defend themselves.

11. Possibilities of obtaining desired information by other means (Explain in detail): Only other plausible means ... Since the organization is new (announced 3/12/64).

12. Risks of detection involved: Negligible to none.

13. Probable length of technical surveillance: Unknown.

14. Request made for technical surveillance by any outside agency (name specific officials, title and agency): Not known.

15. Remarks: Recommend approval of installation.

16. Recommendation of Assistant Director.

4/22/64
Airtel
To: SAC, New York (105–8999)
From: Director, FBI (100–399321)

MALCOLM K. LITTLE
INTERNAL SECURITY NOI, CONFIDENTIAL

Provided full security is assured, authority is granted to install tesur on the residence of Little, 23–11 97th Street, East Elmhurst, Queens, New York telephone number OL 1–6320. Advise time and date of installation and symbol number, Sulet justification 30 days after installation and each three months thereafter.

April 22, 1964
6/4/64
AIRTEL
To: Director, FBI (100–399321)
FROM: SAC, NEW YORK (105–8999), CONFIDENTIAL
SUBJECT: MALCOLM K. LITTLE aka

(00:New York
ReBuairtel dated 4/22/64.
Tesur on MALCOLM K. LITTLE, 23–11 97TH Street, East Elmhurst, Queens, NY, telephone number OL 1–6320, installed at 4:00 p.m., 6/3/64.

UNITED STATES GOVERNMENT

Memorandum

TO: DIRECTOR, FBI, DATE 7/2/64
FROM: SAC, NEW YORK (105–8999)
SUBJECT: JUSTIFICATION FOR CONTINUATION OF
TECHNICAL OR MICROPHONE SURVEILLANCE
RE: Title MALCOLM K. LITTLE, aka

1. Name of person or organization on whom surveillance placed: MALCOLM K. LITTLE.

2. Address where installation made. Also give exact room number or area covered: 23–11 97th Street, East Elmhurst, Queens, New York (single family dwelling)

3. Location of monitoring plant:

4. Dates of initial authorization and installation: Authorized 4/22/64 Installed 4:00 p.m., 6/3/64

5. Previous and other installations on the same subject (with dates and places): None.

6. If installation is a technical surveillance, answer following questions:

7. If a microphone surveillance involved, state number of microphones actually used and location of each: No.

8. Is the installation part of _____? If so, give symbol of other side of the combination: No.

9. Specific examples of valuable information obtained since previous report with indication of specific value of each item and the date information received. State what use was made of each item involved: See attached.

10. Could above information have been obtained from other sources and by other means? No.

11. _____?

12. Has security factor changed since installation?

13. Any request for the surveillance by outside agency (give name, title and agency): No.

14. _____?

15. _____?

16. Personnel
    Costs_____?

17. Remarks (By SAC): It is recommended that this source be continued in view of the prominence of LITTLE as a militant figure in the civil rights field, particularly as the leader of the Muslin Mosque, Inc and the organization of Afro-American Unity. Recommendation by Assistant Director: This technical surveillance is in the single family dwelling occupied by Malcolm K. Little, 23–11 97th Street, East Elmhurst, Queens, New York. It was first installed on 6/3/64. Little is a former national official of the Nation of Islam (NOI) who broke with that organization on 3/8/64 and formed Muslim Mosque, Incorporated (MMI) which he announced would be a broadly based black nationalist movement for Negroes only. Little has urged Negroes to abandon the doctrine of nonviolence and advocated that Negroes should form rifle clubs to protect their lives and property. At MMI rallies, Little has surrounded himself by guards armed with rifles and there have been numerous incidents recently involving gun-wielding MMI members where violence has been averted only by timely police action. At an MMI rally on 6/28/64, Little announced the formation of a new nonwhite civil rights action group called the "Organization of Afro-American Unity" with headquarters at MMI headquarters in New York City the aim of which would be to bring the United States racial problems before the United Nations and which would engage in civil rights demonstrations using the theme "by any means necessary."

In the past 30 days this technical surveillance has furnished valuable information on Little's travel plans, on the new Organization of Afro-American Unity, facts concerning the arrest of MMI members in Boston on a weapons charge following an altercation with Boston NOI members and information on a threat to Little's life by a person unknown. It also furnished information that Little was sending an assistant to Phoenix and Los Angeles to contact two women who had illegitimate children by Elijah Muhammad, NOI leader. Public announcement of these children by Little has caused the virtual state of war now existant (cq) between the NOI and MMI. On 6/30/64 information war between the NOI and MMI. On 6/30/64 information was received that Little sent telegrams to civil rights leaders Dr. Martin Luther King and James Foreman offering to send his followers to teach self-defense to Negroes if the Government did not provide Federal troops for protection.

All of the above information was furnished immediately to the Bureau and was disseminated to the Department and interested agencies. The Domestic Intelligence Division concurs with the recommendation of SAC, New York, that this installation be continued for additional three months.

UNITED STATES GOVERNMENT

Memorandum

DATE: July 28, 1964
TO: Mr. W. C. Sullivan
From: Mr. F. J. Baumgardner
SUBJECT: MUSLIM MOSQUE, INCORPORATED INTERNAL SECURITY—MMI

Reference is made to memorandum C. D. DeLoach to Mr. Mohr, dated 7/25/64, captioned "Racial Riots," and specifically to the last recommendation concerning establishment of additional technical and photographic surveillance coverage Malcolm X Little and the Muslim Mosque, Incorporated (MMI)

In connection with this matter it is noted Malcolm X Little is out of the U.S. on a tour of African nations and is not expected to return until 8/15/64. We presently have technical coverage on the residence of Malcolm X Little which is producing considerable valuable information. The New York Office has conducted surveys to determine whether additional installations are feasible . . .

A survey was also conducted by New York regarding the feasibility of installing microphone surveillances both at Little's residence and at the hotel. New York points out that the headquarters of MMI will be moved as soon as Little returns to the U.S. and such installations at this time would be impractical. New York also points out that microphone surveillances could not be monitored at the hotel or nearby . . . New York points out that the wife and child of Little are constantly at his residence and there are a number of Negroes constantly around the residence. Little has also maintained guards at his residence since receiving threats of bodily harm. Monitoring of microphone surveillances on the residence of Little could not be handled in the immediate neighborhood. Microphone coverage is not feasible at his residence.

CONFIDENTIAL
UNITED STATES GOVERNMENT

Memorandum
To: Director, FBI, 10/2/64
FROM: SAC, NEW YORK

It is recommended that this source be continued in view of the prominence of LIT-TLE as a militant figure in the civil rights field, particularly as the leader of the Muslim Mosque Inc., and the Organization of Afro-American Unity. Plus the fact that source recently advised that MALCOLM, who has been in Egypt since July, 1964, at the expense of the Egyptian Government, and expected to return to New York on 11/15/64, has been appointed to the board of the Supreme Council governing Islamic affairs and is qualified to spread Islam in America among the Afro-Americans . . .

Source has furnished the following valuable information on dates indicated:

7/3/64 Information that MALCOLM notified New York City Police Department that an attempt was made on his life.

7/4/64 Information that MALCOLM and his followers were attempting to make a big issue out of the reported attempt on MALCOLM's life in order to get the Negro people to support Him. (Police believe complaint on an attempt on MALCOLM's life was a publicity stung by MALCOLM) (Teletype to Bureau 7/4/64) . . .

Source: Freedom of Information request, Federal Bureau of Investigation, Department of Justice. http://vault.fbi.gov/malcolm-little-malcolm-x/malcolm-little-malcolm-x-hq-file-01-of-27/view.

Brown v. Board of Education (1954)

Considered one of the most important Supreme Court cases in American history, the Brown *case effectively reversed the course of American legal history on racial issues, and in the process likewise reversed the course of American society and race relations for future generations. It abolished the separate-but-equal doctrine established by* Plessy v. Ferguson *and* Cumming v. Richmond County Board of Education, *and opened all the nation's public schools to integration.*

May 17, 1954
APPEAL FROM THE UNITED STATES DISTRICT COURT FOR THE DISTRICT OF KANSAS

Syllabus
Segregation of white and Negro children in the public schools of a State solely on the basis of race, pursuant to state laws permitting or requiring such segregation,

denies to Negro children the equal protection of the laws guaranteed by the Four-teenth Amendment—even though the physical facilities and other "tangible" fac-tors of white and Negro schools may be equal.

1. The history of the Fourteenth Amendment is inconclusive as to its intended effect on public education.

2. The question presented in these cases must be determined not on the basis of conditions existing when the Fourteenth Amendment was adopted, but in the light of the full development of public education and its present place in American life throughout the Nation.

3. Where a State has undertaken to provide an opportunity for an education in its public schools, such an opportunity is a right which must be made available to all on equal terms.

4. Segregation of children in public schools solely on the basis of race deprives children of the minority group of equal educational opportunities, even though the physical facilities and other "tangible" factors may be equal.

5. The "separate but equal" doctrine adopted in Plessy v. Ferguson . . . has no place in the field of public education.

6. The cases are restored to the docket for further argument on specified ques-tions relating to the forms of the decrees.

MR. CHIEF JUSTICE [Earl] WARREN delivered the opinion of the Court.

These cases come to us from the States of Kansas, South Carolina, Virginia, and Delaware. They are premised on different facts and different local conditions, but a common legal question justifies their consideration together in this consolidated opinion.

In each of the cases, minors of the Negro race, through their legal representatives, seek the aid of the courts in obtaining admission to the public schools of their com-munity on a nonsegregated basis. In each instance, they had been denied admission to schools attended by white children under laws requiring or permitting segrega-tion according to race. This segregation was alleged to deprive the plaintiffs of the equal protection of the laws under the Fourteenth Amendment. In each of the cases other than the Delaware case, a three-judge federal district court denied relief to the plaintiffs on the so-called "separate but equal" doctrine announced by this Court in Plessy v. Ferguson. . . . Under that doctrine, equality of treatment is accorded when the races are provided substantially equal facilities, even though these facilities be separate. In the Delaware case, the Supreme Court of Delaware adhered to that doctrine, but ordered that the plaintiffs be admitted to the white schools because of their superiority to the Negro schools.

The plaintiffs contend that segregated public schools are not "equal" and cannot be made "equal," and that hence they are deprived of the equal protection of the laws. Because of the obvious importance of the question presented, the Court took jurisdiction. Argument was heard in the 1952 Term, and reargument was heard this Term on certain questions propounded by the Court.

Reargument was largely devoted to the circumstances surrounding the adoption of the Fourteenth Amendment in 1868. It covered exhaustively consideration of the Amendment in Congress, ratification by the states, then-existing practices in racial segregation, and the views of proponents and opponents of the Amendment. This discussion and our own investigation convince us that, although these sources cast some light, it is not enough to resolve the problem with which we are faced. At best, they are inconclusive. The most avid proponents of the post-War Amendments undoubtedly intended them to remove all legal distinctions among "all persons born or naturalized in the United States." Their opponents, just as certainly, were antagonistic to both the letter and the spirit of the Amendments and wished them to have the most limited effect. What others in Congress and the state legislatures had in mind cannot be determined with any degree of certainty.

An additional reason for the inconclusive nature of the Amendment's history with respect to segregated schools is the status of public education at that time. In the South, the movement toward free common schools, supported by general taxation, had not yet taken hold. Education of white children was largely in the hands of private groups. Education of Negroes was almost nonexistent, and practically all of the race were illiterate. In fact, any education of Negroes was forbidden by law in some states. Today, in contrast, many Negroes have achieved outstanding success in the arts and sciences, as well as in the business and professional world. It is true that public school education at the time of the Amendment had advanced further in the North, but the effect of the Amendment on Northern States was generally ignored in the congressional debates. Even in the North, the conditions of public education did not approximate those existing today. The curriculum was usually rudimentary; ungraded schools were common in rural areas; the school term was but three months a year in many states, and compulsory school attendance was virtually unknown. As a consequence, it is not surprising that there should be so little in the history of the Fourteenth Amendment relating to its intended effect on public education.

In the first cases in this Court construing the Fourteenth Amendment, decided shortly after its adoption, the Court interpreted it as proscribing all state-imposed discriminations against the Negro race. The doctrine of "separate but equal" did not make its appearance in this Court until 1896 in the case of Plessy v. Ferguson . . . involving not education but transportation. American courts have since labored with the doctrine for over half a century. In this Court, there have been six cases involving the "separate but equal" doctrine in the field of public education. In Cumming v. County Board of Education . . . and Gong Lum v. Rice . . . the validity of the doctrine itself was not challenged. In more recent cases, all on the graduate school level, inequality was found in that specific benefits enjoyed by white students were denied to Negro students of the same educational qualifications. . . . In none of these cases was it necessary to reexamine the doctrine to grant relief to the Negro plaintiff. And in Sweatt v. Painter . . . the Court expressly reserved decision on the question whether Plessy v. Ferguson should be held inapplicable to public education.

In the instant cases, that question is directly presented. Here, unlike Sweatt v. Painter, there are findings below that the Negro and white schools involved have been equalized, or are being equalized, with respect to buildings, curricula, qualifications and salaries of teachers, and other "tangible" factors. Our decision, therefore, cannot turn on merely a comparison of these tangible factors in the Negro and white schools involved in each of the cases. We must look instead to the effect of segregation itself on public education.

In approaching this problem, we cannot turn the clock back to 1868, when the Amendment was adopted, or even to 1896, when Plessy v. Ferguson was written. We must consider public education in the light of its full development and its present place in American life throughout the Nation. Only in this way can it be determined if segregation in public schools deprives these plaintiffs of the equal protection of the laws.

Today, education is perhaps the most important function of state and local governments. Compulsory school attendance laws and the great expenditures for education both demonstrate our recognition of the importance of education to our democratic society. It is required in the performance of our most basic public responsibilities, even service in the armed forces. It is the very foundation of good citizenship. Today it is a principal instrument in awakening the child to cultural values, in preparing him for later professional training, and in helping him to adjust normally to his environment. In these days, it is doubtful that any child may reasonably be expected to succeed in life if he is denied the opportunity of an education. Such an opportunity, where the state has undertaken to provide it, is a right which must be made available to all on equal terms.

We come then to the question presented: Does segregation of children in public schools solely on the basis of race, even though the physical facilities and other "tangible" factors may be equal, deprive the children of the minority group of equal educational opportunities? We believe that it does.

In Sweatt v. Painter . . . in finding that a segregated law school for Negroes could not provide them equal educational opportunities, this Court relied in large part on "those qualities which are incapable of objective measurement but which make for greatness in a law school." In McLaurin v. Oklahoma State Regents . . . the Court, in requiring that a Negro admitted to a white graduate school be treated like all other students, again resorted to intangible considerations: " . . . his ability to study, to engage in discussions and exchange views with other students, and, in general, to learn his profession." Such considerations apply with added force to children in grade and high schools. To separate them from others of similar age and qualifications solely because of their race generates a feeling of inferiority as to their status in the community that may affect their hearts and minds in a way unlikely ever to be undone. The effect of this separation on their educational opportunities was well stated by a finding in the Kansas case by a court which nevertheless felt compelled to rule against the Negro plaintiffs:

Segregation of white and colored children in public schools has a detrimental effect upon the colored children. The impact is greater when it has the sanction of the law, for the policy of separating the races is usually interpreted as denoting the inferiority of the negro group. A sense of inferiority affects the motivation of a child to learn. Segregation with the sanction of law, therefore, has a tendency to [retard] the educational and mental development of negro children and to deprive them of some of the benefits they would receive in a racial[ly] integrated school system.

Whatever may have been the extent of psychological knowledge at the time of Plessy v. Ferguson, this finding is amply supported by modern authority. Any language in Plessy v. Ferguson contrary to this finding is rejected.

We conclude that, in the field of public education, the doctrine of "separate but equal" has no place. Separate educational facilities are inherently unequal. Therefore, we hold that the plaintiffs and others similarly situated for whom the actions have been brought are, by reason of the segregation complained of, deprived of the equal protection of the laws guaranteed by the Fourteenth Amendment. This disposition makes unnecessary any discussion whether such segregation also violates the Due Process Clause of the Fourteenth Amendment.

Because these are class actions, because of the wide applicability of this decision, and because of the great variety of local conditions, the formulation of decrees in these cases presents problems of considerable complexity. On reargument, the consideration of appropriate relief was necessarily subordinated to the primary question—the constitutionality of segregation in public education. We have now announced that such segregation is a denial of the equal protection of the laws. In order that we may have the full assistance of the parties in formulating decrees, the cases will be restored to the docket, and the parties are requested to present further argument on Questions 4 and 5 previously propounded by the Court for the reargument this Term. The Attorney General of the United States is again invited to participate. The Attorneys General of the states requiring or permitting segregation in public education will also be permitted to appear as amici curiae upon request to do so by September 15, 1954, and submission of briefs by October 1, 1954.

It is so ordered.

Source: Brown v. Board of Education, 347 U.S. 483 (1954).

From "The Southern Manifesto: Declaration of Constitutional Principles" (1956)

In the wake of the Brown *decision, numerous southerners displayed their unwillingness to comply with the Supreme Court's order to desegregate their schools. In Mississippi, White Citizens' Councils were formed with the aim of maintaining segregation through economic and political pressure. These councils rapidly spread across the South. At the same time, the Ku Klux Klan enjoyed a revival, and arch-segregationist politicians won a series of victories over more moderate candidates.*

The following document, "The Southern Manifesto," provides a sense of the breadth of southern resistance to desegregation. Largely the work of Senator Samuel J. Ervin Jr. of North Carolina, the "Manifesto," which was read into the Congressional Record, *was endorsed by nearly all of the South's leading citizens, including 100 congressmen from 11 states of the old Confederacy. Even though the "Manifesto" called for using only lawful means to resist desegregation, some contend that it legitimated extralegal forms of resistance.*

The unwarranted decision of the Supreme Court in the public school cases is now bearing the fruit always produced when men substitute naked power for established law.

The Founding Fathers gave us a Constitution of checks and balances because they realized the inescapable lesson of history that no man or group of men can be safely entrusted with unlimited power. They framed this Constitution with its provisions for change by amendment in order to secure the fundamentals of government against the dangers of temporary popular passion or the personal predilections of public office-holders.

We regard the decision of the Supreme Court in the school cases as a clear abuse of judicial power. It climaxes a trend in the Federal Judiciary undertaking to legislate, in derogation of the authority of Congress, and to encroach upon the reserved rights of the States and the people.

The original Constitution does not mention education. Neither does the 14th amendment nor any other amendment. The debates preceding the submission of the 14th amendment clearly show that there was no intent that it should affect the system of education maintained by the States. . . .

In the case *Plessy v. Ferguson* in 1896 the Supreme Court expressly declared that under the 14th amendment no person was denied any of his rights if the States provided separate but equal public facilities. This decision has been followed in many other cases. It is notable that the Supreme Court, speaking through Chief Justice Taft, a former President of the United States, unanimously declared in 1927 in *Lum vs. Rice* that the "separate but equal" principle is "within the discretion of the State in regulating its public schools and does not conflict with the 14th amendment."

This interpretation, restated time and again, became a part of the life of the people of many of the States and confirmed their habits, customs, traditions, and way of life. It is founded on elemental humanity and common sense, for parents should not be deprived by Government of the right to direct the lives and education of their own children. . . .

This unwarranted exercise of power by the Court, contrary to the Constitution, is creating chaos and confusion in the States principally affected. It is destroying the amicable relations between the white and Negro races that have been created through 90 years of patient effort by the good people of both races. It has planted hatred and suspicion where there has been heretofore friendship and understanding.

Without regard to the consent of the governed, outside agitators are threatening immediate and revolutionary changes in our public-school systems. If done, this is certain to destroy the system of public education in some of the States.

With the gravest concern for the explosive and dangerous condition created by this decision and inflamed by outside meddlers:

We reaffirm our reliance on the Constitution as the fundamental law of the land.

We decry the Supreme Court's encroachments on the rights reserved to the States and to the people, contrary to established law, and to the Constitution.
We commend the motives of those States which have declared the intention to resist forced integration by any lawful means.

We appeal to the States and people who are not directly affected by these decisions to consider the constitutional principles involved against the time when they too, on issues vital to them, may be victims of judicial encroachment.

Even though we constitute a minority in the present Congress, we have full faith that a majority of the American people believe in the dual system of government which has enabled us to achieve our greatness and will in time demand that the reserved rights of the States and of the people be made secure against judicial usurpation.

We pledge ourselves to use all lawful means to bring about a reversal of this decision which is contrary to the Constitution and to prevent the use of force in its implementation.

In this trying period, as we all seek to right this wrong, we appeal to our people not to be provoked by the agitators and troublemakers invading our States and to scrupulously refrain from disorder and lawless acts.

Source: Congressional Record, 84th Cong., 2nd sess., March 12, 1956, 4460–64, 4515–16.

From President Dwight D. Eisenhower, Radio and Television "Address to the American People on the Situation in Little Rock" (September 24, 1957)

In response to the Brown *decision, the school board in Little Rock, Arkansas, developed a plan for gradually desegregating its public schools, beginning with the enrollment of nine black students at Central High School. As the fall of 1957 approached, however, public opposition to the plan grew. Governor Orval Faubus, who sought to shore up his support among arch-segregationists, incited much of this opposition.*

On the first day of school, the National Guard, under Faubus's orders, blocked Elizabeth Eckford, one of the nine, from entering Central High and allowed a white mob to taunt, harass, and nearly lynch her.

This action, in combination with Faubus's defiance of a federal court order commanding that the school implement the desegregation plan, compelled President Eisenhower to act. Initially, Ike met with Faubus at the president's summer retreat in Newport, Rhode Island, where he negotiated what he thought was a peaceful resolution to the crisis. When Faubus reneged on his agreement to allow the desegregation of Central High—by withdrawing all troops from Little Rock, thus leaving the black students at the mercy of white mobs—Eisenhower determined he had to intervene. In a televised address, excerpted below, the president explained his decision to send federal troops to Little Rock. Observing that defiance of the law by white mobs was damaging America's image abroad, he declared that he had a constitutional obligation to maintain law and order. While the bulk of the forces were withdrawn shortly after the initial crisis, some federal troops remained in Little Rock for the entire school year.

My fellow citizens . . . I must speak to you about the serious situation that has arisen in Little Rock. . . . In that city, under the leadership of demagogic extremists, disorderly mobs have deliberately prevented the carrying out of proper orders from a federal court. Local authorities have not eliminated that violent opposition and, under the law, I yesterday issued a proclamation calling upon the mob to disperse.

This morning the mob again gathered in front of the Central High School of Little Rock, obviously for the purpose of again preventing the carrying out of the court's order relating to the admission of Negro children to that school.

Whenever normal agencies prove inadequate to the task and it becomes necessary for the executive branch of the federal government to use its powers and authority to uphold federal courts, the President's responsibility is inescapable.

In accordance with that responsibility, I have today issued an Executive Order directing the use of troops under federal authority to aid in the execution of federal law at Little Rock, Arkansas. This became necessary when my Proclamation of yesterday was not observed, and the obstruction of justice still continues.

It is important that the reasons for my action be understood by all our citizens. As you know, the Supreme Court of the United States has decided that separate public educational facilities for the races are inherently unequal and therefore compulsory school segregation laws are unconstitutional. . . .

During the past several years, many communities in our southern states have instituted public school plans for gradual progress in the enrollment and attendance of school children of all races in order to bring themselves into compliance with the law of the land.

They thus demonstrated to the world that we are a nation in which laws, not men, are supreme. . . .

Now let me make it very clear that federal troops are not being used to relieve local and state authorities of their primary duty to preserve the peace and order of the community. . . .

The proper use of the powers of the Executive Branch to enforce the orders of a federal court is limited to extraordinary and compelling circumstances. Manifestly, such an extreme situation has been created in Little Rock. This challenge must be met and with such measures as will preserve to the people as a whole their lawfully protected rights in a climate permitting their free and fair exercise.

The overwhelming majority of our people in every section of the country are united in their respect for observance of the law—even in those cases where they may disagree with that law. . . .

A foundation of our American way of life is our national respect for law.

In the South, as elsewhere, citizens are keenly aware of the tremendous disservice that has been done to the people of Arkansas in the eyes of the nation, and that has been done to the nation in the eyes of the world.

At a time when we face grave situations abroad because of the hatred that communism bears toward a system of government based on human rights, it would be difficult to exaggerate the harm that is being done to the prestige and influence, and indeed to the safety, of our nation and the world.

Our enemies are gloating over this incident and using it everywhere to misrepresent our whole nation. We are portrayed as a violator of those standards of conduct which the people of the world united to proclaim in the Charter of the United Nations. There they affirmed "faith in fundamental human rights" and "in the dignity and worth of the human person" and they did so "without distinction as to race, sex, language or religion."

And so, with deep confidence, I call upon the citizens of the State of Arkansas to assist in bringing an immediate end to all interference with the law and its processes. If resistance to the federal court orders ceases at once, the further presence of federal troops will be unnecessary and the City of Little Rock will return to its normal habits of peace and order and a blot upon the fair name and high honor of our nation in the world will be removed.

Thus will be restored the image of America and all its parts as one nation, indivisible, with liberty and justice for all.

Source: Public Papers of the Presidents of the United States, Dwight D. Eisenhower, 1957 (Washington, DC: GPO, 1958).

Jackie Robinson: Letter to President Kennedy (1961)

Baseball player and civil rights advocate Jackie Robinson's lack of support for John F. Kennedy's bid for the presidency led to an angry exchange with Kennedy's younger brother, Robert Kennedy. Robinson felt that Kennedy was playing both sides in supporting civil rights and sit-ins while at the same time courting bigoted southerners. In this letter, Robinson shares his optimism for Kennedy's leadership but urges him to pick up the pace in his administration's agenda to support civil rights.

February 9, 1961
The President
The White House

My dear Mr. President:

I believe I now understand and appreciate better your role in the continuing struggle to fulfill the American promise of equal opportunity for all.

While I am very happy over your obviously fine start as our President, my concern over Civil Rights and my vigorous opposition to your election is one of sincerity. The direction you seem to be going indicates America is in for great leadership, and I will be most happy if my fears continue to be proven wrong. We are naturally keeping a wondering eye on what will happen, and while any opposition or criticism may not be the most popular thing when you are leading so well, you must know that as an individual I am interested because what you do or do not do in the next 4 years could have a serious effect upon my children's future.

In your letter to me of July 1, 1960, you indicated you would use the influence of the White House in cases where moral issues are involved. You have re-iterated your stand, and we are very happy. Still, we are going to use whatever voice we have to awaken our people. With the new emerging African nations, Negro Americans must assert themselves more, not for what we can get as individuals, but for the good of the Negro masses.

I thank you for what you have done so far, but it is not how much has been done but how much more there is to do. I would like to be patient Mr. President, but patience has caused us years in our struggle for human dignity. I will continue to hope and pray for your aggressive leadership but will not refuse to criticise if the feeling persist that Civil Rights is not on the agenda for months to come.

Source: National Archives.

From John F. Kennedy, "Address on Civil Rights" (June 11, 1963)

John F. Kennedy's election to the presidency in 1960 and his reputation for political courage and vigor raised the hopes of millions of African Americans. Yet, for two years, President Kennedy let the African American community down. Not wanting to jeopardize the rest of his domestic and foreign policy agenda, which depended on white southern support, he neither proposed significant civil rights legislation nor spoke to the nation about its racial problems. Even when faced with crises such as the Freedom Rides and the University of Mississippi's refusal to enroll James Meredith, President Kennedy tended to equivocate.

Yet the civil rights struggle did not retreat from the streets, keeping the pressure on Kennedy to live up to his promise to promote civil rights and to desegregate public housing in particular. On the evening of June 11, 1963, he delivered a nationally televised speech, one of the most significant discussions of racial matters by a president in American history. In the speech, Kennedy demanded that the nation honor its moral principles and called for sweeping civil rights legislation. In November 1963, however, he was assassinated in Dallas, Texas, his proposed civil rights bill still bottled up in Congress.

Good evening my fellow citizens. This afternoon, following a series of threats and defiant statements, the presence of Alabama National Guardsmen was required on the campus of the University of Alabama to carry out the final and unequivocal order of the United States District Court of the Northern District of Alabama.

The order called for the admission of two clearly qualified young Alabama residents who happened to have been born Negro.

That they were admitted peacefully on the campus is due in good measure to the conduct of the students of the University of Alabama who met their responsibilities in a constructive way.

I hope that every American, regardless of where he lives, will stop and examine his conscience about this and other related incidents.

This nation was founded by men of many nations and backgrounds. It was founded on the principle that all men are created equal, and that the rights of every man are diminished when the rights of one man are threatened.

Today we are committed to a worldwide struggle to promote and protect the rights of all who wish to be free. And when Americans are sent to Vietnam or West Berlin we do not ask for whites only.

It ought to be possible, therefore, for American students of any color to attend any public institution they select without having to be backed up by troops. It ought to be possible for American consumers of any color to receive equal service in places of public accommodation, such as hotels and restaurants, and theaters and retail stores without being forced to resort to demonstrations in the street.

And it ought to be possible for American citizens of any color to register and to vote in a free election without interference or fear of reprisal.

It ought to be possible, in short, for every American to enjoy the privileges of being American without regard to his race or his color.

In short, every American ought to have the right to be treated as he would wish to be treated, as one would wish his children to be treated. But this is not the case.

The Negro baby born in America today, regardless of the section or the state in which he is born, has about one-half as much chance of completing high school as a white baby, born in the same place, on the same day. . . . twice as much chance of becoming unemployed . . . a life expectancy which is seven years shorter. . . .

This is not a sectional issue. Difficulties over segregation and discrimination exist in almost every city . . . producing . . . a rising tide of discontent that threatens the public safety.

Nor is this a partisan issue. In a time of domestic crisis, men of goodwill and generosity should be able to unite regardless of party or politics.

This is not even a legal or legislative issue alone. It is better to settle these matters in the courts than on the streets, and new laws are needed at every level. But law alone cannot make men see right.

We are confronted primarily with a moral issue. It is as old as the Scriptures and is as clear as the American Constitution. The heart of the question is whether all Americans are to be afforded equal rights and equal opportunities; whether we are going to treat our fellow Americans as we want to be treated.

If an American, because his skin is dark, cannot eat lunch in a restaurant open to the public; if he cannot send his children to the best public school available; if he cannot vote for the public officials who represent him; if, in short, he cannot enjoy the full and free life which all of us want, then who among us would be content to have the color of his skin changed and stand in his place?

Who among us would then be content with the counsels of patience and delay? One hundred years of delay have passed since President Lincoln freed the slaves, yet their heirs, their grandsons, are not fully free. . . .

And this nation, for all its hopes and all its boasts, will not be fully free until all its citizens are free.

We preach freedom around the world, and we mean it. And we cherish our freedom here at home. But are we to say to the world—and more importantly to each other—that this is the land of the free, except for the Negroes. . . .

Now the time has come for this nation to fulfill its promise. The events in Birmingham and elsewhere have so increased the cries for equality that no city or state or legislative body can prudently choose to ignore them.

The fires of frustration and discord are burning in every city, North and South. Where legal remedies are not at hand, redress is sought in the streets in demonstrations, parades and protests, which create tensions and threaten violence—and threaten lives.

We face, therefore, a moral crisis as a country and a people. It cannot be met by repressive police action. It cannot be left to increased demonstrations in the streets. It cannot be quieted by token moves or talk. It is time to act in the Congress, in your state and local legislative body, in all of our daily lives.

It is not enough to pin the blame on others, to say this is a problem of one section of the country or another, or deplore the facts that we face. A great change is at hand, and our task, our obligation is to make that revolution, that change peaceful and constructive for all.

Those who do nothing are inviting shame as well as violence. Those who act boldly are recognizing right as well as reality.

Next week I shall ask the Congress of the United States to act, to make a commitment it has not fully made in this century to the proposition that race has no place in American life or law. . . .

But legislation, I repeat, cannot solve this problem alone. It must be solved in the homes of every American in every community across our country.

In this respect, I want to pay tribute to those citizens, North and South, who've been working in their communities to make life better for all. They are acting not out of a sense of legal duty but out of a sense of human decency. Like our soldiers and sailors in all parts of the world, they are meeting freedom's challenge on the firing line and I salute them for their honor—their courage. . . .

We have a right to expect that the Negro community will be responsible, will uphold the law. But they have a right to expect that the law will be fair, that the Constitution will be color blind, as Justice Harlan said at the turn of the century.

Source: Public Papers of the Presidents of the United States, John F. Kennedy, 1963 (Washington, DC: GPO, 1964).

George Wallace: Inaugural Address (1963)

By 1964, Alabama governor George Wallace had become the most notorious white supremacist in the nation. In the 1950s, Wallace had run for governor as a popu-list/moderate. He lost and vowed "never to be out-niggered again." A fiery orator and a masterful politician, Wallace not only defended the southern way of life, but he reached out to whites in the North with subtle and not-so-subtle racist appeals. In 1964, he entered several presidential primaries and did remarkably well in a handful of border and northern states. In 1968, running as an independent candi-date for president, he won a larger percentage of the vote than any third-party can-didate for president since Theodore Roosevelt. Four years later, running as a Democrat, he strung together a series of primary victories, only to have his cam-paign cut short by a bullet from an would-be assassin, which left him paralyzed and unable to complete his run for the White House. His most famous speech, his first Inaugural Address of January 14, 1963, is excerpted below, a speech that fea-tures Wallace's defiant defense of segregation and populist tone.

Governor Patterson, Governor Barnett . . . fellow Alabamians:

. . . This is the day of my Inauguration as Governor of the State of Alabama. And on this day I feel a deep obligation to renew my pledges, my covenants with you . . . the people of this great state.
General Robert E. Lee said that "duty" is the sublimest word in the English lan-guage, and I have come, increasingly, to realize what he meant. I SHALL do my duty to you, God helping . . . to every man, to every woman . . . yes, and to every child in this State. . . .

Today I have stood, where once Jefferson Davis stood, and took an oath to my peo-ple. It is very appropriate then that from this Cradle of the Confederacy, this very heart of the Great Anglo-Saxon Southland, that today we sound the drum for free-dom as have our generations of forebears before us done, time and again down through history. Let us rise to the call of freedom-loving blood that is in us and send our answer to the tyranny that clanks its chains upon the South. In the name of the greatest people that ever trod the earth, I draw the line in the dust and toss the gauntlet before the feet of tyranny . . . and I say . . . segregation now . . . segregation tomorrow . . . segregation forever.

The Washington, D.C. school riot report is disgusting and revealing. We will not sacrifice our children to any such type of school system—and you can write that down. The federal troops in Mississippi could better be used guarding the safety of the citizens of Washington D.C., where it is even unsafe to walk or go to a ball game—and that is the nation's capitol. I was safer in a B-29 bomber over Japan during the war in an air raid, than the people of Washington are walking in the White House neighborhood. A closer example is Atlanta. The city officials fawn for political reasons over school integration and THEN build barricades to stop residential integration—what hypocrisy!

Let us send this message back to Washington . . . that from this day we are standing up, and the heel of tyranny does not fit the neck of an upright man . . . that we intend to take the offensive and carry our fight for freedom across the nation, wielding the balance of power we know we possess in the Southland. . . . that WE, not the insipid bloc voters of some sections will determine in the next election who shall sit in the White House . . . that from this day, from this minute, we give the word of a race of honor that we will not tolerate their boot in our face no longer. . . .

Hear me, Southerners! You sons and daughters who have moved North and West throughout this nation. We call on you from your native soil to join with us in national support and vote, and we know wherever you are, away from the hearths of the Southland, that you will respond, for though you may live in the farthest reaches of this vast country, your heart has never left Dixieland.

And you native sons and daughters of old New England's rock-ribbed patriotism, and you sturdy natives of the great Midwest, and you descendants of the Far West flaming spirit of pioneer freedom, we invite you to come and be with us, for you are of the Southern mind, and the Southern spirit, and the Southern philosophy. You are Southerners too and brothers with us in our fight. . . .

To realize our ambitions and to bring to fruition our dreams, we as Alabamians must take cognizance of the world about us. We must re-define our heritage, re-school our thoughts in the lessons our forefathers knew so well, first hand, in order to function and to grow and to prosper. We can no longer hide our head in the sand

and tell ourselves that the ideology of our free fathers is not being attacked and is not being threatened by another idea, for it is. We are faced with an idea that if centralized government assumes enough authority, enough power over its people that it can provide a utopian life, that if given the power to dictate, to forbid, to require, to demand, to distribute, to edict and to judge what is best and enforce that will of judgment upon its citizens from unimpeachable authority, then it will produce only "good" and it shall be our father and our God. It is an idea of government that encourages our fears and destroys our faith, for where there is faith, there is no fear, and where there is fear, there is no faith. . . .

Not so long ago men stood in marvel and awe at the cities, the buildings, the schools, the autobahns that the government of Hitler's Germany had built . . . but it could not stand, for the system that built it had rotted the souls of the builders and in turn rotted the foundation of what God meant that God should be. Today that same system on an international scale is sweeping the world. It is the "changing world" of which we are told. It is now called "new" and "liberal." It is as old as the oldest dictator. It is degenerate and decadent. As the national racism of Hitler's Germany persecuted a national minority to the whim of a national majority, so the international racism of liberals seek to persecute the international white minority to the whim of the international colored majority, so that we are footballed about according to the favor of the Afro-Asian bloc. But the Belgian survivors of the Congo cannot present their case to the war crimes commission . . . nor the survivors of Castro, nor the citizens of Oxford, Mississippi.

It is this theory of international power politic that led a group of men on the Supreme Court for the first time in American history to issue an edict, based not on legal precedent, but upon a volume, the editor of which has said our Constitution is outdated and must be changed and the writers of which, some had admittedly belonged to as many as half a hundred communist front organizations. It is this theory that led this same group of men to briefly bare the ungodly core of the philosophy in forbidding little schoolchildren to say a prayer. . . .

This nation was never meant to be a unit of one but a unit of the many, that is the exact reason our freedom-loving forefathers established the states, so as to divide the rights and powers among the many states, insuring that no central power could gain master control.

In united effort we were meant to live under this government, whether Baptist, Methodist . . . or whatever one's denomination or religious belief, each respecting the others right to a separate denomination. And so it was meant in our political lives . . . each . . . respecting the rights of others to be separate and work from within the political framework. . . .

And so it was meant in our racial lives, each race, within its own framework has the freedom to teach, to instruct, to develop, to ask for and receive deserved help from others of separate racial stations. This is the great freedom of our American founding fathers. But if we amalgamate into the one unit as advocated by the communist philosophers, then the enrichment of our lives, the freedom for our development, is gone forever. We become, therefore, a mongrel unit of one under a single all powerful government and we stand for everything and for nothing.

The true brotherhood of America, of respecting separateness of others and uniting in effort, has been so twisted and distorted from its original concept that there is small wonder that communism is winning the world.

We invite the Negro citizens of Alabama to work with us from his separate racial station, as we will work with him, to develop, to grow. . . . But we warn those, of any group, who would follow the false doctrine of communistic amalgamation that we will not surrender our system of government, our freedom of race and religion, that freedom was won at a hard price and if it requires a hard price to retain it, we are able and quite willing to pay it. . . .

We remind all within hearing of the Southland that . . . Southerners played a most magnificent part in erecting this great divinely inspired system of freedom, and as God is our witness, Southerners will save it.

Let us, as Alabamians, grasp the hand of destiny and walk out of the shadow of fear and fill our divine destiny. Let us not simply defend but let us assume the leadership of the fight and carry our leadership across the nation. God has placed us here in this crisis. Let us not fail in this our most historical moment. . . .

Source: Alabama Department of Archives and History.

Civil Rights Act (1964)

The following excerpt is from the Civil Rights Act of 1964, a landmark in American legal history that provided much of the legal basis for the modern civil rights movement. Enacted on July 2, 1964, the law is lengthy and covers many areas of discrimination, most notably voting rights and segregation. Although it was originally passed to protect the rights of African Americans, sections of the law have since been used by a variety of groups in their fight against discrimination.

AN ACT to enforce the constitutional right to vote, to confer jurisdiction upon the district courts of the United States to provide injunctive relief against discrimination in public accommodations, to authorize the Attorney General to institute suits to protect constitutional rights in public facilities and public education, to extend the Commission on Civil Rights, to prevent discrimination in federally assisted programs, to establish a Commission on Equal Employment Opportunity, and for other purposes.

Be it enacted by the Senate and House of Representatives of the United States of America in Congress assembled. That this Act may be cited as the "Civil Rights Act of 1964."

TITLE I—VOTING RIGHTS
Section 101.
Section 2004 of the Revised Statutes (42 U.S.C. 1971), as amended by section 131 of the Civil Rights Act of 1957 (71 Stat. 637), and as further amended by section 601 of the Civil Rights Act of 1960 (74 Stat. 90), is further amended as follows:

(a) Insert "1" after "(a)" in subsection (a) and add at the end of subsection (a) the following new paragraphs:
"(2) No person acting under color of law shall—
    "(A) in determining whether any individual is qualified under State law or laws to vote in any Federal election, apply any standard, practice, or procedure different from the standards, practices, or procedures applied under such law or laws to other individuals within the same county, parish, or similar political subdivision who have been found by State officials to be qualified to vote;
    "(B) deny the right of any individual to vote in any Federal election because of an error or omission on any record or paper relating to any application, registration, or other act requisite to voting, if such error or omission is not material in determining whether such individual is qualified under State law to vote in such election; or
    "(C) employ any literacy test as a qualification for voting in any Federal election unless (i) such test is administered to each individual and is conducted wholly in writing, and (ii) a certified copy of the test and of the answers given by the individual is furnished to him within twenty-five days of the submission of his request made within the period of time during which records and papers are required to be retained and preserved pursuant to Title III of the Civil Rights Act of 1960 (42 U.S.C. 1974-74e; 74 Stat. 88): Provided, however, That the Attorney General may enter into agreements with appropriate State or local authorities that preparation, conduct, and maintenance of such tests in accordance with the provisions of applicable State or local law, including such special provisions as are necessary in the preparation, conduct, and maintenance of such tests for persons who are blind or otherwise physically handicapped, meet the purposes of this subparagraph and constitute compliance therewith.

"(3) For purposes of this subsection—

"(A) the term 'vote' shall have the same meaning as in subsection (e) of this section;

"(B) the phrase 'literacy test' includes any test of the ability to read, write, understand, or interpret any matter."

(b) Insert immediately following the period at the end of the first sentence of subsection (c) the following new sentence: "If in any such proceeding literacy is a relevant fact there shall be a rebuttable presumption that any person who has not been adjudged an incompetent and who has completed the sixth grade in a public school in, or a private school accredited by, any State or territory, the District of Columbia, or the Commonwealth of Puerto Rico where instruction is carried on predominantly in the English language, possesses sufficient literacy, comprehension, and intelligence to vote in any Federal election."

(c) Add the following subsection "(f)" and designate the present subsection "(f)" as subsection "(g)":

"(f) When used in subsection (a) or (c) of this section, the words 'Federal election' shall mean any general, special, or primary election held solely or in part for the purpose of electing or selecting any candidate for the office of President, Vice President, presidential elector, Member of the Senate, or Member of the House of Representatives."

(d) Add the following subsection "(h)":

"(h) In any proceeding instituted by the United States in any district court of the United States under this section in which the Attorney General requests a finding of a pattern or practice of discrimination pursuant to subsection (e) of this section the Attorney General, at the time he files the complaint, or any defendant in the proceeding, within twenty days after service upon him of the complaint, may file with the clerk of such court a request that a court of three judges be convened to hear and determine the entire case. A copy of the request for a three-judge court shall be immediately furnished by such clerk to the chief judge of the circuit (or in his absence, the presiding circuit judge of the circuit) in which the case is pending. Upon receipt of the copy of such request it shall be the duty of the chief judge of the circuit or the presiding circuit judge, as the case may be, to designate immediately three judges in such circuit, of whom at least one shall be a circuit judge and another of whom shall be a district judge of the court in which the proceeding who instituted, to hear and determine such case, and it shall be the duty of the judges so designated to assign the case for hearing at the earliest practicable date, to participate in the hearing and determination thereof, and to cause the case to be in every way expedited. An appeal from the final judgment of such court will lie to the Supreme Court.

"In any proceeding brought under subsection (c) of this section to enforce subsection (b) of this section, or in the event neither the Attorney General nor any defendant files a request for a three-judge court in any proceeding authorized by this subsection, it shall be the duty of the chief judge of the district (or in his absence, the acting chief judge) in which the case is pending immediately to designate a judge in such district to hear and determine the case. In the event that no judge in the district, or the acting chief judge, as the case may be, shall certify this fact to the chief judge of the circuit (or, in his absence, the acting chief judge) who shall then designate a district or circuit judge of the circuit to hear and determine the case.

"It shall be the duty of the judge designated pursuant to this section to assign the case for hearing at the earliest practicable date and to cause the case to be in every way expedited."

TITLE II—INJUNCTIVE RELIEF AGAINST DISCRIMINATION IN PLACES OF PUBLIC ACCOMMODATION

Section 201.

> (a) All persons shall be entitled to the full and equal enjoyment of the goods, services, facilities, privileges, advantages, and accommodations of any place of public accommodation, as defined in this section, without discrimination or segregation on the ground of race, color, religion, or national origin.
> (b) Each of the following establishments which serves the public is a place of public accommodation within the meaning of this title if its operations affect commerce, if discrimination or segregation by it is supported by State action:

(1) any inn, hotel, motel, or other establishment which provides lodging to transient guests, other than an establishment located within a building which contains not more than five rooms for rent or hire and which is actually occupied by the proprietor of such establishment as his residence;

(2) any restaurant, cafeteria, lunchroom, lunch counter, soda fountain, or other facility principally engaged in selling food for consumption on the premises, including, but not limited to, any such facility located on the premises of any retail establishment; or any gasoline station;

(3) any motion picture house, theater, concert hall, sports arena, stadium or other place of exhibition or entertainment; and

(4) any establishment (A) (i) which is physically located within the premises of any establishment otherwise covered by this subsection, or (ii) within the premises of which is physically located any such covered establishment, and (B) which holds itself out as serving patrons of such covered establishment.

(c) The operations of an establishment affect commerce within the meaning of this title if (1) it is one of the establishments described in paragraph (1) of subsection (b); (2) in the case of an establishment described in paragraph (2) of subsection (b), it serves or offers to serve interstate travelers or a substantial portion of the food which it serves, or gasoline or other products which it sells, has moved in commerce; (3) in the case of an establishment described in paragraph (3) of subsection (b), it customarily present films, performances, athletic teams, exhibitions, or other sources of entertainment which move in commerce; and (4) in the case of an establishment which move in commerce; and (4) in the case of an establishment described in paragraph (4) of subsection (b), it is physically located within the premises of, or there is physically located within its premises, an establishment the operations of which affect commerce within the meaning of this subsection. For purposes of this section, "commerce" means travel, trade, traffic, commerce, transportation, or communication among the several States, or between the District of Columbia and any State, or between any foreign country or any territory or possession and any State or the District of Columbia, or between points in the same State but through any other State or the District of Columbia or a foreign country.

(d) Discrimination or segregation by an establishment is support by State action within the meaning of this title if such discrimination or segregation (1) is carried on under color of any law, statute, ordinance, or regulation; or (2) is carried on under color of any custom or usage required or enforced by officials of the State or political subdivision thereof; or (3) is required by action of the State or political subdivision thereof.

(e) The provisions of this title shall not apply to a private club or other establishment not in fact open to the public, except to the extent that the facilities of such establishment are made available to the customers or patrons of an establishment within the scope of subsection (b).

Section 202.
All persons shall be entitled to be free, at any establishment or place, from discrimination or segregation of any kind on the ground of race, color, religion, or national origin, if such discrimination or segregation is or purports to be required by any law, statute, ordinance, regulation, rule, or order of a State or any agency or political subdivision thereof.

Section 203.
No person shall (a) withhold, deny, or attempt to withhold or deny, or deprive or attempt to deprive, any person of any right or privilege secured by section 201 or 202, or (b) intimidate, threaten, or coerce, or attempt to intimidate, threaten, or coerce any person with the purpose of interfering with any right or privilege

secured by section 201 or 202, or (c) punish or attempt to punish any person for exercising or attempting to exercise any right or privilege secured by section 201 or 202, or (b) intimidate, threaten, or coerce, or attempt to intimidate, threaten, or coerce any person with the purpose of interfering with any right or privilege secured by section 201 or 202, or (c) punish or attempt to punish any person for exercising or attempting to exercise any right or privilege secured by section 201 or 202.

Section 204.
(a) Whenever any person has engaged or there are reasonable grounds to believe that any person is about to engage in any act or practice prohibited by section 203, a civil action for preventive relief, including an application for a permanent or temporary injunction, restraining order, or other order, may be instituted by the person aggrieved and, upon timely application, the court may, in its discretion, permit the Attorney General to intervene in such civil action if he certifies that the case is of general public importance. Upon application by the complainant and in such circumstances as the court may deem just, the court may appoint an attorney for such complainant and may authorize the commencement of the civil action without the payment of fees, costs, or security.
(b) In any action commenced pursuant to this title, the court, in its discretion, may allow the prevailing party, other than the United States, a reasonable attorney's fee as part of the costs, and the United States shall be liable for costs the same as a private person.
(c) In the case of an alleged act or practice prohibited by this title which occurs in a State, or political subdivision of a State, which has a State or local law prohibiting such act or practice and establishing or authorizing a State or local authority to grant or seek relief from such practice or to institute criminal proceedings with respect thereto upon receiving notice thereof, no civil action may be brought under subsection (a) before the expiration of thirty days after written notice of such alleged act or practice has been given to the appropriate State or local authority by registered mail or in person, provided that the court may stay proceedings in such civil action pending the termination of State or local enforcement proceedings.
(d) In the case of an alleged act or practice prohibited by this title which occurs in a State, or political subdivision of a State, which has no State or local law prohibiting such act or practice, a civil action may be brought under subsection (a): Provided, That the court may refer the matter to the Community Relations Service established by title X of this Act for as long as the court believes there is a reasonable possibility of obtaining voluntary compliance, but for not more than sixty days: Provided further, That upon expiration of such sixty-day period, the court may extend such period for an additional period, not to exceed a cumulative total of one hundred and twenty days, if it believes there then exists a reasonable possibility of securing voluntary compliance.

Section 205.

The Service is authorized to make a full investigation of any complaint referred to it by the court under section 204(d) and may hold such hearing with respect thereto as may be necessary. The Service shall conduct any hearings with respect to any such complaint in executive session, and shall not release any testimony given therein except by agreement of all parties involved in the complaint with the permission of the court, and the Service shall endeavor to bring about a voluntary settlement between the parties.

Section 206.

(a) Whenever the Attorney General has reasonable cause to believe that any person or group of persons is engaged in a pattern or practice of resistance to the full enjoyment of any of the rights secured by this title, and that the pattern or practice is of such a nature and is intended to deny the full exercise of the rights herein described, the Attorney General may bring a civil action in the appropriate district court of the United States by filing with it a complaint

(1) signed by him (or in his absence the Acting Attorney General),

(2) setting forth facts pertaining to such pattern or practice, and

(3) requesting such preventive relief, including an application for a permanent or temporary injunction, restraining order or other order against the person or persons responsible for such pattern or practice, as he deems necessary to insure the full enjoyment of the rights herein described.

(b) In any such proceeding the Attorney General may file with the clerk of such court a request that a court of three judges to be convened to hear and determine the case. Such request by the Attorney General shall be accompanied by a certificate that, in his opinion, the case is of general public importance. A copy of the certificate and request for a three-judge court shall be immediately furnished by such clerk to the chief judge of the circuit (or in his absence, the presiding circuit judge of the circuit) in which the case is pending. Upon receipt of the copy of such request it shall be the duty of the chief judge of the circuit or the presiding circuit judge, as the case may be, to designate immediately three judges in such circuit, of whom at least one shall be a circuit judge and another of whom shall be a district judge of the court in which the proceeding was instituted, to hear and determine such case, and it shall be the duty of the judges so designated to assign the case for hearing at the earliest practicable date, to participate in the hearing and determination thereof, and to cause the case to be in every way expedited. An appeal from the final judgment of such court will lie to the Supreme Court.

In the event the Attorney General fails to file such a request in any such proceeding, it shall be the duty of the chief judge of the district (or in his absence, the acting chief judge) in which the case is pending immediately to designate a judge in such district to hear and determine the case. In the event that no judge in the district is available to hear and determine the case, the chief judge of the district, or the acting chief judge, as the case may be, shall certify this fact to the chief judge of the circuit (or in his absence, the acting chief judge) who shall then designate a district or circuit judge of the circuit to hear and determine the case.

It shall be the duty of the judge designated pursuant to this section to assign the case for hearing at the earliest practicable date and to cause the case to be in every way expedited.

Section 207.

(a) The district courts of the United States shall have jurisdiction of proceedings instituted pursuant to this title and shall exercise the same without regard to whether the aggrieved party shall have exhausted any administrative or other remedies that may be provided by law.

(b) The remedies provided in this title shall be the exclusive means of enforcing the rights based on this title, but nothing in this title shall preclude any individual or any State or local agency from asserting any right based on any other Federal or State law not inconsistent with this title, including any statute or ordinance requiring nondiscrimination in public establishments or accommodations, or from pursuing any remedy, civil or criminal, which may be available for the vindication or enforcement of such right.

TITLE III—DESEGREGATION OF PUBLIC FACILITIES
Section 301.
(a) Whenever the Attorney General receives a complaint in writing signed by an individual to the effect that he is being deprived of or threatened with the loss of his right to the equal protection of the laws, on account of his race, color, religion, or national origin, by being denied equal utilization of any public facility which is owned, operated, or managed by or on behalf of any State or subdivision thereof, other than a public school or public college as defined in section 401 of title IV hereof, and the Attorney General believes the complaint is meritorious and certifies that the signer or signers of such complaint are unable, in his judgment, to initiate and maintain appropriate legal proceedings for relief and that the institution of an action will materially further the orderly progress of desegregation in public

facilities, the Attorney General is authorized to institute for or in the name of the United States a civil action in any appropriate district court of the United States against such parties and for such relief as may be appropriate, and such court shall have and shall exercise jurisdiction of proceedings instituted pursuant to this section. The Attorney General may implead as defendants such additional parties as are or become necessary to the grant of effective relief hereunder.

(b) The Attorney General may deem a person or persons unable to initiate and maintain appropriate legal proceedings within the meaning of subsection (a) of this section when such person or persons are unable, either directly or through other interested persons or organizations, to bear the expense of the litigation or to obtain effective legal representation: or whenever he is satisfied that the institution of such litigation would jeopardize the personal safety, employment, or economic standing of such person or persons, their families, or their property.

Section 302.

In any action or proceeding under this title the United States shall be liable for costs, including a reasonable attorney's fee, the same as a private person.

Section 303.

Nothing in this title shall affect adversely the right of any person to sue for or obtain relief in any court against discrimination in any facility covered by this title.

Section 304.

A complaint as used in this title is a writing or document within the meaning of section 1001, title 18, United States Code.

TITLE IV—DESEGREGATION OF PUBLIC EDUCATION

Section 401. Definitions

As used in this title—

(a) "Commissioner" means the Commissioner of Education.

(b) "Desegregation" means the assignment of students to public schools and within such schools without regard to their race, color, religion, or national origin, but "desegregation" shall not mean the assignment of students to public schools in order to overcome racial imbalance.

(c) "Public school" means any elementary or secondary educational institution, and "public college" means any institution of higher education or any technical or vocational school above the secondary school level, provided that such public school or public college is operated by a State, subdivision of a State, or governmental agency within a State, or operated wholly or predominantly from or through the use of governmental funds or property, or funds or property derived from a governmental source.

(d) "School board" means any agency or agencies which administer a system of one or more public schools and any other agency which is responsible for the assignment of students to or within such system.

Section 402. Survey and Report of Educational Opportunities

The Commissioner shall conduct a survey and make a report to the President and the Congress, within two years of the enactment of this title, concerning the lack of availability of equal educational opportunities for individuals by reason of race, color, religion, or national origin in public educational institutions at all levels in the United States, its territories and possessions, and the District of Columbia.

Section 403. Technical Assistance

The Commissioner is authorized, upon the application of any school board, State, municipality, school district, or other governmental unit legally responsible for operating a public school or schools, to render technical assistance to such applicant in the preparation, adoption, and implementation of plans for the desegregation of public schools. Such technical assistance may, among other activities, include making available to such agencies information regarding effective methods of copying with special educational problems occasioned by desegregation, and making available to such agencies personnel of the Office of Education or other persons specially equipped to advise and assist them in coping with such problems.

Section 404. Training Institutes

The Commissioner is authorized to arrange, through grants or contracts, with institutions of higher education for the operation of short-term or regular session institutes for special training designed to improve the ability of teachers, supervisors, counselors, and other elementary or secondary school personnel to deal effectively with special education problems occasioned by desegregation. Individuals who attend such an institute on a full-time basis may be paid stipends for the period of their attendance at such institute in amounts specified by the Commissioner in regulations, including allowances for travel to attend such institute.

Section 405. Grants

(a) The Commissioner is authorized, upon the application of a school board, to make grants to such board to pay, in whole or in part, the cost of—
   (1) giving to teachers and other school personnel inservice training in dealing with problems incident to desegregation, and
   (2) employing specialists to advise in problems incident to desegregation.

(b) In determining whether to make a grant, and in fixing the amount thereof and the terms and conditions on which it will be made, the Commissioner shall take into consideration the amount available for grants under this section and the other

applications which are pending before him; the financial condition of the applicant and the other resources available to it; the nature, extent, and gravity of its problems incident to desegregation; and such other factors as he finds relevant.

Section 406. Payments

Payments pursuant to a grant or contract under this title may be made (after necessary adjustments on account of previously made overpayments or underpayments) in advance or by way of reimbursement, and in such installments, as the Commissioner may determine.

Section 407. Suits By the Attorney General

(a) Whenever the Attorney General receives a complaint in writing—

(1) signed by a parent or group of parents to the effect that his or their minor children, as members of a class of persons similarly situated, are being deprived by a school board of the equal protection of the laws, or

(2) signed by an individual, or his parent, to the effect that he has been denied admission to or not permitted to continue in attendance at a public college by reason of race, color, religion, or national origin, and the Attorney General believes the complaint is meritorious and certifies that the signer or signers of such complaint are unable, in his judgment, to initiate and maintain appropriate legal proceedings for relief and that the institution of an action will materially further the orderly achievement of desegregation in public education, the Attorney General is authorized, after giving notice of such complaint to the appropriate school board or college authority and after certifying that he is satisfied that such board or authority has had a reasonable time to adjust the conditions alleged in such complaint, to institute for or in the name of the United States a civil action in any appropriate district court of the United States against such parties and for such relief as may be appropriate, and such court shall have and shall exercise jurisdiction of proceedings instituted pursuant to this section, provided that nothing herein shall empower any official or court of the United States to issue any order seeking to achieve a racial balance in any school by requiring the transportation of pupils or students from one school to another or one school district to another in order to achieve such racial balance, or otherwise enlarge the existing power of the court to insure compliance with constitutional standards. The Attorney General may implead as defendants such additional parties as are or become necessary to the grant of effective relief hereunder.

(b) The Attorney General may deem a person or persons unable to initiate and maintain appropriate legal proceedings within the meaning of subsection (a) of this section when such person or persons are unable, either directly or through other interested persons or organizations, to bear the expense of the litigation or to obtain effective legal representation: or whenever he is satisfied that the institution of such litigation would jeopardize the personal safety, employment, or economic standing of such person or persons, their families, or their property.

(c) The term "parent" as used in this section includes any person standing in loco parentis. A "complaint" as used in this section is a writing or document within the meaning of section 1001, title 18, United States Code.

Section 408.

In any action or proceeding under this title the United States shall be liable for costs the same as a private person.

Section 409.

Nothing in this title shall prohibit classification ad assignment for reasons other than race, color, religion, or national origin.

TITLE V—COMMISSION ON CIVIL RIGHTS
Section 501.
Section 102 of the Civil Rights Act of 1957 (42 U.S.C. 1975a; 71 Stat. 634) is amended to read as follows:
"rules of procedure of the commission hearings

"Sec. 102.

(a) At least thirty days prior to the commencement of any hearing, the Commission shall cause to be published in the Federal Register notice of the date on which such hearing is to commence, the place at which it is to be held and the subject of the hearing. The Chairman, or one designated by him to act as Chairman at a hearing of the commission, shall announce in an opening statement the subject of the hearing.

"(b) A copy of the Commission's rules shall be made available to any witness before the Commission, and a witness compelled to appear before the Commission or required to produce written or other matter shall be served with a copy of the Commission's rules at the time of service of the subpoena, etc.

"(c) Any person compelled to appear in person before the Commission shall be accorded the right to be accompanied and advised by counsel, who shall have the right to subject his client to reasonable examination, and to make objections on the record and to argue briefly the basis for such objections. The Commission shall proceed with reasonable dispatch to conclude any hearing in which it is engaged. Due regard shall be had for the convenience and necessity of witnesses.

"(d) The Chairman or Acting Chairman may punish breaches of order and decorum by censure and exclusion from the hearings.

"(e) If the Commission determines that evidence or testimony at any hearing may tend to defame, degrade, or incriminate any person, it shall receive such evidence or testimony or summary of such evidence or testimony in executive session. The Commission shall afford any person defamed, degraded, or incriminated by such evidence or testimony an opportunity to appear and be heard in executive session, with a reasonable number of additional witnesses requested by him, before deciding to use such evidence or testimony. In the event the Commission determines to release or use such evidence or testimony in such manner as to reveal publicly the identity of the person defamed, degraded, or incriminated, such evidence or testimony. In the event the Commission determines to release or use such evidence or testimony in such manner as to reveal publicly the identity of the person defamed, degraded, or incriminated, such evidence or testimony, prior to such public release or use, shall be given at a public session, and the Commission shall afford such person an opportunity to appear as a voluntary witness or to file a sworn statement in his behalf and to submit brief and pertinent sworn statements of others. The Commission shall receive and dispose of requests from such person to subpena additional witnesses.

"(f) Except as provided in sections 102 and 105(f) of this Act the Chairman shall receive and the Commission shall dispose of requests to subpena additional witnesses.

"(g) No evidence or testimony or summary of evidence or testimony taken in executive session may be released or used in public sessions without the consent of the Commission. Whoever releases or uses in public without the consent of the Commission such evidence or testimony taken in executive session shall be fined not more than $1,000, or imprisoned for not more than one year.

"(h) In the discretion of the Commission, witnesses may submit brief and pertinent sworn statements in writing for inclusion in the record. The Commission shall determine the pertinency of testimony and evidence adduced at its hearings.

"(i) Every person who submits data or evidence shall be entitled to retain or, on payment of lawfully prescribed costs, procure a copy or transcript thereof, except that a witness in a hearing held in executive session may for good cause be limited to inspection of the official transcript of his testimony. Transcript copies of public sessions may be obtained by the public upon the payment of the cost thereof. An accurate transcript shall be made of the testimony of all witnesses at all hearings, either public or executive sessions, of the Commission or of any subcommittee thereof.

"(j) A witness attending any session of the Commission shall receive $6 for each day's attendance and for the time necessarily occupied in going to and returning from the same, and 10 cents per mile for going from and returning to his place of residence. Witnesses who attend at points so far removed from their respective residences as to prohibit return thereto from day to day shall be entitled to an additional allowance of $10 per day for expenses of subsistence, including the time necessarily occupied in going to and returning from the place of attendance. Mileage payments shall be tendered to the witness upon service of a subpena issued on behalf of the Commission or any subcommittee thereof.

"(k) The Commission shall not issue any subpena for the attendance and testimony of witnesses or for the production of written or other matter which would require the presence of the party subpenaed at a hearing to be held outside of the State wherein the witness is found or resides or is domiciled or transacts business, or has appointed an agent for receipt of service of process except that, in any event, the Commission may issue subpenas for the attendance and testimony of witnesses and the production of written or other matter at a hearing held within fifty miles of the place where the witness is found or resides or is domiciled or transacts business or has appointed an agent for receipt of service of process.

"(l) The Commission shall separately state and currently publish in the Federal Register (1) descriptions of its central and field organization including the established places at which, and methods whereby, the public may secure information or makes requests; (2) statements of the general course and method by which its functions are channeled and determined, and (3) rules adopted as authorized by law. No person shall in any manner be subject to or required to resort to rules, organization, or procedure not so published."

Section 502.

Section 103(a) of the Civil Rights of Act of 1957 (42 U.S.C. 1975b(a); 71 Stat. 634) is amended to read as follows:

"Sec. 103.

(a) Each member of the Commission who is not otherwise in the service of the Government of the United States shall receive the sum of $75 per day for each day spent in the work of the Commission, shall be paid actual travel expenses, and per diem in lieu of subsistence expenses when away from his usual place of residence, in accordance with section 5 of the Administrative Expenses Act of 1946, as amended (5 U.S.C. 73b-2; 60 Stat. 808)."

Section 503.

Section 103(b) of the Civil Rights of Act of 1957 (42 U.S.C. 1975b(b); 71 Stat. 635) is amended to read as follows:
"(b) Each member of the Commission who is not otherwise in the service of the Government of the United States shall serve without compensation in addition to that received for such other service, but while engaged in the work of the Commission, shall be paid actual travel expenses, and per diem in lieu of subsistence expenses when away from his usual place of residence, in accordance with the provisions of the Travel Expenses Act of 1949, as amended (5 U.S.C. 835–42; 63 Stat. 166)."

Section 504.

Section 104(a) of the Civil Rights of Act of 1957 (42 U.S.C. 1975c(a); 71 Stat. 635) as amended, is further amended to read as follows:
    "Duties of the Commission

"Sec. 104. (a) The Commission shall—

"(1) investigate allegations in writing under oath or affirmation that certain citizens of the United States are being deprived of their right to vote and have that vote counted by reason of their color, race, religion, or national origin; when writing, under oath or affirmation, shall set forth the facts upon which such belief or beliefs are based;

"(2) study and collect information concerning legal developments constituting a denial of equal protection of the laws under the Constitution because of race, color, religion or national origin or in the administration of justice;

"(3) appraise the laws and policies of the Federal Government with respect to denials of equal protection of the laws under the Constitution because of race, color, religion or national origin or in the administration of justice;

"(4) serve as a national clearinghouse for information in respect to denials of equal protection of the laws because of race, color, religion or national origin or including but not limited to the fields of voting, education, housing, employment, the use of public facilities, and transportation, or in the administration of justice;

"(5) investigate allegations in writing under oath or affirmation, that citizens of the United States are unlawfully being accorded or denied the right to vote, or to have their votes property counted, in any election of presidential electors. Members of the United States Senate, or of the House of Representatives, as a result of any patterns or practice of fraud or discrimination in the conduct of such election; and

"(6) Nothing in this or any other Act shall be construed as authorizing the Commission, its Advisory Committees, or any person under its supervision or control to inquire into or investigate any membership practices or internal operations of any fraternal organization, any college or university fraternity or sorority, any private club or any religious organization."

(b) Section 104(b) of the Civil Rights Act of 1957 (42 U.S.C. 1975c(b); 71 Stat. 635), as amended, is further amended by striking out the present subsection "(b)" and by substituting therefor:

"(b) The Commission shall submit interim reports to the President and to the Congress at such times as the Commission, the Congress or the President shall deem desirable, and shall submit to the President and to the Congress a final report of its activities, findings, and recommendations not later than January 31, 1968."

Section 505.
Section 105(a) of the Civil Rights Act of 1957 (42 U.S.C. 1975d(a); 71 Stat. 636) is amended by striking out in the first sentence thereof "$50 per diem" and inserting in lieu thereof "$75 per diem."

Section 506.

Section 105(f) and section 105(g) of the Civil Rights Act of 1957 (42 U.S.C. 1975d (f) and (g); 71 Stat. 637), are amended to read as follows:

"(f) The Commission, or on the authorization of the Commission any subcommittee of two or more members, at least one of whom shall be of each major political party, may, for the purpose of carrying out the provisions of this Act, hold such hearings and act at such times and places as the Commission or such authorized subcommittee may deem advisable. Subpenas for the attendance and testimony of witnesses or the production of written or other matter may be issued in accordance with the rules of the Commission as contained in section 102 (j) and (k) of this Act, over the signature of the Chairman of the Commission or of such subcommittee, and may be served by any person designated by such Chairman. The holding of hearings by the Commission, or the appointment of a subcommittee to hold hearings pursuant to this subparagraph, must be approved by a majority of the Commission, or by a majority of the members present at a meeting at which at least a quorum of four members is present.

"(g) In case of contumacy or refusal to obey a subpena, any district court of the United States or the United States court of any territory or possession, or the District Court of the United States for the District of Columbia, within the jurisdiction of which the inquiry is carried on or within the jurisdiction of which said person guilty of contumacy or refusal to obey is found or resides or is domiciled or transacts business, or has appointed an agent for receipt of service of process, upon application by the Attorney General of the United States shall have jurisdiction to issue to such person an order requiring such person to appear before the Commission or a subcommittee thereof, there to produce pertinent, relevant and nonprivileged evidence if so ordered, or there to give testimony touching the matter under investigation; and any failure to obey such order of the court may be punished by said court as a contempt thereof."

Section 507.

Section 105 of the Civil Rights Act of 1957 (42 U.S.C. 1975d; 71 Stat. 636), as amended by section 401 of the Civil Rights Act of 1960 (42 U.S.C. 1975d(h): 74 Stat. 89), is further amended by adding a new subsection at the end to read as follows:

"(i) The Commission shall have the power to make such rules and regulations as are necessary to carry out the purposes of this Act."

TITLE VII—EQUAL EMPLOYMENT OPPORTUNITY

Section 701.

For the purposes of this title—

(a) The term "person" includes one or more individuals, labor unions, partnerships, associations, corporations, legal representatives, mutual companies, joint-stock companies, trusts, unincorporated organizations, trustees, trustees in bankruptcy, or receivers.

(b) The term "employer" means a person engaged in an industry affecting commerce who has twenty-five or more employees for each working day in each of twenty or more calendar weeks in the current or preceding calendar year, and any agent of such a person, but such term does not include (1) the United States, a corporation wholly owned by the Government of the United States, an Indian tribe, or a State or political subdivision thereof, (2) a bona fide private membership club (other than a labor organization) which is exempt from taxation under section 501(c) of the Internal Revenue Code of 1954: Provided, That during the first year after the effective date prescribed in subsection (a) of section 716, persons having fewer than one hundred employees (and their agents) shall not be considered employers, and, during the second year after such date, persons having fewer than seventy-five employees (and their agents) shall not be considered employers, and, during the third year after such date, persons having fewer than fifty employees (and their agents) shall not be considered employers: Provided further, That it shall be the policy of United States to insure equal employment opportunities for Federal employees without discrimination because of race, color, religion, sex or national origin and the President shall utilize his existing authority to effectuate this policy.

(c) The term "employment agency" means any person regularly undertaking with or without compensation to procure employees for an employer or to procure for employees opportunities to work for an employer and includes an agent of such a person; but shall not include an agency of the United States, or an agency of a State or political subdivision of a State, except that such term shall include the United States Employment Service and the system of State and local employment services receiving Federal assistance.

(d) The term "labor organization" means a labor organization engaged in an industry affecting commerce, and any agent of such an organization, and includes any organization of any kind, any agency, or employee representation committee, group, association, or plan so engaged in which employees participate and which exists for the purpose, in whole or in part, of dealing with employers concerning grievances, labor disputes, wages, rates of pay, hours, or other terms or conditions of employment, and any conference, general committee, joint or system board, or joint council so engaged which is subordinate to a national or international labor organization.

(e) A labor organization shall be deemed to be engaged in an industry affecting commerce if (1) it maintains or operates a hiring hall or hiring office which procures employees for an employer or procures for employees opportunities to work for an employer, or (2) the number of its members (or, where it is a labor organization composed of other labor organizations or their representatives, if the aggregate number of the members of such other labor organization) is (A) one hundred or more during the year after the effective date prescribed in subsection

(a) of section 716, (B) seventy-five or more during the second year after such date or fifty or more during the third year, or (C) twenty-five or more thereafter, and such labor organization—

(1) is the certified representative of employees under the provisions of the National Labor Relations Act, as amended, or the Railway Labor Act, as amended;

(2) although not certified, is a national or international labor organization or a local labor organization recognized or action as the representative of employees of an employer or employers engaged in an industry affecting commerce; or

(3) has chartered a local labor organization or subsidiary body which is representing or actively seeking to represent employees of employers within the meaning of paragraph (1) or (2); or

(4) has been chartered by a labor organization representing or actively seeking to represent employees within the meaning of paragraph (1) or (2) as the local or subordinate body through which such employees may enjoy membership or become affiliated with such labor organization; or

(5) is a conference, general committee, joint or system board, or joint council subordinate to a national or international labor organization, which includes a labor organization engaged in an industry affecting commerce within the meaning of any of the preceding paragraphs of this subsection.

(f) The term "employee" means an individual employed by an employer.

(g) The term "commerce" means trade, traffic, commerce, transportation, transmission, or communication among the several States; or between a State and any place outside thereof; or within the District of Columbia, or a possession of the United States; of between points in the same State but through a point outside thereof.

(h) The term "industry affecting commerce" means any activity, business, or industry in commerce or in which a labor dispute would hinder or obstruct commerce or the free flow of commerce and includes any activity or industry "affecting commerce" within the meaning of the labor-Management Reporting and Disclosure Act of 1959.

(i) The term "State" includes a State of the United States, the District of Columbia, Puerto Rico, the Virgin Islands, American Samoa, Guam, Wake Island, the Canal Zone, and Outer Continental Shelf lands defined in the Outer Continental Shelf Lands Act.

Section 702. Exemption

This title shall not apply to an employer with respect to the employment of aliens outside any State, or to a religious corporation association, or society with respect to the employment of individuals of a particular religion to perform work connected with the carrying on by such corporation, association, or society of its religious activities or to an educational institution with respect to the employment of individuals to perform work connected with the educational activities of such institution.

Section 703. Discrimination Because of Race, Color, Religion, Sex, or National Origin

(a) It shall be an unlawful employment practice for an employer—

(1) to fail or refuse to hire or to discharge any individual, or otherwise to discriminate against any individual with respect to his compensation, terms, conditions, or privileges of employment, because of such individual's race, color, religion, sex, or national origin; or

(2) to limit, segregate, or classify his employees in any way which would deprive or tend to deprive any individual of employment opportunities or otherwise adversely affect his status as an employee, because of such individual's race, color, religion, sex, or national origin.

(b) It shall be an unlawful employment practice for an employment agency to fail or refuse to refer for employment, or otherwise to discriminate against, any individual because of his race, color, religion, sex, or national origin, or to classify or refer for employment any individual on the basis of his race, color, religion, sex, or national origin.

(c) It shall be an unlawful employment practice for a labor organization—

(1) to exclude or to expel from its membership, or otherwise to discriminate against, any individual because of his race, color, religion, sex, or national origin;

(2) to limit, segregate, or classify its membership, or to classify or fail or refuse to refer for employment any individual, in anyway which would deprive or tend to deprive any individual of employment opportunities, or would limit such employment opportunities or otherwise adversely affect his status as an employee or as an applicant for employment, because of such individual's race, color, religion, sex, or national origin; or

(3) to cause or attempt to cause an employer to discriminate against an individual in violation of this section.

(d) It shall be an unlawful employment practice for any employer, labor organization, or joint labor-management committee controlling apprenticeship or other training or retraining, including on-the-job training programs to discriminate against any individual because of his race, color, religion, sex, or national origin in admission to, or employment in, any program established to provide apprenticeship or other training.

(e) Notwithstanding any other provision of this title, (1) it shall not be an unlawful employment practice for an employer to hire and employ employees, for an employment agency to classify, or refer for employment any individual, for a labor organization to classify its membership or to classify or refer for employment any individual, or for an employer, labor organization, or joint labor-management committee controlling apprenticeship or other training or retraining programs to admit or employ any individual in any such program, on the basis of his religion, sex, or national origin in those certain instances where religion, sex, or national origin is a bona fide occupational qualification reasonably necessary to the normal operation of that particular business or enterprise, and (2) it shall not be an unlawful employment practice for a school, college, university, or other educational institution or institution of learning to hire and employ employees of particular religion if such school, college, university, or other educational institution or institution of learning is, in whole or in substantial part, owned, supported, controlled, or managed by a particular religion or by a particular religious corporation, association, or society, or if the curriculum of such school college university or other educational institution or institution of learning is directed toward the propagation of particular religion.

(f) As used in this title, the phrase "unlawful employment practice" shall not be deemed to include any action or measure taken by an employer, labor organization, joint labor-management committee, or employment agency with respect to an individual who is a member of the Communist Party of the United States or of any other organization required to register as a Commission-action or Commission-front organization by final order of the Subversive Activities Control Board pursuant to the Subversive Activities Control Act of 1950.

(g) Notwithstanding any other provision of this title, it shall not be an unlawful employment practice for an employer to fail or refuse to hire and employ any individual for any position, for an employer to discharge any individual from any position, or for an employment agency to fail or refuse to refer any individual for employment in any position, if—

(1) the occupancy of such position, or access to the premises in or upon which any part of the duties of such position is performed or is to be performed, is subject to any requirement imposed in the interest of the national security of the United States under any security program in effect pursuant to or administered under any statute of the United States or any Executive order of the President; and

(2) such individual has not fulfilled or has ceased to fulfill that requirement.

(h) Notwithstanding any other provision of this title, it shall not be an unlawful employment practice for an employer to apply different standards of compensation, or different terms, conditions, or privileges of employment pursuant to a bona fide seniority or merit system, or a system which measures earnings by quantity or quality of production or to employees who work in different locations, provided that such differences are not the result of an intention to discriminate because of race, color, religion, sex, or national origin, nor shall it be an unlawful employment practice for an employer to give and to act upon the results of any professionally developed ability test provided that such test, its administration or action upon the results is not designed, intended or used to discriminate because of race, color, religion, sex or national origin. It shall not be an unlawful employment practice under this title for any employer to differentiate upon the basis of sex in determining the amount of the wages of compensation paid or to be paid to employees of such employer if such differentiation is authorized by the provisions of section 6(d) of the Fair Labor Standards Act of 1938, as amended (29 U.S.C. 206 (d)).

(i) Nothing contained in this title shall apply to any business or enterprise on or near an Indian reservation with respect to any publicly announced employment practice of such business or enterprise under which a preferential treatment is given to any individual because he is an Indian living on or near a reservation.

(j) Nothing contained in this title shall be interpreted to require any employer, employment agency, labor organization, or joint labor-management committee subject to this title to grant preferential treatment to any individual or to any group because of the race, color, religion, sex, or national origin of such individual or group on account of an imbalance which may exist with respect to the total number or percentage of persons of any race, color, religion, sex, or national origin employed by an employer, referred or classified for employment by any employment agency or labor organization, admitted to membership or classified by any labor organization, or admitted to, or employed in, any apprenticeship or other training program, in comparison with the total number or percentage of persons of such race, color, religion, sex, or national origin in any community, State, section, or other area, or in the available work force in any community, State, section, or other area.

Section 704. Other Unlawful Employment Practices

(a) It shall be an unlawful employment practice for an employer to discriminate against any of his employees or applicants for employment, for an employment agency to discriminate against any individual, or for a labor organization to discriminate against any member thereof or applicant for membership, because he has opposed any practice made an unlawful employment practice by this title, or because he has made a charge, testified, assisted, or participated in any manner in an investigation, proceeding, or hearing under this title.

(b) It shall be an unlawful employment practice for an employer, labor organization, or employment agency to print or publish or cause to be printed or published any notice or advertisement relating to employment by such an employer or membership in or any classification or referral for employment by such a labor organization, or relating to any classification or referral for employment by such an employment agency, indicating any preference, limitation, specification, or discrimination, based on race, color, religion, sex, or national origin, except that such a notice or advertisement may indicate a preference, limitation, specification, or discrimination based on religion, sex, or national origin when religion, sex, or national origin is a bona fide occupational qualification for employment.

Section 705. Equal Employment Opportunity Commission

(a) There is hereby created a Commission to be known as the Equal Employment Opportunity Commission, which shall be composed of five members, not more than three of whom shall be members of the same political party, who shall be appointed by the President by and with the advice and consent of the Senate. One of the original members shall be appointed for a term of one year, one for a term of two years, one for a term of three years, one for a term of four years, and one for a term of five years, beginning from the date of enactment of this title, but their successors shall be appointed for terms of five years each, except that any individual chosen to fill a vacancy shall be appointed only for the unexpired term of the member whom he shall succeed. The President shall designate one member to serve as Chairman of the Commission , and one member to serve as Vice Chairman. The Chairman shall be responsible on behalf of the Commission for the administrative operations of the Commission, and shall appoint, in accordance with the civil service laws, such officers, agents, attorneys, and employees as it deems necessary to assist it in the performance of its functions and to fix their compensation in accordance with the Classification Act of 1949, as amended. The Vice Chairman shall act as Chairman in the absence or disability of the Chairman or in the event of a vacancy in that office.

(b) A vacancy in the Commission shall not impair the right of the remaining members to exercise all the powers of the Commission and three members thereof shall constitute a quorum.

(c) The Commission shall have an official seal which shall be judicially noticed.

(d) The Commission shall at the close of each fiscal year report to the Congress and to the President concerning the action it has taken; the names, salaries, and duties of all individuals in its employ and the moneys it has disbursed; and shall make such further reports on the cause of and means of eliminating discrimination and such recommendations for further reports on the cause of and means of eliminating discrimination and such recommendations for further legislation as may appear desirable.

(e) The Federal Executive Pay Act of 1956, as amended (5 U.S.C. 2201–2209), is further amended—

(1) by adding to section 105 thereof (5 U.S.C. 2204) the following clause: "(32) Chairman, Equal Employment Opportunity Commission"; and

(2) by adding to clause (45) of section 1069a) thereof (5 U.S.C. 2205 9a)) the following: "Equal Employment Opportunity Commission (4)."

(f) The principal office of the Commission shall be in or near the District of Columbia, but it may meet or exercise any or all its powers at any other place. The Commission may establish such regional or State offices as it deems necessary to accomplish the purpose of this title.

(g) The Commission shall have power—

(1) to cooperate with and, with their consent, utilize regional, State, local, and other agencies, both public and private, and individuals;

(2) to pay to witnesses whose depositions are taken or who are summoned before the Commission or any of its agents the same witness and mileage fees as are paid to witnesses in the courts of the United States;

(3) to furnish to persons subject to this title such technical assistance as they may request to further their compliance with this title or an order issued thereunder;

(4) upon the request of (i) any employer, whose employees or some of them, or (ii) any labor organization, whose members or some of them, refuse or threaten to refuse to cooperate in effectuating the provisions of this title, to assist in such effectuation by conciliation or such other remedial action as is provided by this title;

(5) to make such technical studies as are appropriate to effectuate the purposes and policies of this title and to make the results of such studies available to the public;

(6) to refer matters to the Attorney General with recommendations for intervention in a civil action brought by an aggrieved party under section 706, or for the institution of a civil action by the Attorney General under section 707, and to advise, consult, and assist the Attorney General on such matters.

(h) Attorneys appointed under this section may, at the direction of the Commission, appear for and represent the Commission in any case in court.

(i) The Commission shall, in any of its educational or promotional activities, cooperate with other departments and agencies in the performance of such educational and promotional activities.

(j) All officers, agents, attorneys, and employees of the Commission shall be subject to the provisions of section 9 of the Act of August 2, 1939, as amended (the Hatch Act), notwithstanding any exemption contained in such section.

Source: Civil Rights Act of 1964. Public Law 88-352. *U.S. Statutes at Large*, 78 (1964): 241.

From Fannie Lou Hamer, "Testimony before the Credentials Committee of the Democratic National Convention," Atlantic City, New Jersey (1964)

In early 1964, SNCC decided to undertake a major campaign in Mississippi known as Freedom Summer. Its coordinators put forth two main goals, the opening of Freedom Schools and the establishment of the Mississippi Freedom Democratic Party (MFDP). Encouraged by several prominent liberals, most notably Joe Rauh, counsel for the United Automobile Workers union and a leader of the Americans for Democratic Action, the MFDP decided to challenge the legitimacy of the "regular" Democratic Party's delegation from Mississippi at the Democratic National Convention in Atlantic City in the summer of 1964. The MFDP's challenge climaxed with the testimony of Fannie Lou Hamer, a middle-aged Mississippi sharecropper and one of the leaders of the MFDP. Fearing that the

MFDP's challenge would undermine his support among white southerners, President Lyndon B. Johnson pressured the Credentials Committee to offer the group a compromise of two at-large delegates at the 1964 convention. (There were sixty-eight members in the full Mississippi delegation.) While most moderates and liberals supported this offer, the MFDP rejected the plan, terming it tokenism. In the wake of this confrontation, many civil rights activists never fully trusted LBJ or his liberal allies again, and the liberal coalition that had prospered during the first half of the decade began to fall apart.

Mr. Chairman, and the Credentials Committee, my name is Mrs. Fannie Lou Hamer, and I live at 626 East Lafayette Street, Ruleville, Mississippi, Sunflower County, the home of Senator James O. Eastland, and Senator Stennis.

It was the 31st of August in 1962 that 18 of us traveled 26 miles to the county courthouse in Indianola to try to register to try to become first-class citizens. We was met in Indianola by Mississippi men, Highway Patrolmen and they allowed two of us to take the literacy test at the time. After we had taken the test and started back to Ruleville, we was held up by the City Police and the State Highway Patrolmen and carried back to Indianola where the bus driver was charged that day with driving a bus the wrong color.

After we paid the fine among us, we continued on to Ruleville, and Reverend Jeff Sunny carried me the four miles in the rural area where I had worked as a time-keeper and sharecropper for 18 years. I was met there by my children, who told me the plantation owner was angry because I had gone down to try to register.

After they told me, my husband came, and said the plantation owner was raising cain because I had tried to register and before he quit talking the plantation owner came, and said, "Fannie Lou, do you know—did Pap tell you what I said?" And I said, "Yes sir." He said, "I mean that. . . . If you don't go down and withdraw . . . well—you might have to go because we are not ready for that." . . .

And I addressed him and told him and said, "I didn't try to register for you. I tried to register for myself."

I had to leave that same night.

On the 10th of September, 1962, 16 bullets was fired into the home of Mr. and Mrs. Robert Tucker for me. That same night two girls were shot in Ruleville, Mississippi. Also Mr. Joe McDonald's house was shot in.

And in June, the 9th, 1963, I had attended a voter registration workshop, was returning back to Mississippi. Ten of us was traveling by the Continental Trailways bus. When we got to Winona, Mississippi, which is Montgomery County, four of the people got off to use the washroom. . . . I stepped off the bus to see what was happening and somebody screamed from the car that four workers was in and said, "Get that one there," and when I went to get in the car, when the man told me I was under arrest, he kicked me.

I was carried to the county jail and put in the holding room. They left some of the people in the booking room and began to place us in cells. I was placed in a cell with a young woman called Miss Euvester Simpson. After I was placed in the cell I began to hear sounds of licks and screams. I could hear the sounds of licks and horrible screams, and I could hear somebody say, "Can you say, yes, sir, nigger?" "Can you say yes, sir?"

And they would say horrible names. She would say, "Yes, I can say yes, sir." . . . They beat her, I don't know how long, and after a while she began to pray and asked God to have Mercy on those people. And it wasn't long before three white men came to my cell. One of these men was a State Highway Patrolmen and he asked me where I was from, and I told him Ruleville; he said, "We are going to check this."

And they left my cell and it wasn't too long before they came back. He said, "You are from Ruleville all right," and he used a curse word, he said, "We are going to beat you until you wish you was dead."

I was carried out of that cell into another cell where they had two Negro prisoners. The State Highway patrolmen ordered the first Negro to take the blackjack. The first Negro prisoner ordered me, by orders from the State Highway Patrolmen, for me to lay down on a bunk bed on my face, and I laid on my face.

The first Negro began to beat, and I was beat by the first Negro until he was exhausted, and I was holding my hands behind at this time on my left side because I suffered polio when I was six years old. After the first Negro had beat until he was exhausted the state Highway Patrolman ordered the second Negro to take the blackjack. The second Negro began to beat and I began to work my feet, and the State Highway Patrolmen ordered the first Negro who had beat to set on my feet to keep me from working my feet. I began to scream and one white man got up and began to beat me in my head and tell me to hush.

One white man—my dress had worked up high, he walked over and pulled my dress down and he pulled my dress back, back up. . . .

All of this on account we want to register, to become first-class citizens, and if the Freedom Democratic Party is not seated now, I question America, is this America, the land of the free and the home of the brave where we have to sleep with our telephones off the hooks because our lives be threatened daily because we want to live as decent human beings, in America?

Source: American Rhetoric, http://www.americanrhetoric.com/speeches/fannielouhamercredentialscommittee.htm.

Lyndon B. Johnson: Voting Rights Speech (1965)

On March 15, 1965, President Lyndon B. Johnson delivered this speech to a joint session of Congress, urging them to pass the Voting Rights Act of 1965, a crucial civil rights bill that Johnson had strongly endorsed since its inception.

Mr. Speaker, Mr. President, Members of the Congress:

I speak tonight for the dignity of man and the destiny of democracy.

I urge every member of both parties, Americans of all religions and of all colors, from every section of this country, to join me in that cause.

At times history and fate meet at a single time in a single place to shape a turning point in man's unending search for freedom. So it was at Lexington and Concord. So it was a century ago at Appomattox. So it was last week in Selma, Alabama.

There, long-suffering men and women peacefully protested the denial of their rights as Americans. Many were brutally assaulted. One good man, a man of God, was killed.

There is no cause for pride in what has happened in Selma. There is no cause for self-satisfaction in the long denial of equal rights of millions of Americans. But there is cause for hope and for faith in our democracy in what is happening here tonight.

For the cries of pain and the hymns and protests of oppressed people have summoned into convocation all the majesty of this great Government—the Government of the greatest Nation on earth.

Our mission is at once the oldest and the most basic of this country: to right wrong, to do justice, to serve man.

In our time we have come to live with moments of great crisis. Our lives have been marked with debate about great issues; issues of war and peace, issues of prosperity and depression. But rarely in any time does an issue lay bare the secret heart of America itself. Rarely are we met with a challenge, not to our growth or abundance, our welfare or our security, but rather to the values and the purposes and the meaning of our beloved Nation.

The issue of equal rights for American Negroes is such an issue. And should we defeat every enemy, should we double our wealth and conquer the stars, and still be unequal to this issue, then we will have failed as a people and as a nation.

For with a country as with a person, "What is a man profited, if he shall gain the whole world, and lose his own soul?"

There is no Negro problem. There is no Southern problem. There is no Northern problem. There is only an American problem. And we are met here tonight as Americans—not as Democrats or Republicans—we are met here as Americans to solve that problem.

This was the first nation in the history of the world to be founded with a purpose. The great phrases of that purpose still sound in every American heart, North and South: "All men are created equal"—"government by consent of the governed"—"give me liberty or give me death." Well, those are not just clever words, or those are not just empty theories. In their name Americans have fought and died for two centuries, and tonight around the world they stand there as guardians of our liberty, risking their lives.

Those words are a promise to every citizen that he shall share in the dignity of man. This dignity cannot be found in a man's possessions; it cannot be found in his power, or in his position. It really rests on his right to be treated as a man equal in opportunity to all others. It says that he shall share in freedom, he shall choose his leaders, educate his children, and provide for his family according to his ability and his merits as a human being.

To apply any other test—to deny a man his hopes because of his color or race, his religion or the place of his birth—is not only to do injustice, it is to deny America and to dishonor the dead who gave their lives for American freedom.

THE RIGHT TO VOTE

Our fathers believed that if this noble view of the rights of man was to flourish, it must be rooted in democracy. The most basic right of all was the right to choose your own leaders. The history of this country, in large measure, is the history of the expansion of that right to all of our people.

Many of the issues of civil rights are very complex and most difficult. But about this there can and should be no argument. Every American citizen must have an equal right to vote. There is no reason which can excuse the denial of that right. There is no duty which weighs more heavily on us than the duty we have to ensure that right.

Yet the harsh fact is that in many places in this country men and women are kept from voting simply because they are Negroes.

Every device of which human ingenuity is capable has been used to deny this right. The Negro citizen may go to register only to be told that the day is wrong, or the hour is late, or the official in charge is absent. And if he persists, and if he manages to present himself to the registrar, he may be disqualified because he did not spell out his middle name or because he abbreviated a word on the application.

And if he manages to fill out an application he is given a test. The registrar is the sole judge of whether he passes this test. He may be asked to recite the entire Constitution, or explain the most complex provisions of State law. And even a college degree cannot be used to prove that he can read and write.

For the fact is that the only way to pass these barriers is to show a white skin.

Experience has clearly shown that the existing process of law cannot overcome systematic and ingenious discrimination. No law that we now have on the books—and I have helped to put three of them there—can ensure the right to vote when local officials are determined to deny it.

In such a case our duty must be clear to all of us. The Constitution says that no person shall be kept from voting because of his race or his color. We have all sworn an oath before God to support and to defend that Constitution. We must now act in obedience to that oath.

GUARANTEEING THE RIGHT TO VOTE

Wednesday I will send to Congress a law designed to eliminate illegal barriers to the right to vote.

The broad principles of that bill will be in the hands of the Democratic and Republican leaders tomorrow. After they have reviewed it, it will come here formally as a bill. I am grateful for this opportunity to come here tonight at the invitation of the leadership to reason with my friends, to give them my views, and to visit with my former colleagues.

I have had prepared a more comprehensive analysis of the legislation which I had intended to transmit to the clerk tomorrow but which I will submit to the clerks tonight. But I want to really discuss with you now briefly the main proposals of this legislation,

This bill will strike down restrictions to voting in all elections—Federal, State, and local—which have been used to deny Negroes the right to vote.

This bill will establish a simple, uniform standard which cannot be used, however ingenious the effort, to flout our Constitution.

It will provide for citizens to be registered by officials of the United States Government if the State officials refuse to register them.

It will eliminate tedious, unnecessary lawsuits which delay the right to vote.

Finally, this legislation will ensure that properly registered individuals are not prohibited from voting.

I will welcome the suggestions from all of the Members of Congress—I have no doubt that I will get some—on ways and means to strengthen this law and to make it effective. But experience has plainly shown that this is the only path to carry out the command of the Constitution.

To those who seek to avoid action by their National Government in their own communities; who want to and who seek to maintain purely local control over elections, the answer is simple:

Open your polling places to all your people.
Allow men and women to register and vote whatever the color of their skin.
Extend the rights of citizenship to every citizen of this land.

THE NEED FOR ACTION

There is no constitutional issue here. The command of the Constitution is plain.

There is no moral issue. It is wrong—deadly wrong—to deny any of your fellow Americans the right to vote in this country.

There is no issue of States rights or national rights. There is only the struggle for human rights.

I have not the slightest doubt what will be your answer.

The last time a President sent a civil rights bill to the Congress it contained a provision to protect voting rights in Federal elections. That civil rights bill was passed after 8 long months of debate. And when that bill came to my desk from the Congress for my signature, the heart of the voting provision had been eliminated.

This time, on this issue, there must be no delay, no hesitation and no compromise with our purpose.

We cannot, we must not, refuse to protect the right of every American to vote in every election that he may desire to participate in. And we ought not and we cannot and we must not wait another 8 months before we get a bill. We have already waited a hundred years and more, and the time for waiting is gone.

So I ask you to join me in working long hours—nights and weekends, if necessary—to pass this bill. And I don't make that request lightly. For from the window where I sit with the problems of our country I recognize that outside this chamber is the outraged conscience of a nation, the grave concern of many nations, and the harsh judgment of history on our acts.

WE SHALL OVERCOME

But even if we pass this bill, the battle will not be over. What happened in Selma is part of a far larger movement which reaches into every section and State of America. It is the effort of American Negroes to secure for themselves the full blessings of American life.

Their cause must be our cause too. Because it is not just Negroes, but really it is all of us, who must overcome the crippling legacy of bigotry and injustice.

And we shall overcome.

As a man whose roots go deeply into Southern soil I know how agonizing racial feelings are. I know how difficult it is to reshape the attitudes and the structure of our society.

But a century has passed, more than a hundred years, since the Negro was freed. And he is not fully free tonight.

It was more than a hundred years ago that Abraham Lincoln, a great President of another party, signed the Emancipation Proclamation, but emancipation is a proclamation and not a fact.

A century has passed, more than a hundred years, since equality was promised. And yet the Negro is not equal.

A century has passed since the day of promise. And the promise is unkept.

The time of justice has now come. I tell you that I believe sincerely that no force can hold it back. It is right in the eyes of man and God that it should come. And when it does, I think that day will brighten the lives of every American.

For Negroes are not the only victims. How many white children have gone uneducated, how many white families have lived in stark poverty, how many white lives have been scarred by fear, because we have wasted our energy and our substance to maintain the barriers of hatred and terror?

So I say to all of you here, and to all in the Nation tonight, that those who appeal to you to hold on to the past do so at the cost of denying you your future.

This great, rich, restless country can offer opportunity and education and hope to all: black and white, North and South, sharecropper and city dweller. These are the enemies: poverty, ignorance, disease. They are the enemies and not our fellow man, not our neighbor. And these enemies too, poverty, disease and ignorance, we shall overcome.

AN AMERICAN PROBLEM

Now let none of us in any sections look with prideful righteousness on the troubles in another section, or on the problems of our neighbors. There is really no part of America where the promise of equality has been fully kept. In Buffalo as well as in Birmingham, in Philadelphia as well as in Selma, Americans are struggling for the fruits of freedom.

This is one Nation. What happens in Selma or in Cincinnati is a matter of legitimate concern to every American. But let each of us look within our own hearts and our own communities, and let each of us put our shoulder to the wheel to root out injustice wherever it exists.

As we meet here in this peaceful, historic chamber tonight, men from the South, some of whom were at Iwo Jima, men from the North who have carried Old Glory to far corners of the world and brought it back without a stain on it, men from the East and from the West, are all fighting together without regard to religion, or color, or region, in Viet-Nam. Men from every region fought for us across the world 20 years ago.

And in these common dangers and these common sacrifices the South made its contribution of honor and gallantry no less than any other region of the great Republic—and in some instances, a great many of them, more.

And I have not the slightest doubt that good men from everywhere in this country, from the Great Lakes to the Gulf of Mexico, from the Golden Gate to the harbors along the Atlantic, will rally together now in this cause to vindicate the freedom of all Americans. For all of us owe this duty; and I believe that all of us will respond to it.

Your President makes that request of every American.

PROGRESS THROUGH THE DEMOCRATIC PROCESS

The real hero of this struggle is the American Negro. His actions and protests, his courage to risk safety and even to risk his life, have awakened the conscience of this Nation. His demonstrations have been designed to call attention to injustice, designed to provoke change, designed to stir reform.

He has called upon us to make good the promise of America. And who among us can say that we would have made the same progress were it not for his persistent bravery, and his faith in American democracy.

For at the real heart of battle for equality is a deep-seated belief in the democratic process. Equality depends not on the force of arms or tear gas but upon the force of moral right; not on recourse to violence but on respect for law and order.

There have been many pressures upon your President and there will be others as the days come and go. But I pledge you tonight that we intend to fight this battle where it should be fought: in the courts, and in the Congress, and in the hearts of men.

We must preserve the right of free speech and the right of free assembly. But the right of free speech does not carry with it, as has been said, the right to holler fire in a crowded theater. We must preserve the right to free assembly, but free assembly does not carry with it the right to block public thoroughfares to traffic.

We do have a right to protest, and a right to march under conditions that do not infringe the constitutional rights of our neighbors. And I intend to protect all those rights as long as I am permitted to serve in this office.

We will guard against violence, knowing it strikes from our hands the very weapons which we seek—progress, obedience to law, and belief in American values.

In Selma as elsewhere we seek and pray for peace. We seek order. We seek unity. But we will not accept the peace of stifled rights, or the order imposed by fear, or the unity that stifles protest. For peace cannot be purchased at the cost of liberty.

In Selma tonight, as in every—and we had a good day there—as in every city, we are working for just and peaceful settlement. We must all remember that after this speech I am making tonight, after the police and the FBI and the Marshals have all gone, and after you have promptly passed this bill, the people of Selma and the other cities of the Nation must still live and work together. And when the attention of the Nation has gone elsewhere they must try to heal the wounds and to build a new community.

This cannot be easily done on a battleground of violence, as the history of the South itself shows. It is in recognition of this that men of both races have shown such an outstandingly impressive responsibility in recent days—last Tuesday, again today,

RIGHTS MUST BE OPPORTUNITIES

The bill that I am presenting to you will be known as a civil rights bill. But, in a larger sense, most of the program I am recommending is a civil rights program. Its object is to open the city of hope to all people of all races.

Because all Americans just must have the right to vote. And we are going to give them that right.

All Americans must have the privileges of citizenship regardless of race. And they are going to have those privileges of citizenship regardless of race.

But I would like to caution you and remind you that to exercise these privileges takes much more than just legal right. It requires a trained mind and a healthy body. It requires a decent home, and the chance to find a job, and the opportunity to escape from the clutches of poverty.

Of course, people cannot contribute to the Nation if they are never taught to read or write, if their bodies are stunted from hunger, if their sickness goes untended, if their life is spent in hopeless poverty just drawing a welfare check.

So we want to open the gates to opportunity. But we are also going to give all our people, black and white, the help that they need to walk through those gates.

THE PURPOSE OF THIS GOVERNMENT

My first job after college was as a teacher in Cotulla, Tex., in a small Mexican-American school. Few of them could speak English, and I couldn't speak much Spanish. My students were poor and they often came to class without breakfast, hungry. They knew even in their youth the pain of prejudice. They never seemed to know why people disliked them. But they knew it was so, because I saw it in their eyes. I often walked home late in the afternoon, after the classes were finished, wishing there was more that I could do. But all I knew was to teach them the little that I knew, hoping that it might help them against the hardships that lay ahead.

Somehow you never forget what poverty and hatred can do when you see its scars on the hopeful face of a young child.

I never thought then, in 1928, that I would be standing here in 1965. It never even occurred to me in my fondest dreams that I might have the chance to help the sons and daughters of those students and to help people like them all over this country.

But now I do have that chance—and I'll let you in on a secret—I mean to use it. And I hope that you will use it with me.

This is the richest and most powerful country which ever occupied the globe. The might of past empires is little compared to ours. But I do not want to be the President who built empires, or sought grandeur, or extended dominion.

I want to be the President who educated young children to the wonders of their world. I want to be the President who helped to feed the hungry and to prepare them to be taxpayers instead of taxeaters.

I want to be the President who helped the poor to find their own way and who protected the right of every citizen to vote in every election.

I want to be the President who helped to end hatred among his fellow men and who promoted love among the people of all races and all regions and all parties.

I want to be the President who helped to end war among the brothers of this earth.

And so at the request of your beloved Speaker and the Senator from Montana; the majority leader, the Senator from Illinois; the minority leader, Mr. McCulloch, and other Members of both parties, I came here tonight—not as President Roosevelt came down one time in person to veto a bonus bill, not as President Truman came down one time to urge the passage of a railroad bill—but I came down here to ask you to share this task with me and to share it with the people that we both work for. I want this to be the Congress, Republicans and Democrats alike, which did all these things for all these people.

Beyond this great chamber, out yonder in 50 States, are the people that we serve. Who can tell what deep and unspoken hopes are in their hearts tonight as they sit there and listen. We all can guess, from our own lives, how difficult they often find their own pursuit of happiness, how many problems each little family has. They look most of all to themselves for their futures. But I think that they also look to each of us.

Above the pyramid on the great seal of the United States it says—in Latin —"God has favored our undertaking."

God will not favor everything that we do. It is rather our duty to divine His will. But I cannot help believing that He truly understands and that He really favors the undertaking that we begin here tonight.

Source: Public Papers of the Presidents of the United States: Lyndon B. Johnson, 1965. Vol. I, entry 107 (Washington, DC: GPO, 1966), 281–87.

Arthur Fletcher, "Remarks on the Philadelphia Plan" (1969)

As the twentieth century drew to a close, the American public perceived affirmative action as the most enduring legacy of the civil rights movement. But where and how affirmative action originated remains shrouded in myth and half-truths. Affirmative action was not one of the central goals of Martin Luther King Jr., SNCC, CORE, or, for that matter, the NAACP. Conservative proclamations to the contrary, neither was it the result of a liberal cabal. On the contrary, affirmative action as public policy was most fully developed in 1969 by members of the Nixon administration, most specifically via the Philadelphia Plan.

Unlike the desegregation of schools, for which a single document, the Brown *decision, stands out, the same cannot be stated for affirmative action. No single court case, speech, law, or article enunciated the goals of this policy. Nonetheless, the following remarks, made by Assistant Secretary of Labor Arthur Fletcher in*

406 | Primary Documents

June 1969 on the signing of the Philadelphia Plan, help us understand the policy. The plan aimed at increasing the number of minority construction workers on federally funded projects in Philadelphia. It became a model for affirmative action plans in other regions and industries, both in the private and public sectors. As Fletcher's boss, Secretary of Labor George Shultz, insisted, the plan did not allow for quotas or the lowering of standards. While the particulars of the Philadelphia Plan were never reviewed by the Supreme Court, in 1978, the court upheld, 5–4, in the case University of California Regents v. Bakke, *the constitutionality of affirmative action in principle, while at the same time ruling 5–4 against the specific program implemented by the medical school at the University of California at Davis, because it had established quotas.*

It is most appropriate that a plan for equal employment opportunity should bear the title "Philadelphia Plan" and should be inaugurated in this city. Philadelphia and its people have a great heritage of freedom which is rich in historical events known to every school child throughout the Nation. It was here in this city that the Declaration of Independence was signed and it was here freedom's ring was heard for the first time. It was here that the Constitution of our country guaranteeing freedom for all was drafted.

A vital freedom guaranteed by our Constitution is the right to equal participation in the economic processes of our society. This freedom has been denied to groups within our country. This denial of fundamental participation in the advantages of capitalism has even been institutionalized in our society.

The Federal Government cannot contribute to this denial of rights through blind acceptance of customs and traditions which eliminate the contributions and talents of groups of people. *The Federal Government has an obligation* to see that every citizen has an equal chance at the most basic freedom of all—*the right to succeed.*

Millions of dollars at every level of Government are being spent to correct the symptoms of the denial of this right in our society but almost no effort has been made in the past to affect this problem at its source—where Federal dollars enter the area economy.

These Federal dollars—part of which are Black, Puerto Rican, Mexican-American, and others—enter [the] local economy primarily through Federal contracts. Once these dollars pass the "Gateway" of contracting procedures— the Federal Government has no further control over them. Through the "multiplier" effect experienced by imported money in the regional economy and the existence of institutionalized segregation—the Federal Government can be pictured as contributing to the denial of the right to succeed for substantial groups of people. No amount of money spent by whatever level of Government to correct this situation can be justified after the fact.

The most fair, economical and effective point to address this problem is at the beginning—the time of contracting.

My office is dedicated to this proposition. I view this concept as being in harmony with the highest principles guaranteed by our Constitution and the sound economic cornerstones of our capitalist system. It is good business for the Government, for industry, for labor and for all the people of this country.

With this background firmly in mind, I now want to tell you about the Philadelphia Plan.

The Philadelphia Plan applies to all Federal and federally-assisted construction contracts for projects in excess of $500,000. The plan at the present time is to apply to the Philadelphia area including Bucks, Chester, Delaware, Montgomery, and Philadelphia counties, and goes into effect on July 18, 1969. It is also anticipated that the plan will be put into effect in all the major cities across the Nation as soon as possible.

The plan is aimed at increasing minority participation in designated trades. These trades are:

Iron workers
Plumbers, pipefitters
Steam fitters
Sheetmetal workers
Electrical workers
Roofers and water proofers
Elevation construction workers

The named trades have been singled out for special emphasis because in the past these trades, at least in the Philadelphia area, have been operating without significant minority participation.

Within the plan's presently established geographical boundaries, the Office of Federal Contract Compliance will, with the assistance of representatives from the Federal contracting agencies, determine definite standards for minority participation in each of the trades named and to be used on a construction project. The standard for each trade will be included in the invitation for bids or other solicitation used for every Federally-involved construction contract. The standards will specify the range of minority manpower utilization expected for each of the named trades and such standards must be maintained during the performance of the construction contract.

The standards are to be determined in each instance by applying the following major criteria:

1. The current extent of minority group participation in the trade

2. The availability of minority group persons for employment in such trade

3. The need for training programs in the area and/or the need to assure demand for those in or from existing training programs

4. The impact of the program upon the existing labor force.

When the contractor submits his bid he must include in the bid an acceptable affirmative action program. This program must contain acceptable goals for the use of minority manpower in each of the trades named within the ranges established in the invitations for bids.

The standards within the ranges established must be met by each of the named trades. There is no provision for combining trades or for obtaining an acceptable cumulative total. Failure to meet an established standard will result in the bid being rejected. In no case will there be any negotiation over provisions of the specific goals submitted by a bidder after opening of bids and prior to the award of the contract.

After the contract is awarded post-award reviews will be conducted to determine whether the goals pledged by the contractor are being met. You may rest assured that these reviews will be thorough, that they will be as frequent as is necessary, and that they will uncover any instances of non-compliance.

Perhaps I should pause at this point to discuss the concept of goals or standards for percentages of minority employees contained in the Philadelphia Plan.

Let me start by saying it would have been much better in our history if segregation had not occurred. But it has. This is a fact. None of us—white or black—like to talk about it—much less admit it. But there it remains—it won't go away.

Segregation didn't occur naturally—it was imposed. In that process quotas, limits, boundaries were set. Sometimes written—sometimes unpublished. But official or informal the effect was total, decisive, and I might add—contrary to the American sense of fair play.

Large segments of our society were oppressed by these rules and institutions until they believed it was impossible to change them. With the increasing wealth of our economic system—the gap—visible to any thinking man—between white and black—employed and unemployed—rich and poor—was growing wider and wider.

Contrary to the poet—hope does *not* spring eternal. Hope—and, therefore, the commitment to try to succeed—is directly related to the chances of success. Impossible dreams are not long sustained by anyone—white or black.

Visible, measurable goals to correct obvious imbalances are essential:

1. To provide targets or incentives for setting objectives and measuring achievements under the contracts.

2. To build the hope of the disadvantaged that the institutions that have suppressed them are willing to commit themselves to their aid and to back their pledges in definitive terms.

Fair play and definitive agreements concerning working conditions, promotional opportunities, ratios of skilled craftsmen to trainees, recognition of bargaining groups and seniority security are now an acceptable and respected tradition in our world of commerce. This was not always so. It developed in stormy times and created great feelings of anxiety, threat and insecurity.

The disadvantaged of this country are now asking that the opportunities achieved through this great movement be extended to include them. No more. No less.

It might be better, admittedly, if specific goals were not required—certainly the black people of America understand taboos—but it is imperative that we face facts and dedicate ourselves to ending discrimination in employment in this country.

What is at stake here is something more than equal employment opportunity in a specific industry or named trades. What is at stake is our basic system of Government itself. Persons in the minority communities must be assured that results can be obtained by working within the framework of the existing governmental system. The Office of Federal Contract Compliance must translate the dreams and ambitions of a large segment of our population into every day realities. This means job opportunities in at least every trade and industry which does substantial business with the Federal Government. The time for speculation has ended and the hour for action is now.

Source: Philadelphia Plan Document, U.S. Department of Labor, No. 6, Department of Labor Library, Washington, DC.

Index

Bold page numbers refer to the main entries.

About the Editor

PETER B. LEVY, PhD, is professor in the Department of History and Political Science at York College, York, Pennsylvania. His published works include: *Civil War on Race Street: The Civil Rights Movement in Cambridge, Maryland*; *Let Freedom Ring: A Documentary History of the Civil Rights Movement*; and *The New Left and Labor in the 1960s*. He earned his doctorate in history from Columbia University.